OpenVMS with Apache, OSU, and WASD

OpenVMS with Apache, OSU, and WASD

Alan Winston

Digital Press
An imprint of Elsevier Science
Amsterdam • Boston • London • New York • Oxford • Paris • San Diego
San Francisco • Singapore • Sydney • Tokyo

Digital Press is an imprint of Elsevier Science.

Recognizing the importance of preserving what has been written, Elsevier Science prints its books on acid-free paper whenever possible.

Library of Congress Cataloging-in-Publication Data

A catalogue record for this book is available from the Library of Congress

ISBN 1-55558-264-8

British Library Cataloguing-in-Publication Data

A catalogue record for this book is available from the British Library.

The publisher offers special discounts on bulk orders of this book.
For information, please contact:

Manager of Special Sales
Elsevier Science
200 Wheeler Road
Burlington, MA 01803
Tel: 781-313-4700
Fax: 781-313 4882

For information on all Digital Press publications available, contact our World Wide Web home page at: http://www.digitalpress.com or http://www.bh.com/digitalpress.

Transferred to Digital Printing 2008.

To Deborah, with love, for many reasons.

Contents

Introduction **xi**

1 Why Run a Web Server on VMS? **1**

1.1 VMS clustering 1
1.2 Reliability 2
1.3 Security 2
1.4 You already have it 3
1.5 Can VMS do what I need? 3

2 VMS and the Web **5**

2.1 Beginnings 5
2.2 OSU 6
2.3 Apache 6
2.4 WASD and others 7

3 Web Options **9**

3.1 CSWS 9
3.2 OSU 11
3.3 WASD 12
3.4 Which should you use? 13

4 Installation Issues **15**

4.1 Preinstallation 15
4.2 Installation guides 19

5 Basic Configuration and Server Control 35

5.1 CSWS 35
5.2 OSU 38
5.3 WASD 39
5.4 Basic configuration 40
5.5 Starting and stopping 50
5.6 Command-line control 56
5.7 Web-based control 63

6 Encrypted/Secure Communications: HTTPS Protocol Support 67

6.1 HTTPS 67
6.2 Installation 78
6.3 Configuration 86

7 Managing Access to Your Server Resources 97

7.1 Mapping resources 97
7.2 Authentication 117
7.3 Access controls 135

8 Providing User Personal Web Directories 151

8.1 User directories: pro and con 151
8.2 Implementing userdirs 152

9 Multihosting and Multihoming 161

9.1 Why multihosting? 161
9.2 Multihosting/multihoming configuration 162

10 Indexing and Searching Your Site 171

10.1 Why index? 171
10.2 VMSindex and Lynx Crawl 172
10.3 SWISH-E 175
10.4 HT://DIG 179

11 Cache and Proxy **183**

11.1 Cache and proxy 183
11.2 Cache management 185
11.3 Proxy management 193

12 Managing and Understanding Your Server Logs **203**

12.1 Customizing your logging 203
12.2 Log-file formats and locations 204
12.3 Log-file rotation 211
12.4 Unavoidable ambiguities and user tracking 213
12.5 Error logs 216
12.6 Tools to interpret your logs 218

13 Dynamic Content: Directory Browsing and Server-Side Includes **237**

13.1 Directory browsing 237
13.2 Dynamic content with SSI 259
13.3 Configuring SSI 260
13.4 SSI directives 262

14 Running CGI Programs **281**

14.1 CGI defined 281
14.2 Environment variables 284
14.3 Necessary HTTP headers 293
14.4 Configuration for CGI 293
14.5 CGI environment 296
14.6 Languages for CGI 306

15 RDB Database Access from CGI Scripts **313**

15.1 RDB Web Agent 313
15.2 Embedded RDO or SQL module language 315
15.3 Perl, DBI, and DBD::RDB 315
15.4 Python and the RDB plug-in 322
15.5 Java 323

16 Useful Freeware CGI Scripts **325**

16.1 Serving VMS MAIL files 325
16.2 Sending mail from forms 327
16.3 System management functions 329
16.4 Presenting documentation 330

17 High-Performance Scripting Options **333**

17.1 Issues 333
17.2 Options 335
17.3 Conclusion 348

18 User-Edited Web Pages **349**

18.1 File-naming standards 349
18.2 File layout 350
18.3 Alternatives to FTP 351

19 User-Developed CGI Scripts **355**

19.1 CSWS/Apache 356
19.2 OSU 356
19.3 WASD 361

Appendix A: Perl **363**

Appendix B: Python **369**

Appendix C: PHP **375**

Appendix D: Apache **379**

Appendix E: Annotated Sample Configuration Files **383**

Index **439**

Introduction

This book is intended for people considering running a Web server on an OpenVMS system. This includes OpenVMS hobbyists, professional system administrators, and software developers working on VMS systems. My assumption is that readers are already somewhat familiar with VMS systems and may or may not have any exposure to UNIX/LINUX, Web servers, or freeware tools originating in the UNIX/LINUX world. Although I will endeavor not to make the text unnecessarily confusing for the VMS neophyte, I am not including a VMS primer; that would make the book both unwieldy and tedious.

The goal of this book is to provide a detailed introduction to the VMS-based Web servers under current active development. The reader may expect to learn the features and capabilities of those Web servers, and gain an understanding of the issues common to all three (and, in some cases, to all Web server installations). The capability-oriented organization of the book will also assist in conversions from one server to another by showing the differences and similarities in the ways the servers address the same issues.

All three servers covered run from text-based configuration files. Although I touch on GUI-based configuration tools from time to time, generally I simply show the text files. This will more clearly represent what's actually going on in each file, as well as making it easier to compare the configurations of the three servers. In many chapters, a narrative section on the main topic is followed by example excerpts from the configuration files for each server. The annotated example configurations in the appendices should also help to make the meanings and differences clear.

The exigencies of formatting for book publication may have resulted in some of the examples wrapping at the wrong places. Be wary of this.

1

Why Run a Web Server on VMS?

To ask the question posed by the title of this chapter is, in effect, nearly the same as asking "Why should I buy a book about running a Web server on VMS?" So if you're standing in the aisle at a bookstore trying to make up your mind, read on. The answers are different depending on whether you're considering starting up a huge Web-based enterprise from scratch, looking to add Web access to the data you already have, or running a hobbyist site. If you're starting up a huge Web-based enterprise, you might want to show this chapter to your management.

The reasons to choose VMS as a Web platform if you're starting from scratch include reliability, availability, stability, scalability, security, and ease of administration, all of which boil down to VMS and VMS clustering technology. Clusters were invented for VMS and have been available on that operating system since the 1980s. Other operating systems are starting to catch up, but VMS clustering capability continues to be developed and will probably retain its technological lead for some time to come.

1.1 VMS clustering

If you absolutely, positively must have access to your data all the time, you can get that capability with VMS-based computers. With VMS cluster technology and shareable RAID storage, multiple systems can access your databases or plain files simultaneously, with access arbitrated at a fine-grained level by the distributed lock manager. If you're set up with volume shadowing, losing a physical disk still leaves you with an on-line copy of the information. Losing a system just distributes the load over the other systems in the cluster. If you're really on the high end, you can do clustering over dedicated wide area network links and have your data centers miles apart; in this instance, losing a data center will just distribute the load over your other data centers. (This is the "disaster-tolerant" configuration.)

You don't need to reserve a system as the "backup" server; you can load-balance over all your cluster member systems and get full use from your hardware investment. Your cluster doesn't have to come down altogether when you do an operating system upgrade; "rolling upgrades" are supported, which let you shut down and upgrade one system at a time. The cluster can share user authorization files, configuration files, and so on, enabling the system manager to manage dozens of systems with little more effort than it takes to manage a single one.

Clustering is very scalable. In a well-designed cluster, if the load is getting too big for the existing systems, you can buy another system, configure it as a cluster member, and have it start taking its share of the load, all without ever having to suffer an outage. Even a small cluster with three nodes can give high availability; you never have to go down altogether for operating system upgrades, and a single hardware failure won't take you off the air. Because you still have two systems remaining, you can fix the failed system and bring it back online, again without having a visible outage.

1.2 Reliability

VMS has had more than 20 years of development targeted at environments in which reliability is very important. It runs chip foundries, factories, railroad switch yards, banks, cell phone billing, laboratories, and hospitals, environments in which computer availability is mission critical.

VMS was designed, rather than just growing or being patched together, and the design has rarely been compromised by, say, having to support existing Windows applications, or by putting graphics display code into the kernel where it can crash the system. It doesn't crash by itself, absent hardware failures or really serious misconfiguration. User-mode code doesn't usually require recompilation to run on later operating system releases; VMS 1.0 binaries still work on VAXes running 7.2.

1.3 Security

The culture in VMS engineering is such that you just don't do things like taking input into a buffer without checking the length of the input, which is something that has caused UNIX systems untold problems and is the enabling problem for the famous Code Red virus on Windows systems. Even if you did write a program that allowed user input to overrun a buffer, your process would blow up when it got outside its own memory area, rather than having a chance to compromise the OS itself.

This feature makes VMS less vulnerable to compromise from outside than other popular systems. Even if sendmail ran on it, it wouldn't be vulnerable to the famous sendmail bug, in which overflowing an unchecked buffer with specific values gave the attacker the ability to execute arbitrary code. But sendmail doesn't run on VMS and neither do many other well-known vulnerable applications. The VMS separation of program and data space means that arbitrary code can't overwrite the stack and execute, but buffer overflows can still occur—especially in software ported from UNIX. VMS does a good job of containing the damage.

The bright side of Digital Equipment Corporation's failure to market VMS effectively in the 1990s is that most of the bad guys are unfamiliar with it. You can find cookbook instructions on the Web for cracking Windows and UNIX systems, but those don't exist for modern versions of VMS. (I wouldn't ordinarily try to sell "security-through-obscurity," but this obscurity comes in addition to a robust security model with a fine-grained privilege structure that's been built into VMS from the start.) A properly administered VMS Web server isn't going to display any defaced pages.

There hasn't been a virus or worm that affected VMS since the famous Morris worm of 1987, which knew how to exploit an unsecured DECnet default account. Since then systems are locked down by default, rather than getting installed wide open and requiring a system manager to close the holes. VMS is a C2 rated operating system, following formal evaluation by the NCSC.

1.4 You already have it

The other obvious reason to run a Web server on VMS is that you already have VMS. Your departmental server is a VMS system, and you want to Web-enable some of your applications, or you're a hobbyist with a home or club server. You don't need to be sold on VMS; you already run it. This book is also for you. If you have it, why bring in a security hazard such as a Windows Web server, or a LINUX box you don't already know how to manage? Why mess with expensive cross-platform middleware to get your data to a Web server running on a different box?

1.5 Can VMS do what I need?

That's the question this book is meant to answer. After some discussion of the history of each currently supported Web server, we'll look at broad functional questions, such as "How do I do X?" and give the answers for each server. (On some servers, sometimes, the answer will be "You can't.") You can compare your Web-service requirements with what's available on VMS and decide for yourself whether VMS can do the job.

I hope you'll phrase questions in terms of functional requirements (e.g., "Can VMS provide dynamic database-driven pages?") rather than in terms of specific products (e.g., "Can VMS run ColdFusion?") because, while the capabilities are there, the fact that VMS is a minority platform means that some of the specific commercial products aren't available. Often, open source products that do the same things have been ported to VMS, so there are ways to accomplish this.

The strategy of incorporating open source technology brings a nice benefit: platform-independence. Apache, Perl, PHP, and Java are all platform-independent technologies, which makes it easier to find experienced people for Web development, allows easy porting of applications from UNIX systems, and allows bespoke development on low-cost platforms with deployment on VMS.

According to Macromedia, the next generation ColdFusion Server ("Neo") will rely on underlying Java technology for ColdFusion application services. This will broaden the number of platforms that support ColdFusion and opens the door to a potential VMS port in the future.

Halcyon Software has a Java-based implementation of ASP technology called "Instant ASP" (iASP), which one of the CSWS developers got running in test under CSWS—this shows how Java technology is bringing more capabilities to VMS.

At the time of writing, VMS Engineering is working on the DII COE project, a Defense Department–mandated effort to bring a full Posix-compliant UNIX environment to VMS. When this is complete, there will be fewer barriers to porting commercial UNIX code to VMS. Maybe Cold Fusion will run on VMS eventually. In the meantime, PHP does quite a good job. Altogether, VMS provides a robust, secure, scalable environment, with a good complement of tools available to meet your Web-service needs.

2

VMS and the Web

In a way, this chapter also answers the question "Why VMS?" A short answer is "Because it was there from the start."

2.1 Beginnings

As you may well recall, Tim Bernars-Lee at CERN, the European high-energy physics laboratory, invented the Web as a convenient means of sharing high-energy physics information stored in different forms on diverse servers. VMS systems were big players in the scientific community. (They'd been preeminent in the middle 1980s, but the price/performance of RISC-based UNIX workstations compared with that of the VAXes, which were the only VMS platform at the time, meant that the price-sensitive and performance-hungry scientific market was buying a lot of those as well.) So CERN developed Web servers for UNIX, for IBM machines, and for VMS.

The Web uses the HyperText Transfer Protocol (HTTP), so a typical name for a Web server is HTTPd, with the "d" standing for "daemon." (A "daemon"—an essential concept on UNIX systems—is a program that runs in the background, listening until it recognizes that it needs to do something, then doing it.) The first HTTPd was developed at CERN; and the first non-European Web server was installed at SLAC[1] in December 1991 (running on an IBM mainframe). My site started running the CERN HTTP server on VMS in 1993 (on a VAX 8700).

A basic Web server, one that just takes requests and serves files, isn't that hard to write. The requirements begin to get exponentially more complicated when the server needs to provide dynamic content in various ways; when it needs to support encrypted communication; when it needs to handle heavy loads gracefully; and when it needs to be robust and secure in the

1. www.slac.stanford.edu

face of hacking attempts and badly behaved browser software. The Web actually started before the Internet went commercial, and the environment for Web servers changed considerably when that happened.

CERN eventually needed to spend its money on the Large Hadron Collider and ceased WWW software development after December 1994. (The CERN server can still be found on the OpenVMS Freeware CD.) Various computer science and physics sites had already developed browsers, including SLAC; the National Center for Supercomputing Applications had already developed Mosaic (whose developers went on to found Netscape) and produced an NCSA HTTPd; but development on that product stopped when the primary author, Rob McCool, left. NCSA HTTPd was the most popular server on the Web, but Webmasters now had to develop their own patches, changes, fixes, and enhancements without any coordination, and the program was wandering in different directions.

2.2 OSU

In 1994 came the first release of an excellent freeware server on VMS, which I have used at my site since 1995: the Ohio State University DECthreads HTTP server (OSU) written by David Jones. It has been actively enhanced and maintained ever since.

2.3 Apache

In February 1995, a group of Webmasters "got together" via mailing list to support the NCSA HTTPd product. They combined their patches and bug fixes, and by April 1995 they made the first official public release of the Apache server (version 0.6.2). Because of all the patches, it was "a patchy server"—I'm afraid that's where the name came from.

The Webmasters developed a methodology for making changes to the core, a method of "lazy consensus," in which no changes could be checked into the archive without a number of "Yes" votes and an absence of "No" votes. You got voting rights by being recognized as a useful contributor to Apache development.

Using this methodology for working together, the Apache group started improving the server. Version 0.7 involved various new features, but version 0.8 had a new server architecture incorporating features for speed (e.g., spinning off new processes before they were needed) and extensibility (e.g., a clearly defined application programming interface [API] and a modular structure). After lots more work, Apache version 1.0 came out in December 1995, extensively tested, ported to lots of UNIX platforms, and adequately documented. Within a year, it was the most popular server on the Web, and it has held that leadership position since. Some 6 million sites run Apache, including Amazon.com, Hewlett-Packard, the *Financial Times*, and the English royal family (www.royal.gov.uk).

Apache runs on Linux, FreeBSD, on other UNIX variants, on Windows NT, MacOS X, OS/2, and now on OpenVMS. Compaq, VMS's proprietor at the time, created the Apache port. The current version is CSWS 1.2 (based on Apache 1.3.20, mod_ssl 2.8.4, and OpenSSL 0.9.5a). The CSWS engineers are working with the Apache Software Foundation to get their port checked in to the official CVS repository.

Apache 2.0, currently in test, is a rewritten server organized with the platform-specific services isolated in the Apache run-time library (APR) and multiprocessing modules (MPM). The rest of the code is platform-independent. This should considerably simplify the process of porting 2.0 for a later release of CSWS.

2.4 WASD and others

In 1995 came the release of Process Software's Purveyor, a commercial Web server for VMS. Support was dropped in 1999. (It can still be purchased on an "as-is" basis or downloaded and run for free by hobbyists, but source code is not available.) At this writing, the Multinet Web site[2] is still running Purveyor, and Compaq's own site[3] didn't switch from Purveyor to Apache until September 2001. This book doesn't cover Purveyor because it's unsupported and not under active development; for the same reason I don't cover the port of Netscape FastTrack Server to VMS. (The retirement and end-of-support date for FastTrack is December 31, 2001, on OpenVMS Alpha V7.1-2 and June 30, 2002, for OpenVMS Alpha V7.2-1 and V7.2-2.) Also in 1995, TGV (the company that originated Multinet) produced the Cheetah Web server but dropped it in 1997. VMS was not proving a profitable market for commercial Web server software. It's not entirely clear that a profitable market for Web server software exists anywhere, with the ubiquitous availability of free alternatives. (I would have said "free high-quality alternatives," but that wouldn't have covered IIS.) Figure 2.1 illustrates the Web server timeline.

2. multinet.process.com
3. www.openvms.compaq.com

1991	1993	1994	1995	1996	1997	1998	1999	2000
First Web server at CERN—runs on IBM, UNIX, VMS First North American Web site at SLAC (on IBM-VM)	My site adopts CERN server on VMS	CERN server no longer supported on VMS NCSA Server released, grows into Apache OSU Server version 1 released.	Purveyor released on VMS Cheetah released on VMS Apache 1.0	HFRD Server (later WASD) released.	Cheetah is dropped	Netscape FastTrack Server on VMS	Purveyor no longer supported	CSWS/Apache 1.0 on VMS.

Figure 2.1 *Web server timeline.*

In 1996 Mark Daniel in Australia came out with the first public release of the WASD (initially HFRD) server, which had been working inside the High Frequency Radar Division of the Defense Science and Technology Organization for some 18 months before that. Both OSU and WASD were adopted fairly widely and have grown user communities; both are still under active development.

3

Web Options

At this stage in history, the real options for VMS Web serving are CSWS/Apache, OSU, and WASD. (There are still some vocal adherents of Purveyor from Process Software, but it doesn't really make much sense to start any new project on a server that's neither Open Source nor supported, no matter how solidly it works.) Here's an overview of what the three programs offer.

3.1 CSWS

Compaq Secure Web Server (CSWS) is an official, Compaq-supported port of Apache, the most popular Web server on the planet. It's available for download from the OpenVMS Web page (www.openvms.compaq.com/openvms/products/ips/apache/csws.html). If you have a support contract for VMS, you have support for Apache, so you can call in if you find bugs. It comes as a PCSI kit and is extremely easy to install, delivering compiled images that are ready to go, so you don't need to have a C compiler on your system. (I will endeavor to use "CSWS" when referring to the VMS port in particular, and "Apache" for how Apache generally works.)

The most widely used add-ons for Apache are probably mod_ssl, FrontPage extensions, mod_php, and mod_perl. Compaq has ported mod_ssl and mod_perl, created a supported port of Perl, created a new module for OpenVMS user authorization, added a module that lets you run CGI programs written for the OSU Web server, added mod_php in the 1.2 beta release, and added mod_rewrite as well. There are dozens of modules available for Apache on other platforms; it's hoped that a VMS community will develop around Apache/CSWS and port more of the modules. (I'd certainly like to see mod_python, since there's a VMS port of that scripting language. There was a port of mod_python for an early version of Python.) There is at present no port of the FrontPage extensions to VMS.

Mod_include, the server-side include module, is part of the core, so CSWS can do very full server-side includes that incorporate some scripting logic. CSWS can run Java servlets (if Java's installed), and Compaq also makes Tomcat/Jakarta, the Java application server, available on VMS. (Jakarta won't be discussed in much detail in this book.)

Perl is the amazingly capable scripting/glue language that, in addition to a lot of data manipulation and system management applications, turned out to be perfect for Web programming through the Common Gateway Interface. mod_perl embeds a persistent copy of the Perl interpreter into Apache, with two good effects: When the server needs to process a Perl script, it doesn't have to spend the time to fire up a separate process and load Perl from disk. It can handle the request faster and with less overall system load. In addition, it means that Apache can be extended with Perl modules, instead of being limited to writing, compiling, and linking additional C modules. (The mod_perl interface exposes enough of the Apache internal state to Perl that Perl modules can be involved in Apache's internal processing.)

A Perl module such as Apache::ASP brings Active Server Pages functionality, developed for Microsoft's IIS, to Perl. mod_perl in CSWS 1.1 works only with the version of Perl it was built with (5.5.3), which is not the most up-to-date version; still, with some ingenuity you can use later versions of Perl in CGI scripts but not with mod_perl. The CSW 1.2 has a CSWS_PERL and mod_perl that use Perl 5.6.1, which is the most current stable Perl version as this is written, although Perl development continues apace. See Appendix A for more about Perl history and capability. PHP is the PHP HyperText Processor, the most popular Web-templating language; see Appendix C for more about PHP's history and capability.

There are more add-ons and modules for Apache than for any other Web server, but they aren't supported by Compaq. Just because something runs on UNIX or Windows Apache doesn't mean it will necessarily work on VMS at all or without considerable porting effort, but it will probably be easier to get something that exists working than to build something from scratch. Some things that are fairly standard on UNIX Apaches (e.g., using the Berkeley database manager for authentication files) aren't supported on VMS; I'll point these instances out as we come to them.

The VMS Apache port runs only on Alpha, not on VAX. It requires VMS 7.2-1 or higher. In order to maximize portability, the port doesn't radically change the Apache core very much. As a result, it doesn't really take advantage of many of VMS's unique features—exceptions include that processes use shared memory to communicate rather than keeping a scoreboard file on disk and the use of Galactic shared memory for SSL session cache—and doesn't wring out the last possible bit of performance from the hardware.

CSWS doesn't offer a Web-based administration tool. (There are a number of third-party add-ons that do this on UNIX.) Most configuration will be done by editing the configuration file.

3.2 OSU

The Ohio State University DECthreads HTTP Server, developed by David Jones, is available from http://kcgl1.eng.ohio-state.edu/www/doc/serverinfo.html. Jones also wrote a freeware secure shell server for VMS, the first available SSH server on VMS as far as I know. (Multinet and TCPware include SSH servers, but TCP/IP Services doesn't offer one, and no plans to offer one have been announced so far.)

You can get OSU to run on VAX or Alpha with any version from 5.5-2 on up. (For versions of VMS higher than 7.2 you need to run OSU 3.6b or higher. The current version as of this writing is OSU 3.9b, with 3.10alpha in alpha test.) OSU uses threading to handle concurrent Web requests. If you're running a multiprocessor box and a version of VMS recent enough to handle kernel threads properly, you can take advantage of your CPU investment by automatically running different threads from the same image concurrently on any available processor. (OSU is really good at exposing bugs in VMS's threading implementation, and you may need to turn off kernel threading in the server. Also, the threading model has changed a couple of times, so if you're on an old-enough VMS version you may need to run an old version of OSU.)

To communicate with CGI worker processes, OSU uses DECnet internally—that is, without going outside the server box. (There's a hack that uses VMS mailboxes instead, but that isn't in common use and is really intended only for testing.) Because of the DECnet method, the scripting environment isn't completely standard, and scripts developed for other Web servers often need a small DCL wrapper to work properly. (An exception is made for Perl scripts; the environment sends the right stuff out on the DECnet link and makes the necessary assignments before invoking Perl.) OSU has some support for persistent scripting environments, ranging from using DECnet tweaking to keep the script processes around a long time to a special Webperl image to a High-Performance Script Server process pool manager that accelerates compiled programs linked with the HPSS shareable image. This server can run Java servlets on an Alpha with Java installed. OSU has also has very capable and flexible authentication and access control options.

OSU has no built-in SSL support; you have to build OpenSSL and then create an SSL_ENGINE or SSL_TASK process that communicates with OSU over DECnet, such as a CGI. (This is extremely finicky to set up but works very solidly once it's going; it's discussed in greater detail in Chapter 6.) You definitely need a C compiler if you're going to have encrypted communication support for OSU, and it's a good idea to have one anyway, as there are enough combinations of operating system levels and VMS TCP/IP products that it may be difficult to find a precompiled version of OSU with everything you need.

OSU has very configurable and sophisticated file caching, which gives it an advantage over serving pages just from disk. Some MicroVAX systems serve hundreds of thousands of pages a month, and the cache can help considerably in reducing the system load. Pulling something from memory is a lot cheaper than pulling it from disk.

Documentation is somewhat sketchy. There are example configuration files and some on-line documentation of what they mean, and some users have put up documentation Web pages. Digital Press expects to release an OSU manual in 2002. Quite a lot of server configuration can be done via a Web form, although I prefer editing the configuration files, and most of my examples will be in the form of edited configuration files.

Support is by volunteer effort on the VMS-WEB-DAEMON mailing list. If you have a question or problem, you can raise it on the list and will often get an answer back very promptly, day or night. (Some of the contributors are on different continents, so there's effectively 24-hour coverage.) Jones himself reads the list and answers questions when he's available. I've been using OSU since 1994 and have generally been very happy with it.

3.3 WASD

Mark Daniel developed WASD (then HFRD) for internal use at the High Frequency Radar Division of the Defense Science and Technology Organization, and it was in use for some 18 months before being released to the public. The High Frequency Radar Division of the Defense Science and Technology Organization changed its name to Wide Area Surveillance Division, so the package became WASD; later the division became Surveillance Systems Division, but WASD was too well known to change to SSD, and it might have been too easily confused with the secure shell daemon (SSHD). It's available from http://wasd.vsm.com.au. WASD runs on VAX or Alpha.

The idea with WASD was to be a really good VMS-only server; Mark Daniel says, "I suffered a bit of a VMS cringe when amongst my UNIX colleagues (VMS was and is perceived to be a bit slow and cumbersome), so I have also endeavored to make WASD as fast and efficient as I could, avoiding C run-time library and even RMS code layers where it was feasible and worth it. I also wanted a similarly tight scripting environment and have spent a lot of time honing this aspect."

Although everybody's usage varies, WASD seems to be the fastest server available, getting as much performance as possible from the system. WASD supports a number of scripting environments: standard CGI; CGIplus (each with callouts that can request the server to perform certain functions for the CGI and then resume processing); ISAPI (the fast application program interface developed for Microsoft's IIS); a framework for a persistent run-time environment that you can customize to make your own application permanently available, and a Perl processor that takes advantage of this; plus a CGIUTL utility that simplifies the job of DCL scripts. All of these goodies are supplied with object code, but for customization you'll need a C compiler. There's support for Java servlets on Alpha with Java installed, and there's also an OSU compatibility mode. WASD also allows the execution of DCL commands from within server-side include statements in HTML code.

WASD offers server administration and some statistics via a Web form, or you can edit the configuration file manually. To get SSL working you install a separate kit, which includes the OpenSSL object libraries into the WASD directory tree, and then run a script to link. You don't need to make any source code changes. It is also possible to link WASD against the object libraries of an existing OpenSSL installation. This is easier than OSU but marginally harder than CSWS.

3.4 Which should you use?

The answer to the question "Which should I use?" is always "It depends." If you're running on a VAX, CSWS isn't an option, so you'll need to choose between OSU and WASD. If your Webmaster already understands Apache, use CSWS. If you need to squeeze out the last bit of performance, use WASD. If your site policies won't let you use software without a support contract, use CSWS (or go to a third-party provider of OSU or WASD support). If you're not afraid of compiling source code and want a very stable server with a knowledgeable user base, use OSU. If being "industry standard" matters to you—being able to buy O'Reilly handbooks, *Dummy's Guides*, and so on—go with CSWS, but be prepared to find out that the stuff they document isn't in the VMS version, or at least be prepared to have to figure out file names and the like. If you don't have a C compiler, don't use OSU. If you're stuck on a less-current version of VMS (such as the very stable 6.2 or 6.2-1H1), Apache is out of the picture.

In most cases, everything will matter somewhat to you, so you're going to have to prioritize (i.e., figure out what matters most or how much to weight each factor). All of these servers are available for free, so you do have the comforting option of downloading each one and trying it out, seeing how well it works in your environment, and finding out which one you find most congenial to maintain. You can even run them all at once, on different TCP/IP ports, serving the same or different documents.

4

Installation Issues

Before making a decision about which Web server to choose for your production server, I strongly encourage you to install at least one and play with it. (You could qualify or disqualify Web servers based on the information in this book, but you still shouldn't make a final decision without a real evaluation in your own environment. If you're a hobbyist with a home setup, you don't have to do a full-scale evaluation, or at least you don't have to persuade your management that you made the right decision. However, you still need to go through some preinstallation process to give yourself the best chance of a successful installation. Some of the advice I give here, as in the rest of this book, is more relevant for some readers than for others.

After working through the steps in this chapter, you should have a running copy of the Web server of your choice, which you can then refine and configure more fully following the advice in subsequent chapters.

4.1 Preinstallation

4.1.1 VMS version

CSWS requires at least version 7.2-1 of OpenVMS on Alpha to run. OSU will work back to VMS 5.5-2 on VAX; WASD goes back pretty far as well. (Version 7.2-1 of WASD included special code to enable PERSONA functionality on VMS 6.0 and 6.1; this wasn't provided with the OS until version 6.2.)

The caution with the OSU DECthreads Server is that it was extremely good at exposing thread bugs; you don't get kernel threads (threads as independently scheduleable entities within a process that can be run simultaneously on different processors in an symmetric multiprocessing system) that work right until sometime in the version 7 timeframe. OpenVMS 7.1 introduced kernel threads. OpenVMS 7.2-1 brought persona-based security profiles to kernel threads. (The absence of these resulted in some baroque complications in OSU and WASD. Prior to 7.2-1 kernel threads shared a common security profile.) Therefore, if you have an SMP system and want OSU to work it as hard as possible, you'd better get a recent VMS release. As I write, OSU is at 3.10alpha (that's "three.ten," which followed 3.9c); if you're on a version of VMS earlier than 7.2, you can't use higher than 3.6, but all versions back to the first are available on the OSU Web site (and can be browsed through Dave Jones's targazer script or downloaded as entire archives).

If you're running OSU you need a C compiler. (You can download pre-compiled object files for WASD and link them on your system.) You should get a C compiler anyway if you want to be able to build any other tools. If you have VAX C, get DEC C (now Compaq C). Your VAX C license will work for DEC C, and it's a much better and more standard compiler; it will make your life much, much easier when you go to build other packages. If you're on a VMS version before 6.2, you should download and install the "Backport" C library from Compaq; this will also make your development life easier. A C license is included in the hobbyist and educational layered products license; commercial users can buy single-user C licenses for less than $1,000.

4.1.2 TCP/IP software

Because VMS was developed before the broad spread of TCP/IP software, TCP/IP is an add-on to the operating system rather than an integrated component. Third parties developed TCP/IP for VMS before Digital did, and Digital's offering (originally UCX for "Ultrix Connection") was for a long time really inferior to the third-party products. Process Software was the original developer of TCPware, and they are now also the owners and maintainers of Multinet, first sold by TGV, then by Cisco when Cisco acquired TGV (apparently to get the expertise of the designers rather than the product), and finally by Process. (Wollongong was a respectable TCP/IP package for VMS, but it was eventually sold to Attachmate, which let it wither, and now it's a dead product.) There was also a Carnegie-Mellon freeware package, but it doesn't seem to be maintained now; in any case, Process and Compaq both provide free hobbyist licenses for their software, so few people have any interest in the CMU-IP package any longer. As far as I can tell, it never worked on Alpha anyway. Version 5 of the UCX package, renamed "TCP/IP Services for VMS," is considerably more useful and robust than the earlier versions; much of it is a port from the Tru-64 UNIX IP components. With version 5, TCP/IP Services becomes a serious option for heavy-duty IP use (although I'm told UCX 4.2 was pretty adequate).

Now the three realistic options for IP software are Multinet and TCPware from Process and TCP/IP Services (UCX) from Compaq. If you buy a new server, you'll probably get a license bundle that includes UCX as well as VMS. If you're a hobbyist user, you can get a free hobbyist license for any of the three. New features for Multinet and TCPware are usually developed together; Process writes newer stuff, such as their IMAP server, so that it'll be compatible with either one. There's no longer a significant difference in robustness among the three packages, so if you're picking an IP package ab initio, you'll have to compare on cost and features. Multinet includes an SSH (Secure Shell—essentially encrypted Telnet) server; UCX doesn't, and Compaq has announced no plans to support one. UCX already has support for IPv6, the next-generation Internet; Process doesn't plan to introduce such support until customers ask for it, and so on.

The good news is that they all work pretty well for Web service. CSWS is written to work with UCX, but the developers are also working with Process to make sure it runs on Multinet and TCPware. (For CSWS you need to run at least Multinet 4.3 with patches; 4.4 will be out by the time this book is published, and that should work with CSWS out of the box.) One minor gotcha with the UCX 5 transition is that logical names beginning with UCX$, such as UCX$DEVICE, got changed to TCPIP$whatever, and the UCX compatibility in Multinet at least didn't get updated in time, so you need to define the TCPIP$ names yourself, at least in Multinet 4.3.

4.1.3 Disk space

If you're contemplating doing any serious Web serving, you're probably prepared to devote a few gigabytes of disk to it, unless you're on an old microVAX system where the amount of disk you can support is pretty limited. I'll note the sizes of files in the installation dialogs. If you're developing an e-commerce application, you should be thinking about cluster-attached storage, or even storage area network, and that should get you into terabytes of storage, so the amount of space the software takes up won't be a question.

If you expect to get really substantial traffic, you want your executables and configuration files on a disk that is neither the system disk (where the CSWS installation will put it by default) nor a disk with files that you'll be serving; ideally, they should be on a controller different from either. The system disk is typically the most heavily loaded disk in the system (especially if your page files are located there), and working from the same disk as your data files means that you'll be in contention with yourself and shuttling the disk heads around. It's not that big an issue for the main executable image of the Web server, since that will typically get loaded into memory on startup and stay memory resident throughout, requiring no more disk access, but it may be significant when you spin up new processes to execute CGIs. This isn't worth worrying about for low-traffic hobbyists, but it definitely matters for high-traffic, performance-intensive sites. For those sites, you might want to consider putting configuration and log files on RAM disks (shadowed to real disk so you don't lose the data upon system crash). (The benefit of the RAM disk is considerably reduced if it's accessed via MSCP by multiple cluster members in separate boxes, but if you have a large Galaxy system and put the disk in Galactic shared memory, it can be a big win.)

However, if you just want to know whether you have enough disk space to play with this stuff at all, I can say that my Apache installation is about 17 MB, Compaq's Perl is about 20 MB, and Compaq's PHP is about 3 MB. WASD is about 33 MB, including about 5 MB of excellent documentation. OSU is about 12.5 MB total. Perl, from the Perlbuild kit—which comes with many useful built-in modules that Compaq's Perl doesn't offer—takes up about 60 MB. Python takes up about 43 MB. (Of course, you'll need more than the installed space available, since you've got to have room for a compressed archive—ZIP file or SFX_EXE—and its expansion at the same time, but not necessarily on the same disk.) Basically, 40 MB free should be good enough to install any of the Web servers in a minimal configuration, and 100 MB will let you install most other tools. Even at hobbyist prices you ought to be able to devote a 1-gig drive to your server installation, and that'll be more than you need, strictly speaking (although less than you want, since they don't make fast 1-gig drives).

4.1.4 Network issues

If you're running a departmental system that you want to make accessible to the world at large—the situation at my laboratory—you need to talk to your sitewide network administrators. They may have a firewall up that will block access from offsite, which pretty much defeats the purpose of having a Web server. VMS has an enviable security record, and if you're a competent system manager you should be able to make a case to have them poke a hole in the firewall for your system or systems. Sometimes they are unwilling to open the standard Web ports (port 80 for HTTP, 443 for HTTPS) but will leave higher ports (8000 or 8080 for HTTP, 8443 for HTTPS) open; you can work with that if you know what ports are available. It's much better to use the standard Web ports if you can.

If your site runs scans on port 80 all over the internal network to make sure nobody's running a vulnerable Microsoft IIS server, they'll find your VMS system. Therefore, you should definitely talk to site security people before you start the project; otherwise, you'll be talking to them after they've found your "rogue" server, and you'll start from a disadvantage.

If you're running a home system over DSL and don't have a nice DNS name, you can get usable ones for free in the domains owned by dyndns.org just by signing up with them. This will also leave your system locatable in the event you have to change DSL providers, since your numeric IP address is just about guaranteed to change under those conditions. The dyndns.org service is intended for people who want to run servers and don't even have a static numeric IP address, but you can use it even if your IP address doesn't change from boot to boot. hudson.dyndns.info (my server) is a much nicer name than anything your DSL provider will give you by default. Actually, I registered three names: hudson.dyndns.info, alanwinston.homeip.net, and, my favorite, vms.kicks-ass.net. In later examples I'll show how I provide different content depending on with which name you reach my system.

You can start your installation and testing before making your system visible to the outside world, and it's probably a good idea to do so—one less thing to worry about. However, in some environments it can take months to get firewall changes approved, so you should at least start this process in parallel with installation and configuration. If you give your network people a heads-up as early as possible, it may make them feel more collegial.

If you're intending to run a high-traffic Web site, you may want to look at co-location facilities, multiple high-bandwidth pipes to the Internet, off-loading the most heavily hit content to Akamai, using a specialized Web cache device from Inktomi, and so on. I won't go into detail here because these are issues with high-traffic Web sites, not issues with VMS-based Web sites.

4.2 Installation guides

4.2.1 Downloads

I've generally used Mozilla 0.9.4–0.9.8 to download kits for this book. The browser runs pretty well on VMS. There are some problems with it, however. You may find yourself compelled to use a PC, Mac, or UNIX browser to get the files inside your firewall, and then FTP to get the kits onto your VMS system. If you do this, remember to use binary (or image) mode to transfer the files to VMS; ASCII mode will mess up the kits beyond easy repair.

4.2.2 CSWS

There are separate kits for CSWS Apache, Perl, mod_perl, mod_java, and PHP. You can get the kits from the CSWS home pages, at http://www.openvms.compaq.com/products/ips/apache/csws.html. (Perl is a separate and prerequisite kit from mod_perl; PHP and mod_php come in the same kit.) While you'll see mod_jserv up on the site, you don't want it—this has been superseded by mod_java (Jakarta), which adds Java Server Pages to the server-side Java capability provided by mod_jserv.

The files you download are self-extracting compressed archive files; you run them to create a PCSI install kit. You can download the self-extracting kit with any name you like; it will still (by default) extract the expanded kit with the name PCSI needs to see. These were the kits for version 1.2 beta; as you can see, I downloaded the PHP with a shorter name. The names you see with a different version will be different (Note: directory output is rewrapped to fit on the page.)

```
$ dir

Directory DKB0:[CSWS_KITS]

CPQ-AXPVMS-CSWS-T0102--1.PCSI-DCX-AXPEXE;1
 14382/14382 17-DEC-2001 09:21:15.50 (RWED,RWED,RE,)
CPQ-AXPVMS-CSWS_JAVA-V0100--1.PCSI-DCX-AXPEXE;1
 10501/10503 17-DEC-2001 00:04:34.86 (RWED,RWED,RE,)
CPQ-AXPVMS-CSWS_PERL-T0101--1.PCSI-DCX-AXPEXE;1
 2507/2508 16-DEC-2001 23:59:38.74 (RWED,RWED,RE,)
CPQ-AXPVMS-PERL-T0506-1-1.PCSI-DCX-AXPEXE;1
 19158/19158 16-DEC-2001 23:57:09.82 (RWED,RWED,RE,)
csws_php_pcsi.exe;1
 2994/2994 16-DEC-2001 23:55:29.10 (RWED,RWED,RE,)

Total of 5 files, 49542/49545 blocks.
```

To decompress one of these kits, run it.

```
$
$! Decompressing the downloaded self-extracting executable.
$
$ run CPQ-AXPVMS-CSWS-T0102--1.PCSI-DCX-AXPEXE;1
```

```
FTSV DCX auto-extractable compressed file for OpenVMS (AXP)
FTSV V3.0 -- FTSV$DCX_AXP_AUTO_EXTRACT
Copyright (c) Digital Equipment Corp. 1993

Options: [output_file_specification
[input_file_specification]]
```

The decompressor needs to know the file name to use for the decompressed file. If you don't specify any, it will use the original name of the file before it was compressed and create it in the current directory. If you specify a directory name, the file will be created in that directory. Decompress into (file specification):

```
Opening and checking compressed file...
Decompressing (press Ctrl-T to watch the evolution)...
Creating decompressed file...
Original file specification: ROOT$:[APACHE.KIT]CPQ-AXPVMS-
CSWS-T0102--1.PCSI;1
Decompressed file specification: DKB0:[CSWS_KITS]CPQ-
AXPVMS-CSWS-T0102--1.PCSI;1
Successful decompression, decompression report follows:
File Size: 14381.07 Blocks, 7190.53 Kbytes, 7363107 bytes
Decompression ratio is 1 to 1.60 ( 60.43 % expansion )
Elapsed CPU time: 0 00:00:03.95
Elapsed time : 0 00:00:05.44
Speed : 254329.83 Blocks/min, 127164.91 Kbytes/min,
2170281.25 bytes/sec
```

And you can see here that a larger file has been created.

```
$ dir

Directory DKB0:[CSWS_KITS]
CPQ-AXPVMS-CSWS-T0102--1.PCSI;1
 23072/23073 17-OCT-2001 17:41:14.54 (RWED,RWED,RE,)
CPQ-AXPVMS-CSWS-T0102--1.PCSI-DCX-AXPEXE;1
 14382/14382 17-DEC-2001 09:21:15.50 (RWED,RWED,RE,)
CPQ-AXPVMS-CSWS_JAVA-V0100--1.PCSI-DCX-AXPEXE;1
 10501/10503 17-DEC-2001 00:04:34.86 (RWED,RWED,RE,)
CPQ-AXPVMS-CSWS_PERL-T0101--1.PCSI-DCX-AXPEXE;1
 2507/2508 16-DEC-2001 23:59:38.74 (RWED,RWED,RE,)
CPQ-AXPVMS-PERL-T0506-1-1.PCSI-DCX-AXPEXE;1
 19158/19158 16-DEC-2001 23:57:09.82 (RWED,RWED,RE,)
csws_php_pcsi.exe;1
 2994/2994 16-DEC-2001 23:55:29.10 (RWED,RWED,RE,)

Total of 6 files, 72614/72618 blocks.
$
```

Under certain circumstances on ODS-5 disks, the PCSI kit will be created with a name in lowercase letters. PCSI can't deal with that, so you need to rename the kit to uppercase, with

```
$ RENAME whatever-the-kit-is.pcsi WHATEVER-THE-KIT-IS.PCSI
```

If you want to install the bare server, you can do it now; I'd expect you'd rather install all the kits. To have the mod_perl installation work, you need to install Perl first.

```
$ product install perl /source=dkb0:[csws_kits] -
_$ /destination=dkb0:[compaq_perl]
```

After a successful installation, you need to define some logicals so that the next install can find where Perl is. (I recommend installing Craig Berry's prebuilt Perl kit even if you're going to run mod_perl, because it has a lot of useful modules that have had their VMS compilation issues sorted out, and you can install them into the Compaq Perl tree. At the moment Compaq's Perl and this one are the same version [5.6.1], but there'll likely be a prebuild for 5.8 before Compaq gets its own out; the 5.6.1 prebuild was more than a year ahead of Compaq's. Anyway, if you've already got the prebuilt Perl up, you probably have definitions for PERL_ROOT and PERLSHR that point to it, so you need to overwrite them.)

```
$ define/job/translation=concealed PERL_ROOT -
dkb0:[compaq_perl.PERL5_006_01.]
$ define/job PERLSHR PERL_ROOT:[000000]PERLSHR.EXE
```

You need to define these logicals in some way that will propagate to other processes. A plain define won't be seen in the process that PCSI creates.

```
$ define/job
```

will be visible to all the subprocesses. You could also do

```
$ define/system
```

but if you have a systemwide definition for the prebuilt Perl, this will wipe that out.

```
$ define/job
```

will work without breaking anything else.

You can certainly install one product at a time, like this:

```
$ product install csws /source=dkb0:[csws_kits] -
_$ /destination=dkb0:[apache$common]
```

But there's little reason not to do them all together. Leave out any you don't want to use. You need to have Java installed and configured if you're going to install CSWS_JAVA; you can get it from http://www.compaq.com/java/download/index.html.

```
$product install csws,csws_java,csws_perl,csws_php
_$ /source=dkb0:[csws_kits]
-$ /destination=dkb0:[000000]

The following products have been selected:
 CPQ AXPVMS CSWS T1.2 Layered Product
 CPQ AXPVMS CSWS_JAVA V1.0 Layered Product
 CPQ AXPVMS CSWS_PERL T1.1 Layered Product
 CPQ AXPVMS CSWS_PHP T1.0 Layered Product
```

This will install all the products at once.

After that you need to run APACHE$CONFIG to get Apache running at all. It will create an account/user name for the server to run under.

```
$ @sys$manager:apache$config

 Compaq Secure Web Server V1.1 for OpenVMS Alpha
 [based on Apache]
```

This procedure helps you define the parameters and the operating environment required to run the Compaq Secure Web Server on this system.

```
[Creating OpenVMS username "APACHE$WWW" ]
[Starting
HUDSON$DKB0:[APACHE$COMMON.APACHE]APACHE$ADDUSER.COM]
```

You will be prompted for a name that goes in the owner field of the APACHE$WWW account, a password for the account, and a UIC [group,member] number for the account. Pick a group that doesn't have other user names already established in it, since that could cause unexpected results (e.g., the server being able to serve files owned by those other users who have G:RE protection). Servers are usually given the first unused group, starting at [377,*] and working down. Do not go below SYSGEN parameter MAXSYSGROUP (since members of such groups automatically get system access.)

Other questions include whether you want to define the system-wide logical names APACHE$SPECIFIC, APACHE$COMMON, and APACHE$ROOT. (You probably do, unless you have some unusual requirement to run multiple instances of Apache—not just multiple processes, but multiple instances—which isn't even required to run multiple virtual hosts on multiple IP addresses.)

You'll also be asked whether to enable MOD_SSL and whether to specify any command-line arguments for the server. (This is useful for mildly tricky stuff such as testing configuration files or making temporary changes with defines, but you probably don't need to do it in the permanent configuration.)

Add

```
@SYS$STARTUP:apache$startup
```

to your systartup_vms.com and

```
@sys$startup:apache$shutdown
```

to your syshutdwn.com files so that Apache will start on system boot. If you're going to run MOD_PERL and don't have a DEFINE/SYSTEM of PERL_ROOT and PERLSHR that'll point to the right Perl image, go to the Apache login directory and add

```
$ define/job/translation=concealed PERL_ROOT -
dkb0:[compaq_perl.PERL5_006_01.]
$ define/job PERLSHR PERL_ROOT:[000000]PERLSHR.EXE
```

to the LOGIN.COM file there.

To start Apache "by hand" now, do

```
$ @SYS$STARTUP:APACHE$STARTUP
```

Run

```
@SYS$MANAGER:APACHE$JAKARTA_CONFIG
```

to configure Jakarta (CSWS_JAVA). By default, Jakarta runs as SYSTEM, but you should make it run as APACHE$WWW; so pick Option 1 from the configuration menu.

```
Enter the OpenVMS account name for Jakarta (Tomcat)
[SYSTEM]: apache$www
```

Set the owner of the Java files to apache$www. Look in SYS$MANAGER:SYLOGIN.COM to make sure that you don't run

```
$ SET TERMINAL/INQUIRE
```

on any but interactive processes, since this will fail when Jakarta starts.

```
$ @SYS$STARTUP:APACHE$JAKARTA_STARTUP
```

will start Jakarta; you can add that or a slight variant

```
$ file := SYS$STARTUP:APACHE$JAKARTA_STARTUP.COM
$ if f$search("''file'") .nes. "" then @'file'
```

to

```
SYS$MANAGER:SYSTARTUP_VMS.COM,
```

and similarly add

```
$ file := SYS$STARTUP:APACHE$JAKARTA_SHUTDOWN.COM
$ if f$search("''file'") .nes. "" then @'file'
```

to

```
SYS$MANAGER:SYSHUTDWN.COM
```

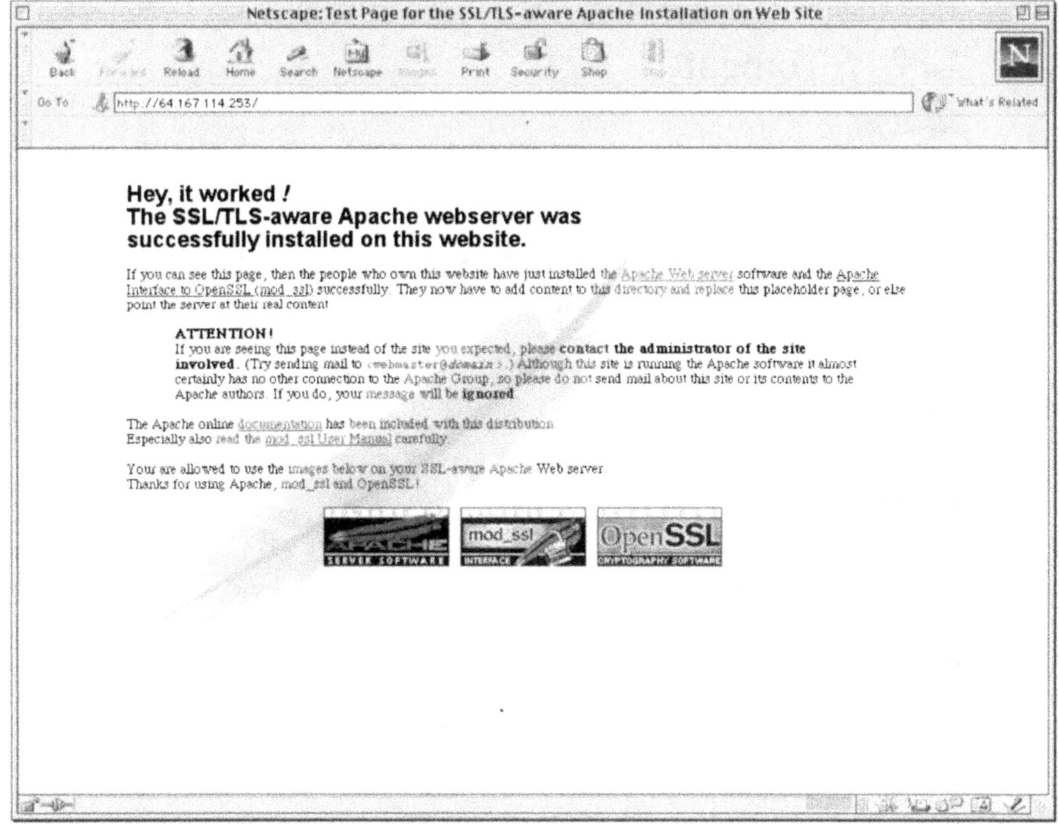

Figure 4.1 *The default Apache startup page.*

Point your browser to HTTP://yourhost.yourdomain.tld/ and you should see the standard Apache startup page, as shown in Figure 4.1.

HTTP://yourhost.yourdomain.tld:8080/ should show the Tomcat startup page, as shown in Figure 4.2.

Edit

```
APACHE$COMMON:[CONF]HTTPD.CONF
```

and look for the "include" lines for the mod_ssl, mod_perl, and mod_php configurations (assuming that you chose to install them). The installation should have automatically inserted them at the bottom of the file. (Later,

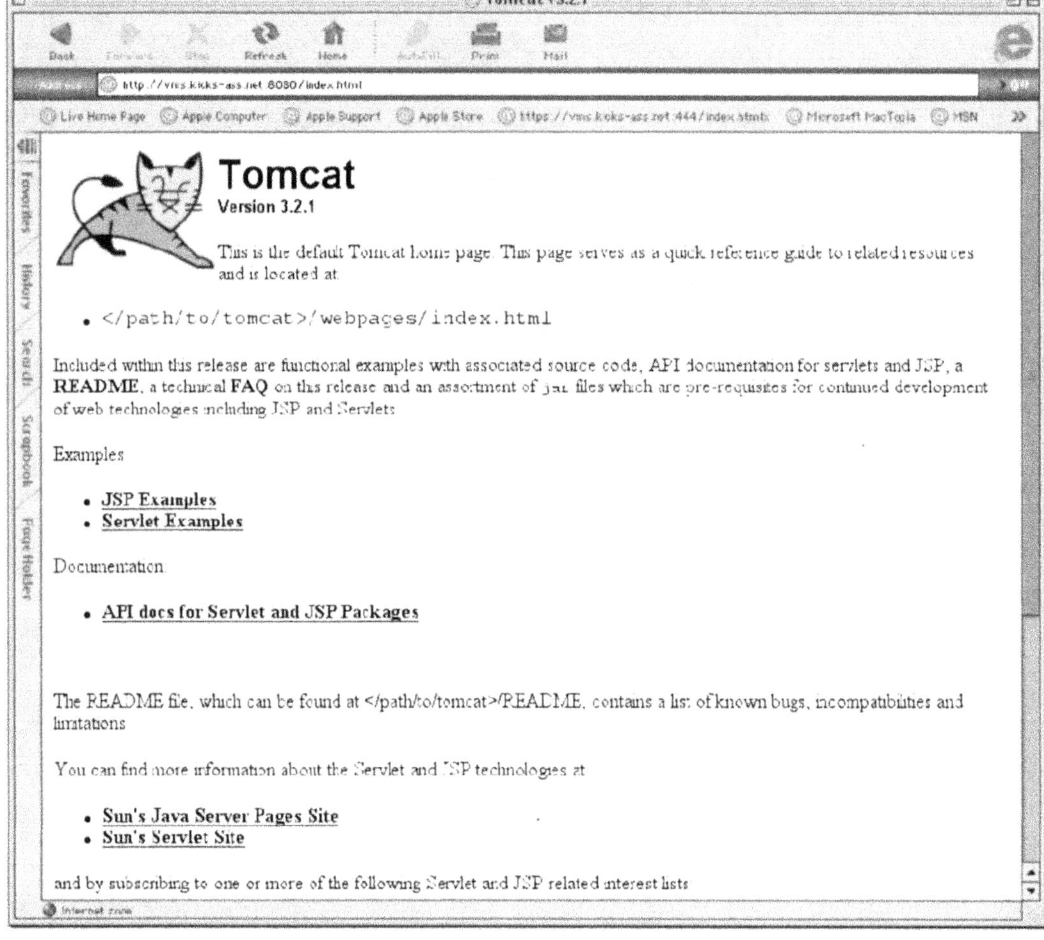

Figure 4.2 *The default Tomcat/Jakarta startup page.*

you'll be happier if you've moved the mod_ssl include up near the top.) If they're not there, insert them.

You can now test the mod_perl configuration by pointing your browser to this test page: http://yourserver.yourdomain.tld/perl/perl_rules.pl. See Figure 4.3.

Similarly, to determine whether or not mod_php is working, look at http://yourserver.yourdomain.tld/php/php_rules.pl. See Figure 4.4.

You should now have a working CSWS/Apache server, although all it will serve right now is the Apache documentation set. If you have an existing set of files you want to serve, you can edit HTTPD.CONF and add

```
DocumentRoot "/deviceorlogicalname/directoryname"
```

to point there, but make sure Apache$WWW can read them.

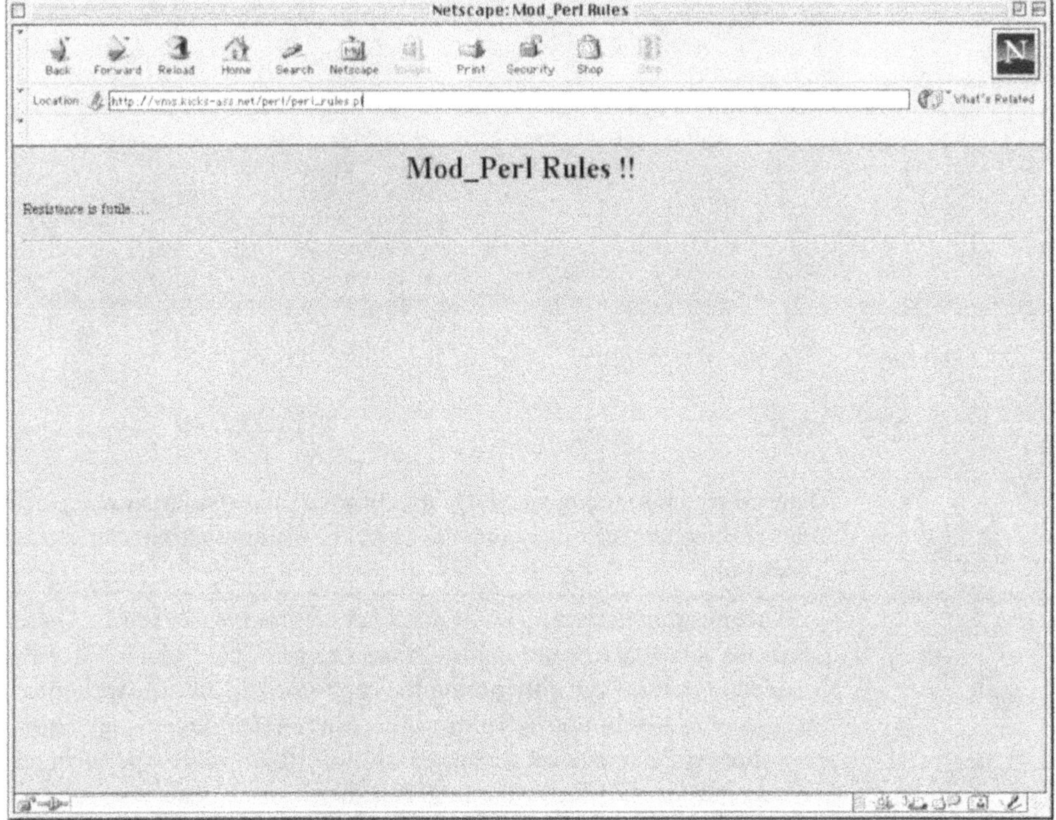

Figure 4.3 *The mod_perl test page.*

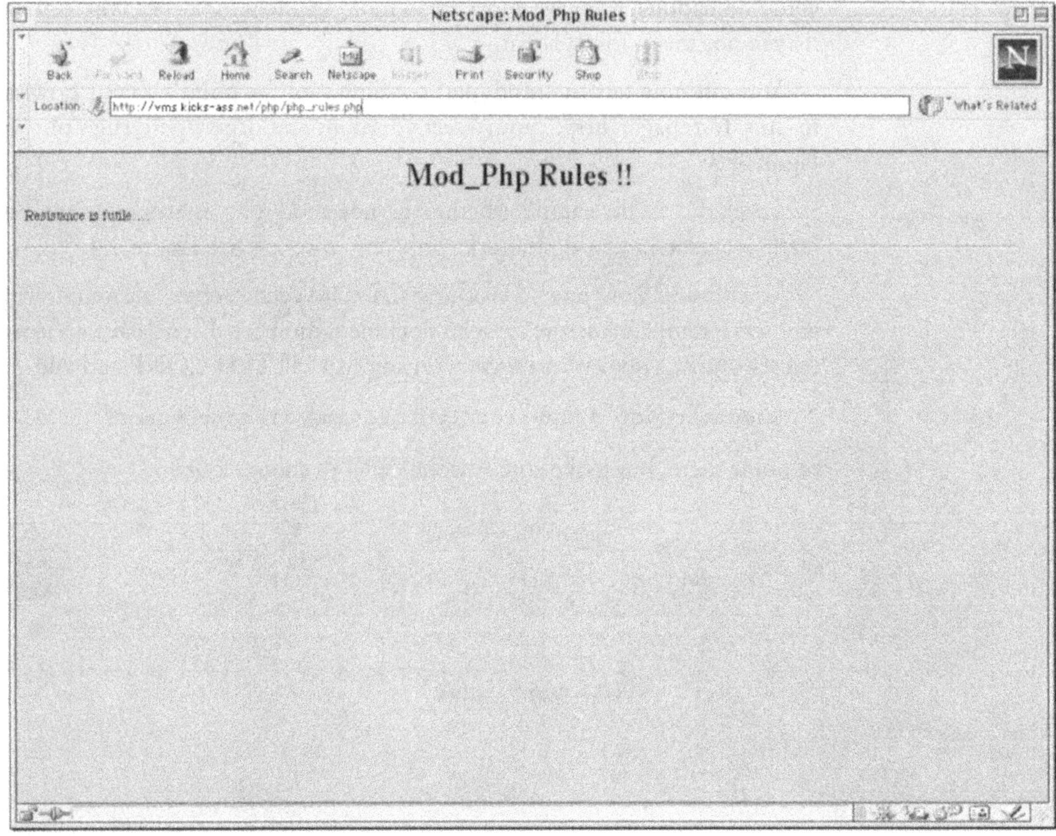

Figure 4.4 *The mod_php test page.*

4.2.3 OSU

These directions are suggested by, but enhanced and somewhat reorganized from, Brian Reed's directions at http://www.iron.net/www/userguide/index.html.

Download the server as a .ZIP or .TAR file from http://kcgl1.eng.ohio-state.edu/www/doc/serverinfo.html. (You can get UNZIP and TAR2VMS from the freeware CD, either using the copy that's distributed with operating system distributions or from the OpenVMS home page, http://www.openvms.compaq.com/freeware.) I use ZIP, but that's a personal preference. Put the ZIP file in the root directory in which you want to install the server software. I've made that DKB0:[OSU].

```
$ dir

Directory DKB0:[OSU]

HTTP_SERVER_3-10.ZIP
 2549/2550 5-FEB-2002 03:07:35.32 (RWED,RWED,RE,)
Total of 1 file, 2549/2550 blocks.

$ unzip "-V" http_server_3-10.ZIP
```

(The "-V" option retains whatever version numbers the files were zipped up with, rather than making all the files version 1. This doesn't make a lot of real difference.) ZIP will create and populate a set of subdirectories to your root directory; these are [.BASE_CODE], [.BIN], [.CGI-BIN], [.FORK_CODE], [.JAVA_CODE], [.PROXY_CODE], [.PVBIN], [.SCRIPT_CODE], [.SERVERDOC], [.SYSOSF], and [.SYSTEM]. Configuration files and server executables typically live in [.SYSTEM], sources for distribution-provided CGI programs and CGI infrastructure in [.SCRIPT_CODE], and CGI programs in [.BIN].

To build the server image (which requires a C compiler), choose a name based on which IP software you're running

```
$ SET DEFAULT [.BASE_CODE]
```

and then the appropriate one of

```
$ @BUILD_MULTINET ! for MULTINET
$ @BUILD_TCPWARE ! for TCP
$ @BUILD_UCXTCP ! for UCX or TCP/IP Services
$ @BUILD_TWGTCP ! for Pathway (Wollongong, then Attachmate)
$ @BUILD_CMUTCP ! for CMU TCP/IP
```

Move over to [-.SCRIPT_CODE] and execute

```
$ @BUILD_SCRIPTS_tcpip-name
```

Before you can run the server, you need to create a server account and set up some DECnet proxies. (It's actually possible to run the server interactively out of a user account, but that isn't a good long-term approach. It's also possible to run it without DECnet, but the author of the software doesn't recommend it; the MBXnet protocol [communicating via mailboxes] is included only for testing purposes.)

To create the account, do

```
$ SET DEFAULT SYS$SYSTEM ! not necessary if SYSUAF is
defined.
```

```
$ RUN AUTHORIZE ! or AUTHORIZE if DCL$PATH includes
SYS$SYSTEM
UAF>ADD HTTP_SERVER -
/DEVICE=disk_you_put_the_directory_on -
/DIRECTORY=[OSU]/PASSWORD=make_up_a_password -
/FILLM=18/BIOLM=18/PRCLM=15/DIOLM=18 -
/ASTLM=20/BYTLM=32000/JTQUOTA=4096 -
/WSDEF=2000/WSQUO=4000/WSEXTENT=32767 -
/PGFLQUO=150000 -
/PRIV=(TMP MBX,NET MBX)/DEFPRIV=(TMP MBX,NET MBX)
UAF>
```

The account doesn't have to be named HTTP_SERVER. On VAX, if the SYSGEN parameter VIRTUALPAGECNT is smaller than the /PGFLQUO qualifier, the server will only get VIRTUALPAGECNT pages, so you may need to edit MODPARAMS.DAT to increase VIRTUALPAGECNT and run AUTOGEN to make it take effect. If the various PQL_Mxxxx working set parameters (which define the minimum working set quotas for processes) are larger than those you've specified, the values from PQL_Mxxxx will be used rather than those from the UAF.

If you're not running DECnet, you'll have to start it and may need to install it. On VMS versions prior to 6, the command was

```
@SYS$STARTUP:STARTNET
```

For more recent versions, see the documentation. Note that you have to start DECnet Phase IV before you start an IP product, because it changes the hardware address of your Ethernet card, which it can't do after the IP software is already using it. So if you're not already running DECnet, you'll need to reboot. A complete DECnet installation and management guide is outside the scope of this book.

Because OSU uses DECnet to communicate with the processes that run CGI scripts and because SYSTEM needs to be able to tell it to start, you need to define some DECnet proxies. If you've never defined a DECnet proxy before, you'll need to create the proxy file.

```
UAF> CREATE/PROXY
```

Now you can add the proxies:

```
UAF>ADD/PROXY 0::http http/DEFAULT
UAF>ADD/PROXY 0::system http
```

(0 is DECnet shorthand for the current system, so this enables passwordless login from the HTTP account on this system to itself, and from the SYSTEM account to itself. If your proxy file is shared clusterwide, the 0::

notation means that the same proxies are defined on each system, whereas if you included a node name, you'd be defining proxies *from that node* to each system.)

On really old DECnet Phase IV systems, you may need to tell DECnet that you've updated the proxy file. This shouldn't hurt, in any case.

```
$MCR NCP SET KNOWN PROXIES ALL
```

At this stage, you can download Brian Reed's TEST_SERVER.COM and run it to see whether your configuration is basically okay, but it's not an essential part of the installation or startup. Get it from http://www.iron.net/www/userguide/test_server.com. Before you start it up, make sure HTTP_STARTUP.COM is readable by the server account, either via W:RE protection, an Access Control List entry, or making OSU the owner of the

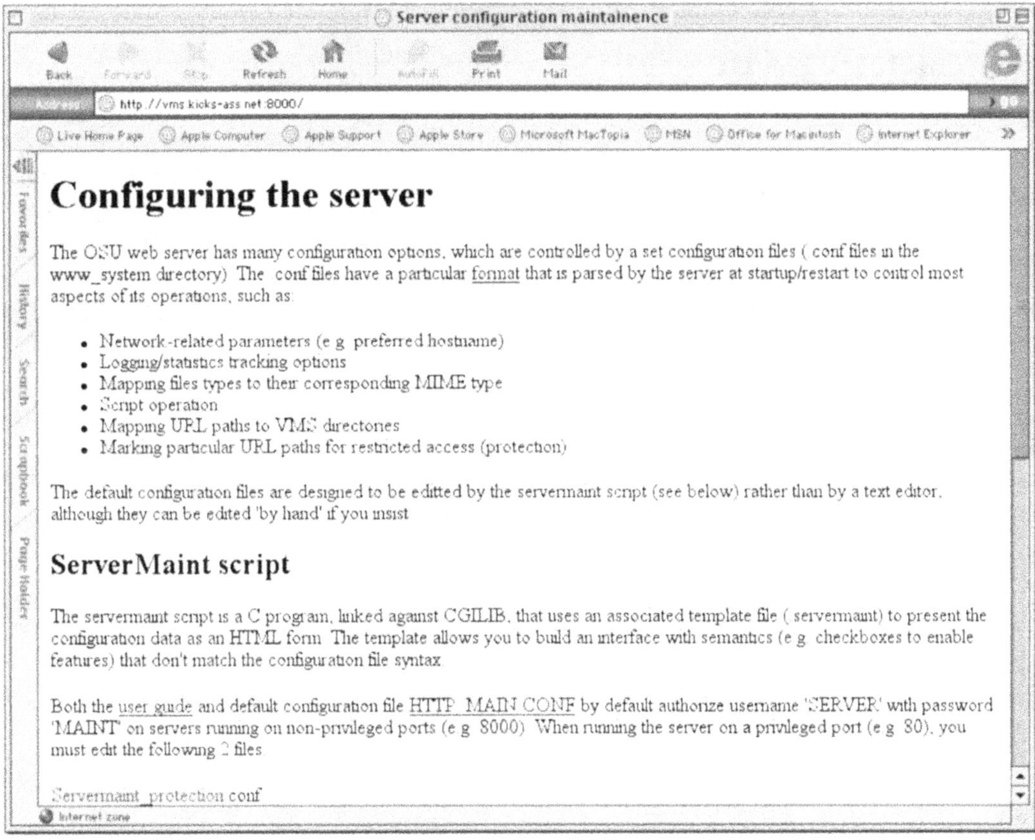

Figure 4.5 *OSU default page.*

file. (If you've been editing in the SYSTEM account, you may end up with SYSTEM owning the file even though you think it's something else.)

You can also just start it up:

```
$ @device:[directory.SYSTEM]HTTP_STARTUP account-name
```

(While the rest of this could be done from any suitably privileged account, this must be done from the SYSTEM account, or at least from an account that has a proxy to the server account.) The startup will define the /SYSTEM logicals WWW_ROOT and WWW_SYSTEM.

If DECnet is configured to allow it, you should now have a running OSU server. You can add the startup command to your system configuration. There isn't a Web server shutdown command file to include in SYSHUTDWN. Point a browser at your server and you should see something similar to the page shown in Figure 4.5.

4.2.4 WASD

Go to the WASD download page (http://wasd.vsm.com.au/wasd/) and pick your nearest mirror site. Download the zipped WASD kit, currently HTROOT_721.ZIP (for a full kit including both VAX and Alpha object files); there's a beta of version 8 out already. If you want SSL support, you can get precompiled binaries of current OpenSSL objects as WASDOPENSSL096C_AXP.ZIP (or WASDOPENSSL096C_VAX.ZIP). Put the zip files in a handy directory, say [WASD].

```
$ UNZIP "-V" HTROOT_721
$ UNZIP "-V" WASDOPENSSL096C_AXP.ZIP
```

This creates the [.HT_ROOT] subdirectory, with the whole tree underneath it. (You can promote this to a root directory by RENAMing

```
$device_name:[WASD]HT_ROOT.DIR $device_name:[000000]
```

but you don't have to do that.

```
$ SET DEFAULT [.HT_ROOT]
$ @INSTALL ! no SSL support
```

or

```
$ @INSTALL SSL ! SSL support
```

This will ask you if you want to compile and link or just link the provided objects. (I always feel better about compiling, since I then have some independent confirmation that [1] the sources provided actually do compile and [2] there are probably no poorly concealed backdoors in the software. Although, in fact, I rarely take the time to desk-check thousands of lines of code for possible bad behavior, I feel fairly confident with a well-known package that someone other than the developer will have looked at the code at some point. In the course of writing this book, I've looked at a lot of surce code and not found any trapdoors.)

At any rate, if this is a new install of WASD, the install script creates all the executables and then runs the server (from the account you're installing from); if all goes well, you can see the server test page on port 7080.

It runs in PROMISCUOUS mode, a mode basically intended just for these circumstances. It will accept any user=name/password combination

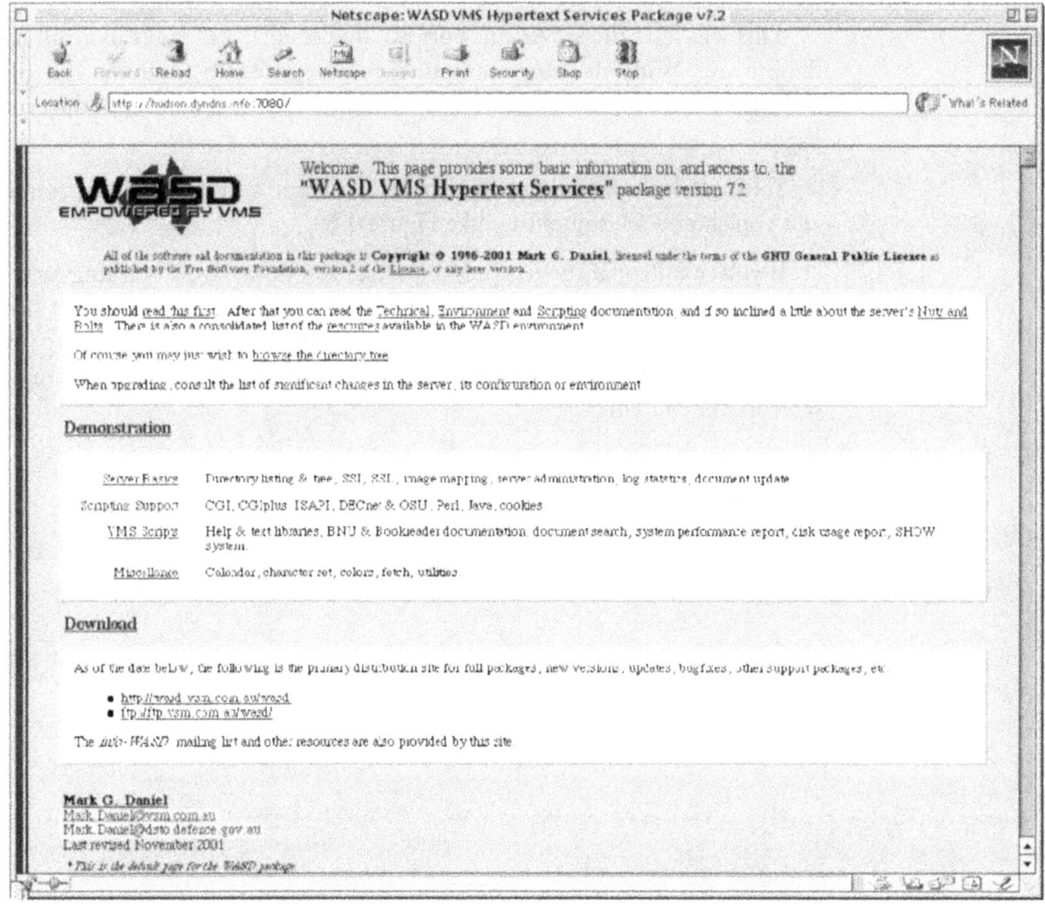

Figure 4.6 *The WASD test page.*

for authentication in this mode. Hit CTRL-Y when you've checked out the server using a browser. Then the procedure will create an HTTP$SERVER account; you'll need to provide a UIC. As I mention in the OSU install, this should be a group without any other users (so you don't get any unexpected results from GROUP:RE protection) and of a higher number than the SYSGEN parameter MAXSYSGROUP, since anything with a lower number than MAXSYSGROUP has implicit system privilege.

Make sure that the HTTP$SERVER account has access to its own files. You can get it running (in a very minimal mode) with

```
$ DEFINE HT_ROOT /TRANSLATION=CONCEALED -
device_name:[WASD.HT_ROOT.]
$ @HT_ROOT:[LOCAL]STARTUP
```

This will start the server (on port 80, by default); and you can again use the browser. Without being configured to give access to anything, it'll give an "ERROR 403 - Access denied, by default." message, and serve the error pages.

You now have a working WASD server. Point a browser at your server and you should see something like Figure 4.6.

If you've followed the instructions here, you now have a working server, whether it's CSWS, OSU, or WASD. In the next chapter, you'll learn how to read and understand the configuration files and to start and stop the servers; we'll then take the first steps toward making these servers actually serve useful content.

5

Basic Configuration and Server Control

Ultimately, the configurations of each of the VMS Web servers come down to a few text files. In this chapter we'll discuss the file names and locations for each server, and, more important, give an overview of the underlying concepts and structure of each file. This will be vital in understanding the configuration file excerpts given as examples throughout the rest of the book. We'll also discuss some of the most basic configuration directives, the ones that tell the servers what ports to listen to, where to find the files to serve, and how to redirect browsers to the right location for content that has moved. Finally, we'll discuss command-line control and Web-based control for each server.

Simultaneous with or after reading this chapter, I suggest browsing through the annotated sample configuration files in the appendices. This chapter plus the annotated sample files can give you a quick start in getting a server up to play with.

5.1 CSWS

The main CSWS configuration file is HTTPD.CONF, usually found in APACHE$COMMON:[CONF]HTTPD.CONF. There are other files in APACHE$COMMON:[CONF]. (If you're looking at an Apache book for UNIX, it will tell you that you can specify a different location for the configuration files as a command-line argument when starting Apache. That's not an available option under VMS, and APACHE$COMMON is a sensible location anyway. Apache books will also tell you about various third-party Apache configuration tools, but they won't work with VMS either.)

Individual modules (mod_perl, mod_ssl, mod_php) have their own configuration files, which are referenced from HTTPD.CONF with include statements. HTTPD.CONF-DIST has the completely uncustomized default configuration file. HTTPD.CONF-DIST-NW (NetWare) and HTTPD.CONF-DIST-WIN (Windows) can be safely ignored on VMS. ACCESS.CONF-DIST and SRM.CONF-DIST can also be ignored; these are prototypes for files whose functionality is better put in HTTPD.CONF. HIGHPERFORMANCE.CONF-DIST has some configuration hints that work on UNIX and don't work on VMS—is there a /dev/null on your system? MAGIC. is a data file for MOD_MAGIC, which enables the Web server to guess the appropriate file type for an unknown file based on the "magic numbers" at the beginning of the file—or would, if MOD_MAGIC were supported on VMS. You're better off making sure files have appropriate names and using MIME types. The MIME.TYPES file provides a default mapping of file extensions to MIME types; you can add more either by editing MIME.TYPES or by using the `AddType` directive in HTTPD.CONF—although Compaq recommends using `AddType` because MIME.TYPES is repaced with each upgrade. (To shorten all this, the only supplied configuration files you need to worry about are HTTPD.CONF, MOD_PERL.CONF, MOD_PHP.CONF, and MOD_SSL.CONF.)

HTTPD.CONF has server-level directives, which affect the whole server, and container directives, which affect only the things contained in them. (You can also scatter per-directory configuration and authentication information out in files in the relevant directories, which you have to be careful not to serve out to the world.) Container directives look a bit like HTML code, with a tag to start them and another one to finish. It's worth mentioning here that the directives in Apache/CSWS are case-sensitive; those in OSU and WASD typically are not.

The general form is:

```
<Container conditions>
directives that apply to this container
</Container>
```

The directives are `Limit`, `LimitExcept`, `Directory`, `DirectoryMatch`, `Files`, `FilesMatch`, `Location`, `LocationMatch`, and `VirtualHost`. The `Limit`, `LimitExcept`, `Files`, and `FilesMatch` directives can be nested inside other container directives.

`Directory` lets you specify either a directory or a wildcard-matched series of directories to which the commands inside will apply; `DirectoryMatch` does the same but uses regular expressions—which are emphatically not the wildcards VMS users are used to—to specify directories that can match.

```
<Directory /$disk1/stuff/*>
order allows deny
deny from all
allow from 127.0.0.1
</Directory>
```

`Files`, as you'd guess, lets you specify either a file or a wildcard-matched series of files to which the commands inside will apply; `FilesMatch` does the same with a regular expression.

`Location` is similar to `Directory`, except with URLs rather than physical directory names; the directives inside are applied before the server maps the URL into a directory, and `LocationMatch` is a version of `Location` that uses regular expressions.

`Limit` is about HTTP methods and is mostly used to grant or restrict access to particular groups. If you want to allow someone at a particular node to PUT (upload) Web pages into a directory, you can do:

```
<Limit PUT>
order deny, allow
deny from all
allow from the-ip-address-you-like
</Limit>
```

which disallows everybody except the ip-address-you-like and then allows that one. (But if you want to use it to disallow all methods, you need to exhaustively list all methods, including any custom ones.) To put a restriction on all but a few methods without listing them exhaustively, use `LimitExcept`; the following directive says that you have to be an authenticated user to do anything but GET.

```
<LimitExcept GET>
require valid-user
</LimitExcept>
```

You'll see a lot of container directives throughout the book, so I won't give you examples of them all now.

CSWS can also take instructions from files distributed throughout the document tree; .htaccess files (the typical UNIX dot-file format for configurations) allow restrictions on access and specifying options for automatically generated directory listings. CSWS can also use different password files to secure different parts of the document tree and these can be located in different places.

5.2 OSU

The OSU configuration files as delivered look pretty confusing. They're actually designed to run through a preprocessor in the server to generate the full configuration file. The reason for this is that the server has come with a Web-based configuration aid for many years, and that configuration aid requires this preprocessor format. You can use the Web-based administration tool, you can hand-edit the files with preprocessor stuff in them, and you can stick nonpreprocessor directives into the config file along with the preprocessor directives.

Most experienced users of the OSU server edit their configuration files by hand. The config files live in the [.SYSTEM] subdirectory of the Web server directory. Preprocessor code looks like this:

```
.ITERATE Welcome $welcome_file
.NEXT index.html
.NEXT welcome.html
.NEXT index.htmlx
```

The preprocessor iterates from the `.ITERATE` command through all the `.NEXT`s, each time plugging the actual parameter into the placeholder in the iterate statement. This ends up translated as

```
Welcome index.html
Welcome welcome.html
Welcome index.htmlx
```

(That particular command specifies what files to look for in each directory when the URL specifies the directory but does not specify a file, serving the first one found. If index.html, welcome.html, and index.htmlx all exist, index.html will get served, but if index.html doesn't exist, welcome.html will get served. You can, of course, specify .htm files as well, if your users are all using PC-based HTML editors. You could also just type in this translation directly.)

```
.DEFINE $placeholder parameter
```

works like a C preprocessor macro, more or less—further appearances of the placeholder in `.EXPAND` commands will be replaced by the parameter.

```
.EXPAND $placeholder [$placeholder2 ...]
```

Most of my examples will have the expanded directives, not the preprocessor code.

The config files that come with OSU and are enabled by default are HTTP_MAIN.CONF (the main file), HTTP_SUFFIXES.CONF (MIME types and in some cases presentation scripts), HTTP_PATHS.CONF (URL path to directory path translation and access control), and HTTP_MANAGE.CONF (configuration for both the Web-based and command-line server management interfaces). HTTP_SCRIPTS.CONF specifies how scripts in different virtual directories are run, HTTP_DIRECTORY configures the MST-based directory browser (the thing that generates clickable listings of directories that don't have a welcome file in them), FASTCGI.CONF configures the optional FASTCGI script execution environment, ISAPI.CONF configures the ISAPI script execution environment, and WWWJEXEC.CONf configures the Java execution environment.

Additional configuration files are .PROT files (which specify access controls and are invoked in the HTTP_PATHS.CONF file) and files that allow tuning of automatically-generated directory listings. In my configuration the .PROT files are in the server root directory, not in the document tree, but actually they can be placed anywhere the server account has read access to. Some additional configuration can be done through the use of logical names, and a little bit more—mostly setting log file levels—can be done from a command-line utility after server startup.

5.3 WASD

WASD's configuration files typically look like this:

```
[DirectiveName]
stuff to do with that directive
more stuff to do with that directive

[SomeOtherDirectiveName]
```

or

```
[DirectiveName] Attribute
```

or

```
[[SchemeServiceName]]
```

or

```
[[SchemeServiceName:Port]]
```

when configuring virtual services.

The configuration files you get out of the box are HTTPD$CONFIG.CONF (essential serverwide configuration information); HTTPD$AUTH.CONF (info relating to authorization and authentication); HTTPD$MAP.CONF (mapping URLs to file names, mostly); and HTTPD$MSG.CONF, which allows you to specify values for server-generated messages in different languages. (If you're aiming only at English speakers, you'll generally leave this one alone.)

You can also define an HTTPD$SERVICE.CONF, which lets you configure different services in more detail than you can in the HTTPD$CONFIG.CONF. HTTPD$SERVICE.CONF typically looks like this:

```
[[SchemeServiceName1:Port]]
attribute
attribute
[Directive]attribute
[Directive]attribute
[[SchemeServiceName2]]
attribute
attribute
[Directive]attribute
[Directive]attribute
```

Some configuration can be done by setting systemwide logical names. Some can also be done from the command line at server startup, and there's also a GUI administration utility. (Note that the GUI administrator was somewhat broken in 7.2-1, but is fixed in the advance copy of 7.2-2 I was given, and will surely be working in version 8, which is likely to be out by the time this book is published. If you have 7.2-1 and want to use Web-based server administration, you should upgrade.)

5.4 Basic configuration

Basic configuration elements include ways to tell the server what TCP/IP port to listen on, where to find your document tree or trees, what host name the server should consider itself to be running on, and how to bring in or block out additional document trees.

5.4.1 Ports and hostnames

The default port for the HTTP transport is 80; for the HTTPS transport it is 443. If you are an unprivileged user and want to run a Web server process, you can't use ports below 1024, so may need to use 8000, 8001, or 8443. (Even if you're a privileged user, if your site has port 80 blocked at the firewall, you may need to use a higher-numbered port.) If you're doing a test installation and don't want to mess up the existing installation, you may need some other port than the default. It is, nonetheless, preferable to use 80 and 443 if you can. You can also set your servers up to listen on multiple ports, so if you have an old port 8001 installation you can run on port 80 as well but not lose people who have port 8001 bookmarked.

You'd think you wouldn't need to tell a server what its name was, but it's helpful in constructing self-referential URLs and e-mail addresses for server administrators, as seen in error messages. It's rarely the case that the server has only one name in the DNS; most people want the server to respond to yourhost.yourdomain.tld and www.yourdomain.tld. If you're running in a cluster with a cluster alias, you want to be sure to use the cluster alias rather than the individual system's name so that the requests you generate can be satisfied by the least busy cluster member, rather than keeping the user tied to the same system even if it's busy or becomes unavailable. So, trust me, you want a host name. (This chapter is on basic configuration; if you want to have multiple hosts with different names on your server, refer to Chapter 9.)

In CSWS, the relevant directives are in HTTPD.CONF and MOD_SSL.CONF.

```
ServerName server.domain.tld
Port port-number
Listen [ip-address:]port-number
```

(Listen directives are cumulative; there's one in HTTPD.CONF for the HTTP port and another one in MOD_SSL.CONF for the HTTPS port [or ports].) While the Listen directive, as the name suggests, tells the server what port(s) to listen for, the Port directive says what port to use in constructing self-referential external URLs, as, for example, in filling out HREFs that are specified relative to the current document.

In OSU, the host-name command is hostname.

```
hostname server.domain.tld
```

Until version 3.10alpha there were only two ports supported—the cached port and the noncached port. (The noncached port could be handy in viewing changes to documents as soon as the changes have been made, rather than waiting for a cache sweep to find that the document had been updated. However, it's the port that ended up being used for HTTPS support, which just adds to the overhead of HTTPS on OSU.) With 3.10alpha you can have up to eight ports in play at once, and you can run HTTPS on a cached port for better performance.

You can specify the ports you want listened to in the HTTPD_MAIN.CONF file, although these can be overridden by putting different values in the server startup command. In the file, put

```
port cached-port[/[+][:][scheme]] [noncached-port [/[+][:]scheme]]
```

By default, this looks like:

```
port 80 443
```

Add additional port commands to add more ports. The second one on a line will always be a noncached port. If, for some reason I can't currently imagine, you want to specify more noncached ports than cached ports, you can respecify one of the cached ports and OSU will recognize and ignore the duplication.

```
port 8000 8001
port 8000 8002
```

If you just give a bare port number, OSU defaults to running HTTP on it, not HTTPS, unless it's 443. OSU notices whether the port is the standard port for that protocol or not, and marks it if it isn't, but you can also save it the trouble by marking it yourself with a ':'. (This matters because it tells the server whether to include the port number in self-referential URLs.) You can give it a plus sign to indicate that keep-alives are supported in the protocol, which is by default true for HTTP and false for HTTPS. A whole-hog full specification of standard and variant ports, including a cached variant HTTPS port, would look like this:

```
port 80/+http
port 443/https
port 8001/+:http
port 8443/:https
```

In the 3.10 alpha release, there's no easy way to actually get the ports in the configuration file honored; the ports specified as arguments to HTTP_STARTUP will override the first two ports in the configuration file, and if you leave those arguments blank, HTTP_STARTUP will substitute defaults for them. You may be able to finesse this by defining WWW_SERVER_PORTS to make the port list yourself.

(The problem is that if these are privileged ports—value less than 1024—OSU won't have the privilege to allocate them itself and needs SYSTEM to do it in the startup, but SYSTEM doesn't read the OSU config files so doesn't know about them.) This should be sorted out by the time 3.10 becomes the production version. As I read the source code, the rule-file parser will also substitute the value of a logical name or global symbol at the time of startup, so if you wanted to you could put

```
port MY_WEIRD_PORT_SPEC
```

in HTTP_MAIN.CONF and then do

```
$ DEFINE /SYSTEM MY_WEIRD_PORT_SPEC "8444/:https"
```

before starting or restarting the server and get that value substituted. It seems to me that this feature would rarely be valuable, and it is definitely not what you'd consider basic configuration.

When you start the server with the HTTP_STARTUP command procedure, there are six parameters: the name of the server account (e.g., HTTP_SERVER); the name of the startup log file (as distinct from the access log; this is where any configuration errors will be reported); the name of the main configuration file (typically http_main.conf); the cached port (typically 80); the no-cache port (typically 443); and the value for WWW_SYSTEM, where all the files will be found. Values specified for ports in the HTTP_STARTUP invocation take precedence over values in the config file.

For basic configuration in WASD, these questions are all handled in the `[Services]` directive in HTTPD$CONFIG.CONF. For more advanced configurations, you can use a separate file in HTTPD$SERVICE.CONF.

```
[Services]
[scheme:]node-name or numeric ip[:portnumber|*]
```

Scheme defaults to HTTP:, port defaults to 80 for HTTP or 443 for HTTPS, so this looks like:

```
[Services]
server.domain.tld
https://server.domain.tld
```

for default ports, and looks like

```
server.domain.tld:8001
https://server.domain.tld:8443
```

for nonstandard ports.

The first service you list will be the "standard" name for the server (although this can be overridden by service in virtual service configuration). You may want to do the following:

```
[Services]
www.server.domain.tld
https://www.server.domain.tld
server.domain.tld:
https://server.domain.tld
```

if you want the server name to show up with the "www" included. An important note if you do not want the server to run on port 80 is that it's possible to wildcard everything in a service definition; a simple '*' as the server name will result in your having a service that's bound to port 80 unless you explicitly specify something else. If you don't specify any services, WASD will start up listening on port 80.

5.4.2 Document trees and index files

In general, you're likely to have one document tree where a lot of your HTML documents can be found along with other stuff scattered over your file system, some of which you want to serve out and most of which you don't. It all has to be mappable by a URL whose document part starts with "/". (URLs, "uniform" or "universal" resource locators, are supposed to be platform independent, but they are, in fact, extremely reminiscent of the UNIX file system.) As you may know, everything in UNIX (including devices) is a file, and everything is in a single file system depending from "/". "/dev" is the directory that is actually devices. Disk-based file structures can be mounted into the file system at different places. There's no difference in how you specify a directory or subdirectory or file; they're all files. VMS people are used to device-logical:[directory.subdirectory]file.type (e.g., $DISK1:[WASD.HT_ROOT.LOCAL]HTTPD$CONFIG.CONF), but for all of the Web servers you need to get used to making the mental translation into /device-logical or /rooted-logical/directory/subdirectory/file.type (or, in extreme cases, such as the Apache log files, "/file_type").

My first advice is to do yourself a favor. Define a rooted logical that specifies the base Web directory you want to use, and do all the definitions in terms of that logical. (That way you can move it to another disk later, or even make it a search list and use multiple disks, without having to reconfigure the Web server.)

```
$ DEFINE $WEB $DISK1:[WEB.]/SYSTEM/EXEC/TRANSLATION=CONCEALED
$ DEFINE $WEB_ROOT $WEB:[ROOT]
```

You'll also need to tell the server which file to display if the URL specifies a directory but not a file. (If it ends in a slash, it specifies a directory; if it doesn't end in a slash, it still might specify a directory.) Should it display an INDEX.HTML, a WELCOME.HTML, or what? (Although we won't talk about server-side includes until a later chapter, there are reasonable grounds for including .SHTML and .HTMLX files—files containing server-side includes—in the list.)

CSWS defines the default Web document directory as apache$root:[htdocs] and places the Apache documentation in there as well. I think it's less confusing to separate your site documents from the Apache docs, but you still want to be able to reach them.

Here's the changes to HTTPD$CONF to serve your own files from the Web_root directory tree and still be able to reach the Apache documents.

```
DocumentRoot /$Web_root/ # or /$disk1/Web/root/

<Directory "/$Web_root">
       Options Indexes MultiViews
       AllowOverride None
       Order allow,deny
       Allow from all
</Directory>

DirectoryIndex index.html index.shtml welcome.html index.htm welcome.htm
```

(That `DirectoryIndex` command means that whenever Apache gets a directory specification, it will search in order for index.html, index.shtml, welcome.html, index.htm, and welcome.htm, displaying the first one of those it finds. If you're expecting to serve up mostly PC-created files, you might want to put the index.htm [and welcome.htm files, if you'll allow that] first in the list, since putting the likeliest ones first will save processing time.)

By changing the document root you've made Apache unable to find the cute file-type icons it uses for automatically generated directory browsing, so you'll want to fix that as well as making the documents available.

The Alias directive is

```
Alias URLstring directory-or-file-name
```

Here's what to put into HTTPD.CONF:

```
Alias /icons/ "/apache$root/icons/"
Alias /docs/ "/apache$common/htdocs/manual/"

<Directory "/apache$root/icons">
       Options Indexes
       AllowOverride None
       Order allow,deny
       Allow from all
```

```
</Directory>
<Directory "/apache$common/htdocs">
       Options Indexes MultiViews
       AllowOverride None
       Order allow,deny
       Allow from all
</Directory>
```

(You need the `Directory` containers to tell Apache that it's permitted to serve the contents of these directories; I'll explain this in detail in Chapter 7.)

In OSU, you set the equivalent of the root directory with the Pass command. These go in the HTTP_PATHS.CONF file. (Pass combines transmuting the URL component and giving access to the file, assuming the server itself has access; the similar map command transmutes the URL file component but doesn't give access.)

```
pass url-file-component(wildcard permitted) translated-value

pass / /$Web_root/index.html # or whatever file you choose.
pass /* /$Web_root/*
```

(`Pass`, `map`, and `fail` commands are processed in the order found in the http_paths file, so if you want to be able to serve anything that isn't directly under $Web_root, you'll need a pass command for it that appears prior to the "`pass /* /$Web_root/*`" command.)

HTTP_PATHS.CONF already, by default, has several useful `pass` and `map` commands for server demonstrations and documentation.

The `pass /` specified the precise welcome file for your root directory, but for other directories you can give more options by using the `Welcome` command in http_main.conf. (If you specify the scriptserver directory browser—this is covered in greater detail in Chapter 13—you'll have to configure this in HTTP_DIRECTORY.CONF.) The syntax is

```
Welcome filename.ext
```

and this is cumulative, so you can do

```
Welcome index.html
Welcome welcome.html
Welcome index.htmlx
Welcome welcome.htmlx
Welcome index.htm
Welcome welcome.htm
```

and the server will check for files in that order whenever the URL points it to a directory rather than a full file name. As in Apache, try to get the order so that the likeliest files pecs show up first.

In WASD, edit the HTTPD$MAP.CONF file to accomplish these goals. The items here are mapping rules, not directives, which is why their syntax is different from the [directive] syntax. There are three syntaxes for the pass rule:

```
pass template
pass template result
pass template "numeric_status message-text"
```

In your out-of-the-box HTTPD$MAP.CONF file, you want to comment out (with a '#') the

```
pass /ht_root/*
```

because that allows any unauthorized user to browse your configuration files.

```
pass /* /$Web_root/*
```

will reset your document root without taking away access to the WASD docs, which are in /ht_root/doc/.

Specify the welcome page choices (which apply at the "/" level in WASD, unlike OSU) with the [Welcome] directive in HTTPD$CONFIG.CONF

```
[Welcome]
index.html
welcome.html
index.htmlx
welcome.htmlx
index.shtml
welcome.shtml
index.htm
welcome.htm
```

5.4.3 Customized error messages and Webmaster address

You could, in fact, stop here, start your server, and experience the mild thrill of seeing your documents being served. But it might be better at this stage to do some more configuration. You can make each of these servers offer helpful Web pages for each HTTP status code that turns up, and, further, optionally have those pages identify which server has produced the error code, and optionally have the pages provide an address to e-mail you to tell you about the problem.

In Apache, make these changes to the HTTPD.CONF file:

```
ServerAdmin your-account@your.domain.tld
```

(You may want to set up forwarding from Webmaster@your.domain.tld to your account and use Webmaster here, rather than revealing your identity.) By default, Apache will produce a reasonable error page (see Figure 5.1). Whether or not it identifies itself as Apache is up to you.

```
ServerSignature On|Off|Email
```

`ServerSignature Email` will generate error pages that say what version of Apache is running on what system, and the system name is actually a

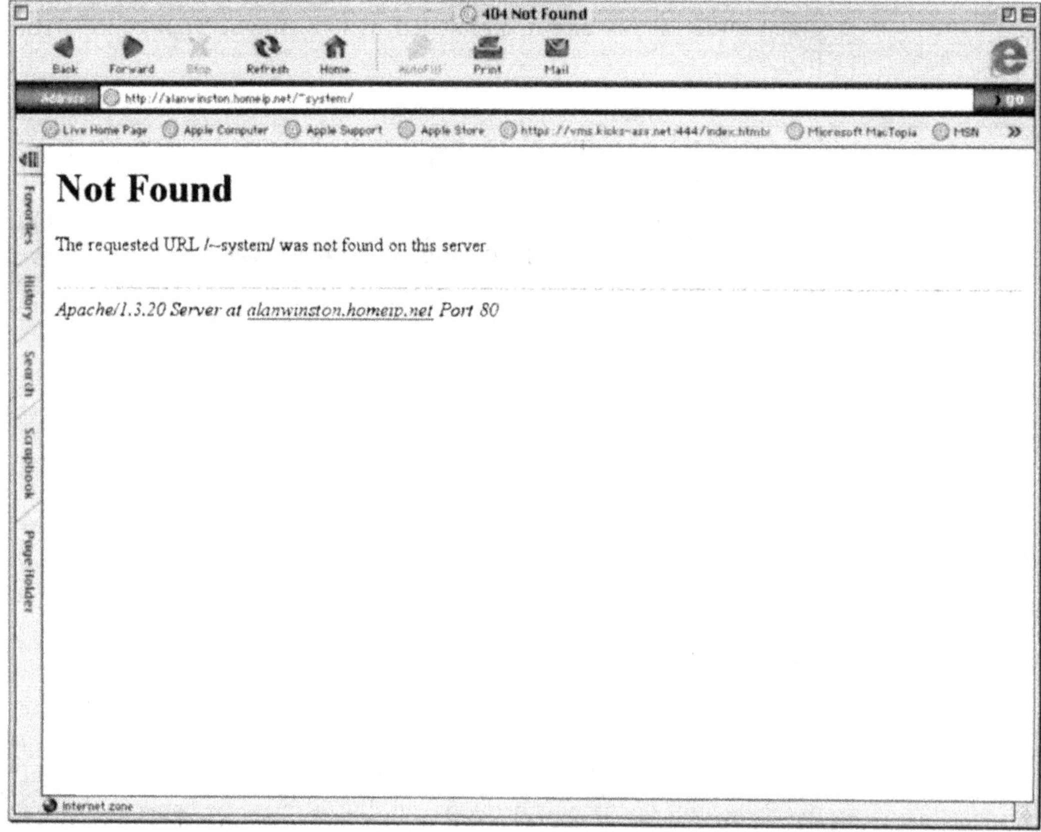

Figure 5.1 *Apache error page with signature.*

mailto: link to the `ServerAdmin` address. `"On"` will do the same thing without the mailto:; `"Off"` won't do it at all. (This is arguably more secure, since a potential attacker doesn't get the extra clue of what Web server this is, but I'd be more concerned about this if I were running IIS.)

If you want to do something fancy with errors, Apache lets you do a lot, although we're getting out of the realm of basic configuration. The magic directive is

```
ErrorDocument error-code response
```

If response begins with a double quote ("), what follows will be taken as a literal string, which the server will write out; this can be plain text or HTML embedded in the config file. (Lines can be continued with backslashes.) If it doesn't begin with a quote, response is considered to be a local or remote URL. If it begins with HTTP or HTTPS, Apache will issue a redirect to that URL. If it begins with a slash, Apache processes it like any other URL; that means it can be a CGI program as well as an HTML page. Once you get to that stage, your response can be arbitrarily complex.

In OSU, there's no equivalent to the ServerAdmin function, but there's support for the ErrorPage command, which uses symbolic names for the error codes.

You can have different actions for protection failures, open failures (a sample script is provided), rule failures, CGI problems, and others. And, of course, if you're producing error pages, you may as well include your e-mail address of choice. The errorpage command goes in HTTP_PATHS.CONF

```
errorpage protfail | openfail | rulefail | cgiprotocol |
| code4 response
```

In WASD, the server administrator e-mail is configured in HTTPD$CONFIG.CONF with the `[ServerAdmin]` directive.

```
[ServerAdmin] user@server.domain.tld
```

Whether this will be included in error reports is determined by the `[ServerSignature]` directive:

```
[ServerSignature] ENABLED | EMAIL | DISABLED
```

`DISABLED` (the default) suppresses the signature altogether, `ENABLED` appends a report of which server on which host produced the message, and `EMAIL` makes the host name into a mailto: link to the value specified in `[ServerAdmin]`.

WASD plugs error codes into a template that's found in the HTTPD$MSG.CONF file, so the result of any error will be an HTML page. The [ServerReportBodyTag] directive lets you specify the HTML <BODY> tag that will be plugged into that template, letting your error messages share at least some of your site's "look and feel." You can also edit the template to include graphics, font choices, and the like to make the messages really match the rest of your site, but this will cause you trouble if you do multihosting because the change is made on a serverwide basis.

```
[ServerReportBodyTag] String
```

(If you specify this, it needs to at least say <BODY>, but could be <BODY BGCOLOR="#00FFFF"> or even call in a cascading style sheet.)

Your basic configuration is complete, and your server should now be ready to serve your own documents.

5.5 Starting and stopping

To start Apache, invoke sys$startup:apache$startup.com. (This procedure can accept parameters; the default value for P1 is START, which instructs Apache to start in a detached process, which is how you ordinarily want to run it. The second parameter is a file in which startup configuration information is stored; this defaults to sys$manager:apache$config.dat, or the value of a logical name APACHE$CONFIG_FILE.) If you want to start Apache running in your current process—most likely because you're debugging configuration files—use the parameter RUN. This is potentially dangerous if you're running from a privileged account.

To shut down Apache, invoke sys$startup:apache$shutdown.com. (Again, this can accept parameters, but defaults to SHUTDOWN.)

To get Apache to reread the configuration files as though it were starting cleanly, you can invoke either apache$startup.com or apache$shutdown.com and use the parameter GRACEFUL, if you don't want to break existing requests, or the parameter RESTART, if you don't care about existing requests.

Both procedures are actually front ends to another procedure, apache$config.com, which has more options available; these are discussed in the following section.

To start OSU, invoke HTTP_STARTUP.COM from the [OSU.SYSTEM] directory. HTTP_STARTUP.COM takes six parameters, in the following order: the name of the account under which OSU will run; the name of the error log file (which defaults to HTTP_SYSTEM, but can be defined as [for example] www_root:[logs]http_errors.log if you want to put your log files in a different directory; the configuration file name; the primary port; the nocache port; and a directory path to have www_system defined as:

```
$ HTTP_STARTUP HTTP_SERVER HTTP_ERRORS.LOG HTTP_MAIN.CONF
80 443 -
WWW_ROOT:[SYSTEM]
```

(I generally create another startup file that calls HTTP_STARTUP with the parameters it needs, so that I can just type @OSU_STARTUP without worrying about the rest.) OSU doesn't require any special shutdown, but if you want to be sure it flushes its log files before it exits, use the privrequest program (discussed in the following section) to issue a shutdown.

```
$ privrequest comm-port-number SHUTDOWN [port if not 80]
```

If you just want it to reread the configuration files, do

```
$ privrequest comm-port-number RESTART [port if not 80]
```

WASD startup is accomplished by invoking [HT_ROOT.LOCAL] STARTUP.COM, which invokes [HT_ROOT. LOCAL]SERVER_START UP.COM and in turn [HT_ROOT.LOCAL]LOCAL_STARTUP.COM to bring in local customizations.

If you're running multiple services on multiple nodes from the same [HT_ROOT], you can create STARTUP_SERVER_nodename.COM or even STARTUP_SERVER_nodename_port.COM files to customize which services to run from which nodes. The least-interruptible version is just to run all services on all nodes in the cluster and use DNS load-balancing to direct the clients to the least heavily loaded machine at any given moment, but there are legitimate reasons to run different services. (If you have two production nodes and two development nodes in the cluster, you don't want the development nodes running potentially broken versions of the services the outside world can see.)

You can also start WASD running in your process.

```
$ MC $HT_EXE:HTTPD_SSL
```

will start it up, and complaints about the configuration file will go directly to your screen. This is handy when you're making radical configuration changes and want to debug them quickly, but this is a dangerous habit to get into if you're running from a privileged account.

There are a number of possible command-line options that affect the behavior of the server if used at server startup; edit your STARTUP_LOCAL or your STARTUP_SERVER_nodename.com to bring these into play. (This list is closely based on section 5.3 of the server documentation, with my own comments interleaved.)

```
/ACCEPT=host1.domain.tld,host2.domain.tld
```

The argument is a comma-separated list of hosts/domains allowed to connect to the server; connects from everywhere else are rejected.

```
/REJECT=host1.domain.tld,host2.domain.tld
```

Alternatively, use `/REJECT` to disallow certain hosts/domains and allow everybody else.

```
/ALL[=servergroupname]
```

At startup, this assigns a server to a specific group of servers (for cluster-wide server control and proxy cache management). If the string isn't specified, it becomes part of the cluster-wide ALL group.

```
/AUTHORIZATION=[SSL,ALL]
```

The "SSL" keyword causes all authentication (both SYSUAF and HTA database) to be available only via "HTTPS:" requests—thus guaranteeing that no passwords will be exchanged in plain text. (Of course, this works only if you are using the SSL-enabled version of the server; see Chapter 6 for a fuller discussion of SSL and Chapter 7 for authentication.)

The `ALL` keyword will make the server deny access to any path that isn't explicitly authorized, thus reversing the default of allowing access to any path that isn't protected against access in some way.

```
/CGI_PREFIX=string
```

The value here will be used as the beginning of each CGI symbol name accessible to scripts. (Use this to allow scripts written for other servers to get the symbol names they expect. Default is "WWW_", a tradition established by the CERN VMS server.)

```
/DETACH=dcl-procedurename/USER=username
```

On VMS 6.2 and later, this causes the server to create a detached process executing the specified dcl-procedurename operating as the specified user name.

```
/FILBUF=number
```

This specifies the number of bytes in the read buffer for files open for processing (i.e., menu files, image mapping configuration files, preprocessed HTML files, etc., not direct file transfers), which you're likely to be interested in tuning only if you have either extremely large preprocessor files or small available memory that you need to conserve.

```
/FORMAT=formatstring
```

The format string overrides the configuration parameter [LogFormat]; see Chapter 12 for details.

```
/GBLSEC=DELETE=integer
```

At startup, the server creates a permanent global section named by the main port number the server is serving. This section stores accounting and request data and is visible to the server monitor utility, HTTPDMON. If you're experimenting with configurations on different ports, you can burn up too much memory on these global sections. Use this parameter to make them deleteable. This won't be used in a stable configuration.

```
/LOG[=name]
```

enables logging and optionally specifies the log file name. If the name is SYS$OUTPUT, the log entries will show up on your screen. If you're experimenting with log file formats, the combination of /FORMAT and /LOG=SYS$OUTPUT will let you see what you're getting before you edit your configuration files. (If not specified in the config files, logging is disabled by default.)

```
/NOLOG
```

disables logging, overriding the logging directives in the configuration files.

```
/NOMONITOR
```

The HTTPDMON utility (discussed in section 5.6) displays information made available to it by the server. This qualifier disables the update of those data, making HTTPDMON useless. This is of most use on an overloaded server, which needs every possible cycle.

```
/NETBUF=number
```

gives the number of bytes to allocate for the network read buffer, allowing tuning if you run frequent large file uploads.

```
/OUTBUF=number
```

gives the number of bytes in the output buffer (for direct file transfers, buffered output from menu interpretation, HTML preprocessing), allowing tuning if you have buffer overruns from large transfers.

```
/PERIOD= DAILY|
 MONDAY|TUESDAY|WEDNESDAY|THURSDAY|FRIDAY|SATURDAY|SUNDAY|
 MONTHLY
```

overrides the configuration parameter [LogPeriod], which specifies how often to start a new log file: every day, every week on the specified day, or every month.

```
/PERSONA[=rightslist-identifier]
```

enables detached process scripting. If you don't specify a rightslist identifier, scripts can be executed under any account—if they're mapped to do so in the configuration file. If you do specify one, then scripts can be run only under accounts that have been GRANTed that identifier

```
PORT=port-number
```

is primarily useful for command-line control with the /DO qualifier, discussed subsequently. At startup, it overrides the configuration parameter [Port] but will be overridden both by any [Service] specified in the configuration files and by any `/SERVICE=` qualifier.

```
/PRIORITY=number
```

Server process priority. By default, this is 4, which means the server competes on an equal basis with interactive users at their default priority. If your interactive users aren't getting enough compute time, you can set this to 3, which is the default batch priority. Setting this to a higher priority than that of your interactive users (if any) risks slow performance and apparent system lockup if some script gets into a tight loop. It would be extremely inadvisable to set this in the real-time priority range of 17–32.

```
/[NO]PROFILE
```

allows (or, with `/NOPROFILE`, disallows) the use of rightslist-identifier–based file access for users authenticated against the SYSUAF. (This is discussed more fully in Chapter 7. It is irrelevant unless the /SYSUAF qualifier is also present.)

```
/PROMISCUOUS[=password]
```

If the password is omitted, this makes the server accept any user name/password pair for authentication; if a password is included, it requires that to be the password used. This is used for testing, demonstration, and initial server configuration via the Web-based interface. If you're going to do this when you have actual material to serve and some authentication in place, it would be a good idea to use the `/ACCEPT` parameter and restrict connections to the system you plan to use for the demo or the configuration.

```
/SERVICE=scheme://hostname1:port1,scheme://hostname2:port2
```

The argument is a comma-separated service list, which overrides the `[Service]` configuration parameter, primarily useful for starting with some services disabled. (In a cluster configuration in which you share configuration files but offer different services on each node, you can specify services by node using this parameter in the STARTUP_SERVER_nodename.COM file; the server will accept the configuration details of the specified services from the configuration file.)

```
/NOSSL
/SSL[=version]
```

In the `/NOSSL` form, this disables HTTPS/SSL support altogether. In the `/SSL=[version]`, it directs the server to support SSL v2, v3, or (the default) both. It is irrelevant if you haven't built the server with SSL support.

```
/SUBBUF=number
```

gives the number of bytes in a script process's SYS$OUTPUT buffer.

```
/[NO]SWAP
```

controls whether the server process may be swapped out of the balance set. (`/NOSWAP` is the default.) It doesn't disable the use of virtual memory altogether, but keeps the server process from being rolled out of memory entirely, since there is a distinct detriment to response time if the system has to identify some other victim process, swap it out to disk, copy every bit of the server process back from disk to memory, and only then deliver the AST for the read on port 80. It's not inconceivable, on a slow and heavily loaded VAX, that the browser would time out the connection by the time the process was ready to handle it. If your system is really starved for memory and you don't care much about Web server response time, you can enable swapping for the server.

```
/NOSYSUAF
/SYSUAF[=ID,PROXY,SSL,WASD]
```

The `/NOSYSUAF` form (the default) disables SYSUAF authentication altogether. (You can still have password support from the HTA database, but not the VMS user name/password from the SYSUAF.) `/SYSUAF=SSL` enables SYSUAF authentication and forces the password dialog to HTTPS, guaranteeing encryption and making it harder to snoop passwords. `/SYSUAF=PROXY` enables SYSUAF proxying; `/SYSUAF=ID` restricts SYSUAF authentication to accounts holding a particular identifier (see

Chapter 7 for some details); `/SYSUAF=WASD` is deprecated; it makes the "hard-wired" WASD identifier environment available.

```
/VERSION
```

displays the copyright notice and version of the executables.

```
/NOWATCH
/WATCH="category-integer,[client-filter],[service-
filter],[path-filter]"
```

The WATCH facility (discussed subsequently) allows an in-browser view of server processing as it happens. If you want to use it, use neither one of these qualifiers. `/NOWATCH` disables it altogether. `/WATCH=` directs watch output to standard output if running from your process or to the server log if running detached. The category-integer is the bitwise-OR of the categories specified in the ADMIN.H source code header; the easiest way to get it is to set up a WATCH with the categories you want in the Web-based admin program, and then note the parenthetical category integer that shows on the screen in all the WATCH reports.

To shut down WASD, define the HTTPD foreign command (described in the next section), and issue either

```
$ HTTPD/PORT=port-number/DO=EXIT ! exit after finishing
                                 ! current requests
```

or

```
$ HTTPD/PORT=port-number/DO=EXIT=NOW ! immediate shutdown.
```

To make WASD reread the configuration files freshly, do

```
$ HTTPD/PORT=port-number/DO=RESTART ! restart after
                                    ! finishing current requests
```

or

```
$ HTTPD/PORT=port-number/DO=RESTART=NOW ! immediate restart
```

5.6 Command-line control

Now you can start and stop the servers. What other control is available from the command line?

In Apache, all the available functions are implemented through SYS$STARTUP:APACHE$CONFIG.COM. The command is the first parameter, so

```
SYS$STARTUP:APACHE$CONFIG command
```

The commands are as follows:

```
CONFIGURE
```

which runs the configuration dialog you had at server startup; you probably don't want to mess with that.

```
FLUSH
```

which gets the log files on disk up-to-date by telling the server to flush the buffered messages to disk. (Implicit in SHUTDOWN.)

```
GRACEFUL
```

which tells the server to finish existing requests, then reread the configuration file.

```
NEW
```

which tells the server to flush the current buffers, then open new log files. (This can be issued from a batch job to get new files daily, weekly, or monthly, but, in fact, the logging module in Apache lets you specify log file turnover with considerable precision.)

```
READ
```

which reads the APACHE$CONFIG.COM configuration file and defines processwide logical names based on that information. (This function is useful when you want multiple Apaches running with different configuration files on the same system, but in a vanilla configuration you'll never use it.)

```
RESTART
```

which sends a restart signal to the server to reread APACHE$ROOT:[CONF]HTTPD.CONF immediately.

```
RUN
```

which runs the Web server in your current process. (This represents a s security exposure when you run from a privileged account.)

```
SHUTDOWN
```

which stops the Web server process immediately.

```
STOP
```

which stops the Web server process. (Same as SHUTDOWN.)

```
START
```

which starts the Web server as a detached process.

(Incidentally, if you're a UNIX person and you're wondering how a DCL script manages to send a signal to a program, APACHE$CONFIG actually runs a small executable program to send whatever signals it needs to be sending. If you're porting other signal-driven UNIX programs to VMS, you can borrow it; it's somewhat frighteningly named APACHE_KILL and takes two parameters: the process-id to deliver the message to and the message itself. A VMS hacker might be wondering why Apache didn't just declare a control mailbox when it was started to which DCL could just write messages. I presume it was because making Apache create the mailbox and hang a read with read-complete AST on it would do excessively radical things to the structure of the program, and the VMS changes are supposed to fold back into the Apache mainstream. It already expects to get a signal.)

OSU offers the PRIVREQUEST program for some command-line control of the program. Unlike Apache, which sends out-of-band signals to the executing server, PRIVREQUEST sends control messages on a port the server is listening to anyway (80, by default) and gets responses on a port it specifies (usually 931). The central port must be specified in the configuration file.

Define a foreign command, such as

```
$ privrequest :== $www_system:privrequest
```

(That's handy for the LOGIN.COM of the Webmaster's account.)

```
$ PRIVREQUEST 931 HELP
```

This brings back a list of the available commands. If the server isn't running on port 80, you have to specify which port to talk to; for 8001, that command would look like

```
$ PRIVREQUEST 931 HELP 8001
```

(If you don't specify a port, it will use port 80, with unexpected results if you're running some other server on port 80.)

Here are the commands, other than `HELP`.

```
DSPCACHE
```

displays the current entries in the cache. (See Chapter 11 for more information on caching.)

```
INVCACHE
```

invalidates the document cache. This means that the next request for any particular document will have to go out to the disk and check the file headers, possibly resulting in fetching a new copy of the file into cache. I've found this most useful when doing incremental changes to an HTML file on the server. If I want to see my changes right away when the default cache expiration is set to three minutes, I need to invalidate the cache to get the most current version. (This whole area is somewhat problematic, since users tend to panic if they upload a file and can't see it right away; this is one of the reasons for making a nocache port available, but the nocache port has been commandeered to run SSL. It will be handy when the multiple port support in 3.10alpha has matured, since that will allow other nocache ports.)

```
NEWLOG
```

creates a new access log. The name and location of the access log is defined in the configuration file; you can't change it here, but you can make a new one run. This is a handy command to run in batch mode to get a new log file on a daily, weekly, or monthly basis.

```
NEWTRACE[/logger-level]
```

starts a new trace file. (This has the name given as the second parameter in the HTTP_STARTUP.COM. The logger level specifies what you want details of and how you want them; higher levels include lower levels. Use plain `NEWTRACE` to start a new log with the default log level—`/1` for connect/completion logging, `/5` for script diagnostics, and `/11` for a detailed trace of requests as they pass through the rule file (so you can see where you messed up in file mapping.) There are higher levels still, which were probably used for debugging problems in developing ISAPI and FastCGI modules—you can basically find out about them only by reading the source code or by experimenting. `NEWTRACE/11` and higher will make huge log files very quickly, so if you're at all short on disk space watch this closely.

```
RESTART[/timeout]
```

restarts the server after allowing the specified number of seconds (or ten seconds if not specified) for current requests to complete.

```
SHUTDOWN[/timeout]
```

shuts down the server after allowing the specified number of seconds (or ten seconds if not specified) for current requests to complete.

```
STATISTICS[/ZERO]
```

displays counters or resets them to zero. I find myself using this mostly when I'm trying to find out whether my server is alive or not, but it's also useful for getting a handle on your current level of traffic without doing extensive log-file analysis.

5.6.1 WASD

Define the foreign command $HTTPD to either "$HT_EXE:HTTPD" or "$HT_EXE:HTTPD_SSL" depending on whether you're running the SSL-enabled server or not. If the main port for your server isn't 80, your commands will need to include /PORT=whatever-the-main-port-is in order to be delivered. If you want to control all the servers in the cluster, add the /ALL qualifier; if you've defined a group of servers with /ALL=servergroupname in the server startup, you can address just that group by including /ALL=servergroupname in the HTTPD command.

That's actually the server image, so if you just type HTTPD you'll find yourself running a copy of the server from the command line. (It won't do much if you've already got a started server process grabbing the IP requests before your copy gets to them.) You need to use the /DO= qualifier to tell HTTPD to pass the message along to the running server and exit. Again, this discussion follows the server documentation fairly closely.

```
/DO=AUTH=LOAD
```

reloads the authorization rule file (HTTPD$AUTH), enabling any changes made since the last reload. (See Chapter 7.)

```
/DO=AUTH=PURGE
```

The authentication cache may be purged, requiring all subsequent authorization-controlled accesses to reauthenticate. This is helpful if you've disabled some authorizations and want them to lose access right away, or if you've enabled it—for example, when a user has been locked out by automatic break-in evasion for too many invalid password attempts and you've cleared the intrusions.

```
/DO=CACHE=ON
```

enables the file cache (see Chapter 11).

```
/DO=CACHE=OFF
```

disables the file cache.

```
/DO=CACHE=PURGE
```

invalidates the current contents of the file cache so that subsequent accesses will go out to the file system, repopulating the cache with current versions of the file.

```
/DO=DCL=DELETE
```

deletes all scripting processes, whether they're doing work or not. (It may cause browsers to display errors.)

```
/DO=DCL=PURGE
```

deletes idle scripting processes immediately and deletes currently busy ones when they've completed the requests they're working on. (Preferable, unless you've got a script process in a tight loop.)

```
/DO=DECNET=DISCONNECT
```

disconnects all DECnet connections, busy or not. (Relevant for OSU-compatible scripting.) Clients may lose data.

```
/DO=DECNET=PURGE
```

disconnects idle DECnet connections immediately and disconnects currently busy ones once they're done. (Generally preferable.)

```
/DO=LOG=FORMAT=string
/DO=LOG=PERIOD=string
```

changes, respectively, the format and period specification of the access log; this will take effect only after the log file is opened or reopened. (See Chapter 12 for log-file format.) These commands are server-by-server; the `/ALL` qualifier is not available.

```
/DO=LOG=CLOSE
```

closes the access log file(s).

```
/DO=LOG=OPEN
```

opens the access log file(s).

```
/DO=LOG=REOPEN
```

closes and then reopens the access log file(s).

```
/DO=LOG=FLUSH
```

All unwritten log records may be flushed to the access log file(s).

```
/DO=MAP
```

reloads the mapping file (HTTPD$MAP.CONF), enabling the changes made since the last load or reload. (See Chapter 7.)

```
/DO=SSL=CA=LOAD
```

reloads the Certificate Authority verification list—relevant only if you're using X.509 authentication. (See Chapter 7.)

```
/DO=SSL=KEY=PASSWORD
Enter private key password []:
```

If your server key requires a password/passphrase to enable it, as described (and recommended against) in Chapter 6, this command allows you to enter the password.

```
/DO=THROTTLE=RELEASE
/DO=THROTTLE=TERMINATE
```

Request throttling is discussed in Chapter 7. Briefly, throttling allows the Webmaster to specify how many simultaneous requests will be handled for a particular path. Requests in excess of that number go onto a FIFO queue for later processing.

`/DO=THROTTLE=RELEASE` instructs the server to immediately start processing all queue requests. (You might use this if you were throttling requests because you were running a big CPU-intensive job that has now finished and want to allow it all now, or if you just want to see what happens to the server load without request throttling.)

`/DO=THROTTLE=TERMINATE` instructs the server to cancel all queued requests, sending them back a 503 "server too busy" response.

```
/DO=ZERO
```

zeroes the server counters. (These are the counters that you'd see using HTTPDMON or the statistics menu item in the Web-based server admin menu. You'd want to do this to get an immediate handle on current traffic; zero it now and check it a couple of minutes later.)

There are a couple of other command-line things that aren't exactly issuing server commands. You can do proxy cache maintenance activities from the command line, using the `/PROXY` (not `/DO=PROXY`) qualifier; I'll discuss this more fully in Chapter 11. The HTTPDMon utility ($HT_EXE:HTTPDMON) enables real-time monitoring of WASD activity from the command line.

5.7 Web-based control

Apache has no built-in Web-based configuration or control utility. (In the UNIX world, there are various GUI configuration utilities provided by third parties, but they aren't part of the Apache distribution. It's probably a bit much to ask VMS Engineering to port and then support TCL/TK so that we can use an existing TCL/TK-based GUI configurator.) It should be fairly easy to write a CGI that could generate the commands to @SYS$STARTUP:APACHE$CONFIG.COM to issue control messages to start/stop/restart the server, but then it would be fairly dangerous to run CGIs in a sufficiently privileged context to actually do that.

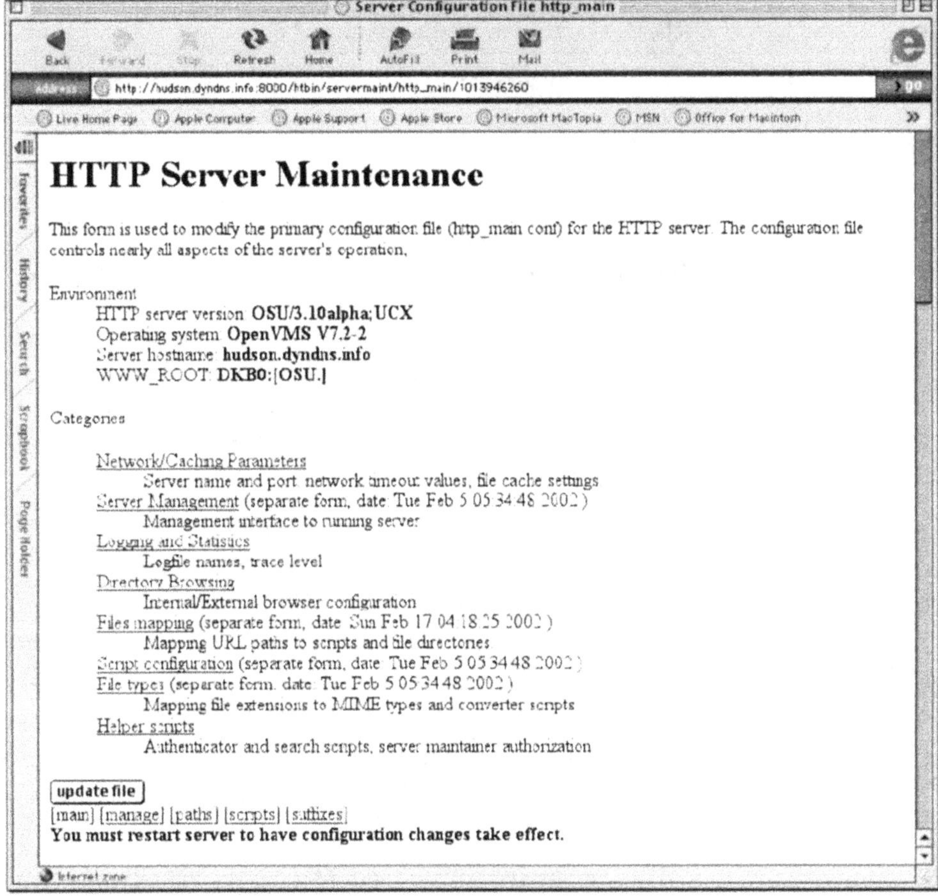

Figure 5.2 *OSU Web-based administration utility—main page.*

OSU provides a Web-based server administration utility. (See Figure 5.2.) By default, this is configured as http://yourserver.domain.tld/demo/servermaint.html (You can also look at http://yourserver.domain.tld/demo/servermaint_userguide.html for advice on using the server maintenance Web-based utility.)

The user name and password for this are, by default, `server` and `maint`, respectively. (The first thing to do when using it is to change the password for access on that page only to something else—you don't want everybody else who uses OSU to know the password that lets them update your configuration.)

Most of the screens simply allow you to update configuration files, but one screen allows the same kind of server control you're able to do with PRIVREQUEST from the command line.

As you can see, from the Web you can stop or restart the server, start a new access log file, or start a new trace file with a different setting of how much information to trace.

Experienced OSU users typically do not use the Web-based configurator, and there are certain things that it just won't do for you—for example, inserting rules into a local-address block if you're multihosting and want to apply specific rules only to certain hosts. (Multihosting is discussed in Chapter 9.) Also, Web-based support for new features tends to lag the release of the new features. New managers should definitely fire it up and poke around, just to get an idea of what's available in the server configuration (although you won't learn much that you didn't get by reading this book).

WASD has an extensive on-line administration utility, which requires some configuration effort to make work. (See Figure 5.3.) Alternatively, to get an idea of what's available, you can just break in.

```
$spawn/wait httpd /promiscuous=password/service=8010
/accept=node-you'll-use
```

This brings up a new copy of HTTPD, willing to accept connections only from the node you specified, running on the port you specified (8010, in the example), willing to authenticate any user name you give it provided you give it the password specified.

This can give you a good idea of what capabilities are available in a fully configured server, which include not only everything you can do from the command line but also configuration file editing, reports, and WATCHing the server processing in real time. However, until you do some authoriza-

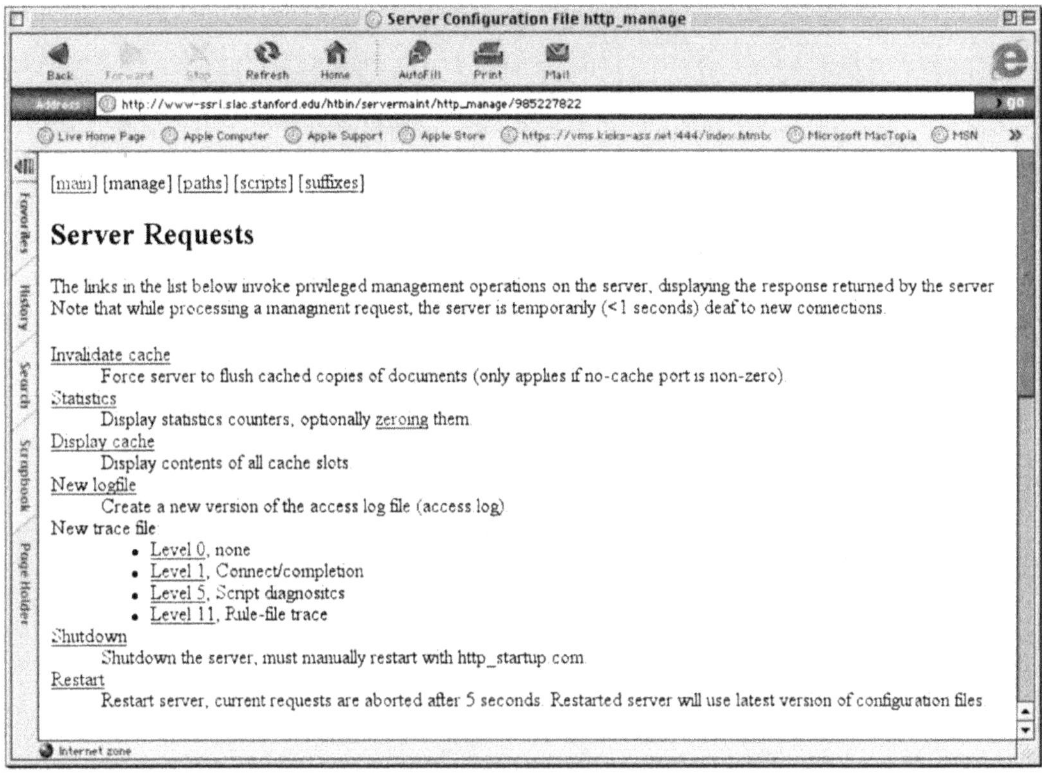

Figure 5.3 *OSU Web-based administrative utility-server commands.*

tion/authentication work (details are discussed in Chapter 7), you won't be able to edit the configuration files or save changes from the Web-based utility. (You will be able to run the reports.)

If you exit or restart at this point, with the server running in a spawned subprocess, the server will just go away rather than restarting.

6

Encrypted/Secure Communications: HTTPS Protocol Support

6.1 HTTPS

6.1.1 Why?

The HyperText Transfer Protocol (HTTP) is intended for the easy interchange of information between systems on multiple platforms. It was designed with the idea that the free sharing of information is good, secrecy is bad, and barriers to communication are to be avoided; overall, it does a good job in embodying these ideals.

Material in HTTP comes over with no attempt at obscurity. Anybody listening in—anyone on your network using a sniffer, any system cracker who may have compromised a system on your network and put its Ethernet card into promiscuous mode so it listens to all the traffic, or any systems person at your Internet Service Provider who monitors your traffic—can see both ends of every dialog conducted over the Web.

This is fine when you're sharing information about the latest results in particle physics or publishing movie times; it's not really a good idea when collecting credit card numbers, passwords, or other confidential information. People found the Web just too attractive as a universal applications platform to leave it exclusively for free sharing of information. Whether you're ordering something by credit card or trying to remotely access your e-mail, you need to provide some information you don't want random strangers to know.

So, HTTPS (S for secure) was invented. This allows both sides of a Web dialog to be encrypted in a cipher negotiated between the browser and the server. (There would be no point in a cipher that was the same for every browser, because then everybody who got the traffic would know how to decipher it.) HTTPS uses the secure session layer (SSL) software, which can use an assortment of different public-key algorithms having colorful names (e.g., RSA, Blowfish, Twofish, and IDEA). SSL code also supports transport layer security (TLS) software. If you're running PMDF-TLS encrypted SMTP you're already running OpenSSL. SSL has been through several versions, and there are browsers that support both version 2 and version 3, so you're best off supporting both.

6.1.2 SSL and PKI

The idea of the secure session layer is to provide a secure wrapper for other protocols. Thus, the same SSL code can support HTTPS and SSH (secure shell, which works like an encrypted Telnet), SCP (secure copy, like an encrypted RCP), and SFTP (encrypted FTP); further, port forwarding in SSH can support X Windows and potentially other protocols. However, "secure" doesn't just mean that it's encrypted (and thus hard for eavesdroppers to understand). It also means that you're talking to who you think you're talking to. (Your credit card information isn't safe if you have a strongly encrypted connection to the wrong site.) SSL supports authentication as well as encryption, and this is where the confusion, annoyance, and expense associated with HTTPS comes in—the rest, which I'm glad to say has eased lately, comes from patents and export restrictions.

This whole system works on "public-key" encryption and authentication methods. (These methods, introduced in 1976 by mathematicians Whitfield Diffie and Martin Hellman, are potentially useful in much broader areas than just the Web and e-commerce, and I expect we'll see a lot more applications for them than we already have. The ones in use now include S/MIME for secure e-mail and code signing for Active-X controls.) Entities are issued key pairs, a private key (which is never shared with anybody), and a public key (which can be given out freely). These are cryptographic inverses of each other, which means that you can encrypt with a public key and decrypt with a private key, but if the keys are of any substantial length, it takes an unfeasibly long time to compute the private key from the public key. So, you can sign something with a private key, and other people can verify that you signed it using your public key. You can encrypt stuff using the recipient's public key, and they can decrypt it using their private key.

Each packet in a dialog is encrypted, but the keys are exchanged only at the beginning, so an eavesdropper would have to catch the whole thing, not just random packets, to even begin to be able to break the encryption. An eavesdropper who has the whole dialog has only the public key, and it's supposed to be too long and slow a process to get from public key to private key. Not an impossible task; just an unwieldy one. (It's not that the encryption can't be broken; it can't be broken while the contents are still interesting. If your traffic is still going to be interesting to the bad guys 30 years from now, you want to use channels you believe can't easily be eavesdropped upon.)

The longer the key, the longer the process of breaking it will take, so a government that wants to be able to read the traffic of its enemies in wartime might plausibly consider strong encryption a weapon that shouldn't be exported. And so the U.S. government did, which led to all kinds of absurdities. This was a problem because it assumed there were no people outside U.S. borders smart enough to code strong encryption themselves; it meant that a T-shirt with a few lines of Perl code was technically a weapon. In addition, it kept U.S. companies from selling strong encryption abroad while European firms could do so; and, relevantly for this book, it meant that browser vendors were obliged to produce U.S. (128-bit encryption) and export (40-bit encryption) versions of their products and servers have to support both. These restrictions were eased in 2000, but the 40-bit browsers are still out there. The usual means for a server to authenticate itself is to present a digital certificate—sometimes called an X.509 certificate because it complies with the X.509 standard promulgated by the International Telecommunications Union—which says not only "this is my name" but also points to a certificate authority (CA) that has validated the certificate by signing it with its private key. Note that users and browsers can also present certificates to authenticate themselves, although this is fairly uncommon within the general Web user population.

How does the browser know to trust the certificate authority? The browser vendor shipped a database of certificate authorities and their public keys along with the browser, and users can also update that database and add other CAs (although the vast majority of them have no idea how to do this or why they'd want to). How did the CAs get in the database? They made deals with the browser vendors to ship their certificates with the browsers. There are two reasons that there isn't a volunteer-run automated CA handing out certificates for free. First, none of the browsers currently deployed would acknowledge them as legitimate authorities, and anybody who used the certificates they issued would have customers frightened by pop-up messages about "a problem with the digital certificate—certificate authority not recognized." (This is the same reason commercial sites don't just generally make themselves a CA and issue themselves the necessary cer-

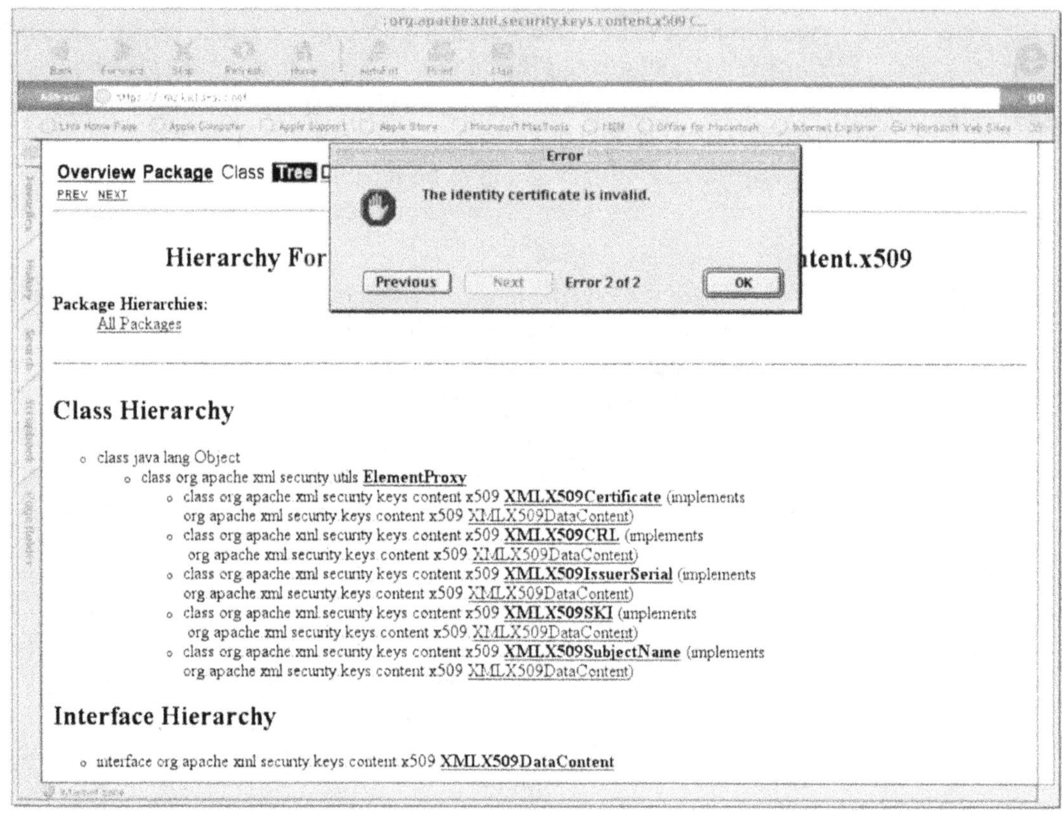

Figure 6.1 *Internet Explorer displays a frightening message.*

tificates—frightening messages from the browser tend to scare off the customers, despite the fact that the encryption is equally good or bad regardless of the validity of the CA.) Second, it actually costs money and effort to verify the identity of the person or organization who's asking you to certify that they are who they say they are, and without the CA making that effort, the authentication value of the certificate is nil.

As for frightening messages, incidentally, it's now generally considered to have been a bad idea that the certificate-authority certificates distributed with Netscape version 3 all expired at midnight on December 31, 1999, making every HTTPS site users tried to access pop up a frightening message about an unknown or expired certificate authority, and giving the people who had to support those users a totally unnecessary Y2K problem. (See Figure 6.1.) Since Netscape 3 was the DEC-supported browser on VMS at the time, this was the only Y2K problem many VMS sites had.

6.1.3 Getting a certificate from a CA

If all your users are technical people who won't panic at browser messages about unrecognized CAs or who can follow instructions to add your CA certificate to their browser database, or if you have control over the machines they'll use to access your site (so you can update their browsers yourself), you can use a self-signed certificate and not have to pay anybody any money. You might want to do this to provide access to your Web applications over insecure networks (e.g., the general Internet) without having passwords flying around in plain text, or just to let people get at their mail using yahMAIL without compromising their passwords. If your CA certificate is in the browser database, you're still safe from being impersonated by some other server—the bad guys shouldn't have your private key. If you teach your users just not to worry about the scary messages, you make them vulnerable to impersonation attacks. Many universities, including MIT and Columbia, have set up their own CAs and installed their certificates in the official university-distributed browser kit.

Otherwise, you're going to have to get a certificate from a commercial provider. Find out whether your organization already has a public key infrastructure (PKI) and arrangements already in place with a CA. If so, you'll have to use whatever procedures the organization has in place for getting a digital certificate. (Organizations can make arrangements with known CAs to receive the delegated authority to issue certificates; the "chain of trust" on those certificates eventually works its way back to a known CA and the browser accepts it without complaint.)

If your organization doesn't have anything in place, it's up to you to do it. Pick a commercial CA and check out their requirements. As an example, I'll use Thawte, a South African company generally considered to have low prices and good service. (They were bought by VeriSign a while ago but still maintain a separate identity and pricing schedule.)

Here's their recommended procedure. Get your documentation together, which means proof that you're the organization you say you are and that you are entitled to use the domain name for which you want the certificate. For incorporated commercial entities, articles of incorporation or state or city documents (business licenses) will work. Partnerships should provide "some form of verifiable proof of the partnership name," which ought to include business licenses. If you're doing business as a particular name, they need a copy of the DBA forms. (All of these documents can be faxed.) Government departments, nongovernment organizations, universities, and university departments need to physically mail an original signed letter on organizational letterhead stationery from the department head (for government departments); the Chief Executive, Chair, or Managing Director (for NGOs); or the Dean or Vice-Chancellor (for university departments). Special interest groups—which I would take to mean unincorporated hobby groups, clubs, international criminal gangs, and the like—need to get in touch with Thawte and discuss individual requirements. Obviously, if you want to register for a certificate as SPECTRE, KAOS, or THRUSH, there'll be some unique needs for verification.

To make a certificate request, you need to install OpenSSL. (More on this follows.) OpenSSL binaries come with CSWS for mod_ssl, and can be downloaded in a separate kit for WASD; for HTTPS support in OSU you'll need either to do a full OpenSSL installation or install the binaries from WASD. Since kits that come from third parties are usually out of date, I recommend installing OpenSSL directly.

These OpenSSL instructions follow those provided by R. A. Byers on his Web site, at http://www.ourservers.net/openvms_ports/openssl/openssl_contents.html; since he keeps them updated, you should go back and read them to see if anything has changed. I have made changes in his directions to match Thawte's requirements.

You have to fill out your configuration files before you can generate certificates or certificate requests. Set your current directory to the SSLROOT directory (where you installed the OpenSSL files). If you've run the OPENSSL_STARTUP.COM, this will be SSLROOT.

```
$ SET DEFAULT SSLROOT:[000000]
```

Create directories to store certificate requests and certificates.

```
$ CREATE/DIRECTORY [.CRL]
$ CREATE/DIRECTORY [.NEWCERTS]
```

You need a file with a few hundred bytes of random data to prime the random number generators in the encryption libraries. A good place to put this is in your [.PRIVATE] directory under the name of RANDFILE., but you could name it anything since you'll define a logical name to point at it. An easy way to get this is to send the output of a long variable command into a file, for example, is as follows:

```
$ SHOW SYSTEM/FULL/OUTPUT=SSLROOT:[PRIVATE]RANDFILE.;
$ DEFINE/SYSTEM/EXEC RANDFILE -
SSLROOT:[PRIVATE]RANDFILE.;
```

Create an empty INDEX.TXT in the SSL root directory.

```
$ CREATE SSLROOT:[000000]INDEX.TXT
^Z
```

Create a file SERIAL. with "01" in it in the SSL root directory.

```
$ CREATE SSLROOT:[000000]SERIAL.
01
^Z
```

Now bring up the OPENSSL.CNF file in your favorite editor and make these changes.

The line that says:

```
dir = sys\$disk:[.demoCA #Where everything is kept
```

should say:

```
dir = SSLROOT:[000000 #Where everything is kept
```

The line that says:

```
RANDFILE = $dir.private].rand # private random number
file
```

should look like

```
RANDFILE = $dir.private]RANDFILE.; # private random
number file
```

and the line that says

```
RANDFILE = $ENV::HOME/.rnd
```

should just be deleted.

Although there are other options, for SSL server certificates only, do this. Find the lines that say

```
# This is OK for an SSL server.
# nsCertType            = server
```

and make them look like this:

```
# This is OK for an SSL server.
nsCertType              = server
```

Now you're ready to generate your certificate request.

```
$ @SSLROOT:[VMS]OPENSSL_UTILS.COM ! Defines the symbol
                                  ! for the OPENSSL utility
```

Use the OPENSSL utility to generate a certificate request.

```
$ OPENSSL
OpenSSL> req -config openssl.cnf -nodes -new -days 365
-keyout newreq_key.pem -out newreq.pem
```

Here's a description of what the parameters mean.

`-req`

This is a certificate request.

`-config`

Use this configuration file.

`-nodes`

Don't DES encode the output key. (Because OSU won't let you specify a passphrase, it won't be able to use a DES-encoded key. Leave the parameter out if you want to use a passphrase on WASD or CSWS.)

`-new`

This is a new request.

`-days`

The number of days the X.509 certificate will be good for.

`-keyout`

File to which to output the key.

`-out`

File to which to output the certificate request.

The program will prompt for some parameter values. For some CAs (not Thawte) you need to answer only one:

```
Common Name (e.g., YOUR name) []:
```

This is not your personal name; this is the name you intend to use as the canonical name for the Web server. So, use www.yourhost.domain.tld if you're going to be in the DNS as www.yourhost.domain.tld; if you expect to be addressed as secure.domain.tld, use that. If you expect to just be called yourhost.domain.tld, use that.

For Thawte, make sure that the company name, state/province, and country that you enter here (or put in your openssl.cnf) exactly match the details in the documentation that you fax or mail to them.

After that, keep pressing return until you get the OpenSSL> prompt; then use CTRL-Z, exit, or quit to get out. You should have two files—the key file (newreq_key.pem) and the certificate request file (newreq.pem). The contents of newreq.pem will look something like this:

```
----BEGIN CERTIFICATE REQUEST----
gibberishgibberishgibberishformanylines
----END CERTIFICATE REQUEST----
```

Despite the .PEM filetype, it's not actually a PEM (privacy-enhanced mail) file, it's just a BASE64-encoded certificate signing request (CSR).

At this point go to the Thawte Web site, http://www.thawte.com/buy/contents.html. You'll cut and paste NEWREQ.PEM into an on-line form at the Thawte site; save the key file, somewhere safe. (If you lose the key file you can't use the certificate when you get it back; this will cost you money.) Also, it wouldn't be a bad idea at this point to request a free test certificate, which will make sure you've got the process working before you spend money on it. Assuming you're going for the real certificate, the Thawte Web site will give you an order number, which you shouldn't lose either, since you'll need it to track the status of your request, generate a subscriber agreement, and download the certificate. Send Thawte the supporting documents by fax or courier. When they're ready to issue the certificate, you'll get e-mail with a URL to download the certificate from. Do so. When you've got it onto your VMS system, append your key to the end of the signed certificate.

```
$ APPEND NEWREQ_KEY.PEM <certificate the CA signed>
```

Then tell the server where to find the certificate (detailed in the following text), and you're set.

6.1.4 Creating a self-signed certificate.

If you're either not going to use a CA certificate or want to get going while you're waiting for your certificate to arrive, you can use OpenSSL to create a self-signed certificate. Here's how. (Again, these instructions follow those provided by R. A. Byers on his Web site at http://www.ourservers.net/openvms_ports/openssl/openssl_contents.html. Assume you've already installed OpenSSL and have run @OPENSSL_STARTUP.) Run SSL-ROOT:[VMS]OPENSSL_UTILS.COM file to define the symbol for the OPENSSL utility.

```
$ @SSLROOT:[VMS]OPENSSL_UTILS.COM
```

Set your default to the SSL root directory.

```
$ SET DEFAULT SSLROOT:[000000]
```

Generate a certificate request using the OPENSSL utility.

```
$ OPENSSL
OpenSSL> req -config openssl.cnf -nodes -new -days 365
-x509 -keyout test_key.pem -out test.pem
```

Here's a description of what the parameters mean.

`-config`

This indicates which configuration file to use.

`-nodes`

Don't DES encode the output key. (Because OSU won't let you specify a passphrase, it won't be able to use a DES-encoded key. Leave the parameter out if you want to use a passphrase on WASD or CSWS.)

`-new`

This is a new certificate request.

`-days`

The number of days the X.509 certificate is good for.

`-x509`

Output an X.509 certificate instead of a regular certificate request.

`-keyout`

File to which to output the key.

`-out`

File to which to output the certificate.

The program will prompt for some parameters, but there's only one you need to answer.

```
Common Name (e.g., YOUR name) []:
```

This is not your personal name, this is the name you intend to use as the canonical name for the Web server. So, use www.yourhost.domain.tld if you're going to be in the DNS as www.yourhost.domain.tld; if you expect to be addressed as secure.domain.tld, use that. If you expect to be called simply yourhost.domain.tld, use that.

Exit the OPENSSL program. You should have two files—the key file and the certificate file. You now need to append the key file (the one you generated when you created the certificate) to the end of the certificate file. (At least you do if you use OSU; Apache lets you specify key and certificate separately if you want.)

```
$ APPEND TEST_KEY.PEM TEST.PEM
```

Verify the certificate.

```
$ OPENSSL
OpenSSL> verify test.pem
```

If OpenSSL confirms that the certificate is okay, you have a working self-signed certificate, and you just need to tell the Web server where to find it. (If it doesn't verify, go back through all the steps and make a new one; that's quicker than trying to figure out what's gone wrong.)

6.1.5 HTTPS dialog

The browser is given an HTTPS URL. It looks the name up in the domain name server to get an IP address and then initiates a dialog with the host at that address, requesting the site certificate. The host passes the browser the site certificate, and the browser looks it over to see if it's acceptable. If the host name on the certificate is different from the host name the browser looked up in the DNS, the browser will complain.

This means that you cannot successfully support name-based multihosting or virtual hosting on standard ports with HTTPS. The certificate must be presented before the browser gets a chance to tell the host what server it was looking for, so the server can't give different certificates based on host names. This is not a VMS restriction and not a restriction of any particular Web server software; it's inherent in the design of the protocol. If HTTPS is going to be a major concern, you'll need to have different numeric IP addresses for each domain you host. While you could try to centralize HTTPS services on one node name and make every domain you host link to that one when HTTPS is desired, this is an unsatisfactory solution if the different services belong to different noncooperating groups, or if you want to do password-based authentication without having passwords flying around in plain text.

There's an ugly work-around, which may or may not actually work for all users. It will work only if the only way users get to your HTTPS connections is by clicking links on the HTTP-served pages. The standard HTTPS port is 443, and that's the only port you can expect the browser to use without your specifying it in the URL. You can run multiple copies of your servers on different ports, each one corresponding to a particular name translation of your IP address; the URLs will have to specify the port (e.g., https://node.domain.tld:8443 for port 8443).

The problem, as I learned when my site didn't allow me to specify port 443 and I had to do HTTPS service on port 8443, is that while some sites leave all the unprivileged ports (ports with numbers greater than 1024) open, other sites block access to ports that aren't the standard ports for well-known services. This means that if you run on 8443, users at those other sites can't reach you. If you have any choice in the matter, run your HTTPS service on port 443, and if you're an ISP hosting multiple noncooperating domains, get each one a separate IP address and use IP-based virtual hosting.

If the certificate is acceptable, the server and browser have a dialog about which encryption algorithms at what strength each one supports; choose a mutually agreeable one, and commence normal HTTP interchange tunneled through the encryption algorithm. (This is, of course, expensive in compute cycles on both host and client sides, in comparison with plain-text communications, so you should use HTTPS only when you need it, if at all possible, especially on a heavily loaded server, or one on a slow pipe. But you need it whenever you're passing passwords back and forth.)

6.2 Installation

To use HTTPS, each server must connect with the SSL library. MOD_SSL interfaces the library with Apache; WASD has an equivalent hookup, and OSU can be connected either intimately (as an MST) or at arm's length (with the SSL task running as a separate process connected to the main server via DECnet.)

6.2.1 CSWS/MOD_SSL

MOD_SSL installs automatically as part of the CSWS installation; that's the argument for calling it Compaq SECURE Web Server. The installation procedure automatically creates a self-signed certificate for you, which will last only 30 days.

Compaq has provided some nice DCL procedures to interface to OpenSSL for certificate handling; these are in APACHE$COMMON:[OPENSSL.COM] and include OPENSSL_AUTO_CERT.COM for automatic creation of a self-signed certificate (used at installation); OPENSSL_SELF_CERT.COM for interactive creation of a self-signed certificate with prompting for organization name; and OPENSSL_RQST_CERT.COM for interactively preparing a certificate request. You can substitute those for the more laborious instructions given above. Also, CSWS is now a recognized server type at VeriSign.

6.2.2 OSU

You need to install OpenSSL to use HTTPS with OSU. (OpenSSL started as SSLEAY, the EAY part because it was coded by Eric A. Young, later joined by Tim Hudson. It became OpenSSL and is now supported on many platforms by a multiperson development team that does regular releases. The code is very widely used, although it still isn't up to version 1.0 yet. If you see references to SSLEAY in documentation, mentally replace them with OpenSSL.)

The installation process used to be quite annoying, but now Richard Levitte, who did the OpenSSL port to VMS, is part of the OpenSSL development team and his changes are folded in to the standard OpenSSL distribution, which includes a MAKEVMS.COM command file for compiling on VMS and an INSTALL.COM for copying the relevant pieces to a production directory tree. Browse to www.openssl.org and download the kit, which will have a name such as OPENSSL-0_9_6C.TAR-GZ;1. (That is, if you download it with Netscape 3.03, which is older than the ODS-5 file system and doesn't know anything about it.) If you use a recent version of Mozilla and download to an ODS-5 disk, the file ends up named openssl-0_9_6C.tar.gz, which also ends up being a problem because the GNU Zip program doesn't understand ODS-5 and is looking for something named .tar-gz in order to work.

Get GZIP (installed as GUNZIP) and VMSTAR from the VMS freeware CD, either the copy that came with your OS distribution or as a download from the www.openvms.compaq.com Web site, and install them.

Here's the routine for preparing and unpacking the kit:

```
$ dir openssl*
Directory DKB0:[CSWS_KITS]
OPENSSL-0_9_6C.TAR-GZ;1  4202/4203 25-JAN-2002 02:53:08.95 (RWED,RWED,RE,)
Total of 1 file, 4202/4203 blocks.
$
$ gunzip openssl*.*
$ dir openssl*.*
Directory DKB0:[CSWS_KITS]
OPENSSL-0_9_6C.TAR;1  22040/22041 25-JAN-2002 02:58:33.29 (RWED,RWED,RE,)
Total of 1 file, 22040/22041 blocks.
```

```
$ rename openssl-0_9_6C.TAR dkb0:[openssl]
$ set def dkb0:[openssl]
$ dir
Directory DKB0:[OPENSSL]
OPENSSL-0_9_6C.TAR;1  22040/22041 25-JAN-2002 02:58:33.29 (RWED,RWED,RE,)
Total of 1 file, 22040/22041 blocks.
$
$ vmstar /extract openssl-0_9_6c.tar
$ set def [.openssl-0_9_6C]
$ dir
Directory DKB0:[OPENSSL.OPENSSL-0_9_6C]
APPS.DIR;1          5/6         25-JAN-2002          03:01:09.51          (RWE,RWE,RE,E)
BUGS.DIR;1          1/3         25-JAN-2002          03:01:24.13          (RWE,RWE,RE,E)
CERTS.DIR;1         2/3         25-JAN-2002          03:01:25.41          (RWE,RWE,RE,E)
CHANGES.;1          52/354      20-DEC-2001          17:20:51.00          (RWED,RWED,RE,)
CHANGES.SSLEAY;1    4/84        22-DEC-1998          23:42:26.00          (RWED,RWED,RE,)
CONFIG.;1           32/33       19-DEC-2001          11:37:41.00          (RWED,RWED,RE,)
CONFIGURE.;1        15/117       6-DEC-2001          05:11:39.00          (RWED,RWED,RE,)
CRYPTO.DIR;1        3/3         25-JAN-2002          03:01:30.56          (RWE,RWE,RE,E)
DEMOS.DIR;1         1/3         25-JAN-2002          03:03:23.54          (RWE,RWE,RE,E)
DOC.DIR;1           1/3         25-JAN-2002          03:03:29.33          (RWE,RWE,RE,E)
E_OS.H;1            28/30        8-NOV-2001          06:36:49.00          (RWED,RWED,RE,)
E_OS2.H;1           2/3          2-MAY-2000          05:15:25.00          (RWED,RWED,RE,)
FAQ.;1              53/54       20-DEC-2001          17:21:03.00          (RWED,RWED,RE,)
INCLUDE.DIR;1       1/3         25-JAN-2002          03:04:00.60          (RWE,RWE,RE,E)
INSTALL.;1          22/24       16-MAY-2001          22:03:47.00          (RWED,RWED,RE,)
INSTALL.COM;1       6/6         11-NOV-1999          17:42:53.00          (RWED,RWED,RE,)
INSTALL.MACOS;1     7/9          1-OCT-2001          07:39:22.00          (RWED,RWED,RE,)
INSTALL.VMS;1       23/24       16-MAY-2001          22:03:47.00          (RWED,RWED,RE,)
INSTALL.W32;1       18/18       22-SEP-2000          19:06:08.00          (RWED,RWED,RE,)
LICENSE.;1          13/15       23-JAN-2001          18:56:13.00          (RWED,RWED,RE,)
MACOS.DIR;1         1/3         25-JAN-2002          03:04:08.96          (RWE,RWE,RE,E)
MAKEFILE.;1         1/3         20-DEC-2001          18:54:43.00          (RWED,RWED,RE,)
MAKEFILE.ORG;1      41/42       14-NOV-2001          02:44:11.00          (RWED,RWED,RE,)
MAKEFILE.SSL;1      41/42       20-DEC-2001          18:54:43.00          (RWED,RWED,RE,)
MAKEVMS.COM;1       49/51       29-OCT-2001          05:05:56.00          (RWED,RWED,RE,)
MS.DIR;1            2/3         25-JAN-2002          03:04:12.80          (RWE,RWE,RE,E)
NEWS.;1             16/18       20-DEC-2001          04:36:39.00          (RWED,RWED,RE,)
OPENSSL.DOXY;1      1/3         28-FEB-1999          09:41:51.00          (RWED,RWED,RE,)
OPENSSL.SPEC;1      16/18       13-NOV-2001          23:42:39.00          (RWED,RWED,RE,)
PERL.DIR;1          1/3         25-JAN-2002          03:04:16.91          (RWE,RWE,RE,E)
README.;1           14/15       20-DEC-2001          17:21:04.00          (RWED,RWED,RE,)
README.ENGINE;1     5/6          1-OCT-2001          07:39:23.00          (RWED,RWED,RE,)
RSAREF.DIR;1        1/3         25-JAN-2002          03:04:19.64          (RWE,RWE,RE,E)
SHLIB.DIR;1         1/3         25-JAN-2002          03:04:20.65          (RWE,RWE,RE,E)
SSL.DIR;1           3/3         25-JAN-2002          03:04:22.15          (RWE,RWE,RE,E)
TEST.DIR;1          4/6         25-JAN-2002          03:04:29.17          (RWE,RWE,RE,E)
TIMES.DIR;1         4/6         25-JAN-2002          03:04:39.36          (RWE,RWE,RE,E)
TOOLS.DIR;1         1/3         25-JAN-2002          03:04:47.54          (RWE,RWE,RE,E)
```

```
UTIL.DIR;1          2/3        25-JAN-2002          03:04:48.76          (RWE,RWE,RE,E)
VMS.DIR;1           1/3        25-JAN-2002          03:04:54.25          (RWE,RWE,RE,E)

Total of 40 files, 974/1032 blocks.
$
```

Here's the actual compilation. In the old days (two years ago), the RSA algorithm was patented and could legally be implemented only in some C code provided by RSA, Inc. The RSAREF parameter was used if you had the code from RSA on your system; NORSAREF if you didn't. Since the RSA patent expired in 2000 (two weeks after RSA, Inc., made it available for free use), RSAREF has become moot, so we compile with NORSAREF. The fifth parameter, UCX, tells whether to link against NETLIB or the UCX library. (NETLIB is a package that presented a uniform interface to the multifarious TCP/IP packages that used to run on VMS. The only packages that make any sense to run now are TCP/IP Services, TCPware, and Multinet, all of which provide a UCX$IPC_SHR library that will work with OpenSSL).

Here's what the OPENSSL install looks like in outline.

```
$ set def [.openssl-0_9_6C]
$
$ @makevms all norsaref nodebug decc ucx
Using DECC 'C' Compiler.
Using UCX or an emulation thereof for TCP/IP
TCP/IP library spec: [-.VMS]UCX_SHR_DECC.OPT/OPT
Creating [.CRYPTO]OPENSSLCONF.H Include File.
Creating [.CRYPTO]BUILDINF.H Include File.
Rebuilding The '[.APPS]MD5.C' And '[.APPS]RMD160.C' Files.
%DELETE-W-SEARCHFAIL, error searching for DKB0:[OPENSSL.OPENSSL-0_9_6C.APPS]MD5.C;*
-RMS-E-FNF, file not found
%DELETE-W-SEARCHFAIL, error searching for DKB0:[OPENSSL.OPENSSL_0_9_6C.APPS]RMD160.C;*
-RMS-E-FNF, file not found
Rebuilding The '[.TEST]*.C' Files.
Rebuilding The '[.INCLUDE.OPENSSL]' Directory.

Building The [.AXP.EXE.CRYPTO]LIBCRYPTO.OLB Library.
No Debugger Information Will Be Produced During Compile.
Compiling With Compiler Optimization.
Using DECC 'C' Compiler.
Compiling Without The RSAREF Routines.
Main C Compiling Command: CC/OPTIMIZE/NODEBUG/STANDARD=ANSI89/NOLIST/PREFIX=ALL/
INCLUDE=SYS$DISK:[]/DEFINE=("FLAT_INC=1",VMS=1,TCPIP_TYPE_UCX,DSO_VMS)/
WARNING=(DISABLE=(LONGLONGTYPE,LONGLONGSUFX))
Main MACRO Compiling Command: MACRO/MIGRATION/NODEBUG/OPTIMIZE
TCP/IP library spec: [-.VMS]UCX_SHR_DECC.OPT/OPT
Compiling On A AXP Machine.
```

```
Using Linker Option File SYS$DISK:[]VAX_DECC_OPTIONS.OPT.
Compiling The uid.c File. (LIBRARY,LIB)
Compiling The MD2 Library Files. (LIBRARY,LIB)
```

and so on, concluding with . . .

```
Building The OPENSSL Application Program.
$
```

Here's the command to copy libraries, configuration files, and so on into another directory tree for production purposes. Once you've done this, you can nuke the SSL, tree if you need the disk space. Quite a lot of it is code and scripts for non-VMS platforms. When you get a later version of SSL you can build that one in its own tree and use this same procedure to put it in your production SSL space. (But note, however, that if you do, this will overwrite your configuration file; therefore, save it before you upgrade.)

```
$ @install dkb0:[production_ssl]
%CREATE-I-CREATED, WRK_SSLROOT:[000000] created
%CREATE-I-CREATED, WRK_SSLROOT:[VAX_EXE] created
%CREATE-I-CREATED, WRK_SSLROOT:[ALPHA_EXE] created
%CREATE-I-CREATED, WRK_SSLROOT:[VAX_LIB] created
%CREATE-I-CREATED, WRK_SSLROOT:[ALPHA_LIB] created
%CREATE-I-CREATED, WRK_SSLROOT:[LIB] created
%CREATE-I-CREATED, WRK_SSLROOT:[INCLUDE] created
%CREATE-I-CREATED, WRK_SSLROOT:[CERTS] created
%CREATE-I-CREATED, WRK_SSLROOT:[PRIVATE] created
%CREATE-I-CREATED, WRK_SSLROOT:[VMS] created
%COPY-S-COPIED, DKB0:[OPENSSL.OPENSSL-0_9_6C]E_OS.H;1
copied to WRK_SSLROOT:[INCLUDE]E_OS.H;1 (28 blocks)
%COPY-S-COPIED, DKB0:[OPENSSL.OPENSSL-0_9_6C]E_OS2.H;1
copied to WRK_SSLROOT:[INCLUDE]E_OS2.H;1 (2 blocks)
%COPY-S-NEWFILES, 2 files created
Installing CRYPTO files.
```

and so on, and so on, concluding with . . .

```
Installing VMS files.
%OPEN-I-CREATED, WRK_SSLROOT:[VMS]OPENSSL_STARTUP.COM;1
created.
%COPY-S-COPIED, DKB0:[OPENSSL.OPENSSL-
0_9_6C.VMS]OPENSSL_UTILS.COM;1 copied to
WRK_SSLROOT:[VMS]OPENSSL_UTILS.COM;1 (3 blocks)
Installation done!
```

At this point you probably want to put

```
$dkb0:[production_ssl.vms]openssl_startup.com "/system"
```

into your system startup so that your SSL root will be defined systemwide.

Your SSL library is built. Now comes the fun part of installing an SSL component into OSU. While there are three different ways to do this, they all start out the same, so I'll go through the common part first. (Again, I'm working from R. A. Byers's instructions at http://www.ourservers.net/openvms_ports/openssl/openssl_contents.html. I've been using these instructions to run various versions of OSU with SSL in a separate task for several years, so I know they're good.)

You'll need to replace a few parts of the OSU server distribution. Point your browser to http://www.ourservers.net/openssl/openssl4.html and follow the links to download newtserver.zip, osu_ssl.zip and wwwssl.zip (unless you're going for the MST version of SSL, in which case you won't need WWWSSL.) You'll also need to have either MMS—the Compaq-licensed make utility, part of DECset—or the free compatible MMK package, which you can get at ftp://ftp.madgoat.com/madgoat/MMK.zip. You'll need to have one of these packages to install Perl extensions or modules later, anyway, so it's good to have this in your toolbox.

Unpack the osu_ssl.zip into the [.BASE_CODE] subdirectory of your OSU directory. (This brings in replacements for some of the linker .OPT files that are in the OSU distribution point to old SSLEAY files.) If you didn't use the shareable-image TCP library options when you built OSU originally, you need to rebuild it using them.

```
$ MMS/MACRO=(SHARE_TCP=xxxx) ! or MMK/
MACRO=(SHARE_TCP=xxxx)
```

where the "xxxx" is one of the following:

CMUTCP	CMU TCP/IP
MULTINET	Multinet TCP/IP
TCPWARE	TCPware TCP/IP
TWGTCP	Pathway TCP/IP
UCXTCP	DEC UCX TCP/IP

Next, unpack the newtserver.zip file into your [.SYSTEM] directory; this replaces the existing tserver_tcpshr_install.com file. Unless you're building the MST version of SSL, unpack the WWWSSL.ZIP file into the root OSU directory, making a WWWSSL.COM file. (This small pure-text file is sent as a ZIP archive because some people have to download using PCs, and if they have Internet Explorer, which doesn't honor MIME-type specifications, it will assume that a .COM file is a PC binary executable and mess it up. ZIPs are reasonably immune to this kind of nonsense.) Edit

WWWSSL.COM so that the SSL_SERVER_CERTIFICATE logical name is defined to point to the file the certificate is in. (Byers recommends putting the certificate into SSLCERTS:—as defined in the OpenSSL startup—and the file name is by default SERVER.PEM.)

Your options are the TASK interface (which works with every combination of a 40- or 128-bit browser and a self-signed or CA-signed server certificate, but which requires a trip through same-system DECnet to get to the server); the ENGINE interface (which supports most browser/certificate combinations and which has the same DECnet trip to cover); and the message-based server thread (MST) interface, which is linked in with the server image and has the best performance but supports the fewest browser/certificate combinations. (As of version 3.10, the MST interface has been altered to support authentication using client certificates; this is not the case with SSL_ENGINE or SSL_TASK.)

All three options work fine with nonexport browsers with 128-bit encryption. If you can rely on all your users having that, you'll be fine. At my site, we need to support users all over the world, including staff who have traveled to conferences in other countries and are using Internet cafes or other systems on which they aren't allowed to install software. Flexibility was more important than getting absolutely optimal performance; therefore, I've always used the TASK interface.

The TASK interface

If you want to use the SSL TASK interface (using the SSLTASK image compiled when you installed OpenSSL), do the following. Compile the DECnet interface to SSL.

```
$ CC TSERVER_SSL.C
$ CC SSL_SERVER_DNET.C
```

Link it.

```
$ MMS TSERVER_SSL.EXE/FORCE/MACRO=(SSL=SSL_SERVER_DNET)
```

That should create a TSERVER_SSL.EXE in your [.SYSTEM] directory. Start the server; if DISK$WORK:[HTTP_SERVER] is your OSU server root, a startup command such as

```
$ @DISK$WORK:[HTTP_SERVER.SYSTEM]HTTP_STARTUP.COM
HTTP_SERVER -
DISK$WORK:[HTTP_LOGS]HTTP_ERROR.LOG -
DISK$WORK:[HTTP_SERVER.SYSTEM]HTTP_MAIN.CONF -
80 443
```

should start you up with an HTTPS service on port 443. If it doesn't work, look in WWWSSL.LOG for clues.

6.2.3 The ENGINE interface

To use the SSL ENGINE interface (using the SSL_ENGINE code provided with the server), do the following. Compile the DECnet interface to SSL and the SSL_ENGINE code.

```
$ CC TSERVER_SSL.C
$ CC SSL_SERVER_DNET.C
$ CC SSL_ENGINE.C
```

You now need to compile the SSL_THREADED.C and BSS_MST.C files as follows:

```
$ CC/STANDARD=ANSI89/PREFIX=ALL/WARNING=DISABLE=DOLLARID -
/INCLUDE=SSLINCLUDE:/DEFINE=("FLAT_INC=1","VMS=1") -
SSL_THREADED.C
$ CC/STANDARD=ANSI89/PREFIX=ALL/WARNING=DISABLE=DOLLARID -
/INCLUDE=SSLINCLUDE:/DEFINE=("FLAT_INC=1","VMS=1") -
BSS_MST.C
```

and link the SSL_ENGINE:

```
$ LINK/NOTRACEBACK/EXE=SSLEXE:SSL_ENGINE.EXE -
SSL_ENGINE.OPT/OPT
```

This puts the SSL_ENGINE code in your installed OpenSSL directory tree, not in your OSU tree. To work properly, this needs to be world-readable, so set the protection:

```
$ SET FILE SSLEXE:SSL_ENGINE.EXE -
/PROTECTION=(S:RWED,O:RWED,G,W:RE)
```

and it needs SYSNAM privilege, so install it as follows:

```
$ INSTALL ADD SSLEXE:SSL_ENGINE.EXE/PRIVS=(SYSNAM)
```

(If you are upgrading OSU, that needs to be INSTALL REPLACE rather than ADD.) You should put this INSTALL command into your server startup script so that it will be executed every time the server starts; if you don't, your HTTPS service will stop working when you next reboot.

Start the server (with the command shown for the TASK interface) and see if it works; if it doesn't, check WWWSSL.LOG for clues. A common problem is having the ownership or the protection on the server certificate set wrong. Remember, you can't make it W:R, because your private key is attached to it, but the OSU account (usually HTTP_SERVER) has to able to read it; anybody else who gets the file can use it to impersonate your server.

6.2.4 The MST interface

In the [.BASE_CODE] directory, compile the TSERVER_SSL.C and SSL_SERVER_MST.C files.

```
$ CC TSERVER_SSL.C
$ CC SSL_SERVER_MST.C Message-based Server Thread
```

Compile the SSL_THREADED.C and BSS_MST.C files as follows:

```
$ CC/STANDARD=ANSI89/PREFIX=ALL/WARNING=DISABLE=DOLLARID -
/INCLUDE=SSLINCLUDE:/DEFINE=("FLAT_INC=1","VMS=1") -
 SSL_THREADED.C
$ CC/STANDARD=ANSI89/PREFIX=ALL/WARNING=DISABLE=DOLLARID -
/INCLUDE=SSLINCLUDE:/DEFINE=("FLAT_INC=1","VMS=1") -
 BSS_MST.C
```

It's normal in this case to get some warnings (-W-) and informational (-I-) compile messages; don't worry about it. Link the MST SSL server.

```
$ MMS TSERVER_SSL.EXE/FORCE/MACRO=(SSL=SSL_SERVER_MST) ! or
MMK
```

You should now see the file TSERVER_SSL.EXE in your OSU [.SYSTEM] directory.

6.2.5 WASD

There isn't really a separate SSL installation process for WASD. At installation time, you need to use the optional WASD OpenSSL kit and install against that as described in Chapter 4, section 4.2.4 or link against your site's existing OpenSSL installation to provide an SSL-enabled WASD image. The WASD OpenSSL kit includes a self-signed test certificate so SSL can be deployed immediately. The [.WASD] directory includes some DCL procedures that make it easy to generate self-signed CA, server, and client certificates.

6.3 Configuration

6.3.1 CSWS/MOD_SSL

MOD_SSL offers global directives that affect the entire Apache installation; per-server directives that apply to either the default server configuration or within a VirtualHost container; and per-directory directives, which can appear not just in the main server config files but in the .htaccess files you may choose to locate in particular directories.

Here's a tip that will save you a little annoyance: mod_ssl.conf is included at the end of HTTPD.CONF by the installation. If you leave it there, any container configuration such as `SSLRequireSSL` that appears above it will keep your server from starting. Move the include of mod_ssl.conf near the top of your HTTPD.CONF, or append all your system configuration below it.

Apache allows different certificates for different IP-based virtual hosts. You can specify those in the mod_ssl.conf include file. The default mod_ssl.conf, incidentally, uses a virtual host container for the default host (with port 443 specified), and has a document root specification in that container. It's a little surprising when you've pointed your document root in the default server to where your actual files are and then go to your site with HTTPS and still see the Apache documentation page.

It is my strongly held opinion that you don't want certificates that require you to enter a passphrase, even though Apache supports it. This would mean that your site couldn't run SSL if the people who knew the passphrases weren't available; if everybody knows the passphrases, they aren't secret, and there's no point in having them. Passphrases make sense if you don't trust the security of your file system—since the encrypted certificate is no good without the passphrase—or the ability of the operating system to keep untrusted users from getting privileges to access resources they're not supposed to. The robust security model of VMS is one of the reasons you're running it; set up your files correctly and don't mess with passphrases. You shouldn't compromise the ability of the platform to boot unattended by requiring operator input to make SSL services work.

(Apache also gives the option of running an arbitrary program to provide the passphrase input, but, in fact, if you're going to have a program know the phrases, or have a program read a file that has the phrases in it, you subvert the point of having passphrases at all.) Apache provides quite a few knobs to twiddle in SSL; on VMS, you mostly don't want to touch them. If you're curious, you can go to modssl.org and read their documentation in detail.

Here are the parameters you care about. (I'll give a brief discussion later of the parameters you don't care about, and why.) In general they can be included at the main server configuration level or in a VirtualHost container.

```
SSLEngine on|off (default off)
```

You need this to use HTTPS at all. This enables or disables use of the SSL/TLS protocol engine for this VirtualHost (or, if you do it for the default server configuration, the main server). Typically, you'd use only the `SSLEngine on` format.

```
SSLCertificateFile      pathto/certificatefilename
SSLCertificateKeyFile   pathto/keyfilename
```

As you'd guess, these directives allow you to specify where your certificate file is located. (If your key is combined with the certificate file, you need only the `SSLCertificateFile` directive; if not, you need the `SSLCertificateKeyFile` directive to tell Apache where the key file is.) If you include these directives in IP-address-based VirtualHost containers, you can specify a different certificate for each VirtualHost. (As already mentioned, this won't work for name-based virtual hosts with the same numeric IP address, because the SSL dialog occurs before the browser can tell the server what host it's looking for.)

```
SSLLog /pathto/filename
SSLLogLevel none | error | warn | info | trace | debug
```

If you want a dedicated log that shows only HTTPS transactions, use `SSLLog` to specify where you want it. A typical path would be `logs/ssl_engine_log` (and that's what's in the CSWS MOD_SSL file by default). `SSLLogLevel` specifies what information you want to see in the SSL log file; if not specified, the default is none. Each level incorporates all the levels shown to the left of it; CSWS gives you `info` by default. Even if you don't have an SSL log, errors will be written to the main Apache log. `trace` is interesting to watch how an SSL dialog unfolds, but you don't want to leave it on all the time—it'll burn a lot of disk space. That's even more true for `debug`.

```
SSLRequireSSL
SSLRequire [arbitrarily-complex boolean-expression]
```

`SSLRequireSSL`, included in any container directive or .htaccess file, forbids non-SSL access to the stuff specified therein. If you use password-based authentication for access to the contents, the password dialog will be SSL-encrypted, which is a good thing.

`SSLRequire`, on the other hand, is like `Require`, the directive that lets you limit access to anything unless any conditions you can specify are met. Potentially, however, it is considerably more complicated, because it has a lot more environment variables to play with. If you want to require that only a particular IP address can get at this container, or get at it only between 9:00 A.M. and 5:00 P.M., or use only SSL version 3 with the Blowfish cipher and a 512-bit key, this is the command you want. I include it here for completeness, but I'll discuss this (and the `Require` command) more fully in Chapter 7.

```
SSLOptions [+-] StdEnvVars | CompatEnvVars | ExportCertData |
                FakeBasicAuth | StrictRequire | OptRenegotiate
```

This can go in a server config, VirtualHost, container, or .htaccess file; if the options specified are preceded with + or -, they are merged with the options already in effect from any higher-level `SSLOptions` specification.

`StdEnvVars` tells Apache to create the standard set of SSL-related environment variables (symbols), which you usually want to do only if you're going to be using them in CGIs or SSIs or possibly in `SSLRequire` statements.

`CompatEnvVars` produces the environment variables for backward compatibility with pre-mod_ssl Apache SSL environments; you're unlikely to need this on VMS unless you've imported CGIs from an old UNIX installation.

`ExportCertData` and `FakeBasicAuth` apply only if you're using client certificates for authentication, which is fairly rare (and is discussed in Chapter 7). `ExportCertData` makes the certificate information available as symbols in the CGI/SSI environment, while `FakeBasicAuth` takes the subject distinguished name (DN) of the client certificate and pretends that the client was authenticated as that user under basic authorization, allowing regular Apache access controls to be used. Since no password is collected, the user name has to be entered in the authorization file—not the SYSUAF but an .htauth file with the password `xxj31ZMTzkVA`, which is the DES-encoded version of the word "password."

`StrictRequire` is designed to keep a `Satisfy any` with other authorized accesses specified from working when `SSLRequire` or `SSLRequireSSL` forbids access; it forces an access failure without looking at the other options permitted in the `Satisfy` command.

`OptRenegotiate` should be used only on per-container specs; it enables optimized SSL connection renegotiation handling. Without this, a full new SSL handshake will occur every time a container is specified that has an SSL directive in it; with it, mod_ssl does parameter checks less often, but still often enough to be safe.

```
CustomLog pathto/filename logformat
```

mod_ssl enhances the `CustomLog` directive (which is technically from mod_log_config, one of the core modules of Apache/CSWS), allowing it to log SSL-related environment variables. The CSWS-distributed mod_ssl.conf has a `CustomLog` defining an SSL_REQUEST_LOG., tracking which protocols and which ciphers were used; it looks like this:

```
CustomLog logs/ssl_request_log \
      "%t %h %{SSL_PROTOCOL}x %{SSL_CIPHER}x \"%r\" %b"
```

The resulting log entries (with the IP address sanitized) look like:

```
[27/Jan/2002:03:29:05 -0800] [IP] TLSv1 EDH-RSA-DES-CBC3-
SHA "GET / HTTP/1.1" 2673
```

Now for the parameters you probably don't want to, or shouldn't, mess with, either because you're unlikely to need them at all or because the default values are good ones. (I don't actually expect good system managers to believe that they aren't important on my word alone, so I explain them anyway.)

```
SSLPassPhraseDialog
```

I don't really believe in passphrases for VMS; they can compromise availability without giving much of an increase in security. Don't use encrypted keys that require passphrases.

```
SSLSessionCache none | dbm:/pathto/file | [c]shm:/pathto/
file[(size)]
SSLSessionCacheTimeout number-of-seconds
SSLMutex none | /pathto/lockfile | | [c]sem
```

If it's told to, Apache will maintain a cache of currently open SSL sessions, which is available to all of the Apache server processes. Modern browsers may issue multiple parallel requests, which can be satisfied by different server processes. If the credentials are cached, each server process doesn't have to go through the whole dialog over again, and you get much better throughput, resulting in pages that load faster. So you want to have a session cache, thus ruling out the `none` option. The `dbm:` parameter isn't actually telling CSW to use a dbm file, but it does let you specify a disk-based table, which is slower than having the session cache in shared memory, which is what shm: gives you; this is what's in the mod_ssl.conf file when you install CSWS. (If you get really, really, heavy SSL use and see performance suffer, you might want to increase the SSL cache size from the default 512,000 bytes, but I'd expect you to do more for SSL performance by splitting the encryption load across more CPUs.)

With version 1.2, there's support for a clusterwide session cache. If your cluster is in a Galaxy box, the session cache can be in Galactic shared memory; specify `cshm:` rather than `shm:` and make sure the size of the datafile is the same everywhere it's referred to. If your cluster combines multiple systems, you can use shared disk storage by specifying `dbm:/pathto/datafile` to a cluster-visible disk and use

```
SSLMutex csem
```

to specify cluster semaphore control. This gives you the performance benefit of a clusterwide shared cache along with the performance drawbacks of having to do disk I/O to get to it. Whether you save or lose time by using disk-based clusterwide SSL session cache is probably highly dependent both on load and I/O speed, and it might be worth some experimentation.

`SSLSessionCacheTimeout` says how many seconds to hold the SSL data in the cache if there's room; the CSWS default is 300 (five minutes), which is what mod_ssl.org suggests. If your users typically put data that are secret enough to require encryption up on their screens and leave it sit for longer than five minutes, you can accommodate that behavior by increasing the `SSLSessionCacheTimeout`.

Since every Apache process can update the SSL Session Cache, they need some way to keep from tripping over each other. `SSLMutex` tells Apache whether to use nothing to direct traffic—which is silly, since it will result in cache corruption the first time two processes try to update the cache at the same time—or a lock file (which is the traditional pathetic UNIX workaround for not having a lock manager and which fails to result in cripplingly bad I/O performance only because the heavily cached file system doesn't guarantee that the file will actually get out to disk when it signals that a write is complete)—or a semaphore if the operating system provides that advanced construct. VMS has had a lock manager for a long, long time, and the `sem` setting (or the `csem` variant) is, therefore, the only one that makes sense; it's the one that CSWS provides out of the box.

```
SSLRandomSeed startup | connect builtin |
/pathto/pseudodevice |/pathto/exe
```

UNIX servers offer pseudodevices that are supposed to provide random values based on events meant to be nondeterministic (e.g., the number and content of I/O operations the system has performed so far); they have names such as /dev/random and /dev/urandom. Those devices have more randomness available when the system has been running awhile—or at least can provide more random bytes—than they do at startup, so on those systems you might want to use different sources of randomness at startup than you do at each new SSL connection. The devices aren't available on VMS, so you either need to use the built-in pseudorandom number generator or roll your own and tell Apache to use it. I'm guessing that nearly everybody will go with the built-in option, and that's what's configured in the CSWS mod-ssl.conf. This works only in the whole-server context, incidentally, not in VirtualHosts.

```
SSLProtocol All | +| - SSLv2 | +|- SSLv3 | + |-TLSv1
```

allows you to specify which SSL protocols you'll support. Unless you want to keep customers or users from talking to you, you'll pick `All`, which is the default. (Mozilla supports TLSv1; Netscape 4.73 and up supports SSLv3, as does Internet Explorer 5.5 and up.) The + or - apply when this command appears in VirtualHost, container, or .htaccess mode, in which the parameters can be merged with those inherited from higher levels.

```
SSLCipherSuite cipher-spec
```

This lets you restrict which ciphers you're willing to support with which SSL protocols, in per-server and per-container contexts and also in .htaccess files. My belief is that most sites want to embrace as many as possible, which is the default. Look up the cipher table on modssl.org if you want to get involved with this.

```
SSLCertificateChainFile pathto/certificatechainfile
```

If your certificate doesn't come directly from a known CA, but rather from an entity that has been delegated the authority by a known CA, you can provide a file consisting of the certificates from the entity that issued your certificate all the way up to a known CA; this directive tells Apache where to find that file.

```
SSLCACertificatePath /path
SSLCACertificateFile filename
```

MOD_SSL supports X.509 client authentication; this is discussed more fully in Chapter. 7

6.3.2 OSU

The SSL configuration for OSU is minimal, and it was covered in the instructions for building in SSL support. For SSL_TASK or SSL_ENGINE, make sure the WWWSSL.COM file specifies where to find the certificate. For MSTs, insert `$ DEFINE/SYSTEM/EXEC` statements for the following logicals into the HTTP_STARTUP.COM file so that they're defined whenever you start the server.

`WWWSSL_MST_THREAD_LIMIT`	Maximum number of SSL threads allowed. (Default is 10)
`WWWSSL_MST_STACK_SIZE`	The stack size for SSL server threads. (Default is 60000)
`WWWSSL_MST_QUEUE_FLAG`	To wait for next available thread or not. (TRUE or FALSE value)
`WWWSSL_MST_CERTIFICATE`	Location of the server's SSL certificate.
`WWWSSL_MST_LOGFILE`	Location to put the MST SSL log file.
`WWWSSL_MST_VERSION`	Which versions of SSL to use: 2, 3, or 23 (Default is 2; 23 supports both.)

Here's an example:

```
$ DEFINE/SYSTEM/EXEC WWWSSL_MST_THREAD_LIMIT 15
$ DEFINE/SYSTEM/EXEC WWWSSL_MST_STACK_SIZE 90000
$ DEFINE/SYSTEM/EXEC WWWSSL_MST_QUEUE_FLAG TRUE
$ DEFINE/SYSTEM/EXEC WWWSSL_MST_CERTIFICATE -
 SSLCERTS:SERVER.PEM
$ DEFINE/SYSTEM/EXEC WWWSSL_MST_LOGFILE -
 DISK$HTTP:[HTTP_LOGS]SSL_MST.LOG
$ DEFINE/SYSTEM/EXEC     WWWSSL_MST_VERSION 23
```

If you put these define statements in your OSU HTTP startup file, you won't be surprised if your HTTP service fails when you next reboot. Start up the HTTPD server (same command as seen in the TASK version) and HTTPS should work. If not, check the file you defined in WWWSSL_MST_LOGFILE for clues.

OSU doesn't need SSL cache configuration directives, because it isn't sharing the information among multiple processes, just multiple threads with the same environment available.

OSU supports the use of exactly one certificate, so don't try to support multiple domains. (There's an ugly hack that allows you to run multiple versions of OSU on different ports, tweaking all the SYSTEM-level logical names into GROUP-level tables; this might let you run the MST SSL version, although only one copy of OSU could be listening to port 443, and the rest would have to specify a nonstandard port. To run multiple copies of SSL_TASK or SSL_ENGINE, you'd need to run OSU under multiple user names so that the DECnet task created to run SSL could have different environments.)

Until the just-released (end of January 2002) 3.10alpha version, OSU did not support authentication through the use of client certificates at all. That version supports it in the MST version only, and the support is described in the release notes as "experimental"; I'll discuss configuration for that in Chapter 7.

6.3.3 WASD

If the WASD server startup finds a certificate in HT_ROOT:[LOCAL]HTTPD.PEM, the startup will automatically define HTTPD$SSL_CERT to point to the certificate file specified. (You can also specify a WASD_SSL_CERT symbol to point to a certificate file before running the startup, and HTTPD$SSL_CERT will end up pointing to that value.) If you do no further configuration, all SSL services will use that certificate. If the key is in a separate file rather than appended to the certificate, you can manually define HTTPD$SSL_KEY to point to the key file. If the key requires a passphrase—which, as I've said previously, I don't think is a good idea—the server will issue a status message saying that it needs to be told the phrase, either to the HTTPDMON utility or, if you've enabled OPCOM logging, to OPCOM. The passphrase can then be entered by a privileged user running the command-line interface to the server:

```
$ HTTPD /DO=SSL=KEY=PASSWORD
Enter private key password []:
```

(The passphrase isn't echoed; you get three tries to get it right before the server carries on with the startup with that service disabled. If there are multiple services with multiple keys with multiple passphrases specified, you need to repeat this dialog and be sure to get it in the right order.)

To specify different SSL services in WASD, you can use a command-line parameter in the server startup (`/SERVICE=`), the `[Service]` header in the file pointed to by the logical HTTPD$CONFIG (which is, by default, HTTPD$CONFIG.CONF), or a separate HTTPD$SERVICE file. (If the startup sees an HT_ROOT:[LOCAL]HTTPD$SERVICE.CONF, it'll define an HTTPD$SERVICE logical name.)

In the HTTPD$CONFIG variant, you define on one line the service name (and port, if it's not the default) for each service you want to support. If no service type is given, it's assumed to be HTTP. If no port is given, it's assumed to be 80 for HTTP and 443 for HTTPS. After the service name, insert a semicolon and then give a cert parameter to locate the appropriate certificate. (This still requires different numeric IP addresses for the different HTTP services, at least the ones on the same ports.)

```
[Service]
yourserver.yourdomain.tld
https://yourserver.yourdomain.tld;cert=ht_root:[local]yourserver.pem
https://otherserver.yourdomain.tld;cert=ht_root:[local]otherserver.pem
https://otherportserver.yourdomain.tld:8443;cert=ht_root:[local]  otherport.pem
```

In the HTTPD$SERVICE variant, there are more directives available. In the HTTPD$SERVICE file, the headers are the service names:

```
[[http://yourserver.yourdomain.tld:80]]

[[https://yourserver.yourdomain.tld:443]]
[ServiceSSLcert]ht_root:[local]servicename.pem
[ServiceSSLkey]ht_root:[local]servicename_key.pem
```

As shown, `SSLcert` points to the location (as a VMS file name, not a UNIXified string with slashes) of the server certificate for this service; `SSLkey` points to the location of the private key file, if you didn't bundle it with the server certificate in a single file.

WASD also supports X.509 certificate authentication and authorization on a per-resource basis. This is discussed more fully in Chapter 7.

7

Managing Access to Your Server Resources

There are two sides to managing access to server resources: the outside and the inside. You need to control who (and how many) entities from outside the system can get at what's on the inside in what way. This brings up the issues of user identification, either anonymously (people coming from particular subnets or domains) or identifiably (through some kind of authentication procedure).

Presented with a URL by the client, the server has to map that into a resource name recognizable by the operating system; determine whether there are any access restrictions on that resource; and, if the access is restricted to particular users, authenticate the requester as one of the users. Resource mapping, access control, and authentication are closely enough intertwined that they should be discussed together.

On the inside, there's presentation, so I'll start by discussing how you map URLs to particular resources along with some related path- or URL-oriented commands. File protection and access control are right in the middle and require some understanding of both sides, so I'll discuss that last.

7.1 Mapping resources

In the basic configuration for each of the servers (discussed in Chapter 5), I described how to specify the document root for each server. (In Apache, that's a DocumentRoot directive; in the other servers, it's a PASS mapping rule, which specifies how /* is interpreted.)

If you just want to serve everything from one document tree, with a URL that exactly matches the subdirectory structure of that document tree and do nothing else, then you may not need to use other mapping rules at all. This is unlikely for any Web site of significant size. In a larger site Webmasters find themselves mapping short URLs rather than long paths, making CGI programs look like HTML files and redirecting requests for documents that have moved to other servers.

In general, on the inside you want to map URLs into file specifications (or sometimes into other URLs). The easiest way is to point "/" at the top of a directory tree and map URLs to file names according to the file-system mapping, but very often you want to do more than that.

The cleanest, most efficient, easiest-to-maintain layout for your file structure may not produce the cleanest layout for URLs, which can get very long very quickly. You can provide easier access and hide your internal structures, which makes life easier for anybody who has to type in a URL and also makes it possible to reorganize your internal structures without disturbing customer bookmarks.

If you're multihosting (see Chapter 9) and want to present different content for each host, you need to point the server-root to different places, which may or may not be in the same directory tree. You can present content from different devices—even from different systems—without exposing that fact to the world. You can send browsers off to other systems to look for content that used to be on yours.

Sometimes it's handy to run scripts without it being obvious that you're doing so. Scripts that generate pages dynamically can be mapped so they look to browsers (and indexers) like indexable static pages.

7.1.1 Apache

Mapping

CSWS 1.2 gives us mod_rewrite, which has an amazing set of capabilities in file mapping. Prior to 1.2, mod_alias was available, and is still useful for bringing in additional document trees that aren't under the document root, as well as handling redirects (and script aliases, which I will discuss later in the book). All of these commands go into HTTPD.CONF. Here are the mod_alias directives.

```
Alias url-prefix filename-prefix
```

This maps URL-prefix (e.g., /tree2) to filename-prefix (e.g., /$disk2/wwwtree). Any URL coming in with /tree2/anyname will be resolved as /$disk2/wwwtree/anyname rather than looking for /tree2 in your main document tree.

```
AliasMatch url-pattern file-system-path
```

This is similar to `Alias` but uses a regular expression for the URL pattern, rather than matching just on the prefix, and substitutes the matched components into the file-system path. Regular expressions are a very nuanced version of wildcarding, which allows you to specify matching on various components. They are a complicated topic; there's an entire O'Reilly book dedicated to them (*Mastering Regular Expressions* by Jeffrey Friedl). Learning about them will repay the Apache Webmaster, but any detailed discussion is beyond the scope of this book. A good tutorial introduction—in the context of Perl programming—can be found at http://www.perldoc.com/perl5.6.1/pod/perlretut.html.

```
Redirect [status] url-prefix [redirect-prefix]
```

Possible values for `status` are `permanent`, `temp`, `seeother`, and `gone`.

This catches URLs starting with a URL prefix (e.g., /temporary) and replaces that with the redirect-prefix (e.g., http://www.otherserver.tld/temporary) and sends that redirection instruction back to the client. The first argument, status, is optional (defaulting to 302—temporary redirect), but if gone is used, you shouldn't include a redirect-prefix. You can also give numeric status values instead of the names; include a redirect-prefix for a 3xx status code and omit it for anything else.

```
RedirectMatch [status]
  url-pattern
  redirect-URL
```

This is similar to `Redirect` but with a regular expression instead of a plain prefix match.

```
ScriptAlias url-prefix file-system-path
```

This has the same syntax as `Alias`, but marks the directory as containing executable CGI scripts. A typical usage example would be a URL prefix of `/cgi-bin` and a file-system-path corresponding to `/$cgi-disk/cgi-bin`. (You could achieve the same effect by using `Alias` and specifying `Options +ExecCGI` in a container directive for that directory or path.)

```
ScriptAliasMatch url-pattern file-system-path
```

This has the same meaning as `ScriptAlias` but uses regular expression for the URL pattern.

Mod_rewrite is a very capable module indeed. For a comprehensive series of examples displaying its capabilities, check out http://httpd.apache.org/docs/misc/rewriteguide.html; and for a full manual, look at http://httpd.apache.org/docs/mod/mod_rewrite.html. One surprising feature is that mod_rewrite directives can be put in per-directory .HTACCESS files (discussed in section 7.3). This is surprising, because it means mod_rewrite hooks into Apache URL processing twice, once at the URL interpretation level and then again after the URLs have been mapped to the file system. Here's a brief introduction to some of the mod_rewrite directives.

```
RewriteEngine on|off
```

This enables or disables the run-time rewrite engine, which is off by default. You must turn this on. The setting is not inherited across virtual hosts (see Chapter 9), so you need to specify this for each virtual host where you intend to use it.

```
RewriteOptions inherit
```

In the future there may be more options specified, but at present only "inherit" is implemented. If used in an .HTACCESS file, it means that RewriteCond and RewriteRule directives of the parent directory are inherited; in a virtual host it means that these directives are inherited from the main server, along with RewriteMap (which I will not discuss here).

```
RewriteLog logfile
```

The log-file specification uses the same syntax as that for any Apache log file, so a typical value would be "logs/rewrite_log". What gets logged depends on RewriteLogLevel.

```
RewriteLogLevel 0|1|2|3|4|5|6|7|8|9
```

The argument to RewriteLogLevel is a verbosity level, where 0 is "log nothing" and 9 is "log everything including debug info."

```
RewriteBase url
```

This is useful for per-directory rewriting (implemented in an .HTACCESS file). Because the .HTACCESS files are processed after Apache mapping has worked its way down to the current directory, the RewriteRule directives in it apply only to local files; the directory-path prefix is stripped off. If you do redirects, the value of the RewriteBase will be prefixed back on to the front of the result of the RewriteRule directives, unless the result begins with HTTP: or HTTPS:, since that's probably a redirect to a different server and should be fully specified. (For example, if files that had formerly been in a user directory (see Chapter 8) were moved to a new directory in the main server root, the user directory could get an .HTACCESS file that specifies a

RewriteBase of "/newdir/" and a RewriteRule that matches all the moved files and says to redirect. mod_rewrite would combine the file specification with the RewriteBase for any file accessed and issue a redirect from the old URL to the new.

```
RewriteCond test-value pattern [[NC|nocase,OR|ornext...]]
```

If a RewriteRule is preceded by one or more RewriteCond directives, it will be executed only if the conditions specified in the RewriteCond have been met and the URL matches the predicate of the RewriteRule. The test string can be a server variable (%{variable-name}) or various other items that require some knowledge of regular expressions to understand. This would let you provide different content for users coming from America Online than for everybody else, using a RewriteCond %{REMOTE_HOST} AOL.COM (You can also negate the pattern with an exclamation point; !AOL.COM would mean "if REMOTE_HOST doesn't match AOL.COM do the next RewriteRule.")

The "NC" or "nocase" flag value makes the comparison with the pattern case insensitive. The "OR" or "ornext" flag means that the truth value of this RewriteCond is ORed with that of the next RewriteCond, rather than the implicit AND that would otherwise be in effect; this makes it easier to have multiple cases that end up executing the same rule.

```
RewriteRule url-pattern new-template [[flag[,flag]]]
```

The instruction says to rewrite everything that matches the URL pattern to match the new template (which may include specific pieces of the URL pattern) and do things according to the flags specified. Among these flags are:

- "R" or "redirect," which terminates rewrite processing and forces the issue of a redirect to the value made from the new-template
- "F" or "forbidden," which generates a 403 error
- "P" or "proxy," which passes the mapped URL on to mod-proxy to be fetched from another system (see Chapter 11)
- "L" or "last," which terminates rewrite processing
- "N" or "next," which bails out of the current round of rewrite processing and starts again from the top with the new URL
- "T" or "type," which can force a particular MIME type
- "NC" or "nocase," which makes the comparison case insensitive

- "S" or "skip," which skips the next rule
- "E" or "env," which lets you set an environment variable that can then be used in subsequent RewriteCond or access control checks

An example

Case-insensitive redirect of any URL containing "othersite" to another site.

```
RewriteRule othersite http://www.othersite.com/ [R,NC]
```

Force a redirect of anything starting with /shortname (including the rest of the path) to /longpath/to/shortname plus the rest of the path, which bails out of rewrite processing immediately. (The $ and $1 syntax are regular expression stuff; $1 refers to the value matched by the .* in the original pattern.)

```
RewriteRule shortname(.*)$ /longpath/to/shortname$1 [L,R,NC]
```

Simply rewrite /shortname to /longpath/to/shortname and restart mapping processing from the top:

```
RewriteRule shortname(.*)$ /longpath/to/shortname$1 [N,NC]
```

Since the file names that URL paths map to are, in fact, case insensitive on VMS, it seems silly not to make any URL mappings case insensitive as well; that's why all my examples include the NC flag.

Content type

Another important component of server presentation is what the server does with files once they're identified. Apache uses the MIME.TYPES file to tell what content type to send back based on the file extension. This can be tweaked or extended by using the AddType directive in HTTPD.CONF.

```
AddType content-type .extension [.extension]
```

To tell Apache that files named something.letter are plain-text files, use

```
AddType text/plain .letter
```

Some files need to be processed by something before they can be presented. The AddHandler directive is used to identify the handling program.

```
AddHandler handler-type .extension [.extension]
```

To tell Apache that .HTMLX files (the standard extension for the OSU preprocessor) and .SHTML (a standard extension for the Apache preprocessor) should both be preprocessed by Apache and presented to the browser as regular HTML files, use the following directives:

```
AddType text/html .shtml .htmlx
AddHandler server-parsed .shtml .htmlx
```

Other values for handler-type include `send-as-is` (used for documents that contain all the HTTP headers they need) and `imap-file` (used for image maps).

7.1.2 OSU

Mapping rules

The mapping directives in OSU are found in HTTP_PATHS.CONF. They can be included inside local address blocks and will apply only to that particular host. Full VMS-style wildcarding—where the asterisk matches anything and can be placed anywhere in the string—is supported in `fail`, `protect`, `hostprot`, `localaddress`, and `filecache` rules. In most other cases, the only wildcard allowed is a single asterisk at the end of the string.

You can get a trace log of mapping activity in detail by using PRIVREQUEST; the command to pass is `NEWTRACE/11`. Examining the HTTP_ERROR.LOG file (or whatever you've named that file) will give you a good idea of the mapping process and will probably show you why any particular mapping rule isn't having the effect you expected. The order of commands in the file is important; the first match on a `PASS` command will bail out of rules file interpretation and look up the file on disk.

```
redirect url-template redirect-template
```

causes the server to issue a redirect if the URL-template is matched. If a wildcard is included in the URL template, the value it matched is replaced in the redirect template. If you've moved the whole /elsewhere directory elsewhere, do

```
redirect /elsewhere/* http://name-of-elsewhere-server.tld/*
```

and the file name in the elsewhere directory gets plugged into the redirect. This can also be used to insist that certain files be accessed only through HTTPS, with

```
redirect http://www.myserver.tld/needsSSL \
https://www.myserver.tld:443/needsSSL
map   url-template    filesystem-path-template
```

The map rule rewrites an incoming URL into another form but does not terminate processing. (What you've mapped it into can fall through to subsequent pass or map commands.) Again, each template can include a wildcard. If you've moved everything from old-directory to new-directory, use the following:

```
map /old-directory/* /new-directory/*
```

to keep from breaking anybody's old bookmarks. To make what appears to be a static Web page actually invoke a script, do

```
map /static-Web-page.html /htbin/scriptname
```

You can use multiple map directives to resolve multiple URLs down to the same file or directory, and then have a single pass (or protect or hostprot) statement to address the whole thing.

```
pass url-template filesystem-template
```

The pass rule operates the same way as the map rule but terminates mapping processing for that URL. If the pass rule is defined incorrectly, it'll send the server out to the file system looking for a file that doesn't exist. Another possibility for the pass rule is to convert URL specs to file specifications that actually refer to files on other systems to which the server has access via a DECnet or NFS proxy. For example,

```
pass /othervax/* /othervax::$disk1/Web_content/*
```

(This will certainly fail if your OSU Web server account doesn't have default proxy access to othervax::. This approach enables you to display current sky images from the VAX controlling the telescope while keeping that VAX safely inside your firewall and not dedicating resources to running a Web server itself.)

```
fail url-template
```

Anything matching the template terminates map processing and returns a 403 error. In the default configuration for the server, a

```
pass / desired-welcome-page
pass /www/* document-root/*
fail /*
```

maps / to the welcome page, causes any /www/* URL to pass to the file system, and anything else to fail. (Other mapping is done with map and pass statements between the first pass and the final fail.) Because there's a separate mapping for the "/" root, any images or pages referenced in that root can't just specify the file name; they have to specify "/www/filename". I find this sufficiently hard to explain to my users that I configure OSU with a catchall

```
pass /* document-root/*
```

at the end of my HTTP_PATHS.CONF and let access to files that aren't really there fail with a 404 (file not found) instead of a 403 (access ruled out); I end up not using the `fail` directive at all. If you have enough traffic that the disk I/O to look up nonexistent directories becomes an issue, you may prefer the /www/ and catchall fail configuration, despite the drawbacks I've mentioned.

Content type

OSU uses MIME types defined in the HTTP_SUFFIXES.CONF file to determine the content-type header it will send. The command for a particular type is

```
suffix .extension representation encoding qualifier
```

So the command to specify the GIF (binary image file) format is

```
suffix .gif image/gif BINARY 1.0
```

(.GIFs, along with most common filetypes, come prespecified by default.)

PHP template pages include

```
suffix .php text/php 8BIT 1.0
```

If the filetype needs to be processed by something else, you use a presentation rule to define the script.

```
presentation content-type processor
```

For PHP template pages, which need the PHP processor run on them before they go to the browser, that's

```
presentation text/php PHP
```

(if the PHP command is defined systemwide or in the OSU account's login.com).

Image maps are specified by default with

```
presentation application/imagemap www_root:[bin]mapimage
```

PDFs or other large files can be usefully downloaded in chunks by some clients if you use the byterange script.

```
presentation application/pdf byterange
```

7.1.3 WASD

Mapping

WASD's mapping rules go in HTTPD$MAP.CONF. They'll look familiar if you're used to OSU mapping. What will look unfamiliar is the addition of conditional mapping statements. They fall somewhere between access control and mapping but are included here for the sake of consistency.

```
REDIRECT template result
```

For a URL that matches the template, substitute the result string. There are four different formats for the result string, all but one of which will generate genuine external redirects. If the result string is just a path specification with no scheme or host name specified (starting with a single slash), the server restarts the request internally.

If the result is a full URL (scheme://server.domain.tld/path with or without a trailing query string "?a=b"), the server instructs the browser to try that new URL as it stands.

If the result string leaves out the scheme: (giving a URL such as //server.domain.tld/path with two leading slashes), the current scheme is defaulted in, so the same redirect statement can redirect HTTP requests to HTTP and HTTPS requests to HTTPS.

If the result includes the scheme but leaves out the host name, the server will default in the current host name, which allows you to redirect requests from HTTP: to HTTPS: for documents that require it, or, if for some reason you want to, you can go the other way and have the same redirect rule work across virtual hosts.

If the result string leaves out the host name as well, giving a URL such as (///path, with three leading slashes), the server defaults in both scheme and host name from the current request, so the same redirect rule can be used for multiple hosts.

If you need to pass query strings in any of the redirects, make the last character of the result string a question mark ("?"). Without that, query strings will be dropped from the redirect.

```
MAP template result
```

(See the foregoing discussion of the map rule for OSU.) Both template and result must be absolute, not relative paths—they must start with a single slash. As with OSU, a match on a map statement doesn't terminate map processing.

```
PASS template [result | "numeric-status [alphanumeric-explanation]"]
```

The pass rule extends the OSU map rule. The form where it's just the template is permitted if file-name translation isn't required (e.g., /ht_root/docs/*, where /ht_root/ is translated as the directory referred to by the system logical HT_ROOT). The WASD pass rule can also return a numeric status and an explanatory string, if desired, or can just refuse the connection.

For example, if you discovered that one of your users had put some inappropriate but popular material in a user directory (see Chapter 8) on your server, you could forestall user-name translation and file access with

```
PASS /~username/* "403 very naughty"
```

or, if you want to frustrate the attempted users, you can use a 1xx or 2xx status code without explanation, which will just drop the connection immediately. (You could also use this version of the pass command to do redirections, by substituting a 3xx code and a URL to redirect, perhaps, to a page describing the institution's policy on inappropriate materials.)

```
FAIL template
```

Similar to the OSU fail, this will terminate map processing and reject the request with an access denied failure.

WASD offers three mapping rules that relate to CGI scripting. Exec and uxec rules map script directories; the script rule maps a specific script.

```
EXEC[+] template [(RTEname)]result
```

The template should include a wildcard so that named scripts will be matched (e.g., " /htbin/*"). The result can have the wildcard substituted in (e.g., " /ht_root/bin/*"). This instructs the server both where to look for files in htbin and that those files should be treated as executables. This means that any script in the directory can be executed, which means that anybody who can contrive to put a file in that directory can get the server to execute anything he or she wants. Make sure permissions are set appropriately.

If the "exec+" form is used, the CGIplus persistent scripting environment will be used. If a Run-Time Environment name is given, that environment (e.g., a persistent Perl process) will be used. (More discussion on CGIplus and RTEs can be found in Chapter 17.)

```
UXEC[+] template [(RTEname)]result
```

works like exec, except that it maps script execution for users (running as that user if the Persona services are enabled). Template looks like "/~*/directory/*", and result looks like "/*/www/cgi-bin/*". (Template could also be "/~specificusername/directory/*", and result would be "/specificdirectory/www/cgi-bin/*".) The first wildcard is for user name, and the second is for the script name. Uxec must always be preceded by a SET rule—for example,

```
SET /~*/www/cgi-bin/* script=as=~
```

(The set rule is discussed subsequently, but this is what instructs the server to run scripts from that directory in the persona of the user it belongs to.)

```
SCRIPT template file-system-path-to-script
```

The script rule maps a URL to a particular file and makes that file executable. This can be used (as in my earlier example) for making a script look like a static Web page—for example,

```
SCRIPT /status.html /cgi-bin/status.pl
```

or for making sure only specific named scripts in particular locations are run. Typically the template will look like " /scriptname/*", and the path to script like "/Web/myscripts/bin/scriptname.exe*"; the wildcards here are to pass along path names on which the scripts should operate.

The final rule, and it's a doozy, is the set rule. Set doesn't actually do any mapping, but it fits logically with the mapping rules because it acts on path ames, instructing the server to adjust the characteristics of the specified path in a wide variety of ways.

```
SET pathname characteristic [ characteristic-2 ...characteristic-n]
```

You can have multiple characteristics for a path in a single SET command; just separate them with a space. You can also have multiple SET commands with additional characteristics. They're processed in the order they appear in the HTTPD$MAP.CONF file, so you can turn a characteristic on for a large tree and then, below it, turn the characteristic off for a subtree within it.

Many of the characteristics are binary, turned on with the characteristic name and off with NOcharacteristic. Some of these characteristics mention attributes we haven't discussed yet, but it makes sense to put a full reference for the set rule in one place.

`AUTHONCE, NOAUTHONCE`

When a request path has both a script and a resource the script acts upon, the server ordinarily checks access to both the script and the resource. `AUTHONCE` makes the server authorize only the original path. `NOAUTHONCE` restores the original behavior.

`CACHE, NOCACHE`

When caching is enabled—see Chapter 11—files are cached by default. `NOCACHE` turns off caching for this path; `CACHE` can turn it back on for a subtree. Of course, a path can be specified down to the level of a particular document.

`CGIPREFIX="desired-prefix"`

Chapter 14 discusses CGI environment variable names. By default, these are prefixed with WWW_, but the prefix can be changed for compatibility with scripts written for other servers. To remove the prefix altogether use `CGIprefix=` with no value.

`CHARSET="charset-specifier"`

This setting can override the default character set parameter ([Charset-Default]), which is sent in the character set parameter of the content-type header for text files. You must specify what charset you want to identify—for example, "charset=ISO-8859-5".

`CONTENT="content-type/parameter"`

Ordinarily the server chooses what content type to put in the header based on the file extension (determined by the `[AddType]` directive in the HTTPD$CONF or an external MIME types file specified in `[AddMime-TypesFile]`). This setting allows that mapping to be overridden for files in the path you specified, as, for example, when you have a lot of text files with a .DOC extension in one particular directory tree; you can specify `"/path-to-DOC-files/*.DOC"` as the template and `"content=text/plain"`, while letting all other .DOC files on the system be served as DECwrite files (the default) or MS-Word files (which is how IE will interpret them regardless of the content-type header).

`EXPIRED, NOEXPIRED`

Files in the path will be sent with headers indicating that they are already expired, so that the browser will automatically fetch them again when they're accessed, rather than coming up with the old version from the browser cache. (This is useful on very dynamic documents; you likely want to use it in conjunction with NOCACHE.)

```
INDEX="format string"
```

The value here is the directory listing format string for directories in the specified path. (See Chapter 13 for more on directory listings.)

```
LOG, NOLOG
```

If you're logging at all, by default you log all accesses. NOLOG will suppress logging to this path. (If you want to know what pages are being loaded but don't particularly want a log entry for every button, ball, or line graphic, you can set NOLOG on the path containing those images. This not only speeds up your logging, it can speed up your log-file analysis.)

```
MAPONCE, NOMAPONCE
```

Once the application of a script, exec, or uxec rule has identified a particular request as a script and mapped it to a path, that path takes another trip through the mapping process in case it needs to be translated again. You can suppress this with a SET path MAPONCE. (You might do this to save some processing effort when an exec directory can be located without further mapping—for example, /ht_root/bin/*.)

```
PROFILE, NOPROFILE
```

If the server has been started with /PROFILE and /SYSUAF (see Chapter 5), it uses SYSUAF authentication and rightslist-based access to server resources. NOPROFILE will enable you to ignore rightslist-based access for the specific path; PROFILE will reenable it. (If the server hasn't been started with the relevant qualifiers, this setting won't do anything—all access is NOPROFILE.)

```
REPORT=[BASIC|DETAILED]
```

This setting changes server-generated reports between BASIC and DETAILED for a particular path.

```
ODS-5, ODS-2
```

ODS-5 warns the server that a path maps to files on an ODS-5 volume and may thus have names that use the Extended File Specification and need to be treated differently; for example, the RMSCHAR setting won't be applied. ODS-2 is the default, so you never actually need to specify it, but it may help you make the mapping rules read more more clearly.

```
RMSCHAR=invalid-replacement-character
```

For ODS-2 paths, the server will replace RMS-invalid characters or syntax with this replacement character. By default, a $ is used; other plausible choices are underscore ("_") and hyphen ("-"), but this will let you specify any alphanumeric character. If you've got files moved from a UNIX system or even NFS served from another system, this may enable you to serve them.

```
SCRIPT=AS=[~|$|username]
```

This applies only if the server was started with the /PERSONA qualifier. This setting instructs the server to run scripts from this path under a user name different from than that of the server. Tilde will run the script as the user specified in the URL after the tilde; dollar sign will run the script as the SYSUAF-authenticated user accessing the script; a user name will run the script as the specified user name. I urge caution in the use of any of these options (and strongly suggest using the /PERSONA=identifier variant, which limits scripting capabilities to accounts that hold the specified identifier).

```
SCRIPT=BIT-BUCKET=hh:mm:ss
```

tells the server how long to allow a script to execute if the client disconnects prematurely, overriding the HTTPD$CONFIG.CONF `[DCLBitBucket-Timeout]` directive.

```
SCRIPT=CPU=hh:mm:ss
```

directs the server to whack script processes in the specified path that have used more than the specified quantity of CPU time, preventing runaway scripts from running forever.

```
SCRIPT=FIND|NOFIND
```

The server ordinarily makes sure scripts exist before trying to run them. However, a script might be executed by a process that knows how to find it by means not available to the server—for example, if the scripts are stored as procedures in a relational database. `NOFIND` tells the server not to bother looking for it, but just to go ahead and execute it.

```
SSI=PRIV|NOPRIV
```

Server-side includes documents (discussed in greater detail in Chapter 13) can contain directives (e.g., <--#exec command-name-->) that are considered privileged, because they could do damage through running a program in server context. The server won't run those directives unless the documents are owned by SYSTEM or the path they're in is set as `PRIV` to allow these directives. Caution is strongly recommended here.

```
SSLCGI=none|Apache_mod_SSL|Purveyor
```

If you're running a CGI script (see Chapter 14) under SSL (see Chapter 6) and the script needs environment variables set to tell it about the SSL environment, this setting tells the server which style of CGI variable should be created: none, Apache's mod-ssl style, or Process Software's Purveyor style. If you need this, go back to HTTPD$CONFIG.CONF and add 2048 to the values of the `[BufferSizeDclCommand]` and `[BufferSize-CgiPlusIn]` directives to account for the extra room taken by the variables.

```
STMLF, NOSTMLF
```

specifies paths for files to be automatically converted to Stream-LF format. Default is no conversion.

```
THROTTLE=parameters
```

controls the concurrent number of scripts to be processed on the path. (This is discussed more fully in Chapter 14.) Options are:

```
"THROTTLE=n,[n,n,n,hh:mm:ss,hh:mm:ss]"
"THROTTLE=FROM=n"
"THROTTLE=TO=n"
"THROTTLE=RESUME=n"
"THROTTLE=BUSY=n"
"THROTTLE=TIMEOUT=QUEUE=hh:mm:ss"
"THROTTLE=TIMEOUT=BUSY=hh:mm:ss"
```

```
TIMEOUT=KEEPALIVE=hh:mm:ss
```

overrides the `[TimeoutKeepAlive]` HTTPD$CONFIG.CONF directive for this path.

```
TIMEOUT=NOPROGRESS=hh:mm:ss
```

overrides the `[TimeoutNoProgress]` HTTPD$CONFIG.CONF directive for this path.

```
TIMEOUT=OUTPUT=hh:mm:ss
```

overrides the `[TimeoutOutput]` in the HTTPD$CONFIG.CONF file.

```
TIMEOUT=hh:mm:ss,hh:mm:ss,hh:mm:ss
```

overrides the `[TimeoutKeepAlive]`, `[TimeoutNoProgress]`, `[Timeout-Output]` directives, in that order, for this path.

Conditional mapping

You can use conditional mapping on paths in the HTTPD$MAP file. Rules using conditional mapping are applied only if criteria other than just the

URL path match are met, which offers immense flexibility and power to the administrator, as well as an opportunity to get really confusing results if you forget what you've done. Conditional processing adds some overhead to the URL path translation. (Because the mapping can control access to the resources, a case could be made for including this in section 7.3, but I've left it here in the mapping section. Possibly, this is the wrong choice.)

Conditionals appear on the same line as the mapping rule to which they refer, following the rule. They are set off by square brackets. A conditional is in the form "specific thing":pattern, and can usefully be read as "if specific thing matches pattern." A rule whose conditional(s) is not met is ignored and doesn't affect subsequent processing. The patterns are specified in the same way as patterns you'd give to the VMS $ DIRECTORY command: a simple, case-insensitive, string comparison, using the asterisk to match any number of characters and a percent sign to match a single character. If the string you're looking to test has a space, tab, asterisk, or left or right square bracket in it, substitute a % sign—you can't match those characters other than by single-character wildcard match—there are no escape characters or encoding.

Multiple conditionals inside one set of square brackets are treated as "OR" conditions; if any of the matches are true, the whole conditional is true. Multiple conditionals in separate sets of square brackets on a single line are treated as "AND" conditions; all must be true for the rule to be applied. An exclamation point preceding the conditional negates it (changes it from "if it matches" to "if it doesn't match"); you can put an exclamation point outside the square brackets to negate the entire sense of a multipart conditional. Here are the conditionals and what they match against.

```
[!]AC:accept-string
```

Contents of the HTTP Accept: header coming from the browser, which details content types the browser is willing to render.

```
[!]AL:accept-language-string
```

Contents of the HTTP Accept-Language: header coming from the browser; you could choose to map different directories or file names to support different languages.

```
[!]AS:accept-charset-string
```

Contents of the HTTP Accept-Charset: header. Again, map to different versions of files to support different character sets.

```
[!]CK:cookie
```

Contents of cookie returned by browser.

```
[!]EX:
```

This is actually a Boolean, rather than a pattern match. EX matches if this path has been set ODS-5 with a SET directive.

```
[!]FO:host-name/address
```

Contents of the "Forwarded:" header, seen if the request is coming to you through a proxy or gateway. You can test for specific values in this header or just put in an * if you want to do something different for all proxied requests.

```
[!]HO:host-name/address
```

That's host-name/address of the client, not the server.

```
[!]HM:host network mask (client mask, see immediately below)
```

To directly quote the WASD documentation, "The host-mask ('HM') directive is a dotted-decimal IP address, a slash, then a dotted-decimal mask. For example, [HM:131.185.250.0/255.255.255.192]. This has a 6- bit subnet. It operates by bitwise-ANDing the client host address with the mask, bitwise-ANDing the network address supplied with the mask, and then comparing the two results for equality. Using this example the host 131.185.250.250 would be accepted, but 131.185.250.50 would be rejected.

```
[!]ME:http-method
```

GET, POST, PUT, and so on.

```
[!]QS:query-string
```

This is the request query string, the part that comes after the "?" in the URL. It's particularly fun to combine the capability of the PASS command to return a status and message you specify with conditional mapping capability against the values in the query string.

```
[!]SC:request-scheme
```

HTTP or HTTPS. Handy for ensuring that certain pages are always viewed encrypted (by using it on a redirect to HTTPS with an SC:HTTP).

```
[!]SN:server-name
```

The name of this server. This is helpful when multiple cluster nodes share the same configuration files. It's potentially confusing if they're all responding to the same cluster alias.

```
[!]SP:server-port
```

The port the browser connected to.

```
[!]RF:referring-URL
```

This is the contents of the (curiously misspelled in the standard) "Referer:" header. If you only want people to be able to get to the download page after getting the "you have successfully filled out the application page," you can use this. Remember, however, that while headers are hard to spoof using standard browsers, they're easy using tools such as wget or the Perl lib-WWW programs, so don't rely on this for anything really important.

```
[!]UA:user-agent
```

The contents of the "User-Agent:" header. This can let you map old browsers off to a version of your pages they can handle. (Let me insert a plea here not to map them off to the "you need the latest and greatest version to see our site at all; download it here!" page, on behalf of everybody who used Netscape 3 on VMS for years and kept getting those pages, which never had a VMS version.) You can also use this conditional to play practical jokes on search engine robots, mapping them each by name to a page very different from the one their users will get when they click on the link back to your site. I can't in good conscience recommend this practice either.

```
[!]VS:host-name/address
```

The host-name header for a name-based virtual server or the numeric IP the client connected to. (This is a synonym for the obsolete HH: conditional, in case you're looking at an old HTTPD$MAP file and trying to figure it out.) Here are some examples.

```
PASS /content/* /browserspecific/MOZILLA/*
[UA:*MOZILLA*][!UA:*MSIE*]
PASS /content/* /browserspecific/IE/* [UA:*MSIE*]
PASS /content/* /generic/*
```

If your pages are optimized for specific browsers (a bad practice, but sometimes the Web designers feel an urgent need for control, which can be obtained only by using browser-specific extensions), you can have multiple versions of your site. Each one has links relative to the "content" directory, which will be where the HTML resides. This will map "content" back to the appropriate directory. IE identifies itself as Mozilla compatible, so it would match the Mozilla mapping if we didn't include the negated Explorer match (although we could avoid this problem by changing the order of the lines). Read the first line as "Pass /content/* as /browserspecific/MOZILLA/* if user-agent matches MOZILLA AND user-agent doesn't match MSIE."

```
PASS /images/* /MacImages/* [UA:*Mac*]
PASS /images/* /PCimages/* ![UA:*Mac*]
```

Because of design and display differences, images optimized on PCs tend to look darker and dingier on Macintoshes. For your site to look its best on each platform, you should have two versions of each image: one optimized for Mac, one for PC. The foregoing example will allow the links in the HTML to refer to the /images/ directory, so you need only one copy of the HTML code, but it will map the /images/links to the right directory, depending on what the user agent says about the platform in identifying itself. There's no consistency here; some say "Mac_PowerPC," some say "Macintosh PPC," but "*MAC*" will match any of them. We can't test for PCs that way, obviously, since *PC* will match the PC in PowerPC and PPC. You could test for *Windows*, but other OSs run on the same hardware and have the same issues.

```
PASS /doc/* /Web/doc/english/* [al:en*]
PASS /doc/* /Web/doc/french/* [ho:*.fr al:fr*]
PASS /doc/* /Web/doc/swedish/* [ho:*.se al:se*]
PASS /doc/* /Web/doc/english/*
```

This example (modified from the WASD documentation) demonstrates mapping based on country-oriented domain or accept-language header. Wherever they are, if English is their first-choice language, they get English. If the host is in France or France is their first-choice language, make it French; similarly for Sweden and Swedish. Otherwise, fall through to English because it's better than nothing, even though not the first choice.

```
PASS /companyspecific/* "403 You can't see that!"
![ho:*.mydomain.TLD]
```

If somebody from a host that isn't in my domain tries to look at my company-specific material, they get told not to. See the WASD documents for more examples.

Content type

WASD uses the `[AddType]` directive in HTTPD$CONFIG.CONF or can use a MIME.TYPES file if specified in the `[AddMimeTypesFile]` directive. The syntax for `[AddType]` is `.extension content-type [; charset] description`. That looks like

```
.HTML "text/html; charset=ISO-8859-1" HyperText Markup
Language
.HTM text/html HyperText Markup Language
.GIF image/gif image (GIF)
```

MIME.TYPES specifications are compatible with those used by Apache. The basic format is content-type extension(s), which looks like

```
application/msword             doc
application/octet-stream       bin dms lha lzh exe class
application/oda                oda
```

but there are some WASD-specific extensions (which are used for descriptions in server-generated directories, among other things). These are hidden in comments; WASD knows they're there because the hash mark (#) comment indicator is followed by an exclamation point. The comments follow the line to which they refer.

```
#! file description
```

A single blank indicates that what's coming is free-form text for directory listings.

```
#!/cgi-bin/script
```

A slash indicates that what follows is the name of a script that should be run automatically whenever the file type is requested—the same thing as an Apache handler or an OSU presentation script.

```
#![alt-tag-text] /path/to/icon.gif
```

A left square bracket is used to specify an icon to be used in directory listings. Since these are mapped against content type, not suffix, they have to be specified only once per content type. The contents of the square brackets will be used as the alt-tag for the icon, so they should be brief.

7.2 Authentication

There are several types of authentication available to Web servers. Structurally, they all work the same way. The client requests a resource that has access controls that require authentication; the Web server asks the client to authenticate (by sending it a "401 Authentication Required" header along with a "realm" or "authentication name"). The browser then asks the user for user name and password (typically in a separate small window on graphical browsers) or gets them from some other source—Internet Explorer running Windows NT talking to an IIS server in the same Windows domain will pass along your authenticated login name without requiring you to enter it, although that example is irrelevant for a VMS-based server—and then assembles a credentials packet, which it sends back to the server. The browser caches the contents of the credentials packet, based on realm and fully qualified server name, so it doesn't have to ask the user over and over again.

Since HTTP is a stateless protocol, the server needs authentication information for each protected page and will ask the browser for it every time. If the browser has the credentials for that realm in its cache, it supplies them.

Unfortunately, there's no way for either the server or the user to tell the browser to forget the credentials it has cached—that is, to log out from the session with the server. If you've provided a user name/password to a Web browser at an Internet cafe, you need to shut down the browser program altogether to be sure that the next person doesn't use your cached authentication to impersonate you. If it's a kiosk with a browser you can't shut down, don't use it for anything for which you have to put in credentials. Another unfortunate effect of caching credentials by server name is that if you refer to a system by different names—foo.bar.tld and www.foo.bar.tld—the browser won't realize these refer to the same system and will have to ask the user for credentials for each of them separately. Of course, if the browser cached by numeric IP address, it would do the wrong thing with multihosted domains that share the same numeric IP, thinking they were all the same server, and it would do a different wrong thing with servers that respond to a cluster alias with different numeric IPs.

The server takes the credentials packet and looks up the user name and password in some authentication database. If it matches and if access to the page isn't disallowed by some other access control, the server returns the page to the browser.

In the BASIC authentication mode the credentials packet with the user name and password is encoded (not encrypted!) in BASE-64. There's nothing secret about this—BASE-64 can be decoded by anybody who wants to. BASIC authentication makes passwords vulnerable to anyone with a sniffer on the line anywhere between the browser and the server. If you're going to use BASIC authentication, it's a particularly good idea to use SSL encryption for it.

DIGEST authentication returns a cryptographic digest of the password using the MD5 algorithm. Not all browsers support this; curiously, the most recent Mozilla does and Netscape 6.2 apparently doesn't. Netscape 4.78 on Macintosh appears to. Basically, you can't count on DIGEST working unless you have control of which browsers the users will use. Anyway, a person with a network sniffer can't just pick the password up from the DIGEST packet, but, by catching the digest of the password, he or she could write a program to pretend to be a browser and resubmit the same credentials. (This class of attack is referred to by security specialists as a "replay" attack. OSU and WASD, at least, defeat this by including a "nonce" value in the credentials request that's used in the encoding of the reply. The next time the request is issued it will have a different nonce value, so replay is ineffectual.)

Furthermore, that same individual with the sniffer can catch everything the server sends; therefore, if the content that comes back is unencrypted, the intruder can read it all, with little difficulty. Even with DIGEST authentication, if you care about the security of your content, use SSL encryption for the whole dialog.

In X.509 authentication the server requests and the browser presents a digital certificate (see Chapter 6 for more on digital certificates), and the server decides whether to accept it based on whether it has expired or whether it was issued by a Certificate Authority the server recognizes (or, at any rate, whether up the chain of issuers there is, somewhere, a CA the server recognizes). If the certificate is accepted, the server can then accept the identity of the person at the other end as authenticated. (Of course, the person at the other end could be a random visitor if a user walked away from his or her PC leaving it logged on, but that's more of a user education issue than a technological one.) The necessary configuration here is to let the server know where to find a file or database of recognized certificate authorities, and how far up the chain you're willing to go. You may want to honor only self-signed certificates, for example, and you don't care if they're presenting a certificate signed by some other system that is also known to Verisign or Thawte.

There are other authentication schemes that allow a single sign-on into a security domain (e.g., Kerberos), require possession of a physical token, or do a retinal scan or fingerprint check. These are not directly supported by any VMS-based Web servers, but I expect such support will be coming as these technologies become more popular. (Most likely, such access systems will have modes in which they can present authentication information to the browser, which will then use one of the authentication methods already in place. Thus, the servers won't have to explicitly contend with new authentication schemes.)

The server may be using one or more of many different authentication databases, regardless of the method used to present the credentials packet. It can validate against the SYSUAF, so the credentials are the same user name and password you can use to log in. It can validate against a special-purpose database that contains Web-only user names and passwords, either in some binary form or as a simple ASCII file.

On UNIX systems Apache modules have been written to check credentials against entries in relational databases, such as Oracle, but these are not currently available on VMS systems. This makes it harder to run pay-for-content sites on VMS without human intervention. If you can authenticate against a relational database, the same CGI script that accepts and validates the credit card information can easily insert the credentials into the database; it's somewhat harder to programmatically update the special-purpose authentication databases. Database access for large numbers of users—thousands or millions—scales well under a good relational database, whereas the plain-text lookup supported by OSU does not. If you're planning to run a pay-for-content site, you might want to look into porting one of the database authorization modules. VMS also doesn't support mod_auth_dbm, which uses the semigeneric DBM file format, for UNIX. VMS never needed the DBM file format because it had indexed files provided for free by RMS; as a result, however, tools layered on top of DBM can require significant porting effort.

In theory, you could authenticate against an LDAP (lightweight directory access protocol) server or by using remote authentication against an NT domain controller (which works for Pathworks and Advanced Server installations), but at present none of these authentication methods is available for VMS. mod_auth_ldap, mod_auth_kerberos, and mod_auth_radius exist for UNIX and could presumably be ported to VMS; indeed, CSWS Engineering has an LDAP authorization module working in the lab now.

Here's how each server manages authentication.

7.2.1 Apache

Password-based authentication

CSWS offers authentication against the SYSUAF using mod_auth_openvms; authentication against BASIC or DIGEST password files using mod_auth (which is part of the Apache core); authentication using X.509 certificates; and anonymous authorization (analogous to anonymous FTP). To use VMS authentication, you need to load the appropriate module; therefore, the following statement needs to go in your HTTPD.CONF before any directive that uses VMS authentication.

```
LoadModule auth_openvms_module/apache$common/modules/
mod_auth_openvms.exe_alpha
```

Authentication and access control directives can be placed in a per-directory .HTACCESS file, unless you configure the directory not to honor such files. This delegates responsibility to the users who own those directories; if you trust them, you can put `[AllowOverrideAuthConfig]` (or `All`) in your container directive.

In the container directive that specifies the resources you're controlling access for (typically `<Location>`, `<Directory>`, or `<Files>`), you can specify the following directives:

```
AuthType Basic|Digest
```

specifies whether to use BASIC or DIGEST for the authorization dialog. (You might think it would make sense to be able to say X.509 here, but with the way Apache modules work, mod_SSL is responsible for all the SSL stuff, and mod_auth, which is responsible for processing this directive, doesn't know anything about X5.09.) Instead, the mod_SSL SSLVerify-Client directive is used to ask the browser to send an X.509 certificate. If you use BASIC authorization, you should use SSLRequireSSL to ensure that the dialog is encrypted.

```
AuthName realm_name
```

This is what's going to show up in the browser window after "Enter user name and password for." Every time the browser tries to get into something with a different realm_name, the user will get a new credentials dialog, so you want to reuse realm_names as much as makes sense. If various different parts of the server directory tree are restricted to authenticated local users, make sure all the realm names for those parts are the same thing, just to minimize annoyance. I find that a useful value is "your VMS account" (in quotes, just as shown). This reminds the users, who may well be logged into some Windows domain with different credentials, which user name and password to put in. Of course, that name should be used only if you mean to do SYSUAF-based authentication.

```
AuthUserOpenVMS On
```

This enables SYSUAF-based authentication for the current container. To disable it, just leave this directive out. If you don't specify `AuthUser-OpenVMS On`, you need to specify some other authentication source.

```
AuthUserFile /path-to-password-file
```

This will authenticate against a special file containing user names and passwords that don't have to match anything in the UAF. You create and maintain the file by using the HTPASSWD.EXE_ALPHA utility. The relevant command-line arguments for HTPASSWD are -c (create a new password file), -m (force MD5 encryption of the password), and -b (take the password from the command line rather than prompting for it—thus, "b for batch"). So you can do

```
$ MC apache$common:[000000]ht_passwd.exe_alpha -
_$ -cmb password-file-name username password
```

and create a password file suitable for DIGEST authentication, populating it with the user name and password you specified; the password is stored in MD5 DIGEST form. You can add user names and passwords to that file by issuing the command with the same format, just leaving off the "c" from the switch. You can maintain multiple password files. You can make files suitable for basic authentication by leaving off the "m" flag. At any rate, the path to this file is what you put into /path-to-passwordfile in AuthUserFile.

```
require valid-user
```

This is technically an access-control directive rather than an authentication directive, but this, or the related require group, is what triggers Apache to actually request the authentication. Valid-user will be determined according to the authentication method you currently have active.

```
AuthGroupFile /path-to-group-file
```

The group file is a plain-text file that looks like

```
group-name1: list-of-usernames
group-name2: list-of-usernames
```

```
require group group-name
```

Again, require is technically access control rather than authentication, but looking ahead, this is the form of the require directive with which you can insist that the user be a member of a particular group. Looking in the AuthGroupFile is how Apache can tell whether that condition is met. The same user name can appear in any number of groups.

Using SSL authentication

```
SSLCARevocationPath /path
SSLCARevocationFile filename
```

SSLCARevocationPath and SSLCARevocationFile are combined to point to lists of certificates the CAs say they've revoked. (You or your organization may well be the CA in this case; you'd revoke a client certificate if the employee it identified had been terminated or if the certificate had been installed on a laptop that had been stolen.) You probably want to make these items serverwide, or at least VirtualHostwide, rather than putting them in every container file in which SSL authentication is used.

```
SSLCACertificatePath /path
SSLCACertificateFile filename
```

If you're going to use client certificates for authentication, you need to be able to verify the certificate authorities they claim to be issued by; the `SSLCACertificatePath` and `SSLCACertificateFile` are combined to point to a file containing the information for the CAs from which you'll accept client certificates. (The reason this file is specified in two parts, path-to-file and file name, in Apache and in other servers, is that they all end up calling an OpenSSL routine, SSL_CTX_load_verify_locations, which wants the path and the file name as two distinct arguments.)

```
SSLVerifyClient none | optional | require | optional_no_ca
```

`SSLVerifyClient` says whether clients need to have certificates. `none` (the default) requires no certificate; `optional` allows the client to present a certificate; `require` means that the client must present a valid certificate; `optional_no_ca` means that the client may present a certificate and if it does, the certificate doesn't have to be signed by a verifiable CA—you'll talk to them anyway. (In fact, however, only `none` and `require` will definitely work with all SSL-enabled browsers.)

```
SSLVerifyDepth number-of-levels
```

`SSLVerifyDepth` specifies how far you'll go up a certificate chain to verify a certificate; `0` works only for self-signed certificates, `1` only for self-signed certificates and CAs already known to you (in the `SSLCACertificateFile`), and so on.

```
SSLOptions [+-] ExportCertData | FakeBasicAuth |StrictRequire
```

(The whole list of options is included in Chapter 6.)

`FakeBasicAuth` will take the subject distinguished name (DN) of the client certificate and pretend that the client was authenticated as that user under BASIC authorization, allowing regular Apache access controls to be used. (Since no password is collected, you may need to edit the password file to put the user name into the authorization file with the password "xxj31ZMTzkVA," which is the DES-encoded version of the word "password".)

ExportCertData makes the certificate information available as symbols in the CGI/SSI environment (which is useful if you are doing complicated things with SSLRequire or you have a CGI to do an LDAP lookup).

StrictRequire is designed to keep a "Satisfy any" with other authorized accesses specified from working when SSLRequire or SSLRequireSSL forbid access; it forces an access failure without looking at the other options permitted in the Satisfy statement. (This will make more sense after reading section 7.3.)

Anonymous authentication

Mod_auth_anon is intended to let you do the same kind of (minimal) authentication anonymous FTP does. Here are the directives for this module:

```
Anonymous list-of-users
```

or

```
Anonymous_NoUserID on
```

Anonymous has a list of user names, one of which must be entered for access to these resources unless Anonymous_NoUserID is set on. (Typical user names include "guest" or "visitor.")

```
Anonymous_MustGiveEmail on|off
```

If on (the default), the person must enter an e-mail address as the password.

```
Anonymous_VerifyEmail on|off
```

If on (the default is off), the e-mail address the person puts in must resemble a real e-mail address, containing an @ symbol and at least one "." No attempt is made to determine that what's entered is indeed a working e-mail address.

```
Anonymous_LogEmail on|off
```

If on (the default is off), the e-mail addresses entered will show up in the access log.

7.2.2 OSU

Password-based authentication

OSU offers authentication against the SYSUAF; against user name/password combinations specified in plain-text protection files; and, starting in

3.10alpha, in client SSL certificates. (There's also a mechanism for making callouts to an external authentication routine, so if you really need to check passwords via LDAP or a database, you can write a shareable image library, including a check_password routine, that will be called if the setup file specifies a domain or if the target user name in the SYSUAF has the external authentication bit set. However, you get only one, so you can't both check against the Windows NT domain and look it up in an Oracle database. For further details see the EXT_AUTHENTICATOR.C source code.)

All the authentication work is done by a separate authenticator process (which keeps the entire server from needing to be installed with elevated privileges; only the authenticator needs it). Three different authenticator programs are provided with the server. Sample_Authenticator is, as it sounds, a skeletal program that doesn't do much; MD5_Authenticator was the first attempt at supporting DIGEST authentication; and EXT_AUTHENTICATOR is the real and current program. By default, the authenticator isn't installed with SYSPRV. If you want to be able to do SYSUAF authentication, you need to do that. Edit HTTP_SYSSTARTUP.COM to comment out or remove the line

```
$ goto auth_install_done
```

because this skips the INSTALL you need.

Access control is managed in plain text .PROT files. Remember that host-based access controls (as distinct from numeric-address–based access controls won't work unless `DNSLookup` is enabled; this is discussed in Chapter 11). The formats of those files are discussed in greater detail subsequently, but in any case, you can specify user name and password for access control as follows:

```
*[@host] *
```

This accepts any SYSUAF-validated user name and password.

```
username[@host] *
```

This allows access only to the specified user name and gets the password from the SYSUAF.

```
username password
```

This requires that the user enter the specific user name and password found in the file.

```
* password
```

This accepts any user name but must match the entered password.

Using SSL authentication

SSL authentication via client certificate has just been implemented with the most recent test release, OSU 3.10alpha. It works only with the threaded SSL server, not with the SSL_Engine or SSL_Task. There's no documentation other than a mention in the release notes that this capability is included, and some comments in the source code.

Reading the source code and the tempm.conf included with the server, I conjecture that you want to include at the end of the HTTP_MAIN.CONF file, localaddress blocks with fake variable names for configuration purposes. (Variables beginning with "@" are ignored by the main rule file parser, which is under the impression that they are configuration variables for the server-maint utility. This mechanism has been overloaded to allow for some SSL configuration.)

```
localaddress @SSL_CA_FILE=vms-full-file-spec-for-CA-file
localaddress @SSL_CA_PATH=/path-to-file
```

If you're going to use client certificates for authentication, you need to be able to verify the certificate authorities they claim to be issued by; the `SSL_CA_FILE` and `SSL_CA_PATH` are combined to point to a file containing the information for the CAs from which you'll accept client certificates.

```
localaddress @SSL_CLIENT_VERIFY=digit
```

`SSL_CLIENT_VERIFY` says whether clients need to have certificates. Don't include at all if you don't want a certificate; "`0`" makes the certificate optional; "`1`" means that the client must present a valid certificate; "`2`" means that the client may present a certificate and, if it does, the certificate doesn't have to be signed by a verifiable CA—you'll talk to them anyway. (But, in fact, only using "`1`" or leaving it out altogether will definitely work with all SSL-enabled browsers.)

```
localaddress @SSL_CHAIN_VERIFY=digit
```

`SSL_CHAIN_VERIFY` specifies how far you'll go up a certificate chain to verify a certificate; `0` works only for self-signed certificates; `1` only for self-signed and CAs already known to you (in the only), and so on.

David Jones, the OSU author, has provided some tools for building an indexed certificate map file that maps X.509 distinguished names to VMS identifiers (user names). You can compile cert_map_manager.c and cert_map.c, link them together with SSL routines using cert_map_manager.opt., and use cert_map_manager to create and populate the file. The commands for the cert_map_manager are

```
$cert_map_manager create [filename]
$cert_map_manager add certfile [identifier] [/noissuer]
$cert_map_manager remove cert-file [identifier]
$cert_map_manager show [/default] [cert-file]
$cert_map_manager set default defspec
```

When you issue a client certificate, you can use this program to associate it with a VMS user name. Because you can break the association with the remove command, OSU doesn't need an SSL_CA_REVOCATION file and path; if the DN isn't associated with a user name, you don't care whether the certificate is valid.

```
localaddress @SSLCERTMAP=full-path-to-certmap-DB
```

Use this to tell the server where the certificate map database is.

To invoke all this, use the `<CERTMAP>0` tag in the protection file; the authenticator will do the mapping and pretend it got the user name and the right password for it from the browser, matching any later user-name directives.

7.2.3 WASD

Password-based authentication

WASD supports the usual forms of authentication as well as some unusual ones. If you want to do any flavor of SYSUAF-based authentication, you must have the /SYSUAF parameter in the server startup. I'd recommend /SYSUAF=SSL, which will guarantee that the credentials dialog is encrypted. /SYSUAF=ID would restrict SYSUAF authentication to accounts holding relevant rightslist identifiers.

/SYSUAF by itself supports any active (non-disusered, non-expired), non-privileged, nonsystem user names for authentication; /SYSUAF=RELAXED allows any active user names at all to go through; and /SYSUAF=PROXY supports the unusual SYSUAF proxying function, which can map remote user names at other hosts into particular VMS user names on your local system as though user name and password had been entered. Combine the values with parentheses around a comma-separated list, such as /SYSUAF=(SSL, PROXY, RELAXED).

If you're using /SYSUAF=ID, the relevant identifiers are as follows:

- WASD_HTTPS_ONLY—if present, it requires SSL for authentication on the particular account (obviously superseded by /SYSUAF=SSL).
- WASD_NIL_ACCESS—if present, it allows authentication against an account even outside of any time restrictions given for the account.
- WASD_PASSWORD_CHANGE—this lets the authenticated user on the account change the SYSUAF password, if the server is set up to allow that.
- WASD_PROXY_ACCESS—this permits proxy access (discussed subsequently).

You can also add the startup qualifier /AUTHORIZE=SSL to make sure that all authentication dialogs are conducted encrypted, not just SYSUAF authentication. (/AUTHORIZE=ALL will let you require that every path that's served be ruled in by a protection rule, rather than just not ruled out; this is probably a good idea for sites with data that should not get out.)

You can authenticate group membership against plain-text list files with an .$HTL extension, placed in the HT_AUTH directory (HT_LOCAL by default). These can be created with any source editor. You can also authenticate against server-specific .$HTA files with user names and passwords. These can be created only via the on-line administration utility; there is no command-line program to create them.

You can also use the (spoofable and somewhat dubious) RFC 1413 authentication, which follows the TCP/IP connection for this user back to the host and asks the ident server on the host who owns it. (This is probably a good idea only on an intranet.) A very detailed X.509-based authentication and access control method is available, and access control allows access by rightslist identifier held by the SYSUAF-authenticated user. As with OSU, WASD also has hooks for an external authentication program in case you need to authenticate via a relational database, an LDAP lookup, or some other scheme.

In the HTTPD$CONFIG.CONF file you may want to set the authorization failure limit, which enables the server to mimic VMS break-in detection and evasion. After a specified number of unsuccessful login attempts (three by default for VMS), even correct user name/password combinations won't be accepted.

```
[AuthFailureLimit] number-of-attempts
```

This prevents your Web server from allowing indefinite numbers of password-guessing attempts and thereby weakening security on your SYSUAF-authenticated users. Once the failure limit is exceeded, a failure count number of minutes must expire before legitimate password checking again occurs (i.e., if five failures occurred, then five minutes after the last attempt, input of correct credentials will result in successful access). If the user calls you and you set that user's password to something known, you can do HTTPD/DO=PURGE=AUTH to clear the authentication cache and allow the user to access the resources.

```
[AuthRevalidateUserMinutes] minutes
```

This forces the browser to demand authentication credentials again after a specified number of minutes. For example, setting this to 600 would allow a user's credentials to be checked once every working day. Such reentering of user name and password has the potential to become very irritating if it is more frequent than is really required.

You specify authentication realms in the HTTPD$AUTH.CONF file. The realm specification is wrapped in square brackets and consists of an optional realm-name string (in quotes if it contains blanks), an equals sign if the realm-name string is specified, an authentication type, and optional qualifiers to the type. (If you leave out the realm name, then the authentication type is the name of the realm as well.)

```
[authorizationtype; full-access-group; read-access-group]
```

Authorization type is

```
"Optional Realm Description"[=type-specific-
identifier]=authenticationtype
```

The optional realm description is what shows up in the browser window when it asks for user name and password; if you're going to use something that doesn't ask for user name and password, you can leave it out. If you leave it out on user name/password-driven lookups, the authentication type will be used as the realm descriptor.

Here are the available authentication types and what they mean. The types that do SYSUAF lookups are VMS and ID. Those that do authentication against a server-specific list or database are LIST and HTA. Other forms are AGENT, HOST, NONE, PROMISCUOUS, RFC 1413, WORLD, and X.509. Here's what they each mean, along with sample syntax for them:

```
"Optional realm description"=EXTERNALAGENT_NAME=agent"
```

If you need to do that LDAP callout or RDB lookup, you can build a program to do so based on the HT_ROOT:[SRC.AGENT]AUTH-AGENT_EXAMPLE.C example program. This runs as a CGIplus persistent script, so you don't take a hit from image activation on every path validation. The script can get realm, group, user names, and plain-text passwords as CGI variables if needed for lookups. The server will look for the agent program in /cgiauth-bin/.

If the script doesn't need the server to issue an authentication request to the client—for example, you want to authenticate by hardware address or biometrics—you can use the param `/NO401` qualifier on the path. Samples follow:

```
["Windows-NT username
/password"=AuthAgentNTLookup=agent;NTfull=HTA;NTread]
```

When you're looking for any path within this realm, the server issues a 401 WWW-Authorize request to the browser, then invokes /cgiauth-bin/AuthAgent_NTLookup.EXE and gets back from it a status on whether that user name and password are authenticated. (Presumably, AuthAgentNT-Lookup validates against a Windows NT domain.) The server checks the NTfull.$HTA database to see whether that authenticated user is in the full access group; failing that, it checks the NTread.$HTA to see whether the user is in the read-only group. If the user is in neither, it makes the request fail.

```
[AuthAgentBiometrics=agent]
path /biometricallyqualifiedstuff/* param="/NO401"
```

This doesn't ask the browser for credentials but does invoke /cgiauth-bin/AuthAgentBiometrics.exe, which then does whatever it has to do to authenticate the user without going back through the browser. For SYSUAF authentication, you can use the VMS authorization type, as follows.

```
[VMS]
```

prompts for user name and password, looks it up in the SYSUAF, and accounts for time/day restrictions.

```
["Your VMS Username and Password"=VMS]
```

This does the same thing, but uses the string "Your VMS Username and Password," which shows in the browser window.

```
[righstlist-identifier=ID]
```

prompts for VMS user name and password and allows access only if that account holds the identifier given in the rightslist-identifier.

```
["Enter your application-specific username/password"=databasename=HTA]
```

The server prompts for user name and password using the description string you entered; it validates against the HT_AUTH:databasename.$HTA database you specified.

```
["Enter your application/specific username/password"=listname=LIST]
```

The server prompts for user name and password using the description string you gave; it validates against HT_AUTH:listname.$HTL plain text list you specified. (This is not generally a good idea.)

```
[EXTERNAL]
```

Will accept any request at all. The understanding is that authorization and authentication will be done by some external agent that you provide. (The example configuration files shows this as being used for CGI program, which can make callbacks to the Web server for help with authentication or authorization if they need it.

```
[NONE]
```

Any request is accepted, no authentication is done, and no user name or realm is set.

```
[PROMISCUOUS]
```

This is available only when the server is running in PROMISCUOUS mode (that is, with the startup parameter /PROMISCUOUS), which usually is not the case. PROMISCUOUS mode should only be used for server testing.

```
[WORLD]
```

passes any request; it doesn't prompt for user name or password and sets the realm and user name value both to "WORLD." (This is helpful when running in /AUTHORIZATION=ALL mode, where you have to explicitly say that the entire world can look at a given path.)

Using SSL authentication

```
[X509]
```

This provides authentication by client certificate. If you want to do this, a few more files come into play. You need a file containing root certificates for all the Certificate Authorities you plan to use; if you put that in HT_ROOT:[LOCAL]CA-BUNDLE_CRT.TXT, the startup will find it there and define HTTPD$SSL_CAFILE to point to it. You can define

Certificate Authority bundles for each service, using the `[ServiceSSL-clientVerifyCAfile]`; you can define for each service whether a verifiable client certificate is required with the `[ServiceSSLclientVerify-Required]` directive.

Alternatively, if you're using the HTTPD$SERVICE file to run multiple services, you can specify this on a per-service basis using:

```
[ServiceSSLclientVerifyCAfile] vms-filename-for-per-
service-Cafile
[ServiceSSLclientVerifyRequired] enable | disable
```

When using X.509 certificates, you generally want to do more than just ask for a certificate; you need to specify which certificates get to have access. By default, WASD takes the fingerprint from the certificate record, which is a 32-digit hexadecimal number. (This is an MD5 digest of the record so it's unique per certificate.) That fingerprint is then used as the user name for access controls, which are discussed in section 7.3. If you'd rather use some other field as the user name (e.g., distinguished-name, e-mail, etc.), you need to tell WASD to do that, using the `param` directive on the path line. For example, `Param="[ru:/CN=]"` says to set the remote-user name to the value in the certificate name field.

There a number of directives that can be passed as parameters and that allow you to tweak some aspects of certificate negotiation. The format for each follows. Please note that in WASD syntax the external square brackets are literal square brackets, not signifying an optional item.

These directives can be set on a per-path basis, overriding any serverwide or servicewide defaults. They also give you a way to talk about values in the certificate record, which can be used for access control.

```
[DP:depth-integer]
```

Verify the certificate's CA chain to this depth (default 10).

```
[LT:minutes]
```

Set the certificate verification lifetime in integer minutes. By default (without specifying this directive), the certificate must be reverified with each new access. When this is specified, the lifetime counter is reset with every new access before the lifetime runs out.

```
[RU:/record-option=]
```

Set the remote-user name based on the specified record from the certificate. Options, not all of which make a lot of sense but are available, include /C—(country name), /CN—(common name), /ST—(state or province), /SP—(also state or province), /L—(locality), /O—(organization), /OU—(organizational unit), /T—(title), /I—(initials), /G—(given name), /S—(surname), /D—(description), /UID—(unique identifier), and Email—(e-mail address).

```
[TO: minutes | EXPIRED]
```

sets the session cache entry timeout (normally five minutes) to the number of minutes specified if any; if "EXPIRED," sets the session cache entry for the current certificate as expired immediately, requiring (and initiating).

SSL renegotiation

```
[VF:NONE | OPTIONAL | REQUIRED]
```

sets CA verification options. With NONE, no certificate is required, and any existing certificate authentication is expired from the cache without triggering a new SSL negotiation. With OPTIONAL, the client must present a certificate (or have one unexpired in session cache), but it doesn't have to be verifiable against known Certificate Authorities. With REQUIRED, a verifiable certificate must be presented or be in session cache.

Ident-based (SYSUAF proxy) authentication

```
[RFC1413]
```

This doesn't prompt; it asks the ident daemon on the other end of the connection for the name of the user who's using that port and takes that as user name. (Of course, there may be no ident daemon, in which case this will fail.) It provides no password authentication. It can be used with SYSUAF proxying to map a remote user name to a local one that is considered to be authenticated.

If /SYSUAF=ID is in effect, user names to be proxied to must hold the rightslist identifier WASD_PROXY_ACCESS. The proxy commands can be applied at realm level or at path level within a realm.

Proxy entries come in three basic formats, each with an optional host or network mask component. The entries can appear directly in HTTPD$AUTH.CONF or can be in a separate file referenced with `[AuthProxyFile]`. If you want them to apply to everything in a realm, put them directly after the realm specifier. If you want to apply to a particular path or set of paths, place them before those paths and put an `[AuthProxy]` directive with no proxy entries right after those paths. (The paths themselves will presumably have access control directives that involve user names.)

You can have multiple proxy entries in a single [AuthProxy] directive, and multiple [AuthProxy] directives with no intervening path specifications all active at the same time. If there's a path specification and then another [AuthProxy], all existing proxy mappings are cleared and only the new one is accepted.

Here are the proxy entry formats. (In these particular WASD formats, square brackets really do indicate optional elements rather than literal brackets.) The SYSUAF_NAME is the VMS user name being mapped to. The REMOTE_NAME is the remote user name (CGI variable WWW_REMOTE_USER).

```
REMOTE_NAME[@HOST|@network/mask]=SYSUAF_NAME
```

Maps a specified remote user name (and optional host/network) onto the specified SYSUAF user name. For example, ALAN@vms.kicks-ass.net=WINSTON maps the Alan account at vms.kicks-ass.net to the WINSTON account on my system. ALAN@134.79.32.0/255.255.255.0=WINSTON maps Alan logged in to any machine on the 134.79.32 network to WINSTON on my system.

```
*[@HOST|@network/mask]=SYSUAF_NAME
```

Maps all remote user names, or all remote user names on particular hosts or networks, to a single specific user name on this system. This is good as a catchall proxy after you've matched other names. `*@vms.kicks-ass.net=GUEST` maps any user on vms.kicks-ass.net to GUEST on your system, *=GUEST maps any user anywhere to GUEST.

```
*[@HOST|@network/mask]=*
```

Maps any remote user names into that same user name on your system. This is handy if you can specify the rest of your VMS cluster easily with a network and mask; if they're coming from there they share a SYSUAF with you and actually are the same people. Otherwise, it's terribly dangerous. If you've set up /SYSUAF=RELAXED, then all people on another system have to do is have an account with the same name as a privileged account of yours in order to be considered to be that user. That doesn't matter too much with path-based authentication until you get to persona-based scripting, but it might be good to disallow mapping of the system account altogether, which you can do with an early `system=-`.

Here's an example set of [AuthProxy] entries taken from the WASD documentation.

```
[RFC1413]
  [AuthProxy] bloggs@131.185.250.1=fred
  [AuthProxy] doe@131.185.250.*=john system=- *@131.185.252.0/24=*
  [AuthProxy] *=GUEST
```

First line: bloggs on system 131.185.250.1 is allowed access as though he'd been UAF authenticated as FRED (assuming FRED has the proxy-access identifier set up.)

Second line: doe on any system in the 131.185.250.* network is JOHN on VMS. `system=-` keeps a remote "system" from being mapped to my local SYSTEM. `*@131.185.252.0/24=*` maps all accounts on all systems in 131.185.250.0 8-bit subnet to the same VMS user name on the server system as they have on the remote system.

Third line: Anybody who hasn't been mapped already is mapped as GUEST.

7.3 Access controls

Just because something's on your server doesn't mean you want the whole world to see it. You may have files that tech support people should be able to see but that customers shouldn't or programs that only certain people should be able to run. (You don't want random strangers updating your phone list, much less writing purchase requisitions.) You probably don't want search engines wasting your resources by trying to run your CGI scripts.

You can restrict or allow access to your pages in a bewildering variety of ways. You can do it based on the IP address it comes from (or portion thereof, such as the subnet or just the domain). If only your on-site users need access to the company-provided pizza-order page, you can allow access only to those with internal IP addresses.

You can require that people get to a page only via another page (even on another site) using the REFERER [sic] header; that they be running a particular browser; that they validate user name and password against your SYSUAF; or that they validate against some external file that's just for that project or that directory (or just that they know the specific password for that file and that directory). You can even do combinations: any on-site user can look at the building plans but off-site users have to authenticate with user name and password to do it.

All that said, if you have stuff on a computer that would put the company out of business or put you in jail if it got out, that computer shouldn't be connected to the Internet at all, much less in any directory a Web server can serve. If it's merely embarrassing material, you might be better off with a separate intranet-only machine on a network that has no Internet connectivity. You don't see a lot of successful break-ins to VMS systems, but it would be silly to put your business or your freedom at risk because of blind faith. VMS systems are a lot less vulnerable to OS security failures (buffer overflows and so on) than many other systems, but they're just as vulnerable to social-engineering and disgruntled-employee attacks as any other kind.

Each of the servers has particular strengths and weaknesses in this area. OSU lets you have different people authenticate in different ways—some against the UAF, some against a file-specific password; CSWS lets you do arbitrarily complicated access-control logic.

7.3.1 Apache

In Chapter 5, I introduced container directives. These are the basic elements of access control in Apache. Which directive you use will determine at what point in processing your access-control directives are applied.

To do it based on URL path, you want `Location` or `LocationMatch`. To do it after alias or rewrite processing has mapped the resource into a file, use `Directory` or `DirectoryMatch`. You can use `Files` or `FilesMatch` either standalone or nested. All of these can be nested inside `VirtualHost` containers, if necessary.

.HTACCESS files can be used in the directories—the same directories you're serving—to control access to those directories. (The actual name of the file is controlled by `AccessFile` in HTTPD.CONF, but people generally don't mess with it.) You don't usually want those to be visible to the world, so you can do a `Files` at the highest level that blocks access to .HTACCESS, and similarly to .HTPASSWD (or whatever you decide to name the password files.) You'll find this in the HTTPD.CONF file you get by default.

```
<Files ~ "^\.ht">
    Order allow,deny
    Deny from all
</Files>
```

(In fact, the tilde format of the `Files` container, which can be read as "matching," is deprecated; for good form this should be `<FilesMatch "^\.ht">` rather than a `Files` directive.)

The directive applies to any files matching that regular expression. The caret means that what follows is at the beginning of the file name; the backslash is an escape character that means that the period is a literal period; and the h and t are literal letters. So this means "any files with names beginning .ht". And what we do with them is deny access to everyone.

This particular instruction could also have been written, using the limited wildcarding available without going to regular expressions, as

```
<Files .HT*>
    Order allow, deny
    Deny from all
</Files>
```

The network-based access control directives in Apache are `Order`, `Allow`, and `Deny`, which can appear inside any container, including a `<Limit>` or `<LimitExcept>`.

```
Allow from SOURCE [SOURCE ...]
```

SOURCE is a full or partial host name or a full or partial numeric IP address or network/netmask pair (192.168.0.0/255.255.0.0) or network/CIDR specification (192.18.0.0/16). For host names, if you want the trailing part (e.g., to allow all the educational sites), you need to include the leading "." on the trailing part (e.g., ".edu"). (If the host name doesn't begin with a dot, Apache thinks it's a whole host name, not a partial one.) You can match only whole tokens in the host name, so "ford.edu" wouldn't match ".stanford.edu". Source can also be `env=VARIABLENAME`, which controls access through the existence or nonexistence of the variable. (The variable would presumably be set through `SetEnvIf` elsewhere in the body of the server config.) Source can also be `all`, which is every system everywhere.

Multiple sources separated by white space are permitted.

```
Deny from SOURCE [SOURCE ...]
```

SOURCE is defined the same way as for Allow.

```
Order  deny, allow | allow, deny | mutual-failure
```

specifies the order in which the other two directives are evaluated, except for `mutual-failure`, which makes `order` irrelevant. (`Mutual-failure` says allow access only for those hosts that are matched by `Allow` and not by `Deny`. So if you had a `Deny from all`, it wouldn't matter what your `Allow` said. `Mutual-failure` isn't used very often.)

The first order (deny, allow) lets you specify the (presumably limited) number of hosts you want to allow access to and disallow the rest, as follows:

```
Order deny, allow
Deny from all
Allow from host-I-like other-host-I-like env=CLUSTERMEMBER
```

The second order (allow, deny) lets you specify the (presumably limited) number of hosts you want to deny access to and welcomes the rest, as follows:

```
Order allow, deny
Deny from .bad-domain.tld env=SPAMSPIDER
Allow from all
```

As I discussed briefly in Chapter 5, Limit is about HTTP methods and is used primarily to grant or restrict access to particular groups. If you want to allow someone at a particular node to PUT (upload) Web pages into a directory, you can do:

```
<Limit PUT>
order deny, allow
deny from all
allow from the-ip-address-you-like
</Limit>
```

which disallows everybody except the ip-address-you-like, and then allows that one. (But if you want to use it to disallow all methods, you need to exhaustively list all methods, including any custom ones.) To put a restriction on all but some methods without listing them exhaustively, use Limit-Except; the directive says that you have to be an authenticated user to do anything but GET.

```
<LimitExcept GET>
require valid-user
</LimitExcept>
```

This brings us to authentication-based access controls, which can be combined with host-based access controls. The relevant commands here are Require, SSLRequire, and Satisfy.

```
Require valid-user | user USERNAME [...] | group GROUPNAME [...]
```

This lets you specify that access requires having a valid user according to whatever authentication method you're using, a list of specific user names, or a member of one of a list of groups—all of which require and trigger an authentication dialog. The necessary support commands were discussed in section 7.2.

```
Satisfy  all | any
```

When you combine host-based access controls and authentication-based access controls, Satisfy lets you determine whether every requirement must be satisfied or just some of them. `all` means that you must meet both host-based and authentication-based controls; `any` means that if you're from an acceptable host, you won't even be asked for user name and password. Unfortunately, this doesn't appear to work with SYSUAF-based authentication; if you specify `AuthUserOpenVMS`, the user will get prompted for a VMS user name and password. If the user doesn't have one, the access fails without the host being checked.

Example

```
<Directory /device/accountinggroup>
Order deny, allow
Deny from All
Allow from .mycompany.tld
<Limit PUT>
 AuthUserOpenVMS On
 AuthGroupfile /device/accountinggroup/groupmembers.txt
 Require group accountingupdate
</Limit>
</Directory>
```

This says that for the accounting group's directory, anyone coming from a host with a name that says it's part of the company's domain can see all the files, and people from outside the domain can't see anything. The only people who can publish files using the PUT method are SYSUAF-authenticated VMS users whose user names are listed in the groupmembers.txt file as part of the accountingupdate group. (As written, anybody can see who this is by looking at the groupmembers.txt file, which is accessible to everybody, but the only people who can replace it via the Web are those who already have update access. Therefore, the group members can add another member to their group without having to bother the Webmaster. (Or they could prankishly remove one another's authorization, which will definitely end up bothering the Webmaster.)

```
SSLRequireSSL
```

SSLRequireSSL, included in any container directive or .HTACCESS file, forbids non-SSL access to the stuff specified therein. If you use password-based authentication for access to the contents, the password dialog will be SSL-encrypted, which is a good thing.

```
SSLRequire  [arbitrarily-complex Boolean-expression]
```

SSLRequire, on the other hand, is a directive that lets you limit access to anything unless any conditions you can specify are met. This is potentially very complicated, because it has a lot more environmental variables to play with. SSLRequire has access to all the mod_SSL variables and all the Apache host variables as well, and it's not limited to SSL-related activities, so you can use it even when certificates aren't involved at all. But this is your only choice for access based on a combination of cipher strength, time of day, and domain name of the e-mail address on the certificate. I'll list the SSL CGI variables in Chapter 14.

Example

```
SSLRequire %{HTTPS_SECRETKEYSIZE} != %{HTTPS_KEYSIZE}
```

(These would be the same in a domestic version of the browser but are different in crippled Export versions. So this denies access to cryptographically weaker browsers.)

OSU

The access controls in OSU are implemented basically through two rules—PROT and HOSTPROT. Each applies the contents of a plain-text protection file (.prot) to a particular path. PROT is for authentication-based protection; HOSTPROT is for host/network-based protection. DEFPROT sets default authentication protection. (I just now learned about DEFPROT by reading the source code. To be honest, in seven years of running an OSU server I have never known that DEFPROT existed and I have never felt the lack. But it's in there, so I'm telling you about it.)

```
DEFPROT path filename
```

sets the default protection file for a path specification, which may include wildcards. The protection file specification may be overridden by a more detailed path specification occurring later in the HTTP_PATHS.CONF configuration file, and won't even be reached if the matching PROTECT or HOSTPROT path spec is encountered earlier.

```
PROTECT path  filename
```

sets the authentication-based protection file for a path specification that may include wildcards. The first PROTECT or HOSTPROT encountered that matches the current path will be applied.

```
HOSTPROT path  filename
```

sets the network-address-based protection file for a path specification that may include wildcards.

Basically, the only difference between using DEFPROT and using a PROTECT with a very general path specification is that DEFPROT can be overridden by a matching PROTECT/HOSTPROT that come after it, and PROTECT can be overridden only by matching PROTECT or HOSTPROT that come before it in the config file.

Here's what the protection files look like. For HOSTPROT, the sample file is LEVEL1.PROT as distributed; I think David Jones's explanatory text speaks for itself.

```
# Example level-1 (hostprot) protection file. This file restricts access to
# the protected documents based upon IP address or host name (host-spec).
# The only recognized command a level 1 protection file can have is limited
# form of maskgroup (getmask):
#
#      maskgroup @host-spec [,@host-spec2,...]
# e.g. maskgroup @128.146.235.50, @*.eng.ohio-state.edu, @128.146.10.*
#
# The ip-address may substitute a wildcard for any octet in the address.
# A host name may substitute the wildcard character (*) for one or more
# labels (labels are delimited by periods).
#
# A host mask may optionally specify the local port number by appending
# a ":port" to the end of the mask (e.g. @*.*.*.*:443).  If a port number
# is present, it must match the target port in addition to the regular
# matching rules. The port match allows you to require certain
# document access to be via a secure protocol (e.g.. SSL).
#
maskgroup @*.*.*.*:443, @*.acs.ohio-state.edu
maskgroup @*.dec.com, @kcgl1.*.ohio-state.edu
```

For PROTECT or DEFPROT, the sample file is LEVEL2.PROT as distributed.

```
# Level 2 example protection file. For the sample authenticator, this
# file is not actually used but is kept as a place holder. For a
# real authenticator, this file has pointers to the password and group
```

```
# definition files as well as other configuration information (scheme
# supported, etc.) for the protection domain being defined.
#
# For the CEL authenticator (1.3), lines have the following formats:
#       # notes                  comment
#       <realm>                 Realm name Set string user sees in username prompt.
#       @host *                  Host address must match
#       user[@host] password     Both user and password must match.
#       user[@host] *            Must match username, password from SYSUAF
#       *[@host] *               Any username, password from SYSUAF
#
# For the MD5 authenticator (test), these additional formats are available:
#       <acl>       (ACE)              Accesss control list entry.
#       <digest> [args]               Set MD5 mode and parameters.  Any subsequent
#                                    username/password pairs will be case-sensitive
#                                     (since client is generating hashes).
#       <cache> timeout               Set refresh time in seconds for file cache.
#
# For the EXT authenticator, these additional formats are available:
#       <xxxx> arg
#       [\\domain\]user[@host] *
#       [\\domain\]*[@host] *
#
<CACHE> 0                    # argument is seconds before expiration.
<CERTMAP> 0                  # Argument is processing options, must be present
<realm>  Sample  Authenticator
#<digest> private="makeup" pwdfile="excess"
<ACL> (ID=PATHWORKS,ACCESS=READ)
<ACL> (ID=CE_ARISS,ACCESS=READ)
#<DEMOTAG1> tcp
#<DEMOTAG3> localhost
#\\Dave\* *                  # Invoke external authenticator.
#
#@*.acs.*.edu *
#*@164.107.183.*:431 *       # local subnet with SSL
#*@*.*.*.*:443 *             # anywhere using SSL and username
#@*.*.*.*:8040 *             # anywhere using port 8040
guest oqobf
```

Examples

```
hostprot */localonly/*    www_system:localonly.prot
```

This takes any path that has */localonly/ anywhere in it and applies the contents of the localonly.prot file to it. (This even works for userdirs, incidentally, and it's very handy if you have material that should be shared broadly on-site and not at all off-site.) The localonly.prot file might look like the following:

```
maskgroup @127.0.0.1, @*.slac.stanford.edu

prot /htbin/stockroom_update*
www_system:stockroom_updaters.prot
```

The stockroom_updaters might look like:

```
<realm>"Your stockroom update account"
StockroomTemp  boguspasswrd  # takes the password from this
                             # file, since this week's temp
                             # won't have a VMS account.
Milo               *         # Use his SYSUAF password
Serena         CuttySark12   # take the password from this
                             # file.
```

Only the users identified in the protection file can gain access to this program and only if they use the correct passwords. You can mix and match authentication sources.

```
exec /protbin/*  www_root:[protbin]
prot /protbin/*  www_system:SYSUAF.PROT
```

The SYSUAF.PROT would look like:

```
<realm>"your VMS account"
* *
```

Any program you put in PROTBIN will require SYSUAF authentication to run, but can be run by any user who can log into the system. (If the particular program needs to limit access further, it will have to do it itself. I have some RDBWeb programs that just have a database table of which users are allowed to do updates and enforce that themselves.)

OSU has no equivalent to the `Require` and `Satisfy` directives in Apache. You can have the server apply only one kind of protection to each object, and if access fails, it won't try anything else. If you want anybody to be able to see a document from on-site, and off-site people to only be able to see it if they are authenticated users, you'll have to write a little program to mediate access to those documents and then map the document items to run the program—for example:

```
map /document-directory/* \
/htbin/access_cntrl.pl?file=document_directory/*
```

7.3.2 WASD

Password-based access control

As I mentioned previously, the configuration file for authorization and access control as well as authentication is in HTTPD$AUTH.CONF. All access control is based on the untranslated path that came in. Paths may not appear in more than one realm in the same virtual service. (So if you want to authenticate the same thing by two different methods, you need different IP addresses, ports, or host names.)

The config file has a realm statement, which looks like

```
[AuthorizationSource [; full-access-grp; read-only-grp]]
```

`AuthorizationSource` is defined in exhaustive detail in section 7.2. Those group specifications are `identifier-or-database=authtype`. Group lists can be defined by those holding a particular rightslist identifier (provided this is a SYSUAF-based authorization source) or those in a particular list or database (which, as I noted previously, must reside in the HT_AUTH: directory).

```
GROUPNAME[= ID|HTA|LIST]
```

In the ID format, GROUPNAME is a rightslist identifier. In the LIST format, GROUPNAME is the plain-text HT_AUTH:GROUPNAME.$HTL list of user names. In the HTA format (which is the default), it's the HT_AUTH:GROUPNAME.$HTA list. Note that if you have two group names, they're the full-access group and the read-access group. If you have one group name and it's an HTA format group, access per person is determined by what access is set for that user name in the HTA database.

If you leave off the groups, everybody who successfully authenticates has read and write access to the paths in the realm unless restricted by the path statements.

Paths within a realm can specify the kind of access that's available for them and restrict further what's available in the realm. Access restrictions specified by the path can include user names, access schemes, full or partial host names, networks, or network/netmask combinations. The path directive is

```
PATH  /path/* restrictions type [param="paramstring"]
```

The access restrictions, which appear in the statement as a list of restrictions separated by commas, are:

Scheme	`http:` or `https:`
Host name	`*.domain.tld` or `server.domain.tld`
Numeric IP	`#11.22.33.44/255.255.255.252` or `#11.22.33.44/16 (subnet)` or `#11.22.33.44` or `#localhost`
User name(s)	`~username`

The `param="paramstring"` is a means of passing additional parameters that apply on a per-path basis to an authenticator process. More on params is provided subsequently.

Example

```
PATH /onlyfromserver/ https:,#localhost,~winston,~alan,r+w
```

This means that path /onlyfromserver/ can be accessed only through SSL, only from a browser running on the same machine, and only by users named WINSTON or ALAN. Those people get read and write access.

SSL and access control in WASD

You can also restrict access to paths based on matching values in the client certificate. (This works only in paths specified in the [X.509] section of the HTTPD$AUTH.CONF, because the other paths don't have certificates to compare against.) You do this by passing conditional statements with the `param=` directive. The syntax and the logical possibilities are the same as for conditional mapping except for requiring `param=` in front. Here are the available conditionals for matching.

```
[CI:string]
```

This indicates the choice of cipher that was negotiated between client and server.

```
[IS:/recordname=string]
```

The `/recordname` parameter matches one of the certificate records shown previously in "authenticating with SSL" for WASD.

```
[IS:string]
```

matches against the entire Issuer (CA) DN.

```
[KS:integer]
```

matches the minimum allowed key size from certificate (in bits).

```
[SU:/recordname=string]
```

matches specified Subject (client) DN record only.

```
[SU:string]
```

matches entire Subject (client) DN. Some examples follow. These are all assumed to be in the [X.509] section of the HTTPD$AUTH.CONF file.

```
/certneeded/quitesecure/* r,param="[KS:128][CI:RC4-MD5
CI:DES-CBC-MD5]"
```

This allows access only to minimum key size of 128 bits and using either the RC4-MD5 or the DES-CBD-MD5 cipher.

```
/mylocalstuff/* r+w,param="[RU:/CN=][IS:/O=My\ Own\
Authority\ Cert]"
```

Take the common-name record as the remote-user name and do it only on certificates granted by my own authority. For more examples consult the WASD docs.

For certificate-based access control, the default user name is the 32-digit fingerprint of the certificate. You can treat this just like a user name, putting it into lists (.$HTL files) to establish group membership. Alternatively, you can use the [RU=/recordname] parameter to take some other record (e.g., CommonName) and get a derived name, which may be a little less intimidating when you're reading the files. However you derive the user name, you can use it in access restrictions, just like a user name derived any other way. Here are some example group lists (closely related to examples in the WASD docs).

```
# FINGERPRINTGROUP.$HTL
# (a file of X.509 fingerprints for access to "/path/requiring/cert/")
AB12D58890013406BBA517418D253CE2  winston@vms.kicks-ass.net
6ADA07108C20338ADDC3613D6D8B159D  just.another@where.ever.com

# CERT_CN.$HTL
# (a file of X.509 remote-user names derived using [RU:/CN=]
Alan_Winston winston@vms.kicks-ass.net
Just_Another just.another@where.ever.com
[X509;FINGERPRINTGROUP=list]
/path/requiring/cert/* r+w
```

(Gives fingerprints listed in FINGERPRINTGROUP full access to the path, restricted to read and write.)

```
[X509;CERT_CN=list]
/path/requiring/cn/* r+w
```

Similarly, gives access to this path, restricted to read and write, to people whose certificate CommonNames are in the CERT_CN.$HTL file. Alternatively, you can use the fingerprint or the CommonName where you'd use any authenticated user name.

```
[X509]
  /httpd/-/admin/* ~106C8342890A1703AAA517317B145BF7,r+w
  /ht_root/local/* ~106C8342890A1703AAA517317B145BF7,r+w
```

Access granted only to the user with this fingerprint on his or her certificate.

```
/other/path/* ~Alan_Winston,r+w,param="[ru:/cn=]"
/yet/another/path/* ~Just_Another,r+w,param="[ru:/cn=]"
```

Access granted to the user whose CommonName from the certificate matches the access restriction list; the param says to get the remote user name from the CommonName field. Again, once you get the remote user set, you can use it just like a SYSUAF user name.

7.3.3 Robots.txt

Search engine companies such as Google or Altavista have crawlers or spiders searching the Web all the time. Most sites have quite a lot of links that it would be pointless for a robot to follow—anything that leads to a form that has to be filled out and "submit" pressed, for example, or material that's highly dynamic. (You don't want to index the every-two-minutes stock quote; you want to index the menu page that gets you to it.) It's to everybody's benefit that the crawlers don't spend their time indexing the wrong stuff and you don't waste your horsepower serving them stuff they can't use.

The convention is that crawlers will ask the server for "/robots.txt" before starting to crawl the server. Robots.txt is an ASCII file containing a list of paths on this server that robots shouldn't follow. (Indexing graphics and the like can be bad news.)

Note that there are badly behaved crawlers out there. E-mail-address mongers have crawlers searching the Web looking for stuff that looks like valid e-mail addresses, which they can compile and sell for the purpose of sending unsolicited commercial e-mail. (If they believe in wasting e-mail bandwidth and everybody else's disk space, there's no reason to think they care about your network and CPU utilization.) Further, in the early days of the Web it occurred to some people that the contents of the robots.txt file might be "secret and possibly embarrassing stuff we don't want the world to see," and they'd have fun retrieving the file and following exactly those links. So you need appropriate access controls on those paths, not just a robots.txt that keeps polite spiders out.

You can put a robots.txt file in your root directory, except in the default configuration of OSU, where the root is mapped to /www/; the spiders don't ask for /www/robots.txt, so the default configuration provides a mapping of /robots.txt to /www/robots.txt. (Robots ask for an all-lowercase "/robots.txt"; if you're doing mapping in CSWS, be sure you're either case-blind or using lowercase.)

The robots.txt file is created according to the Robot Exclusion Standard. It can be maintained with your favorite text editor. The file is composed of records. Each record has one User-Agent line and one or more Disallow lines.

```
User-Agent: * | name-of-specific-agent
Disallow  path
```

(The asterisk is a wildcard, which should match any agent. Alternatively, you can match a specific agent. Agents have names such as googlebot, WebCrawler, and Slurp. There's a registry of Web robots—284 different ones now—at http://www.robotstxt.org/wc/active/html/index.html.) Look in your logs (if you're using an extended format that logs the User-Agent) for more robot names.

Inktomi's Slurp seems to be a fairly typical well-behaved robot. It processes the robots.txt top down. Whichever User-Agent line it encounters first, whether "Slurp" or "*", is the only line it'll process. If you have special instructions for specific robots, they need to precede the "*" User-Agent, which should be the last one in the file, and they need to reiterate all the stuff you want all agents to do.

It's worth pointing out the Wayback Machine at the Internet Archive, www.archive.org. The aim of this project is to keep, online, all the content that ever was on the Web. So far, this is working to a surprising degree. When *MicroTimes*, a magazine for which I did a couple of years' worth of columns, went bust and shut down its Web site, my stuff was still retrievable from the Wayback Machine. Alexa Internet does periodic Web crawling and makes data donations to the Internet Archive. If you want to be sure to be crawled, you can go to www.alexa.com and follow links until you get to a place where you can enter a request to crawl your site. If you want to be sure not to be crawled—if your current content is something that you'd be happier to see lost to history—you can also request not to be crawled and archived. You should also bar ia-archiver (Alexa's user-agent name) and googlebot (which caches your content on its site) in the robots.txt and possibly through mapping rules as well.

```
Disallow: (blank) | filename | directorypath | /
```

`Disallow:` followed by a blank bars nothing and tells the robot it can cruise the whole site. Followed by a bare slash, it bars everything. Followed by a file name, it bars the file name wherever it might be found. Followed by a directory path, it bars that directory path. The directory path is matched left to right against links on this site. There's no explicit wildcard specification, but it's a "greedy" match: `/www` matches /www/index.html, /www.html, /www56/giantrobots.html, and so on.

Typically you'd at least like to bar robots from trying to cruise your script directories, so you can use

```
Disallow: /htbin/# on OSU (same-line comments are legal)
Disallow: /cgi-bin/
# not that the server should allow them out. (this
# comment format is preferred)
Disallow: .HTACCESS
```

If you want to `Disallow` most stuff and allow crawling only a small portion of your site, you might want to consider putting the crawlable stuff in a separate directory, if not a separate server.

Note that browsers as well as robots can retrieve /robots.txt, so if you'd like to see what big complicated /robots.txt files look like, you can retrieve some from your favorite sites.

One problem with /robots.txt is that there's only one per server. Per-directory robots.txt files don't do anything—the robots never request them. You could set up some kind of a batch job to locate and roll up robots.txt files out of all your directories (or at least all those that aren't in the Webmaster's direct control) every couple of days and make an official robots.txt for your site out of it. But there's an alternative that is accessible to users who can put files into Web directories: the Robots <META> tag.

META tags go in the HEAD portion of your HTML document and describe things about the document that don't necessarily get rendered. In this case, the interesting tag is `<META NAME="ROBOTS" CONTENT="[NO]INDEX,[NO]FOLLOW">`.

The contents of `CONTENT` are permutations of `INDEX`, and `FOLLOW`. `INDEX` instructs the robot that it's okay to index this page (e.g., to put this page into the search-engine database); NOINDEX asks it not to do that. FOLLOW encourages the robot to follow the links from this page as it keeps on crawling; NOFOLLOW says to treat this page as a dead end—don't crawl along any links found here. Most, but not all, robots default to "INDEX,FOLLOW" if there is no tag and the path hasn't been ruled out by /robots.txt.

Here are the four legal values of the CONTENT tag; you can have only one of them effective in a document. (It's robot specific whether the first META ROBOTS tag would be processed and scanning would immediately cease or the robot would follow the last one in the file.)

```
<META NAME="ROBOTS" CONTENT="INDEX,FOLLOW">
<META NAME="ROBOTS" CONTENT="NOINDEX,FOLLOW">
<META NAME="ROBOTS" CONTENT="INDEX,NOFOLLOW">
<META NAME="ROBOTS" CONTENT="NOINDEX,NOFOLLOW">
```

Again, these tags have power only over well-behaved robots—they won't do a thing to stop impolite robots from grabbing the pages. Watch your server logs so that you can tell whether rebellious Web crawlers are actually sucking down your entire site. Note the names and use mapping or protection rules to keep these naughty bots from doing you any harm.

8

Providing User Personal Web Directories

8.1 User directories: pro and con

You've probably seen URLs that bring you to personal Web directories. The http://host.domain.tld/~username/ syntax brings you to Web space in a nonprivileged user's personal account. User Web directories are often called userdirs.

Is this a good idea? It depends. In an educational or hobbyist environment, it's likely to be a very good idea. Users can develop their own Web content, take responsibility for it, organize their directories to suit themselves, update whenever they feel like it, and never have to hassle the system manager. Instructors can put assignments or syllabi on their personal Web sites, researchers display digital offprints of papers, and so on. The system manager can plausibly claim that he or she never checks anybody's content, and avoid uncomfortable issues of censorship, quality standards, browser compatibility, and so on. If your institution is teaching a class in Web development, this approach can solve a lot of problems.

In a commercial environment, it's probably a bad idea. If the Web site is your company's Internet storefront, it looks unprofessional to have people putting up digitized pictures from their wedding—and your company probably has a written acceptable-use policy that you'll be responsible for enforcing, or at least required not to subvert. The userdir approach may be useful for providing test Web sites for your authorized Web developers, but you're mostly better off avoiding it.

There are a few additional security risks in user Web directories. (If you've decided to conceal the operating system and hardware type you're running on, and you allow server-side includes in user Web directories, then it's possible that a user would have documents that included that potentially dangerous information; if you allow execution of DCL scripts from within server-side include documents in user Web directories, then any internally available information could be seen outside—if that's a concern, then you shouldn't allow that. You can still have user Web directories—just don't allow execs. You also need to consider whether you want your users to be able to run CGIs directly. One comforting note is that since the users, not the server, own the files in the user directory, they can only be read (and thus served) by the server if VMS file protection allows it, either via W:RE protection or by an ACL permitting access. The server won't be able to accidentally serve out the user's mail files unless he or she puts them in a subtree of the [.www] directory and sets the protection so that anybody on the system can read them.

An alternative to userdirs, which takes a bit more system management time but avoids the funky tilde, and which makes a structure that's a little easier to exercise some central management over, is to set up a user directory tree in your Web space (e.g., $WEB:[USERS...]). Each user, or each user who requests personal space, gets a directory ($WEB:[USERS.THISUSER]), some quota on the $WEB disk, and access by ACL entry to the directory. The system manager has to create the Web directory, issue the quota, and set up the access control list, but this is easy to do as a DCL script and shouldn't take the system manager much time—it can even be automated as part of the account creation process. Once that's done, the user's directory will be available as http://node.domain.tld/users/thisuser/, which looks a little more professional. A real advantage of this structure over userdirs, if you believe the material posted is going to be of some actual use, is that it's much easier to automatically index the material in a structure like this than in user space scattered over multiple trees.

8.2 Implementing userdirs

8.2.1 CSWS

Apache books assume that all your users are in a file system something like /home/users/username. In fact, more typically on VMS, your users may be on $userdisk1:[theirname], or $userdisk2:[groupname.username]. In some cases, their SYS$LOGIN directory won't even be the root of their own directory; at my site, we had some users who were migrated in the early 1980s from the RSX-11 system we ran before we got our first VAX; their original directories were ODS-1 style [ggg,uuu] specifiers. Eventually we put them on ODS-2 disks and changed the numbered directory to [theirname.numbered], but we had to make their SYS$LOGIN directory the numbered directory they were used to. If one of these people needed a userdir, it would be $disk2:[username.numbered.www]. If one of these people had gotten married and changed names and the system manager was too lazy to change the directory name, he or she could be $disk2:[old-username.numbered.www]. (That works fine if the server gets the device and directory information out of the SYSUAF, but will frustrate any other mapping scheme.) You may well have to account for this kind of irregularity in your file structure.

Apache implements userdirs with the `UserDir` directive:

```
UserDir absolute-or-relative-path-name
```

The name used in the example in the default configuration file is public_html; I prefer WWW, which happens to be the default for OSU. To make everybody's ~username directory be the [.WWW] subdirectory of their SYS$LOGIN directory, even if the account name is something different do

```
UserDir www      # relative path name
```

If you want to do userdirs on some other volume than their SYS$LOGIN directories—which requires a community of users who can figure out how to get FTP to change volumes when they're uploading files

```
UserDir      /$userwww_disk/
```

and the tilde translation will turn

```
~username/index.html
```

into

```
/$userwww_disk/username/index.html
```

(And something will break if the users ever change their user names.) For completeness, I'll mention that you can plug the user name into the middle of the path, not just the end, by using a placeholder.

```
UserDir      /$userwww_disk/*/www
```

results in translation of

```
~username/index.html
```

into

```
/$userwww_disk/username/www/index.html
```

Either of these last two approaches is faster than a SYSUAF lookup, so you might want to do it in the extremely unlikely case that you expected very high traffic on a userdir-intensive site. (Maybe if your individual users were all serving porn and warez, this could happen, but it's unlikely in any legitimate business or academic environment.)

You can also implement the above functionality with `AliasMatch` or `RewriteRule` directives (discussed briefly in Chapter 7), since this just says how to translate ~username. But that's getting pretty far away from the point of having userdirs.

Apache lets you enable and disable user directory support for specific users, or for all users.

```
UserDir disable [list of usernames]
```

If you leave out the list of user names, it's disabled for everybody who isn't specifically enabled.

```
UserDir enable [list of usernames]
```

Unless you include the list of user names, this is fairly pointless outside of a VirtualHost container, where you might want to override a serverwide disable. It's still on the confusing side, since a SYSUAF-based userdir scheme can't restrict the users to particular hosts. However, if you felt it looked unprofessional to have userdirs on www.your-ecommerce-site.com but still wanted to provide that service, possibly on staff.your-ecommerce-site.com, you could use this scheme to disable them sitewide and reenable them only in the staff.your-ecommerce-site.com VirtualHost.

With the list of user names, this makes sense if your site policy requires that people sign a document indicating that they understand the requirements to post only content that fits the acceptable-use policy, is legal, doesn't violate copyright, and so on; you can enable them when they sign the document.

Once you've told Apache how to translate the ~username in the URL, you also need to tell it who has access to those documents. The `<Directory>` container on your `DocumentRoot` won't apply—unless you've mapped the userdirs into your regular directory tree, in which case you can skip the next bit. Instead, you'll need to specify something that matches any place the user files are going to end up.

This is where you need to know what your users' sys$login directories look like. If everybody is on one disk, and has a sys$login that looks like

USER$DISK:[username], then you might think you were in business, and that

```
<Directory /user$disk/*/www>
```

will get everyone. Maybe, maybe not. If they're scattered around, you may need multiple directory specifications, or you may be able to do something extremely clever with the regular-expression matching capabilities of <DirectoryMatch>.

My site used to have a bunch of different disks; then we got a RAID array and moved all the user files to that. But we wanted to maintain the appearance of the old disk structure in order to avoid user retraining. We had $DISK1, $DISK2 . . . $DISK6. Now we made one big honking disk, $DATADISK, and put the old disk trees as subdirectories on that: $DATADISK:[DISK1] and so on. $DATADISK, which is in cluster-accessible storage, is actually 9DKA2. I ended up finding a bug in CSWS 1.1, which has been fixed.

```
<Directory /dka2/*/*/www>
```

didn't work because "dka2" wasn't recognized as the same device as "DKA2", which is what $DATADISK translated into. If you have come to rely on this bug for some reason I don't understand, and you insist on having case sensitivity in your user directory device names, you can insert

```
$ DEFINE/PROCESS APACHE$USER_HOME_PATH_UPPERCASE YES
```

in the LOGIN.COM of your APACHE$WWW account.

Eventually I ended up with

```
<Directory /$9$DKA2/*/*/www/>
  AllowOverride FileInfo AuthConfig Limit
  Options MultiViews Indexes IncludesNOEXEC
  <Limit GET POST OPTIONS PROPFIND>
    Order allow,deny
    Allow from all
  </Limit>
  <Limit PUT DELETE PATCH PROPPATCH MKCOL COPY MOVE LOCK
UNLOCK>
    Order deny,allow
    Deny from all
  </Limit>
</Directory>
```

and that worked for me.

`<Directory */www/>` doesn't work, incidentally, because if your directory doesn't begin with a slash, Apache assumes that it's a subdirectory within the `DocumentRoot` tree, which is exactly where your user directories aren't. One potential pitfall with userdirs: If you don't want users running their own scripts, you need to be sure not to include ExecCGI as one of the options on the `<Directory>` or `<DirectoryMatch>` container for the userdir. (They can still have forms that use scripts you provide in a sitewide CGI-BIN directory.) Note the `IncludesNOEXEC` in my example specification; this keeps a user-provided server-side include document from making Apache run an arbitrary program it specifies.

8.2.2 OSU

In processing userdirs, OSU does a straightforward SYSUAF lookup of the user name and maps the given user directory name to that subdirectory of the SYS$LOGIN directory. (I keep saying that instead of SYS$LOGIN:[Web-directory] because this is invalid syntax; SYS$LOGIN isn't a rooted logical.) To enable this, the relevant commands are in HTTP_PATHS.CONF. In the preprocessor form, they're

```
.define userdirenable userdir
.define userdirname www
.define baduserenable #
.define baduser /www_root/serverdoc/baduser.html
```

and

```
.EXPAND $userdirenable $userdirname
.EXPAND $baduserenable /~* $baduser
```

If you want to get something other than the standard 404 status if they enter a user who doesn't exist or doesn't have a userdir, change the value of baduserenable from "#" to "pass." That'll result in these expanded commands:

```
userdir www
pass /~* /www_root/serverdoc/baduser.html
```

If you're worried about people probing your server using ~randomname to determine what user names exist on it in order to launch password-cracking attacks on those user names, you should make the pass /* point to the 404 error page so that they'll get the same results on undefined users as on defined ones who don't have userdirs set up. However, if you're really concerned about that, then you shouldn't allow userdirs at all. And I hope you've already disabled FINGER; further, block your phone directory from off-site access if it includes e-mail addresses that can be mapped to user names on the Web host; and don't allow Telnet access from outside the firewall so that passwords can't be sniffed; and so on. There's a lot of stuff higher on the 'keep-you-up-nights' scale than people probing userdirs for random user names. If you see the same IP address failing on random user names over and over in the access log, adjust your configuration so you won't even talk to that node any more.

Here's a major gotcha: These commands appear in the distributed HTTP_PATHS.CONF below the localaddress blocks. If you put `pass /*` mapping blocks inside the localaddress containers, userdirs won't work. If you have a `pass /*` at the top, userdirs won't work. This isn't a problem with the way the server is configured by default, because the document root is aliased to `/www/*`, and you don't need a `pass /*` command. However, if you're like me and don't like the superfluous-seeming `/www/` and therefore simply replace the `pass /www/* $sitepath` with `pass /* $sitepath`, userdirs won't work because the server will map ~filename as though it were in your $sitepath tree, resulting in a nonexistent file. As a result, to make userdirs work in this configuration, you need to move the userdir commands above any `pass /*` or `map /*`, whether it's in a `localaddress` block or sitewide.

Since OSU will run scripts only from predefined script directories and the server-side includes don't allow you to run arbitrary executables, you don't have to worry about locking down those functions.

OSU gives you a nice command procedure, WWW_SYSTEM: BUILD_USERDIR.COM, which you can customize and make world-readable; then users can run it, and it will create their Web-readable subdirectory set ACLs to allow the server appropriate access, and create an index.html template with their name in it.

8.2.3 WASD

WASD has some restrictions on userdirs. It won't serve user directories for accounts with SYSPRV, DISUSERed accounts, CAPTIVE accounts, or accounts with expired passwords, all for fairly obvious reasons. (If you really want to serve particular accounts that match those criteria, you can use mapping rules for each account to make the Web space available.) OSU and Apache appear to have no such restrictions. (However, in the case of Apache, if you have a `<Directory /SYS$MGR/*>` you deserve what you get, and in either case making SYS$MGR world readable isn't a big win. The restriction to an explicit [.www] subdirectory is probably good enough.)

To provide SYSUAF-mapped userdirs, the following commands go in HTTPD$MAP.CONF:

```
USER /~*/* /*/www/*
REDIRECT /~* ///~*/
PASS /~*/* /user$disk/*/www/*
```

The `USER` command maps ~username/* to /device:[directory.www]*, but doesn't handle the case where the browser sends the URL without a terminal slash. The `REDIRECT` makes the server tell the browser to try it again with a slash. The `PASS` command is required so that the server knows to actually serve the stuff from that directory. (`Redirect` and `Pass` are discussed more fully in Chapter 7.)

The same requirements—that the userdir be world readable or be marked with ACLs to make it usable by the server account—apply. If you have users scattered on multiple disks, you'll need multiple `pass` commands. Don't try defining a search list logical for user$disk and using that; instead; bite the bullet and put in one `PASS` command for each disk with user directories.

Naturally, the `PASS` command for the user directories needs to appear in the file earlier than any applicable catchall `PASS /*` command. If you're doing multihosting or multihoming (see Chapter 9), you can enable user directories either for every service on your server or for a particular virtual host by putting the relevant mapping rules inside the virtual service block in the HTTPD$MAP.CONF file. Be sure to get the `PASS /~*/*` before the catchall `PASS /*` in the virtual service block.

There is some security concern about the ability to have user-generated server-side include documents run arbitrary executable programs in the context of the server through use of the <exec> or <dcl> tags (discussed more fully in Chapter 13).

How big a concern is this? Well, the server account doesn't have SYSPRV, so it's hard even for a malicious user to do a lot of damage to the system at large (although that person could possibly mess up the server configuration). However, if you have things anywhere on your server that can be read by any local user but you don't want them getting out—classic examples are FINGER, or for that matter SHOW USER, which will display currently logged in users, thereby giving a system cracker a little bit of a leg up on guessing user name/password combinations—then the <--#EXEC--> tag can make your server into a tunnel through the firewall, displaying local-only info to anyone in the world. If you've got real secrets, you probably shouldn't be running anything but the Web server on your machine anyway. If you've got stuff you just don't want to have get out, you've got a user-education issue on your hands.

However, WASD lets you fine-tune this. If you enable `[SSIexec]` on the server level, it will, by default, work only on documents that are owned by [1,4], the SYSTEM account. (If malicious users have the ability to modify files owned by SYSTEM, the game is already over—the bad guys own the box.) The SSI processor works on user-owned documents, but if it encounters an <--#exec--> tag in a document not owned by [1,4], it quits interpreting.

If you do want to allow <#exec> access for some non-SYSTEM files, you can use the SET mapping rule for the path—for example:

```
SET /path-to-document/ SSI=PRIV
SET /path-to-document/ SSI=NOPRIV
```

(`SET` is discussed at length in Chapter 7.) Since this does run the risk of giving away the store, you want to do this only on document trees you have good reason to trust, which means you probably don't want to do it on userdirs.

Mark Daniel, the WASD author, recommends configuring your WASD server so that the account that runs scripts is a harmless nonprivileged account that doesn't own the WASD configuration or executable files—a different account altogether. I'll discuss this again when talking about scripting environments, but the brief recipe is to create the scripting account, enable `[DCLDetachProcess]` in HTTPD$CONFIG.CONF, and edit STARTUP_LOCAL.COM to use /PERSONA=scripting-account as a startup qualifier. This is essentially the only way to allow nonvetted scripts—including SSI with <#EXEC> capability—without potentially compromising the security and stability of your system.

9

Multihosting and Multihoming

9.1 Why multihosting?

You want your system/cluster to provide Web service for more than one domain. You could be a VMS-based ISP (e.g., Pageweavers.com in Sacramento, CA), or implementing a server consolidation program, or a hobbyist hosting a personal and a club Web site.

One approach, which is, in my opinion, really ugly, is to assign different sites to different ports on the server. Since people keying in the URL are likely to forget the :8001, they may get presented with the wrong site, and you get a support call. I like this so little that I'm not going to discuss in any detail how to do it.

You can put multiple node names in the Domain Name Server system that all resolve to the same numeric IP address. When modern browsers connect, they remember what alphabetic name they were looking for and tell the server, using the host header. (This is the CNAME, or Canonical Name.) Unfortunately, one of the antique browsers that doesn't support the host header is Netscape 3.03 on VMS; fortunately, as I write, Mozilla has reached a state of sufficient maturity that Compaq is releasing it as the Compaq Secure Web Browser (CSWB). If there's no host header and you haven't configured the server with a default host or an explicit numeric host, results can be surprising.

While you can make the browser issue a redirect to a particular directory tree based on the CNAME, you can also use multihosting configuration to simply serve from the appropriate directory tree. If you don't, you can get unprofessional results. Ultranet, a Massachusetts ISP, provides Web space to the New England Folk Festival Association (NEFFA. WWW.NEFFA.ORG goes to WWW.ULTRANET.COM and shows the Ultranet home page. You have to go to www.neffa.org/~neffa to get the NEFFA information; this inconveniences the NEFFA users over and over.) It's preferable, in my opinion, for the server to recognize what people were trying to connect to (by the CNAME, not the IP address) and give them the appropriate Web root automatically. If your IP package supports it, each node name can have a separate numeric IP address in the DNS, and your system can respond to every relevant numeric IP. (This is multihoming, and it requires some IP configuration effort every time you start or stop hosting a domain, which may require a reboot depending on your IP package.)

Multihosting is supporting different host names with the same numeric IP address. Multihoming is supporting different numeric IP addresses on the same Ethernet interface.

Life gets more complicated if you have to provide HTTPS service for more than one node name. The most you can do with any server is to offer one certificate per numeric-IP/port combination. (You can't do it by CNAME, because the SSL dialog precedes the HTTP dialog; the browser never has a chance to tell the server what host it's looking for.) If you provide the wrong certificate, the browser will complain. (Even with OSU it's possible, with some cleverness, to run multiple instances on different ports using the MST version of SSL and have a different certificate for each instance, but it makes for some slightly odd-looking URLs.)

9.2 Multihosting/multihoming configuration

When you multihost or multihome, you have to be able to configure what's different for each server: host name, document root, log file name and location, and so on. Typically, your multihost configuration will inherit anything from the general server configuration that you don't explicitly override—so, for example, the server documentation directory can be available to every domain you host.

9.2.1 CSWS

Apache thinks of the individual hosts in your multihosting or multihoming configuration as virtual hosts. You configure them with the VirtualHost container directive. (Many Apache books will tell you that VirtualHost can be used only with numeric IP addresses and that you differentiate different CNAMEs by having multiple VirtualHost containers with different ServerNames, after using the NameVirtualHost directive to alert Apache that you'll be doing this. This is not true under CSWS 1.2; you can specify names or numeric addresses in your VirtualHost container.) You do still need the `NameVirtualHost` directive.

Here are the HTTPD.CONF directives:

```
NameVirtualHost numeric-ip[:port]
<VirtualHost cname-or-ip-address[:port]
 [cname-or-ip-address[:port]] >
 [ServerAdmin Webmaster-email-address]
 [DocumentRoot directory-specification]
 [ServerName servername.domain.tld]
 [ErrorLog filespec-for-error-log-for-this-host]
 [CustomLog filespec-for-access-log log-format]
</VirtualHost>
```

The port number is optional in both the `NameVirtualHost` directive and the `VirtualHost` container directive. If you leave it off, it defaults to port 80 (or whatever port you defined with the `Port` directive in the general configuration); if you replace it with "*", your `VirtualHost` will be defined on all the ports that Apache has been told to listen to with the `Listen` directive. (And if you want to, you can define different virtual hosts on the same CNAME or IP based on having different explicit port numbers—but it's not a good idea.)

If you want more than one CNAME or IP to resolve to the same virtual host (a common example of this is www.servername.domain.tld and servername.domain.tld), you can specify both of them in the `VirtualHost` directive. The directives shown within the `VirtualHost` container are all optional; if you don't specify them, this virtual host will inherit the values from the general configuration. You can actually specify almost any directive (the excluded ones are the ones that only make sense systemwide, such as `StartServers`, `BindAddress`, `ServerRoot`, and `NameVirtualHost`) within a `VirtualHost` container, including nesting `Directory` and `File` containers. (See Chapter 7 for details of `Directory` and `File` containers.) The directives are discussed in order in the following paragraphs. The drawback is that this introduces a dependency on the DNS server, which would have been avoided by relying solely on numeric IP addresses.

`ServerAdmin` probably looks a little better—or at least gives away less about your hosting setup—if you set the e-mail address to be at the domain of the virtual host, although you should make sure the e-mail will be delivered there.

`DocumentRoot` is a full directory specification, not one relative to the general server's `DocumentRoot`. One convention on UNIX systems is to put the virtual host's documents into a directory named /www/ server.domain.tld; this won't work at all on ODS-2 disks and will only cause you trouble even on ODS-5 disks. If you want all your virtual hosts in the same directory tree, consider trying /www/server_domain_tld instead. In some senses it's neater to put all the documents in the same directory tree, but there are sometimes good reasons not to do so. Are all the hosts maintained by trustworthy people? Do they all need the same backup regimes? You can certainly manage multiple access to the contents of one directory tree with access control lists and resource identifiers, but it may make your life easier to put customers with larger sets of files on their own disks, or even on virtual disks maintained with VDDriver, which may be less annoying to the system manager than managing disk quotas.

You really need `ServerName` only if you've got more than one CNAME or IP in the `VirtualHost` container; this is what Apache will use in constructing self-referential URLs. (This is also the case if you include a `Port` command.)

For `Errorlog` and `CustomLog`, if you don't include these directives for the `VirtualHost`, logging will be done to the general server's log; if you do specify them, the errors and accesses for the virtual host won't show up in the general log and will be only in the host-specific logs. There are reasons why you'd want to do either; I'd be inclined to combine my `ErrorLogs`, since as the Webmaster I want to know if anything's going wrong with the server, but I would keep the access logs different for each host for easier analysis of traffic by host. There's more information on log file configuration and management in Chapter 12.

If you're doing virtual hosts at all, you should be sure to include a default host. The setup is shown in the HTTPD.CONF that comes with the server, and it looks like this:

```
<VirtualHost _default_:*>
[directives]
</VirtualHost>
```

This will catch any requests that didn't match any of the other virtual hosts; you don't want to leave this undefined. For example, what happens if you're running a browser on the same system as the server and you point it at 127.0.0.1, which is the local host? No host header for CNAMEs and doesn't match your numeric IP address. The default virtual host will catch it.

9.2.2 OSU

OSU thinks of the hosts as local addresses. Your configuration file can include multiple `localaddress` blocks. (Although you can get the blocks set up using the GUI configuration, I have been unable to get them to work correctly that way.)

`localaddress` blocks take two forms, depending on whether this is an IP-based or CNAME-based localaddress.

```
localaddress CNAME server.domain.tld # CNAME based form
localaddress numeric-IP [hostname]   # IP-based form
```

Each `localaddress` block goes on until the next `localaddress` command starts, so the last one specified is

```
localaddress
```

with no name or IP address. That ends the last `localaddress` block and after that commands are interpreted in the context of the general server again. The numeric-IP form instructs the server to listen to that specific IP address, rather than to all; as a result, if you include any specific numeric-IPs (even including 127.0.0.1), you need to include every numeric-IP you want the server to listen to. You can mix and match CNAME-based and numeric-IP-based `localaddresses`, but the CNAMEs won't work unless you have a numeric-IP-based one for at least one of the CNAMES you want to support.

What you find in http_paths.conf are the following preprocessor commands. (Remember that the semicolon indicates the end of a line in the expansion, while the backslash indicates a line continuation in the template.)

```
.ITERATE localaddress cname $hname ;\
AccessLog $cn_logfile $cn_extflags ;\
map / $cn_root_page ;

.next server.domain.tld \
    vms-style-log-file-directory-and-file-name log-file-
format-flag \
    root-page
```

So, for example:

```
.next alanwinston.homeip.net \
$Web_root:[logs]accessaw.log 1 \
/index.htmlx
```

```
.ITERATE localaddress $addr $name ;\
       AccessLog $mh_logfile $mh_extflags ;\
       map / $mh_root
```

(The log file format flag is 0 for "common" format and 1 for extended format, which saves the "referer" [sic], and for user-agent, which isn't on by default because it can make your log files bigger.)

The example says: Respond to the CNAME alanwinston.homeip.net, log accesses into a special log file, and make requests that just have the address and a slash get index.htmlx (a file with some preprocessor directives in it). This is perfectly reasonable if you want all your virtual hosts to serve from the same root directory, but if you want them to be in different directory trees, you need to modify the file. In this case, I changed the template to

```
.ITERATE localaddress cname $hname ;\
AccessLog $cn_logfile $cn_extflags ;\
map / $cn_root_page ;\
pass /* $cn_root_star
.next alanwinston.homeip.net \
$Web_root:[logs]accessaw.log 1 \
/index.htmlx \
/$disk1/alanwinston/*
```

and did my other CNAME-based host configuration the same way. This works fine, but it breaks the PATH portion of the GUI configuration utility. You can make the same changes for the IP-based virtual hosts, or you can just spell out the whole `localaddress` block for either one:

```
localaddress cname server.domain.tld
AccessLog logfilename formatflag
map /index.htmlx
pass /* /rootdirectoryname/*
```

followed by any other server rules you want to have apply to this server only.

Be sure to terminate your last `localaddress` block with

```
localaddress
```

You don't need to configure a special catchall `localaddress`, as in Apache; instead, any unrecognized CNAME will be processed as though it were the host name specified in the general configuration, and go to that root page. The same is true for unrecognized IPs if you didn't use any numeric-IP localaddresses; if you did, the server won't accept any connections on numeric-IP addresses you didn't specify.

9.2.3 WASD

The WASD approach is somewhat different. A virtual host is a virtual service; you specify the services you mean to turn on either in the `[Service]` directive of HTTPD$CONFIG.CONF or in a separate HTTPD$SERVICE.CONF file. While there are specific configurable items (detailed in the following text) for each service, the mapping rules for the service are placed in the HTTPD$MAP.CONF file. (Services can also be specified in the command line using the `/SERVICE` qualifier; this trumps the HTTPD$SERVICE.CONF, which in turn trumps the `[Service]` definitions in the HTTPD$CONFIG.CONF file.)

Service definitions in HTTPD$CONFIG.CONF look like this:

```
[Service]
[scheme://]hostname-or-number[:port]
```

or, by example:

```
[Service]
alanwinston.homeip.net
https://alanwinston.homeip.net
vms.kicks-ass.net:81
https://vms.kicks-ass.net:444
```

Scheme defaults to HTTP and needs to be specified only for HTTPS:; port defaults to 80 if the scheme is HTTP or blank, or to 443 if the scheme is HTTPS. The name is based on the host header from the browser, and if you want to allow connections from an explicit numeric-IP-based lookup you need to define a service for it.

Therefore, my example defines four services: HTTP service for alanwinston.homeip.net on port 80, HTTPS service for alanwinston.homeip.net on port 443, HTTP service for vms.kicks-ass.net on port 81, and HTTPS service for vms.kicks-ass.net on port 444.

The port on the first service you specify will become the port the server listens to for administrative control messages.

If you want to allow any access via unexpected numeric-IP or unconfigured host name to work, you need to do nothing, and the default (server-wide) configuration will apply in those cases. (Remember, anybody anywhere in the world can put your IP address in the domain name server with a host name that implies you're in that person's domain, or with an uncomplimentary host name. If you don't want to be a victim of this, you may want to configure a catchall connection. The downside is that people using the old browsers that don't use the host header will fall through to the same configuration.) If you don't want unexpected accesses to end up at your generally configured home page, use the [ServiceNotFoundURL] directive.

For the default page that comes with the server, make that

```
[ServiceNotFoundURL]
//yourserver.domain.tld/httpd/-/servicenotfound.html
```

Incidentally, remember that just because you defined a name-based virtual service in your server configuration, that's meaningless until it's defined in the DNS, and defining a numeric-IP-based service will have no visible effect until you've configured your IP software to respond to that address. If you want to run different services on different systems in a cluster, you may want to share one configuration file and define all the services on all the systems, using DNS and IP configuration to restrict which systems actually get messages routed to them. This enables you to change the DNS if one of your systems is down and point that traffic to another one without having to reconfigure the server or take any downtime on the node that's picking up the load. If you're supporting additional numeric IPs, you may have to reboot. If you have everything map to the cluster alias IP address, then you can share all your name-based services across the cluster.

If you're doing more than just a couple of services, it makes sense to use the HTTPD$SERVICE.CONF file. Note that the documentation says that the server will not use the file unless the HTTPD$SERVICE logical name is defined to point at it. This is true, but the standard startup command procedure will define the logical name if the file exists. Therefore, if you're using the standard startup and have the file, you will use it. If you don't want to use it, rename or delete it and deassign the logical. (If you do want to use the file and are running the server from the command line for testing purposes, you should remember to define the logical.)

The HTTPD$SERVICE.CONF definitions look like this:

```
[[ [scheme://]servername-or-numeric-ip[:port] ]]
[ServiceBodyTag] string (default: <BODY>)
[ServiceSSLclientVerifyCAfile] string (default: none)
[ServiceSSLclientVerifyRequired] string (default: none)
[ServiceErrorReportPath] string (default: none)
[ServiceIpAddress] dotted-decimal address (default: none)
[ServiceNoLog] ENABLED|DISABLED (default: DISABLED)
[ServiceNoTrack] ENABLED|DISABLED (default: DISABLED)
[ServiceProxy] ENABLED|DISABLED (default: DISABLED)
[ServiceProxyAuth] none|AUTH|LOCAL (default: DISABLED)
```

```
[ServiceProxyCache] ENABLED|DISABLED (default: DISABLED)
[ServiceProxyChain] string (default: none)
[ServiceProxyTrack] ENABLED|DISABLED (default: DISABLED)
[ServiceProxySSL] ENABLED|DISABLED (default: DISABLED)
[ServiceSSLcert] VMS file spec for certificate (default: none)
[ServiceSSLkey] VMS file spec for private key (default: none)
```

All elements except the actual virtual-service definition are optional. The service scheme, name, and port number are enclosed in double square brackets.

I've listed all the possible elements for the sake of completeness, but most of them are discussed in detail in other chapters: the `SSlclient` tags are discussed under SSL authentication in Chapter 7, the `NoLog` and `NoTrack` tags in Chapter 12, and the `SSLcert` and `SSLkey` in Chapter 6.

```
[ServiceBodyTag]
```

This is the contents of the `<BODY>` tag you want to have the server use in server-generated reports and errors for this service. You can set up different background colors and such for the pages to make them fit in with the site. The server does no validation of the contents, so if you want you can add some non-`<BODY>` stuff that will precede the contents of the page as provided by the server. If you want to go to a lot of trouble, you can edit the HTTPD$MSG.CONF file to find the source of the pages and include `<IMG>` tags with relatively specified calls to generically named items—for example, company logos, background images, even cascading style sheets—then adjust this parameter to set the base directory for the included img tags, thus getting different logos or entirely different looking pages for each service. If you don't specify this, you get a plain `<BODY>` tag.

```
[ServiceErrorReportPath]
path-to-error-reporting-SSI-doc-or-script
```

This does the same thing as `[ErrorReportPath]` in the general server configuration (mentioned in Chapter 5). If you want to override the general server configuration's error pages, you can specify this which may be a better idea than subverting the `<BODY>` tag, as mentioned previously.) You can have a Web designer make the report page for this service fit exactly with the rest of the site design. The path is formatted as a URL.

```
[ServiceIpAddress] dotted-decimal address (default: none)
```

Rarely necessary, but if you're running multiple numeric IP addresses (multihomed networking), this binds the service to the specific IP address, rather than working based on the host header.

The careful reader will by now have noticed—or remembered from Chapter 5—that the service definition doesn't include the option to specify a document tree or any protection rules. This is handled in the HTTPD$MAP.CONF file, described in some detail in Chapter 7.

In the HTTPD$MAP.CONF file, you can include a virtual service and include mapping or protection rules that apply only to that service; these can override the general server configuration. An important note: In HTTPD$MAP.CONF, a virtual service specification cannot include the scheme; by the time the mapping portion of the server is at work, it no longer matters whether this is encrypted or unencrypted. If you include a scheme, the mapper won't recognize the service as defined and will not implement the mapping rules you've applied for it. For each virtual service that needs to serve different documents, you'll need to apply a pass rule:

```
[[virtual-service1]]
pass /* /unixified-path-to-doc-tree-for-service-1/*
[[virtual-service2]]
pass /* /unixified-path-to-doc-tree-for-service-2/*
[[*]] # which resets the environment to talking about
      # all services.
```

Here is an example:

```
[[alanwinston.homeip.net]] # this covers all ports on
                           # this hostname
pass /*  /$disk1/Web/alanwinston/*
[[vms.kicks-ass.net:81]]  # covers only the non-standard
                          # port
pass /*  $disk1/vms/*
[[vms.kicks-ass.net:444]] # covers only the non-standard
                          # HTTPS port
pass /*  /$disk1/vmssecret/*
[[*]]
```

The example shows that if you want to provide the same content for both HTTP and HTTPS ports, you can specify the host name without specifying a port, and what remains will apply to both. Alternatively, you can specify a port, and the configuration will apply only to that port. In the example, port 81 shows the standard content from the $DISK1:[VMS] directory, while port 444 shows an entirely different directory: the $DISK1:[VMSSECRET] directory.

10

Indexing and Searching Your Site

10.1 Why index?

It's no good having useful information on your site if your users can't find it. It's hard to predict how they'll look for it, but if you have a full-text index of your pages, you won't have to guess how the users will look for information, and they'll have the best chance to get hold of what they need.

Unless you go to some trouble to prevent it (as described in Chapter 7), your site—or at least those pages that are linked to from elsewhere—is searchable by external search engines. But they won't do this job very effectively.

There are two problems with using external search engines for this function. One is that they can't find files that they don't know are there—if items are present but not linked from pages that the search engine has seen, they can't be seen or indexed. The other problem is that it's more user friendly to offer a search function on your home page than to tell your users to go off to Google for it. (If you decide to use an external search appliance, you can offer a form on your home page that has as its action a script that runs on the appliance in order to get this capacity without running it on VMS.)

If your site is very small, you can, of course, implement a search function that searches through your Web tree for either specific strings (even using plain old DCL SEARCH) or regular expressions (using GNU grep) and returns file names; a small DCL or Perl wrapper would let you convert those to URLs. That's pretty easy; the problem is that it gets very slow very quickly to read every file and look at every line, and all that disk access may slow down your other activity. An indexer reads through all your files once, then builds an index optimized for fast searching. This trades off time for disk space; these index files are typically at least half as large as the files they index. However, the disk space can be on some other drive on some other controller, so accessing it doesn't slow down your regular access; you can even dedicate a separate server to do the indexing and the searches. Also, a proper index-based searcher, unlike grep or $ SEARCH, can do matches based on more than one line of a file—does the whole document contain "X" but not "Y"?

If VMS really takes off as a Web platform, commercial indexers will be ported to or developed for the platform. In the meantime, there are a number of freeware alternatives: VMSindex (alone or in combination with Lynx), SWISH-E, and the newly ported ht://Dig. SWISH-E and ht://Dig are both recent ports, not fully shaken down but still quite usable.

Search tools, CGIs, and the fine points of each would fill a book in themselves. The aim of this chapter is to give you enough information about each of these tools to get you started.

10.2 VMSindex and Lynx Crawl

Ohio University has contributed a toolkit it uses to the OpenVMS freeware CD, on-line at http://www.openvms.compaq.com/freeware/freeware50/lynx-2-8-3/osu.

This is used to index the contents of some 80 different servers. There is a nice write-up of this at http://www.ohiou.edu/pagemasters/memo85/append4.html.

Download the contents of both the index and the Lynx subdirectories. The index portion is Bruce Tanner and Foteos Macrides's VMSindex package, which does extensive indexing of text files, including HTML. The Lynx portion is Richard Piccard's specially tweaked version of the character-based Web browser, Lynx, version 2.8.2, which saves files from the Web in a way that VMSindex can index much more efficiently. The directory also contains Diff output showing the changes, so you can apply them yourself to a more recent version of Lynx if you prefer.

The last time I looked at this, a couple of years ago, the tweaked version was 2.7.something and the current version was 2.8.1; the newer version had Unicode support, and many routines were much, much longer than they had been; I gave up on trying to apply the diffs. I'm glad they've made a more recent version available.

There are some gotchas in building these applications. Unzip the index.zip package. (If you just do unzip without directing the output anywhere, it'll unzip into the current directory rather than a subdirectory.) Unzip the Lynx package (which goes into a subdirectory).

If you're running Multinet, you need to lie to the build procedure to get Lynx to compile. Make sure the header file `UCX$INETDEF.H` is located somewhere the build procedure can find it. I copied MULTINET:[MULTINET_ROOT.INCLUDE.VMS]UCX$INETDEF.H to SYS$LIBRARY:, which seemed to do the trick.

Type `@BUILD.COM` and you'll see:

```
Acceptable TCP/IP agents are
  [1] MULTINET (default)
  [2] UCX
  [3] WIN_TCP
  [4] CMU_TCP
  [5] SOCKETSHR_TCP
  [6] TCPWARE
Agent [1,2,3,4,5,6] (RETURN = [1])
```

Tell it you're running UCX (whether you're running TCP/IP services, Multinet, or TCPware). The problem is that if you admit that you're running Multinet, it will attempt to use a Multinet header file that's incompatible with the DECC libraries, and your compile will fail. This is not the Lynx developer's fault; the Multinet developers have given up trying to track DECC-required changes and don't maintain that header file any longer, so it just drifts further and further out of synch. It's not needed for new development; the DECC library calls just go to the (Multinet-provided) UCXDRIVER and all remains well. This should be enough to let you build Lynx. (To run Lynx, minimally, you need to define `Lynx_dir` to point to where the sample `lynx.cfg` file is.)

To build VMSindex with DECC, don't bother using MMS or MAKE.COM. (First, MMS won't recognize .c files as .C files, so it won't try to build anything if you're on an ODS-5 disk unless you `$ RENAME *.c *.C` before running it. Second, MMS aborts the build when it gets a warning message on line 628 of build_index.C, which seems like an overreaction.) Instead, just use the supplied command procedures

```
$ @COMPILE
$ @LINK
```

and you should get a working build_index.exe and query.exe. (Don't be freaked by the 0-block DECC.OPT file, which seems to be included for symmetry with the VAXC.OPT and GNUC.OPT files.)

Lynx does a nice job of crawling. Based on the freeware readme, you can do

```
$ CRAWL :== "$LYNX_DIR:LYNX -NOPAUSE -CRAWL -TRAVERSAL -REALM"
$ CRAWL http://yourserver.domain.tld
```

and Lynx will start from the top on your server, follow no links that lead off the server (that's what the -REALM flag does), and create in your current default directory a whole bunch of .DAT files with the contents of HTML pages, modified to tag each at the top with THE_URL:url-at-which-this-was-found and THE_TITLE:the-contents-of-the-title-tag. This is fun to watch, because Lynx renders the pages as it's crawling them.

When I tried to use the existing index-building command procedures from the freeware CD against these files, I ended up with a blank index. I couldn't find any documentation in the freeware kit explaining how to build an index based on this output. Don't waste your time trying to use any of the provided command procedures from the freeware CD; they won't work.

I went searching on Google and found this page at Ohio University, which nicely explains how VMSindex works and links to example command procedures. (These were presumably not included in the freeware distribution because they were quite specific to Ohio's setup. Nonetheless, you want them.) The URL of the page is http://ouvaxa.cats.ohiou.edu/vmsindex/index.html. From here, I learned that the incantation to index pages in this format is

```
$ index :== $[where-build-index-is]build_index.exe
$ index -
        [where-the-Lynx-output-is]lnk*.dat.* -
        /output=[where-you-want-the-index]indexname.idx -
        /topic=(text="the_title:",exclude) -
        /wordlength=40 -
        /url=(text="the_url:")
```

If you want to prove to yourself that the documents have, in fact, been indexed, do

```
$ query :== $[where-query.exe-is]
$ query indexname
Enter query: [searchstring]
```

and it will show you the pages that match your search string.

To set up a regular procedure and a Web-based search for your environment, go to http://ouvaxa.cats.ohiou.edu/vmsindex/examples/index.html and download every command procedure shown. None of them will work in your environment without significant modification, but what to change and where should be pretty clear. The search CGI program provided works for OSU; you'll either need to run it under the OSU emulation from other servers or write your own for Apache or WASD.

Be aware that index-building with Lynx and VMSindex is not a process that you can completely automate; you can't just write a batch script, run it every week or month, and expect to have clear full indexes forever. Lynx can hang or crash, so somebody has to baby-sit it—or at least check in on it every so often while it's crawling—and diagnose problems if they occur. Since this process creates a copy of every Web page it crawls, it can demand a lot of disk space; you may need to crawl your site in sections and merge the indexes later. If you do that, you need to keep on top of your site organization, since a new section won't automatically be indexed unless you put in a job to do it. Nonetheless, scrupulously maintained, this can work very well, as the quick response from the Ohio University search page shows.

10.3 SWISH-E

SWISH-E stands for Simple Web Indexing System for Humans—Enhanced. Originally developed by Kevin Hughes, it's now under active development by a large team, with versions for various UNIXes, Windows flavors, OS/2, and even Amiga. The home page is http://www.swish-e.org/, and you can find the documentation and pointers to third-party scripts there.

While the source from the SWISH-E home page includes VMS support files, it may be easier to get the VMS package from the WASD site. This includes precompiled binaries and some VMS-specific instructions. You can find it at http://wasd.vsm.com.au/wasd/. There are AXP and VAX versions there. You need DECC version 6 or better to compile it, but the packages contain precompiled objects.

In addition to SWISH-E itself, the package also contains SWISHESI (pronounced "SWISH-Easy"), Mark Daniel's CGI front end used to do SWISH-E searches. It uses his CGI library to run under Apache, OSU, WASD (of course), and Purveyor if you're using that.

SWISH-E can do file system searching and Web spidering and can use external programs or filters to understand filetypes it doesn't have built in. (Built in are HTML, XML, and plain text.) It can do all kinds of indexing, not just Web indexing.

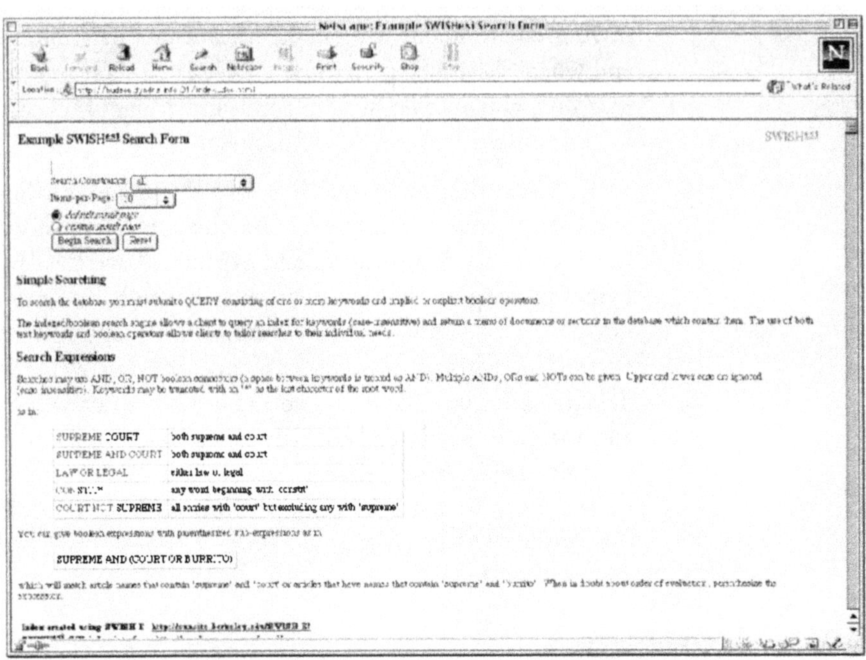

Figure 10.1 *The SWISHESI documentation index search page.*

If you're running WASD, you can use the SWISHESI setup as supplied. Copy the `SWISH-E.EXE` to `HT_EXE`:; rename `[SWISH]` into a subdirectory of `HT_ROOT:[SRC]`; copy INDEX_DOC.HTML to some directory the server can see; and execute `@INDEX_DOC.COM`, which will index the WASD documentation tree into DOC.SWISH_E and DOC.SWISH-E_PROP.

Go to your browser and bring up INDEX_DOC.HTML, as shown in Figure 10.1.

If you select the default results page, the results are as seen in Figure 10.2.

If you select the custom results page, the results are as seen in Figure 10.3.

For other servers, you'll need to put SWISHESI into HTBIN/CGIBIN, set up a path name where it can find the index, edit INDEX_DOC.CONF to index some other set of documents, edit INDEX_DOC.COM to find SWISH-E.EXE in some other location, and change the ACTION items in INDEX_DOC.HTML to refer to the location you've decided upon for the index and results page.

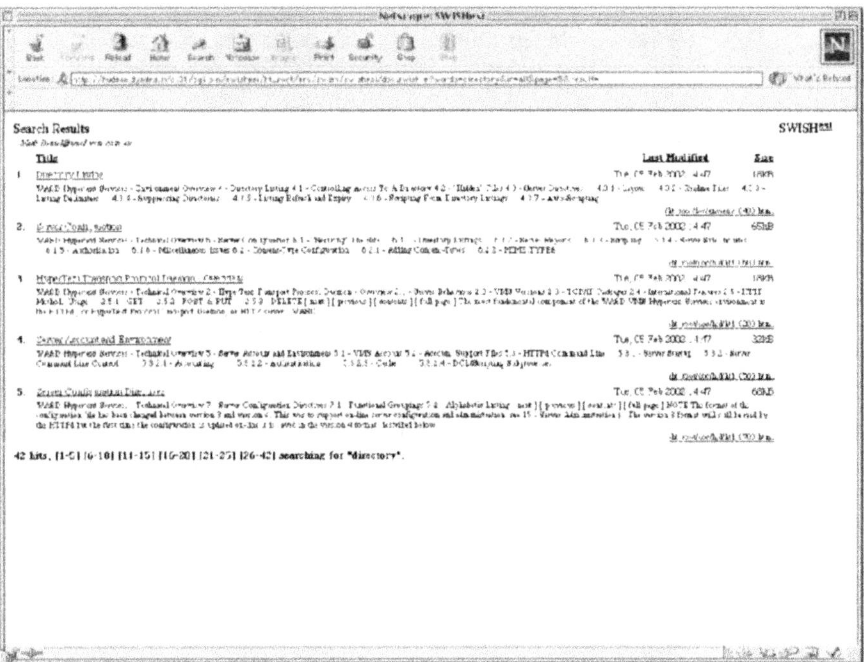

Figure 10.2 *SWISHESI default page layout.*

In any case, when you go to index your own documents, you'll need to edit the appropriate configuration file (whose name is supplied as a command-line parameter to SWISH-E). To index other stuff, you need to make different configuration files. There are fine points that you should read the documentation for, but here are the basic things to change:

```
IndexFile ./doc.swish-e
```

That translates to doc.swish-e in your default directory when you run SWISH-E. Put in a UNIXified file-system path if you want to put the index somewhere else.

```
IndexDir /ht_root/doc/
```

This gives the top-level directory of which to index the documents therein. In theory, this can be a top-level URL to spider. The spidering is done with an external Perl script, swishspider. If you want to try spidering, you need to use the command-line switch "`-S http`", and since the case of the S matters, you need to quote the switch (e.g., "`-S`").

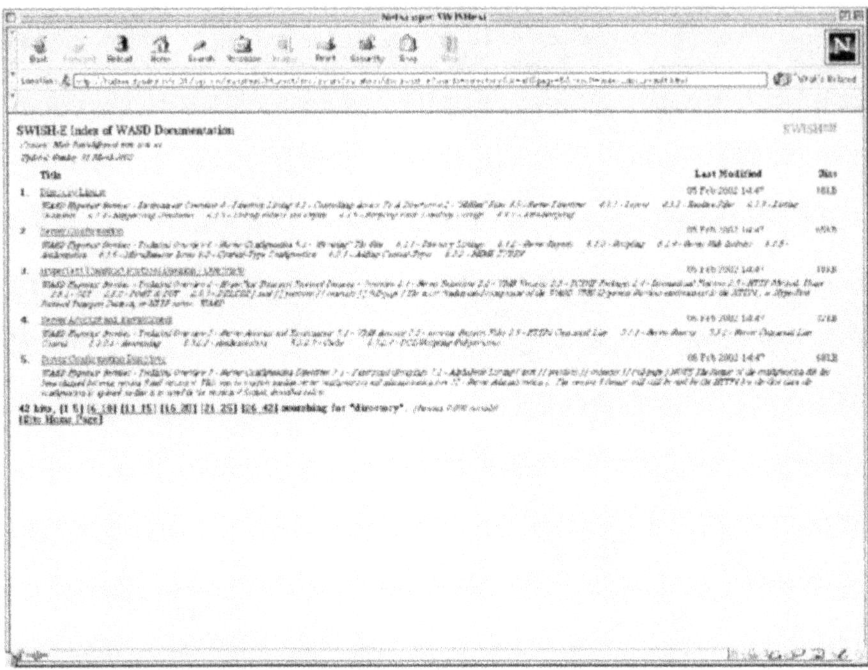

Figure 10.3 *SWISH-E custom results page layout.*

If you can manage something as convenient as a file system path that matches the URL path, as /ht_root/doc/ does, it'll make life easier later. Even when Web-spidering works, it's slower than local direct access.

```
IndexName "WASD Documents"
```

Any string you like, which some presentation scripts will show as the name of the index you're creating.

```
IndexDescription "Example SWISH-E index of WASD
documentation"
```

Any string you like, which some presentation scripts will show as a description of the index you're creating.

```
IndexAdmin "Mark.Daniel@wasd.vsm.com.au"
```

Any name or name and e-mail address, which some presentation scripts will show as a description of the index you're creating.

```
IndexContents HTML .htm .html
```

If your site has server-parsed HTML files, such as .HTMLX, .SHTML, .PHP, or .JSP, you may want to add them here. This line tells SWISH-E to use the HTML parser on files of these types.

10.4 HT://DIG

ht://Dig is a multiplatform suite of Web indexing programs originally developed at San Diego State University. ht://Dig's particular claim to fame is its ability to make various "fuzzy search" indexes, including indexing by soundex and by synonyms. It can also index PDFs by using XPDF to do the rendering for it. You can find samples, the FAQ, and documentation for the UNIX version at http://www.htdig.org; the documentation is also in [.HTDOC] once you've unpacked the kits.

Martin Vorländer has ported version 3.1.5 to VMS. You can find it on his home page, http://www.pdv-systeme.de/users/martinv/. Note that even if you download the source distribution, you need to get both the binary and the data distributions, and unzip them all into the same tree. (With the source distribution you can rebuild and replace the binaries, but you need some files that are only in the binary distribution.)

Be warned that ht://Dig uses the Berkeley "database" for file storage—necessary on UNIX where this was developed because of an absence of native indexed file formats. On UNIX, the Berkeley DB doesn't really understand locking and can get badly messed up if multiple updaters try to access the same database simultaneously. Be careful when indexing not to get your hands crossed. (Multiuser read access isn't a problem.)

To build the package you need to have a copy of the ZLIB library, which isn't included in the ht://Dig package. You can get this from Rick Dyson's Web site; it's included in several of the log file analysis programs (see Chapter 12). You can also get it from the info-ZIP project at http://www.info-zip.org/pub/infozip/zlib/.

Edit SET_BUILD_ENVIRONMENT.COM to define `ZLIB_DIR` to point to a directory with ZLIB in it. To build the package, do

```
$ @SET_BUILD_ENVIRONMENT
$ MMS
```

Read the README.VMS first. The installation directions that follow are closely based on those found there. Note that building the various images leaves them throughout the [HTDIG-3_1_5...] tree and doesn't put them in the [.INSTALL_VMS...] tree, which is where the precompiled binaries are found. To move them to the INSTALL directory, do

```
$ MMS INSTALL
```

All the files needed are in the [.INSTALL_VMS] tree. Its structure is used in all the command procedures and configuration files, but you should be able to make it work with a directory structure suitable to your Web server by defining logical names appropriately.

Move the files in [.BIN] and [.COMMON] to some location and make sure that the [.COMMON] files can be read by the account that runs scripts for your Web server. (You don't want to serve them out, they just need to be reachable by the HTSEARCH CGI program.) Move [.CGI-BIN]HTSEARCH.EXE to a CGI script directory for your Web server, or map that directory as a CGI script location.

Move the files in [.IMAGE] to some location accessible over the Web by the URL "`/htdig_image`" or map that path to point to this directory. (If you want some other name for the path, you can edit `DESCRIP.MMS_MACROS` and change `IMAGE_URL_PREFIX` to the path name you prefer. If you built the package before reading this paragraph, you can edit [.CONF]HTDIG.CONF, [.SEARCH]SEARCH.HTML, and [.COMMON]*.HTML.)

Move [.SEARCH]SEARCH.HTML to some location accessible over the Web. This is a sample search form you can build upon. Adjust the "`/cgi-bin/htsearch`" form action in that file to a path that will find where you put HTSEARCH.EXE. Move [.CONF]HTDIG.CONF to some convenient location and edit it. More on the configuration file is given subsequently.

Create a [.DB] directory on a disk that has lots of free space. Edit SETUP_HTDIG.COM to reflect the choices you've made about where to locate files and execute it. Edit SYSTARTUP_VMS or whatever other arrangements you have for startup to be sure it's included in system startup. Define TMPDIR to a place that has lots of free space.

To index PDF documents, you'll need PDFTOPS.EXE from the XPDF package (on the OpenVMS freeware CD-ROM). Define the symbol pdftops as a foreign command—that is

```
pdftops == "$device:[directory]pdftops.exe"
```

Before you can start searching, you will need to create a search database. A sample script to do this is in [.BIN]RUNDIG.COM. (This is one of the files that's in the binary distribution but not the source.) Martin strongly suggests that you read the comments in RUNDIG.COM so you know what's going on; there's actually quite a lot.

You can do an incremental index update—run through the directories and index any new or updated documents—by editing RUNDIG.COM to remove the "`-i`" option from the call to HTDIG.EXE, and set the "alt" symbol to (or call RUNDIG with) "`-a`".

There are a few configuration file entries you must or should change before doing any work of your own.

```
database_dir:        /htdig_root/db
```

UNIXified path name; if you've done the logical assignments in SETUP_HTDIG, the default assignment will work. Note that if you do specify a device name in the path, you need to escape any dollar signs with a backslash, as in "/user\$disk1/db".

```
start_url:        http://www.htdig.org/
```

If you don't change this to your own site, you'll be indexing the ht://Dig home site, which is probably not what you want.

```
limit_urls_to:        ${start_url}
```

This defaults to the value of start_url, so that you don't go spidering off over the entire Web. This should be read as "limit URLs followed to values containing the following string"; if you make this blank or "http://" you can spider the entire Web if you like. This can be multiple strings.

```
exclude_urls:        /cgi-bin/ .cgi
```

Read this as "don't follow URLs containing any of the following strings." This is typically used to keep from trying to index scripts. If you're indexing an OSU site, you probably want /htbin/ rather than /cgi-bin/; the .CGI extension might be supplemented by `.com`, `.exe`, and `.pl`. This string is matched anywhere in the URL, so be sure to include the "`.`" when you're defining extensions.

```
maintainer:    unconfigured@htdig.searchengine.maintainer
```

Change this to your e-mail address, or at any rate to the e-mail address of somebody who can reasonably respond to requests from a site Webmaster to stop spidering them at peak hours, or whatever. ht://Dig will supply this in response to any identification requests it gets.

The configuration file is worth reading; it has the best comments—explaining what's going on in an unambiguous way—of any config file I've seen recently.

Here's a quick start guide for ht://Dig on CSWS, provided by one of the CSWS engineers.

```
- @HTDIG_ROOT:HTDIG_STARTUP CONFIG        ! Create environment file
- @HTDIG_ROOT:HTDIG_STARTUP               ! Define environment
- $ Edit HTDIG_ROOT:[CONF]HTDIG.CONF      ! Configure search engine controls
- Copy HTDIG_ROOT:[SEARCH]SEARCH.HTML APACHE$COMMON:[HTDOCS] ! Search form
- Copy HTDIG_ROOT:[CGI-BIN]HTSEARCH.EXE APACHE$COMMON:[CGI-BIN]! Search
script
- @HTDIG_ROOT:[BIN]RUNDIG
! Create database and index the site
```

Define aliases for on-line documentation and image directories:

```
Alias /htdig/ "/sys$common/htdig/documentation/"

<Directory "/sys$common/htdig/documentation">
   Options Indexes MultiViews
   AllowOverride None
   Order allow,deny
   Allow from all
</Directory>

Alias /htdig_image/ "/sys$common/htdig/image/"

<Directory "/sys$common/htdig/image">
   Options Indexes MultiViews
   AllowOverride None
   Order allow,deny
   Allow from all
</Directory>
```

Set file protection to `W:RE` on `HTDIG_ROOT:[DB]*.*` database files. Start Apache and point browser at http://<server-name>/search.html.

11

Cache and Proxy

11.1 Cache and proxy

Caching in general is the act of keeping things around where you can access them faster, typically by keeping them in RAM after you've accessed them from disk (and thus amortizing the cost of the disk I/O over multiple accesses). For this to be a win, you need to have enough physical memory available to do it. If you don't, any I/O wins from having the documents in memory are more than offset by the hit from increased paging.

Caching is distributed all over the Web. The second America Online user who looks at your home page in 15 seconds will probably receive a copy of it from America Online's cache, not from your server. But if you're actually getting multiple hits yourself, you want to avoid expensive disk I/O to get the pages and images in question, so you run a cache yourself, keeping the pages in memory.

In some environments it makes sense for the desktop clients to access the wider world through a single gateway—for example, if you have only one high-speed connection to the greater world or if your organization needs to restrict Web access to specific outside sites. In that case, you configure a Web proxy that will collect Web content from outside your local site on behalf of the Web clients, cache the results locally for greater performance, and distribute the results to local clients when they request it.

A Web proxy can also block local clients from getting at outside data, if your organization is required to do that either as diligent stewards of taxpayer-funded bandwidth resources or as Big-Brotheresque censors more concerned with what employees are looking at than with how much work they get done. If, as Webmaster, you can possibly avoid getting involved with blocking access to certain sites because their content is deemed bad or unprofessional, do so. If the site policy is that employees shouldn't use company resources to view porn, then the way to implement that policy is to make viewing porn a firing offense and make sure everybody knows it. It will not be accomplished by your trying to list the name of every porn site and blocking it in your configuration files; there are new porn sites every day. Even if you succeeded in blocking access to every porn site, you'd need to block access to all anonymizing proxy servers, which clever users could use to fetch porn on their behalf. It's a losing battle; stay out of it if you can.

Proxy servers are a big win for large ISPs; if 6,000 AOL users are trying to look at the CNN home page, it's a lot faster if they can all fetch it from a cache in AOL's network than if all their requests have to go round trip to CNN, and it's easier on CNN's servers too. (But you probably would use a dedicated proxy server for this purpose, not overloading the Web server capability.)

Conversely, sometimes you want to serve material from a system inside your corporate firewall to the outside world; rather than open a hole through the firewall to that system, your existing Web server can act as a proxy server, ferrying requests from the outside world to the inside server and returning results. That's called (by some) "reverse proxying." In some cases similar goals can be attained by using DECnet to run tasks on VMS servers that can't get through the firewall and return the results to the Web server system. DECnet isn't an option if what you're trying to do is serve data from Windows NT servers without exposing those servers to IIS viruses, and it might make considerable sense to front-end those with a Web server that laughs off attempted buffer-overflow exploits.

In the case of a proxy, the content you're serving happens not to live on your system, and you have to do an expensive fetch over the Net to get pages, which you may then keep on disk because local disk is likely to be faster than distant Net pages. Once you have the pages you cache them and manage the proxy cache in pretty much the same way as content generated on your own site, although with proxies you have some additional management hints from the original server. (It is, however, entirely possible to proxy and not cache the results.) Since these ideas are so closely linked, we'll cover proxy and caching information together in this chapter.

There are some special-purpose Web proxy server boxes and some freeware proxy server software. Some proxy service capability is also available in Apache, WASD, and OSU.

I must say here that if you really need high-performance dedicated proxying capacity, this is an excellent application for a cheap non-VMS box. Why? Because, in the long term, you don't care about the data. The only thing on a dedicated proxy server that you'd back up would be the configuration information and maybe the log files. The data are all temporary, and are available on the Web. If you have a disk dedicated to proxy cache and lose it, you can just put in another disk and start over; your cache will get repopulated as requests come in. Dedicate a reasonably fast PC with a fast Ethernet interface; throw in lots and lots of memory and some adequately speedy disk, which comes fast, big, and cheap in IDE formats—and remember, you don't care about the data, so IDE's not a big problem—run a CD-based version of LINUX or NetBSD (so your OS directories aren't writeable) or use netboot; put on squid or socks; keep the configuration files on some VMS disk served (read-only) to the cache over NFS; use SSH when you need to connect to the box; and you're in business.

The popular freeware proxy servers don't run on VMS (although there was an attempt to port squid in 1997, and this kind of porting has gotten easier as the C library has gotten more UNIX-compatible, so they may run on VMS someday). The reliability and redundancy of VMS clusters, the security, the extreme competence of the BACKUP utility, the careful flushing to disk of data before RMS reports that a file is closed—the things that give you a warm, comfortable feeling about your Web server and your database running on VMS—are not particularly helpful in a proxy cache environment, where you want speed, which you get from cheapness. Nonproprietary memory is pretty cheap, so you can get a ton of it; big fast, IDE drives are cheap compared with SCSI, so you can get more of those (and some spares to replace them). If this suggestion makes you twitch, remind yourself again that you don't care about the data and it's okay to lose all the data.

However, if you need light-to-medium proxy service, the VMS Web server software can handle it.

11.2 Cache management

Here's the way the caches in Web servers work in general. The Web server has allocated a chunk of RAM (generally at a size you've configured) for cache. The server has to read files into memory before it pushes them out to the client. In fact, if the system or cluster has a significant amount of memory set aside for disk caching, the server's first read of a file may put it into VMS's disk cache, and the next time the server reads the file (within an interval determined by how much other activity there is on your system and how much memory is available), the OS satisfies the file read from the cache if there is no new version of the file and the file header on disk shows that there have been no modifications since the version now in cache was cached.

The Web server sticks the file into memory and puts a pointer to it in a header structure. When a file is requested (e.g., when mapping rules have been applied and the specific file identified), the server checks the cache to see if that file is present, looks at the header to see how old the version in memory is, checks the in-memory configuration structures to see how often the server is supposed to check for new file versions (e.g., "Is the cached version three minutes old yet?"), and, if it's outside that window, checks whether there's a new version of the file. If there isn't, check the headers for the file on disk to see if it's been modified since that time. If there's no new version of the file and the file hasn't been modified, update the cached headers for this file to refresh its expiration time and serve the file out of RAM. If it has been modified, flush the old version and serve and cache the new version with updated headers.

The issues tend to be these: How much memory is available for the cache? Is usage distributed evenly across all the documents you serve or are there some documents or paths in much higher demand than others? Does your free-with-VMS (VCC, VIOC, XFC) or paid-for third-party disk cache program do an adequate job of preventing excessive disk I/O without making the Web server take care of it? (And, if you've got a clusterwide disk cache, does that make it more effective than multiple instances of a Web server, each with its own individual file cache? And is that answer different on a Galaxy system if the file cache can be shared and put in Galactic shared memory?) One thing that a Web server–specific cache does is save on overhead from reading variable-record-length files with the C run-time library. C does a poor job with those files, which are the kind typically created by VMS editors, compared with STM-LF files. If the Web server caches the file contents, the cost of reading the file is potentially amortized over multiple accesses. If the disk cache provides it, the C RTL overhead of reading it is repeated every time.

While OSU and WASD provide some knobs for tuning the in-memory cache organization, odds are poor that you'll see any very substantial change from messing with, for example, the chunk size. So there is no one-size-fits-all answer (except for Apache; see the following subsection). To be optimally effective, you'll not only need to configure cache as sensibly as you can, you'll need to run tests in different configurations to see what the effects actually are.

11.2.1 Apache

Apache 1.3 has no file cache as part of the core distribution. There's an experimental mod_mmap, a memory-based cache for static pages. (In Apache 2.0, where CSWS will eventually be, there's a mod_cache with mod_disk_cache and mod_mem_cache modules; this is also experimental in 2.0, and in any case there's no VMS port of 2.0 yet.) There are a lot of promising-sounding Cache directives; these are all interpreted by mod_proxy and have to do with proxy cache. This is probably because modern UNIX systems do really aggressive disk/file caching, so Apache wouldn't gain much performance benefit from doing it itself.

If your VCC/VIOC/XFC cache isn't doing enough for you and increasing the amount of memory available to it doesn't help enough, perhaps because the most popular documents are also the most frequently updated, you can try putting your most heavily accessed Web files onto a RAM disk so all access is at memory speeds. If that doesn't do enough for you, you can put your VMS box behind a cache appliance.

11.2.2 OSU

In the default configuration, OSU maintains a file cache. Access through the nocache port(s) bypasses the cache and goes straight to the on-disk file system. Information on cache contents and hit rates is available via the PRIVREQUEST command.

The main part of the cache (where the actual data are stored) is divided into chunks of a size you can specify. There's a linked list of headers, also in RAM, that maintain the metadata (file name, file size, expiration time) and point to which chunk(s) the file data are stored in. Every cache entry will take up at least one chunk; the chunk size isn't related to the on-disk record size of the file.

The available knobs that affect the whole cache system are `LIMIT` (largest size in bytes of a file you're willing to cache), `SIZE` (how many bytes of RAM to allocate to the cache), `MAXREC` (size of a chunk in bytes), and `REFRESH` (the maximum number of seconds after a file has been cached that it can be served out without checking the on-disk structure to see whether there's been a new version). `EXCLUDE` specifies a path to exclude from caching.

These directives go in HTTP_MAIN.CONF.

```
FILECACHE SIZE number-of-bytes
```

specifies how much memory to allocate for the file cache (defaults to 1,000,000 bytes).

```
FILECACHE LIMIT number-of-bytes
```

specifies the maximum size of file you're willing to cache (defaults to 48,000).

```
FILECACHE REFRESH minutes:seconds | seconds
```

specifies the number of seconds for which a document can be served from cache without being checked against the on-disk file system. The default is three minutes; you could specify that as 3:00 or 180. You could also specify it as 0; this would force an on-disk check for every file access, but you'd still get some benefit from the cache, since the actual file wouldn't be read if it hadn't changed since the last time.

```
FILECACHE MAXREC number-of-bytes
```

shows in-memory chunk size for cache, (defaults to 4,096). It should be roughly the average size in bytes of files you serve. The criteria for choosing this are a lot like the criteria for choosing cluster size on a disk. The larger the chunk size the faster things theoretically go, since there's less overhead; however, since each cache entry consumes at least one chunk, the larger the chunk size the fewer the things you can cache. If the average size of a served file is significantly smaller than the chunk size, you'll waste a lot of space. Unless you have a very unusual system where, all files to be served are the same size (so there's no dilemma; just set the chunk size to that one file size), you may as well take the default chunk size as a reasonable compromise. Setting `MAXREC` higher than `LIMIT` is guaranteed to waste memory.

```
FILECACHE EXCLUDE template
```

Don't cache files matching this template. You can have multiple instances of this directive, and all will apply. By default the HTTP_PATHS.CONF file has a

```
FileCache exclude *;
```

directive in it. This allows the requester to force an on-disk lookup of a given file by putting a bare semicolon on the end of the path. This template supports full VMS wildcarding. If you had a lot of documents that changed very frequently and getting the most recent version was important, you could do

```
FileCache exclude */dynamic/*
```

and any directory tree, including userdirs, could have a [.DYNAMIC] subdirectory, within which any file would automatically be noncached.

A related directive is `FILEEXPIRE`, which sets expiration date and time on files. This will be reflected in an expires: header when the file is served, but the internal cache will also honor the expiration set by the directive and go out to the file system. This lets you override the cache-wide REFRESH setting for the particular file or path.

```
FILEEXPIRE template EDT
FILEEXPIRE template CDT+|RDT+ time-offset
```

Template is a fully wildcardable path specification, which can get down to a directory, a file name, a file extension, or all the files beginning with a particular string. The second argument says which RMS attribute of the file to base expiration upon. (Do a `$ DIR/FULL` of some file to see these attributes.) "EDT" is the expiration date/time of the file as given by RMS. (This can be set by the creating program, or inherited at creation time from the RETENTION setting of the disk volume; see `$ HELP SET VOLUME /RETENTION` for more info.)

In the second format, time-offset (specified as either a number of seconds or minutes:seconds) is applied to the creation date (CDT+) or revision/modification date (RDT+) of the file to determine the expiration.

```
FileExpire */winston/create* CDT+59:00
```

would cause every file in any tree ending with /winston/ whose name began with "create" to expire 59 minutes after it was created. (Sixty minutes after creation, OSU won't stop serving the file, but it will end up going out to disk to check for a new version every time.)

You can get an understanding of how well your cache is doing with the `PRIVREQUEST` command.

```
$ PRIVREQUEST control-port-# DSPCACHE port-#
```

will display the headers of what's currently cached, showing you paths, expirations, files ize, and how many times the individual files have been served from cache. (If hits are zero it means the file was requested, was served and cached, and hasn't been requested since.)

```
$ PRIVREQUEST control-port-# STAT port-#
```

shows a number of statistics about the current Web server, including some overall file cache information.

```
File Cache Statistics:
   Hit rate: 82.8%

   items: 191189 lookups, 1604/156786 hits (act/lru), 32743/56/0 misses
(new/lock/fail)
    chunks: 486 used (18 dir), 486 total, 92605 alloc attempts
```

What this means is discussed in the following paragraphs.

Lookups are the total number of times the cache has been checked since the last time the statistics were zeroed. The two hit counts are active and least recently used. An active hit is counted when the lookup finds an entry that was concurrently being read by another thread and therefore already on the active list. The least-recently used hits are counted when the lookup finds the item on the least-recently used list of items that are candidates for purging if the cache runs out of memory. When this happens, the entry is moved to the active list.

The number of misses is divided into new, lock, and fail. A "new" miss occurs when a cache lookup doesn't find the entry because it's not in cache; in that case a new entry is created, usually by deleting the oldest entry on the lru list. A "lock" miss occurs when another thread has just created a cache entry for the file and is still loading it into cache. Rather than waiting or serving a potentially incomplete version of the file, the current thread gets the file from disk and doesn't try to cache it. A "fail" miss would be a "new" miss except that the thread couldn't create a new cache entry. If you get a lot of "fail" misses, your cache may be too small.

The chunks line shows how many chunks are used in cache; the (nn dir) says how many are being used as cache headers. (Each header takes around 300 bytes, so a 4,096-byte chunk holds 13 headers; in this example, between 241 and 254 headers are in use.)

Finally, you can force the server to treat every current entry in the cache as stale by using

```
$ PRIVREQUEST [manage-port] INVCACHE [server-port]
```

After receiving this command (also available through the Web-based SERVERMAINT), the server marks all entries as expired. On the next access, the file is checked on-disk. If the modification date hasn't changed and there isn't a new version, the expiration date of the cache entry is updated and the cached data are reused; if the modification times are different, the file contents are loaded anew from disk (or from disk cache).

11.2.3 WASD

Cache control directives go in the HTTPD$CONFIG.CONF file. The WASD cache, like the OSU cache, manages the cache contents in chunks of a size you specify. It attempts to notice what cache entries are often used and thus shouldn't be candidates to be overwritten with other files; you get to specify what "often" is. You can specify the maximum number of cache entries, the maximum size (in kilobytes) of the whole cache, the maximum file size you're willing to cache, and how long cached files can be served without checking them on-disk. As usual with WASD directives, the square brackets are part of the syntax rather than indicating optional components.

```
[Cache] enabled | disabled
```

specifies whether or not to cache at all. Default is enabled.

```
[CacheHashTableEntries] number
```

specifies how many hash table entries (used for speedier indexed lookup into the cache) to allocate; it should be a power of 2 to work well with the algorithm used (and if it isn't, it will be rounded down to the smaller power of 2—for example, anything between 513 and 1,023 will be rounded down to 512). Default is 1,024.

```
[CacheEntriesMax] number
```

specifies how many different files can be cached at once. Default is 200. If this limit is reached, even if the cache size limit is not reached, the cache will not grow.

```
[CacheTotalKBytesMax] number
```

specifies the maximum amount of memory to be used by the cache, in kilobytes. Default is 2,048 (two megabytes). If this limit is reached, even if the CacheEntriesMax number has not been reached, the cache will not grow.

```
[CacheFileKBytesMax] number
```

specifies the largest file you're willing to cache, in kilobytes. Default is 64.

```
[CacheChunkKBytes] number
```

shows the chunk size for cache, in kilobytes. It defaults to 8 (16 blocks). If your files average much smaller or much larger than 16 blocks, you could try adjusting this number; if you cut it in half, double the size of the hash table.

```
[CacheValidatePeriod] HH:MM:SS
```

shows how long a document can be cached before it has to be revalidated against the on-disk structure. Default is 00:01:00 (one minute).

```
[CacheFrequentHits] number
```

shows the total number of hits needed to qualify a cache entry as a candidate for immunity against getting removed to make room for a new entry. Default is 3. See the next directive for discussion.

```
[CacheFrequentPeriod] HH:MM:SS
```

If the server has a new file to cache and is out of room or already at the maximum number of entries, it looks for a victim file to remove. Entries that have been used both frequently and recently are immune. If the entry has been served from cache at least `[CacheFrequentHits]` number of times and the most recent time was within `[CacheFrequentPeriod]`, then the file is considered to be frequently and recently used and will stay in cache. (It will still be revalidated if `[CacheValidatePeriod]` has passed since the last time it was validated.) The default is 00:02:00 (two minutes).

As mentioned in Chapter 7, you can mark a path that you want never to be cached using the `set` directive in HTTPD$MAP.CONF.

```
SET path-template NOCACHE
```

In addition, requests that contain a semicolon always go to disk for the file, and the response is not saved in cache.

From the command line you can do some large-scale cache management:

```
$ HTTPD /DO=CACHE=ON
```

enables caching.

```
$ HTTPD /DO=CACHE=OFF
```

disables caching.

```
$ HTTPD /DO=CACHE=PURGE
```

These capabilities are available from the Web-based administration tool as well. The admin menu has a cache report, which can tell you how good a job the cache is doing. Use the results from that and the suggestions in the server documentation to see if you need to tune your cache; the most productive thing to change is probably the number of hash table entries if you see too many hash collisions.

11.3 Proxy management

In addition to proxying other servers' documents, you have considerable influence over how other proxy servers handle yours. You can include an expires: header, which tells the other servers when they can't safely serve your file from cache and need to fetch a new copy; a cache-control header, which describes in general how caches should handle the document; or for HTTP 1.0 clients, a `Pragma: nocache` header, which tells them not to cache it at all.

Note that browsers typically maintain their own client-side cache so that they don't automatically go out for a new page when the user clicks on "Back," and in some cases won't even do it when the user clicks on "Reload." If your content changes frequently, you'll want to control this behavior with headers. For each server, the options available for proxy-cache management are discussed in the following subsections.

11.3.1 Apache

Mod_proxy is first supported in CSWS 1.2. Capabilities include proxy, reverse proxy, and proxy caching. You can get more information about mod_proxy from the mod_proxy manual at apache.org; look it up at http://httpd.apache.org/docs/mod/mod_proxy.html.

You can be part of a proxy chain, forwarding proxy requests to another proxy server. You can enable or disable proxy support either serverwide or on a virtual host-by-virtual host basis. For proxying (as distinct from reverse proxying) you almost certainly don't want to act as a proxy server for everyone on the entire Internet.

If you're doing forward proxy only (fetching things from the great world for users on your internal network), use a `Directory` container directive to lock down all proxy services to users from your domain.

```
<Directory proxy:*>
Order Deny,Allow
Deny from all
Allow from mydomain.tld
</Directory>
```

The special proxy: directory specification can be extended with the scheme (mod_proxy supports HTTP, HTTPS, and FTP) and/or a wildcarded host name. `<Directory proxy:ftp:*>` will affect only FTP proxying services. `<Directory proxy:http:server.domain.tld>` affects proxying of HTTP requests to server.domain.tld. `<Directory proxy:*:*.domain.tld>` affects proxying of any requests to any server in domain.tld.

If you're going to do reverse proxying (presenting content from servers on the internal network to the outside world), you'll want to use one of the foregoing variants of the `Directory` directive to allow proxy access to hosts you're proxying from `All`. The variant directive will need to appear in the HTTPD.CONFIG file physically before the `<Directory proxy:*>`, which rules out any proxy access to any external user at all.

```
ProxyRequests  on|off
```

enables general proxying (and proxy caching, if configured) if turned on. The default is off. (This setting doesn't affect `ProxyPass` or proxy directives generated by mod_rewrite.)

```
ProxyRemote  match-URL remote-server
```

forwards all requests that match match-URL to the remote proxy server specified (as a partial URL) in remote-server. (If your path through the firewall depends on this other server, you want to pass everything nonlocal to it.) The match-URL can be "*" (for all requests of any kind), a scheme (http:, https:, ftp:), or a partial URL (http://otherdomain.mydomain.tld/ http://proxy.otherdomain.tld/ .) You can use this to make it look as though all the content available via proxy.otherdomain.tld is on your server as otherdomain.mydomain.tld. Since requests are forwarded, they'll come back to this server to get back to the user.

```
NoProxy pattern [pattern ...]
```

"pattern" is a subnet, IP address, host name, or domain name to which the proxy will connect directly, without using one of the forwarding proxies specified in `ProxyRemote`. This is useful primarily to specify other servers on your intranet, since a `ProxyRemote` on the other side of the firewall might not be able to get back in to them. To be sure of overriding patterns matched in `ProxyRemote` put `NoProxy` ahead of it in your configuration file.

```
ProxyBlock pattern [pattern ...]
```

"pattern" is a URL substring, host name, or domain name; you can have as many as you like, separated by spaces. Apache will refuse to proxy to sites matching those patterns, whether by HTTP, FTP, or HTTPS.

```
ProxyPass path URL
```

makes other servers appear to be within your directory tree. Path is the portion of the URL that follows the host name; URL is the other system to map it to. `ProxyPass /CNN/ http://www.cnn.com/` will make it look as though the whole CNN Web site is on your site in the /CNN/ directory.

```
ProxyPassReverse path URL
```

Path and URL have the same meanings as in `ProxyPass`. `ProxyPassReverse` intercepts the Location: headers produced by redirects on a machine being proxied to and rewrites them so that what the browser receives points at your machine. (If you're doing reverse proxy and the internal machines can't be reached from outside the firewall, a redirect to another path on the internal machine would leave the client at a dead end, unable to reach the machine it was redirected to. This directive fixes that problem by mapping redirects into the apparent space of the machine that's visible from outside.)

```
ProxyDomain domain
```

This directive specifies the default domain to which the Apache proxy server will belong. If a request to a host without a domain name is encountered, a redirect to the same host with the configured `Domain` appended will be generated. Useful only in intranet situations.

```
ProxyVia on|off|full|block
```

The Via: header is used to control the flow of proxy requests along a chain of proxy servers. This directive controls the user of that header. off (the default), does nothing special; if Via: headers are present, they're left unchanged. `On` adds a Via: header line to each request and reply, specifying the current host. `full` does the same as `on` and adds the Apache server version as a Via: comment field. `block` will strip out any Via: lines from proxy requests and not generate any new Via: headers.

```
AllowCONNECT port [port ...]
```

enables proxy tunneling (which lets other protocols run over HTTP). By default, HTTPS and news ports (443 and 563) are enabled. To support Telnet proxying, you'd specify port 23. Note that if you have an `AllowCONNECT` directive, only the ports called out in that directive are enabled; if you don't list the HTTPS port, you won't be able to connect to it this way.

```
CacheRoot directory-spec
```

The presence of the `CacheRoot` directive is what enables proxy caching; without it, Apache will proxy (if configured) but not cache. This directory needs to be writeable by Apache$WWW; it should ideally be on a disk and controller, different from your Web server executables or your local content. Remember that directory-specs end with the end of the directory-name, not a slash; this could be /apache$root/cache but not /apache$root/cache/.

```
CacheSize number-of-kilobytes
```

sets the desired—rather than the maximum—space usage of the cache, in kilobytes. Default is 5. The cache may grow bigger than this setting, but garbage collection will be triggered to delete files until the cache shrinks back to this size or below. Make this value no more than 80 percent of the space available.

```
CacheDefaultExpire hours
```

If the document is fetched via a protocol that doesn't have an expires: header (e.g., FTP), it will be assigned a cache lifetime of `CacheDefaultExpire` hours. (Default is 1.) This takes precedence over `CacheMaxExpire` for such documents.

```
CacheMaxExpire hours
```

determines the maximum number of hours you'll keep a document in cache without fetching it again from the original server. This directive takes precedence over a longer-term expires: header in the document. (Default is 24.)

```
CacheLastModifiedFactor factor
```

If the origin HTTP server did not supply an expiration date for the document, the server will estimate one by multiplying the time since last modification by the factor you specify here. (The default is 0.1.) If that gives it more time to live than it would be given by `CacheMaxExpire`, the `CacheMaxExpire` date/time takes precedence.

```
CacheGcInterval decimal-hours
```

is used to perform garbage collection on the cache every specified number of hours. (ninety minutes would be rendered as 1.5 hours). The larger you set `CacheGcInterval`, the likelier it is that cache space utilization will grow past the `CacheSize` you specified.

```
CacheDirLevels number-of-levels
```

sets the number of subdirectories that will be used below the CacheRoot. Default is 3. This probably has file-system performance implications, and I suspect they are different implications depending on what file system you're on, whether on UNIX or VMS (ODS-2 and ODS-5 or NFS-cached).

```
CacheDirLength number-of-characters-per-subdirectory-name
```

Again, this probably has file-system performance implications, but you'll have to experiment to see what they are. Default is 1.

```
CacheForceCompletion percentage
```

If the transfer of a document is canceled—user pushes stop button or closes window—the file will still be cached if it was at least `percentage` complete. `Percentage` is the bare integer—no % sign; default is 90. At 100, only files that were completely delivered will be cached.

```
NoCache *|word|host|domain [word|host|domain] ...
```

The NoCache directive takes a list of words, hosts, and/or domains, separated by spaces. HTTP and nonpassworded FTP documents from matched words, hosts, or domains are not cached by the proxy server. "*" disables caching completely. Partial matches are supported, so if you list "green," that will keep you from caching anything from greenbaypackers.com, greenpeace.org, SimpleGreen.com, or any file with green in the name.

At startup mod_proxy guesses which of the parameters might be host names and does a DNS lookup, caching the IP addresses and treating them as nocache as well. This makes it difficult to cache stuff from one name-based virtual host on a system and not from another.

(I have not discussed the two directives that let you adjust IP buffer size, because one of them isn't implemented until Apache 1.3.24, which is later than the 1.3.20 CSWS version, and because I'm not sure the VMS IP stacks would support it anyway.)

11.3.2 OSU

OSU provides two different tools, both somewhat experimental, for proxying. One is a CGI script that only does proxy (equivalent to `ProxyPass` in Apache); the other is a persistent DECnet object that does the same kind of processing. Neither one caches the result, and neither one leaves a trail in the headers.

The CGI script is proxygw.c, found in the script_code directory. You can build it (along with various other goodies) by setting default to [OSU.SCRIPT_CODE] and then issuing

```
$ @BUILD_UNSUPPORTED.COM
```

Copy or rename proxygw.exe to [OSU.BIN], your CGI directory. Add the following rules:

```
PROXYSCRIPT    /HTBIN/PROXYGW/*
PROXYLOG       /path-to-logfile
```

to your HTTP_MAIN.CONF and give it a try. (Internet Explorer on a PowerBook gave me three choices of proxy types for this; the one labeled "Normal" as distinct from "Tunnel" or "Socks" was the one that worked.) If you leave out the PROXYLOG directive, you'll log into your ACCESSLOG-specified file.

For the full-featured proxy program, setup is a little more complicated. You need to compile and link the proxy_server.c file found in the [.PROXY_CODE] subdirectory. Set default to that subdirectory.

```
$ CC PROXY_SERVER.C /PREFIX=ALL
$ LINK PROXY_SERVER/OPT ! uses the proxy_server.opt
linker options
```

Copy or rename proxy_server.exe into the [.SYSTEM] directory.

Modify your HTTP_STARTUP.COM so that in the part that SYSTEM executes, you

```
$ DEFINE/SYSTEM/EXEC WWW_PROXY_OBJECT WWWPROXY
```

Edit the WWWPROXY.COM file. There's a sample in the [PROXY_CODE] directory, but the real one is in the OSU root directory. Define these logical names:

```
WWW_PROXY_ACCESS
```

This is a multivalued logical containing node::username pairs, which will be authorized to connect to the proxy server. This needs at minimum to be this_node::http_server_account. If you want to have one proxy server accessed by multiple nodes over DECnet, you'll have to put all those values in there.

```
WWW_PROXY_LOCALHOSTS
```

This is a multivalued (comma-separated) list of hosts that are truly local (e.g., hosted by the same host). Include port numbers if necessary. This will tell the server to serve that content directly, not go through proxy processing for it. Defaults (in WWWPROT) to current host name.

```
WWW_PROXY_LOG
```

This is the fully specified name for the log file, including device specification. (WWW_SYSTEM:PROXY.LOG would work.)

```
WWW_PROXY_LOG_LEVEL
```

This is the trace level for logging. Defaults to 0.

```
WWW_PROXY_CLIENT_LIMIT
```

is the maximum number of concurrent clients allowed. Default is 32.

```
WWW_PROXY_TARGET_TIMEOUT
```

is the maximum number of seconds to allow for a remote transaction. Defaults to 600 seconds (ten minutes).

Add the following Web server configuration rules to HTTP_MAIN.CONF.

```
PROXYSCRIPT /proxy_gateway/
EXEC /proxy_gateway/ 0::"0=WWWPROXY"
```

Use HTTP_STARTUP to restart the server and you should have the proxy gateway in place.

Either of these proxy systems runs forward or reverse. If you want to limit proxy access to forward only, use a

```
HOSTPROT proxyfile.prot
```

to limit access to your local network. (See Chapter 7 for details.) If you want to run reverse as well, don't protect the file.

OSU's proxy processors appear to leave the headers pretty much alone.

11.3.3 WASD

As with Apache, WASD capabilities include standard proxy, reverse proxy, and proxy caching. You can specify the directory structure of the on-disk cache, say where it is (RAM disk, if you have lots more memory than you're using otherwise), how much space it should be allowed to use on disk, and when garbage collection should be triggered. WASD mapping and authorization rules provide control over access to the proxy services themselves, as well as to what may be accessed via the proxy, allowing implementation of a site policy on Web access.

Here are WASD's proxy-cache related directives.

```
[ProxyForwardedBy] ENABLED|DISABLED
```

controls the presence of a "Forwarded:" header line added to the request. The added header line would look like "Forwarded: by http://host.name.domain (HTTPd-WASD/n.n.n OpenVMS/AXP Digital-TCPIP SSL)". This is disabled by default.

```
[ProxyHostLookupRetryCount] numeric-count
```

indicates how many times to retry a DNS lookup for the requested site before giving it up. The retries come at five-second intervals; two or three should be sufficient. Default is 0.

```
[ProxyReportLog] ENABLED|DISABLED
```

determines whether to report significant proxy-processing activities, such as cache maintenance.

```
[ProxyReportCacheLog] ENABLED|DISABLED
```

controls reporting of proxy caching activity to the server process log.

```
[ProxyServing] ENABLED|DISABLED
```

enables or disables proxy serving on a whole-server basis, regardless of any proxy services that might be configured.

```
[ProxyCacheFileKBytesMax] file-size-in-kilobytes
```

indicates how big a file has to be before you're not willing to cache it; by default, that's 64KB.

```
[ProxyCacheRoutineHourOfDay] hour|NONE
```

A routine cache purge is equivalent to garbage collection. The server takes a sweep through the cache headers, sees which files have expired and which haven't, and then revalidates the expired files if possible.

The parameter is the integer hour of day to run a routine cache purge. You can leave it blank or set it to something nonnumeric in order to dissuade the server from doing routine purges, which makes it your responsibility to schedule cache purges youself.

```
[ProxyCacheDeviceCheckMinutes] minutes
```

indicates how many minutes apart the server will check the amount of available space on the cache device. If space is not available, then an immediate garbage collection pass is instituted.

```
[ProxyCacheDeviceDirOrg] FLAT256|64X64
```

specifies how the cache-device directories will be organized. `FLAT256` makes a single-level structure with as many as 256 directories below it. `64x64` makes a top level of 64 directories, each with as many as 64 below it. `FLAT256` was a drawback on machines prior to the ODS-2 optimization that had a distinct knee in file-handling performance as soon as the directory got too big to cache in memory.

```
[ProxyCacheDeviceMaxPercent] percentage
```

If the cache device is this full, drastic measures are indicated. The server will only allow this percentage in use on the cache device before a reactive purge is scheduled. When this limit is exceeded, no more cache files are created. Use the bare integer, no percent sign (defaults to 85).

```
[ProxyCacheDevicePurgePercent] percentage
```

indicates what percentage the server will attempt to reduce usage by when a reactive purge is run (defaults to 1).

```
[ProxyCacheNoReloadSeconds] seconds
```

Prevents `pragma: nocache` reloads from actually retrieving the file from the source host until the period expires and limits concurrent reloads of files into cache. Thirty seconds is probably a good value.

```
[ProxyCachePurgeList] hours[, hours, ...]
```

The argument is a comma-separated list of integers specifying the sequence of last accessed period in hours used during proxy cache purging, whether routine or reactive, (default: 168,48,24,8,0). This means that the server will first trim all files with as much time in the cache as the largest number of hours listed, and then go down to the second count if more free space is still needed.

```
[ProxyCacheReloadList] hours[, hours, ...]
```

A list of comma-separated integers representing the sequence of age in hours used when determining whether a cache file's contents should be reloaded (default: 1,2,4,8,12,24,48,96,168). This list actually demarcates a series of ranges that determine the frequency with which a file is refetched, or at least rechecked, from the origin, based on the file's age in cache, upon a request. The default list would result in a file 1.5 hours old being reloaded every hour, 3.25 hours old every 2 hours, 4–8 hours old every 4 hours, and so on. Files not reloaded since the final integer, in this example 168, are always reloaded.

```
[ProxyHostCachePurgeHours] hours
```

specifies the frequency (every *x* hours) at which the cache of host names to IP addresses is purged.

Some proxy maintenance activities can be initiated from the command line, either interactively or in a batch job.

```
$ HTTPD /PROXY=PURGE=ROUTINE
```

initiates a routine purge. Since hours aren't specified, this form uses the hours from `[ProxyCachePurgeList]`.

```
$ HTTPD /PROXY=PURGE=ROUTINE=168
```

specifies the maximum age explicitly, overriding the `[ProxyCachePurge-List]` hours. Anything older than the specified number of hours is removed.

```
$ HTTPD /PROXY=PURGE=REACTIVE=80%,168,48,24,8,0
```

You can initiate a "reactive" purge, which will work down through the list of hours until the space utilization on the device is down to the specified percentage. If you put a number with a percent sign (80%, in the example) in the previous list, that overrides the configured percentage, and the rest of the items are considered to be the list, overriding the `[ProxyCachePurge-List]` value.

```
$ HTTPD /PROXY=CACHE=STATISTICS
```

scans to collect cache statistics. If you really want to tune your proxy cache, you'll monitor your statistics regularly.

12

Managing and Understanding Your Server Logs

Most Web servers, including the ones under discussion here, log accesses in a standard format. (You can generally customize how much information gets logged, and further on I'll discuss the commands for how to do that. If you're considering a customized log-file format, though, you'd better have a plan for what you're going to do with it; many log-file analysis tools understand only the standard formats.)

A typical log entry will have the IP address of the originator, the URL requested, and the status returned. Counting the 200 status lines gives you a rough indication of how many hits you had. However, each page you serve will probably result in multiple entries in the log file—one for the actual page and one each for any images linked in the page.

Apache and WASD offer cookie-based user-tracking features that generate a unique user ID, which you can use to track "visits" rather than hits (this won't work if cookies aren't enabled on the browser). (Some Perl modules exist for session tracking that fall back to URL-encoded IDs if cookies aren't enabled, but they're not core browser functionality so I won't document them here.) In addition to access logs, your server can generate error logs, which are useful in identifying and solving problems.

12.1 Customizing your logging

You can locate your log files where you want them. (In a high-performance configuration you'll want to put them on a different disk and ideally on a controller different from either your Web content or your server executables, since a heavily laden site will generate a lot of I/O in just logging activity.) You can also configure what will be included in your log files, in what format, and how often a new log file will be created (although this turns out to require some cleverness in OSU and Apache).

It's worth pointing out that the server logs are just big sequential ASCII files. They're quite human-readable, and the formats are very portable—you could FTP your log files to a UNIX or Windows machine for analysis, if you wanted. You can do some primitive log-file analysis with the DCLSEARCH command. Web server log-files get big very quickly, since, depending on the format you choose, you might log 80 to 200 bytes worth of data for each file you serve.

You can choose whether to log all access to the server in the same log, to log each virtual hosts/localaddress/service separately, to log different kinds of access (proxying, SSL) separately, and more.

12.2 Log-file formats and locations

Two well-known log-file formats are the Common format, which lists client-IP, user name if available (through ident), user name if available (through HTTP authentication), time request completed, request from client, scheme, status, and number of bytes transferred); the Combined format (which appends Referer and User-Agent to the Common format); and, less well known, the Common_Server format, which is Common with the host name of the server appended to the end. (Common_Server is interesting either when you have a lot of virtual hosts appending to the same log file and you want to break down the requests by virtual host, or when you have multiple cluster nodes, perhaps sharing a cluster alias, appending to the same log file and you want to determine which box serviced which requests—to find out, among other things, if your load-balancing is working.)

Log-file analysis tools can deal happily with any one of these formats, which are provided by most Web servers. If you want to use some other format, Apache and WASD make it easy to do so, but think carefully about why you're doing it and how you'll interpret the files before you customize.

12.2.1 Apache

You can do everything (format, location, decision whether or not to log) with the single `CustomLog` directive, but the `LogFormat` and `TransferLog` directives are also available to you and may make life more convenient when dealing with virtual hosts. (`CookieLog` is also available, but deprecated, so I won't discuss it.)

You can define a format (using either `LogFormat` or `CustomLog`) and give it a nickname by which other log directives can refer to it. If you want the same log formats in every virtual host but different log files, use `Log-`

Format to define the format serverwide and CustomLog to create a new log for each host. (You can also use the LogFormat to set the default format, which will be used by subsequent CustomLog or TransferLog directives.)

A log format string is set off by double quotes, the contents of which are interpreted not unlike a C-language format string. Table 12.1 (taken from the Apache.org on-line docs for mod_log_config) indicates the format specifiers and their meanings. If you're planning to use Common or Combined log formats, you can skip this.

Table 12.1 *Format Specifiers for Apache Logs*

Element	Meaning
%...a:	Remote IP address
%...A:	Local IP address
%...B:	Bytes sent, excluding HTTP headers
%...b:	Bytes sent, excluding HTTP headers. In CLF format (i.e., a "-" rather than a 0 when no bytes are sent).
%...c:	Connection status when response is completed "X" = connection aborted before the response completed "+" = connection may be kept alive after the response is sent "-" = connection will be closed after the response is sent
%...{FOOBAR}e:	The contents of the environment variable FOOBAR
%...f:	File name
%...h:	Remote host
%...H	The request protocol
%...{Foobar}i:	The contents of Foobar: header line(s) in the request sent to the server
%...l:	Remote log name (from identd, if supplied)
%...m	The request method
%...{Foobar}n:	The contents of note Foobar from another module
%...{Foobar}o:	The contents of Foobar: header line(s) in the reply
%...p:	The canonical port of the server serving the request
%...P:	The process ID of the child that serviced the request
%...q	The query string (prepended with a ? if a query string exists, otherwise an empty string)

Table 12.1 *Format Specifiers for Apache Logs (continued)*

Element	Meaning
`%...r:`	First line of request
`%...s:`	Status. For requests that got internally redirected, this is the status of the *original* request --- %...>s for the last.
`%...t:`	Time, in Common log format time format (standard English format)
`%...{format}t:`	The time, in the form given by format, which should be in strftime(3) format (potentially localized)
`%...T:`	The time taken to serve the request, in seconds
`%...u:`	Remote user (from auth; may be bogus if return status [%s] is 401)
`%...U:`	The URL path requested, not including any query string
`%...v:`	The canonical ServerName of the server serving the request
`%...V:`	The server name according to the UseCanonicalName setting

In this table, the ellipses ("...") in the format string are not to be taken literally. They're either omitted entirely (so "%h %u") or can have conditions for inclusion of the item (which, if not met, will replace the item with "-").

The conditions are a comma-separated list of HTTP status codes; you can either match a code from the list or negate the whole list with a leading "`!`". For example, `"%400,501{User-agent}i"` logs the contents of the User-agent header on requests that produced 400 and 501 errors, while `"%!200,304,302{Referer}i"` logs the contents of the Referer header on requests that didn't return some normal status (so you can tell what pages have bad links on them).

Common format looks like this:

```
"%h %l %u %t \"%r\" %>s %b"
```

Combined format looks like this (note the quotes escaped with backslash):

```
"%h %l %u %t \"%r\" %>s %b \"%{Referer}i\" \"%{User agent}i\""

LogFormat format-string nickname
```

In this form, the `LogFormat` directive defines a format string and associates it with a nickname, which can be referred to by other directives. It does not set a default format.

```
LogFormat format-string
LogFormat nickname
```

Either of these forms sets the default log format, either defining the log format or referring to a previously defined log format by nickname.

```
CustomLog file format|nickname [env=[!]environment-
variable]
```

The `CustomLog` directive lets you specify the log file path relative to the `ServerRoot`. (A typical value is logs/accesslog, which puts it in the logs subdirectory; you can make a separate log file subdirectory for each virtual host or adjust the file name per host, as you choose. Unless you're an ISP and your clients want their very own log files to play with, you may as well do all your logging into one log file; it makes management easier, and it's easy enough to break the log out by host later.) Where I have "file," the Apache documentation has "file or pipe"; Apache on UNIX can open a pipe to another program, which can deal with the log in the manner desired. That's not a very VMS-like thing to do.

You can log, or not, based on the value of an environment variable (which can be virtually anything if you use `SetEnvIf`.) Here is an example from the mod_log_config documentation:

```
SetEnvIf Request_URI \.gif$ gif-image
CustomLog gif-requests.log common env=gif-image
CustomLog nongif-requests.log common env=!gif-image
```

The `SetEnvIf` says that if the request matched a regular expression that translates to "ended with .gif", set the gif-image variable to true. The first `CustomLog` logs just the requests for gifs into gif-requests.log; the second logs every request other than those into nongif-requests.log.

```
TransferLog file
```

This directive uses the default format established by the most recent `LogFormat` directive that didn't define a nickname and logs into the file (again relative to `ServerRoot`) specified. It defaults to Common format if no format has been specified.

```
HostNameLookups On|Off
```

Must be on if you want to log host names rather than numeric-IP addresses. (Even with it on, you'll get a certain number of numeric-IPs, either because of DNS failures or because there is no corresponding DNS entry for the host name.)

12.2.2 OSU

In OSU you can specify either Common (the default) or Combined formats; no other options are available. You can include `ACCESSLOG` or `PROXYLOG` directives inside `LOCALADDRESS` blocks to get different logs for each virtual host, either by directory or by file name.

```
ACCESSLOG vms-style-file-name  [0,1]
```

You can have a serverwide access log or a different one for each localaddress block. The file name (e.g., www_system:accesses.log) is mandatory. The optional number (actually a bitmask, but with only two choices it doesn't make much difference) is the choice of format: 0 is the Common file, 1 is the Combined file.

```
PROXYLOG  vms-style-file-name  [0,1]
```

This takes the same arguments as `ACCESSLOG`. If `PROXYLOG` is omitted, proxy requests are logged to the `ACCESSLOG`.

```
DNSLookup On|Off
```

While this parameter affects more than logging—name-driven host-based access control is the other significant aspect—your log files will have only numeric-IP addresses unless `DNSLookup` is `On`. If your server is very heavily loaded, you may want to turn `DNSlookup Off` to save a little processing effort and then postprocess your log files from the numeric-IPs later.

12.2.3 WASD

WASD allows you to pick a name for the log file if you have only a serverwide log file and don't enable periodic log-file rollover. If you have separate logs for each service, `[LogPerService]` lets you specify elements from which a log-file name can be derived, which will include the port number unless you enable `[LogPerServiceHostOnly]`. If you enable periodic logfile rollover, that will also affect the naming scheme, and only the directory you've specified for logging is used in determining the file name.

WASD predefines COMMON, COMMON_SERVER, and COMBINED log formats and also allows user-defined formats. You can specify a log format either in the configuration file with `[LogFormat]` or at startup time with the `/FORMAT=` qualifier. The log-file format string will look curiously familiar to people who've worked with the $FAO system services. The string must begin with the character to use if a specified field is unavailable, typically "-". What goes in a string is either a substitution field (begins with "!") or a formatting character (begins with "\"). (See Table 12.2.)

Table 12.2 *WASD Format Strings*

Element	Meaning
`!AR`	authentication realm (if any)
`!AU`	authenticated user name (if any)
`!BB`	bytes in body (excludes response header)
`!BY`	bytes in response (includes header)
`!CA`	client address
`!CN`	client host name (or address if DNS lookup disabled)
`!EM`	request elapsed time in milliseconds
`!ES`	request elapsed time in fractional seconds
`!ID`	session track ID
`!ME`	request method
`!PA`	request path ONLY (not query string or script)
`!QS`	request query string (if any)
`!RF`	referer (if any)
`!RQ`	complete request string (including script and query string, if any)
`!RS`	response status code
`!SC`	script name (if any)
`!SM`	request scheme (HTTP: or HTTPS:)
`!SN`	server host name
`!SP`	server port
`!TC`	request time (Common log format)
`!TG`	request time (GMT)
`!TV`	request time (VMS format)

Table 12.2 *WASD Format Strings (continued)*

Element	Meaning
`!UA`	user agent
`\0`	a null character (used to define the empty field character)
`\!`	insert an "!"
`\\`	insert a "\"
`\n`	insert a new line
`\q`	insert a quote
`\t`	insert a TAB

The Common log format looks like this:

```
-!CN - !AU [!TC] \q!RQ\q !RS !BY
```

The Combined log format looks like this:

```
-!CN - !AU [!TC] \q!RQ\q !RS !BY \q!RF\q \q!UA\q
```

Here are the relevant directives:

```
[Logging] ENABLED|DISABLED
```

controls whether the server logs anything at all. Defaults to disabled.

```
[LogFormat] COMMON | COMMON_SERVER | COMBINED | custom-format-string
```

defaults to "combined." Overridden by `/FORMAT=` startup qualifier. All logs use the same format string.

```
[LogPerService] ENABLED | DISABLED
```

defaults to `disabled`. If `enabled`, a separate log file is created for each service. Since services running on different ports are different services, port number is included in the log-file name.

```
[LogNaming] NAME | ADDRESS | HOST
```

applies only if `[LogPerService]` is enabled. Directs WASD on naming the per-service log files. NAME says to take the nodename portion of the DNSname of the service (so for `yourserver.yourdomain.tld` it takes "YOURSERVER"); this is the default. HOST takes as much of the full DNSname as will fit in an ODS-2 style file name, possibly

YOURSERVER_YOURDOMAIN_TLD, and ADDRESS takes the numeric-IP, so 192_168_10_0. The port number is appended to this unless

```
[LogPerServiceHostOnly]
```

is enabled.

```
[LogPerServiceHostOnly] ENABLED | DISABLED
```

controls whether per-service log files have port numbers in their names. Disabled (i.e., include port numbers) by default.

```
[LogFile] VMS-style-logfile-name
```

defaults to HT_LOGS:, a logical defined by the server startup to be the HT_ROOT:[LOG] directory, but you can override that. If you put in a log-file name, it may be overridden by other processing, especially log-file rotation processing.

```
[LogFileExtend] 0-65535
```

indicates the number of blocks to have RMS extend the log file by whenever it needs to be extended. Values below 0 (the default) are treated as 0, above 65,535 are treated as 65,535. (If 0, RMS will take the extend quantity set as the default for the WASD process, if any, or systemwide.) Setting this higher helps reduce file-system overhead, because larger extend quantities mean fewer extends but may waste disk space if set too large.

```
[LogExcludeHosts] host[,host...]
```

gives a comma-separated list of hosts not to log activities from. Useful if you want to keep your developers from polluting your page view statistics.

```
[DNSLookup] ENABLE|DISABLE
```

must be enabled to be able to log host names rather than numeric-IP.

12.3 Log-file rotation

12.3.1 Apache

Be careful with the Apache log files. Multiple server processes can update the log file, sometimes interrupting each other, so it's not safe to just rename the existing log to something (or somewhere) else. You need to make a new version, using

```
$ @sys$startup:apache$config NEW
```

(which will produce new versions of all access and errorlog files), then rename or copy the old versions.

```
$ @sys$startup:apache$config FLUSH
```

will flush any existing but unwritten log entries out to the existing log files.

You can set up a periodic batch job to issue the relevant command. (There are various freeware tools resembling UNIX "cron," which will conveniently run jobs at periodic intervals—every hour, every day, every Monday, or first Monday of the month. KRONOS is a good one on the Freeware Tools. This is a good application for that. You don't want to spend a lot of time debugging the code that reschedules the batch job.)

12.3.2 OSU

OSU successfully serializes access to its log file. You can flush and close the current log file with

```
$ privrequest [command-port] NEWLOG [server-port]
```

This can also easily be put in a periodic batch job. (I have a "monthly new logs" file that runs from the system account and does this, also creating a new ACCOUNTNG.DAT and a new AUDIT.LOG.)

Then move whatever.log;-1 to wherever you want it, either through `COPY` or `RENAME`, and if desired run a log-file analysis tool on it.

12.3.3 WASD

WASD will automatically create new log files for you on a daily, weekly, or monthly basis, controlled by the `[LogPeriod]` directive.

```
[LogPeriod] DAILY | weekday-name | MONTHLY
```

(This defaults to blank, or unused.) "Weekday-name" implies a new file every week on Monday, Tuesday, and so on.

The log file changes on the first request after midnight of the new period; in a weekly period, it changes on the first request after midnight of the named day.

An automatically created file will have a name that includes the date on which it was created, in YYYYMMDD format. The directory is taken from the `[LogFile]` directory, and the file name is then made up (if the log is serverwide) of host-name_port_yyyymmdd_ACCESS.LOG. Consequently for a server running on VMS.KICKS-ASS.NET on port 81, the log for

March 2002 would be named VMS_81_200203_ACCESS.LOG. If that server is running multiple services with a log per service and `[LogName]` set to HOST, the log for the same month would be VMS_KICKS-ASS_NET_200203_ACCESS.LOG if `[LogPerServiceHostOnly]` is enabled and VMS_KICKS_ASS_NET_81_200203_ACCESS.LOG if `[LogPerServiceHostOnly]` is disabled.

12.4 Unavoidable ambiguities and user tracking

There are limits to the precision with which the server can log activity. Some of the clients connecting to it may actually be proxy/cache servers. If 50 AOL users are looking at files from your site, you may log only one hit from the AOL proxy server. Your server has only served the files once, but you had 50 page views.

The desire to count actual page views has resulted in various cheesy tactics, such as setting and testing cookies just to make sure the client has to respond with something; this slows things down, and makes some users worry about privacy. (Alternatively, you can mark all your pages with a time-to-live of zero so the proxies won't cache them.) With these tactics, you still can't tell who exactly is trying to talk to you, but you can get a good idea of how many there are. These are supported in Apache and WASD, and I detail them below.

I think it's a better idea not to use that kind of thing and just accept that your logs may somewhat understate your actual hit count. (However, if you're selling banner ads and the number of page views actually matters directly in terms of income, then you might as well use the "transparent .gif" trick. Here, in addition to the link to the vendor's server where the ads reside, on each page with a banner you have a link to a useless but harmless image file that's always expired; the number of hits on that should be equal to the number of hits the banner ad vendor gets from your pages, so you have some rough measure of the page views you're delivering to the vendor.)

Once you get into cookies, you learn that there are different formats for them, starting with the original Netscape-defined format (which included a two-digit year) and going on to a couple of other formats. Not all browsers support all cookie formats. Cookies are available to hosts in a domain range you specify; if you say it's only for your host, then the browser won't return the cookie contents to any other system. If you're running on a cluster, you may want to specify a wider range so that if the next request is load-balanced to another system of yours, you can still identify the user. (You can't do this on CSWS 1.2 but probably can in the next release.)

12.4.1 Apache

All the cookie directives can apply serverwide within a `VirtualHost` container, within a `Directory` container, or within an .htaccess file. I'll refer to realm of applicability as the context.

```
CookieTracking on|off
```

If "on," Apache will send a user-tracking cookie for all new requests applicable to the context. (It recognizes new requests because the old ones return the cookie.)

```
CookieDomain domain
```

This directive was introduced in Apache 1.3.21 so is not available in CSWS 1.2, which tracks Apache 1.3.20. It's highly likely to be available in the next release of CSWS, so I'm including it here.

If this directive is absent, no domain is included in the cookie header field. The domain must begin with a dot and have at least one other dot within it. ".domain.tld" is legal, "server.domain.tld" is not, and neither is ".com". ".domain.tld" instructs the browser to return the contents of the cookie to any host in "domain.tld".

```
CookieExpires time-to-live
```

(In CSWS 1.2 the context is serverwide or virtual host; in later releases it should extend to directory and .htaccess files.)

This sets an expiration period—how far in the future the cookie will expire. It can be rendered either as a bare integer, in which case it's the number of seconds until expiration, or as a quoted string "`[n years] [n weeks] [n days] [n hours] [n minutes] [n seconds]`" where at least one element should be present, so "`10 years`," "`2 weeks 3 days`," "`7 hours 10 minutes 3 seconds`" are all legal.

If you don't specify a `CookieExpires` time-to-live, cookies go away as soon as the browser exits. (If you're really tracking visits rather than trying to find out about individuals, that's the behavior you'd prefer to have. The same person coming back tomorrow is a new visit.)

```
CookieName token
```

If you'd like your cookie to be named something other than "Apache," you can specify that name here. Use normal characters; upper- and lowercase letters, numbers, hyphen, and underscore are all legitimate.

```
CookieStyle Netscape | Cookie | Cookie2 | RFC2109 | RFC2965
```

This enables you to specify what style of cookie you want to use. The default is Netscape, which is the oldest and now deprecated format. Despite there being five styles shown, there are only two actual choices; Cookie is a synonym for RFC 2109, the syntax that came after Netscape; Cookie2 is a synonym for RFC 2965, which is the most current.

To actually log the cookie values, you need to either include the cookie header value in your log files or you can use `CustomLog` to create a separate log file logging just the cookie activity. The field identifier to include in another log specification is `%{cookie}n`,and a complete CustomLog directive for a separate log file named cookielog, logging cookie, request, and time is as follows:

```
CustomLog logs/cookie_log "%{cookie}n %r %t"
```

12.4.2 WASD

Tracking is enabled for the whole server with the `[Track]` directive. If you want to disable it for a particular service, you can use the "`;notrack`" parameter if the service is specified in HTTPD$CONFIG.CONF or the `[ServiceNoTrack] enable` directive in HTTPD$SERVICE.CONF. (It's disabled by default for proxy services, but you can reenable it with "`;track`" or `[ServiceNoTrack] disable`.)

```
[Track] ENABLED | DISABLED
```

enables or disables user-tracking cookies on a serverwide basis. Disabled by default.

```
[TrackMultiSession] ENABLED | DISABLED
```

If tracking is enabled, this enables cookies that (probably) won't go away when the browser shuts down. ("Probably," because some users carefully purge their cookie files, while others carefully don't let browsers write cookies out to files at all, and browsers are permitted to abandon cookies if they run out of disk space. So you can't count on finding these cookies again.)

```
[TrackDomain] domain
```

The domain must begin with a dot and have at least one other dot within it. ".domain.tld" is legal, "server.domain.tld" is not, and neither is ".com". ".domain.tld" instructs the browser to return the contents of the cookie to any host in "domain.tld". If you leave this out, only your server can see the contents of this cookie.

12.5 Error logs

The two things you want to do with error logs are to specify where to put them and to tell the server how much detail to go into. (When you don't have a problem, you don't want too much detail. These things get huge really fast, especially at debug levels, where you may get a line in the log for every comparison of a request with a mapping rule, resulting in hundreds of lines for every request.)

12.5.1 Apache

```
ErrorLog file-path
```

You can have a separate error log for each virtual host or one for the whole server. If the file path begins with a slash, then it's an absolute path so you can do `/otherdevice/logs/logfilename`, and if it doesn't begin with a slash, it's relative to `ServerRoot` so you can do `logs/error.log` if you prefer.

(UNIX allows reporting to syslog or opening a pipe to another process, but since there is no VMS syslog and not many ported programs that expect to read a pipe and write an error log, I'm not detailing that here.)

```
LogLevel emerg | alert | crit | error | warn | notice |
info | debug
```

This can be set for the whole server or by virtual host. The default is "`warn`"; and the recommended level is at least "`crit`". The options are listed in decreasing order of significance; "`emerg`" is emergency, "`crit`" is critical. Each lower level incorporates all the notices that would be seen in the higher level, so `crit` includes `emerg` and `alert`. "`debug`" will give you very large log files.

12.5.2 OSU

The name of the server error log is one of the startup parameters for the server. (In Chapter 5, I show how to set it to HTTP_ERRORS.LOG.) This is only serverwide, not settable by localaddress.

The level of detail for the error/trace log is a numeric parameter; the initial level can be set into the configuration files and dynamically adjusted with the `PRIVREQUEST` program. You can specify a trace-log file separately from the error log by editing the configuration file; you can't specify it in the SERVERMAINT Web-based administrator.

```
TRACELEVEL level [tracelogfile]
```

The trace-log file is optional, and if it is omitted, logging will go into the error log file as defined at startup. Level is a positive integer. Higher numbers will include the trace information shown by lower numbers. Zero (the default) will show only errors; 1 shows connection open and close; 6 shows script execution; and 11 shows the rule file translation steps, which will very quickly get you a large trace file. (Eleven is the highest number I've ever had call to use, but a quick trawl through the source code shows that the highest number referenced is 19, so if you want to see every possible trace message, use a level of 19 or higher.)

To dynamically change the trace level without stopping the server, use

```
$ PRIVREQUEST [manage-port] NEWTRACE/level [port]
```

This will create a new trace log if you've specified a trace log, or a new error log, flushing any buffered errors or traces before closing the old log.

While you can `$TYPE` or `$EDIT` the active error log, you may not see anything interesting for a while; for performance reasons, OSU is pretty lazy about updating the log. If you're trying to solve a particular problem with a high trace level, let it run for a time while you try the request, then issue another NEWTRACE command with a lower level so you can examine the trace.

12.5.3 WASD

WASD does not have a distinct error log file. It reports run-time and other selected errors directly into its process log, and can log significant items to OPCOM and the OPERATOR.LOG file. The WATCH utility (available from the Web-based Admin component or from the command line) takes care of the needs of tracing requests for debugging purposes. The relevant directives for OPCOM logging follow.

```
[OpcomTarget] NONE | messageclass
```

indicates the VMS message class for any OPCOM messages, which is one of: "CARDS," "CENTRAL," "CLUSTER," "DEVICE," "DISKS," "NETWORK," "PRINT," "SECURITY," "TAPES," or "OPER1" through "OPER12."

```
[OpcomAdmin] DISABLED | ENABLED
```

If enabled, this sets up OPCOM logging of ADMIN utility actions.

```
[OpcomAuthorization] DISABLED | ENABLED
```

If enabled, this sets up OPCOM logging of HTTP authorization failures and logouts.

```
[OpcomControl] DISABLED | ENABLED
```

If `enabled`, this sets up OPCOM logging of command-line (HTTPD/DO=) activity; it also reports if an insufficiently privileged account runs the image.

```
[OpcomProxyMaint] DISABLED | ENABLED
```

If enabled, this reports proxy cache maintenance activities.

```
[OpcomHTTPd] DISABLED | ENABLED
```

When enabled, this reports significant server events, such as startup and shutdown.

12.6 Tools to interpret your logs

Before you get all excited about the information you're going to be able to pull out of your logs, go to your browser and read the text posted at http://www.goldmark.org/netrants/Webstats/.

(It's an excellent rant from 1995 about why Web usage statistics are completely meaningless. A bit hyperbolic, but worth knowing about.) Similarly, the ANALOG site has the page http://www.analog.cx/docs/Webworks.html, which explains how the way the Web works defeats any attempt to gain absolute knowledge from your Web log.

12.6.1 LogResolve

`ftp://www-pi.physics.uiowa.edu/~dyson/Webalizer/logresolve.c`

LogResolve is a tool that reads log files (or standard input, or whatever) and copies them to its output with numeric-IP addresses converted into fully qualified domain names. If you have DNS lookups turned off in your Web server, you may want to do this before you analyze your log files.

Actually, even with DNS lookups enabled, you'll get some percentage of numeric-IP addresses in your log file. If, at the time you happened to do your lookup, the relevant DNS—which is often the one at the client's site, since it's likelier to be authoritative for the client's domain than yours is—was busy, down, or otherwise unavailable, your Web server didn't wait around until the DNS was up to serve and log the request. LogResolve can probably fix those, unless the DNS at those sites is coincidentally down when you run it. It can't do much about nodes that were never in the DNS at all, which do, definitely, exist, and running it ex post facto won't tell you with 100 percent certainty what the DNS would have said at the time of the transaction. If the node that looked you up is gone and something else is using the numeric-IP, you'll get the new value, not the old. None of this, actually, should be that big a deal. Just don't have a heart attack if there are entries LogResolve doesn't resolve.

12.6.2 Log-file analyzers

Log-file analysis tools help a lot in pulling comprehensible information from huge log files. They'll answer questions such as "How many unique visitors did I have?" and "What are my most popular pages?" and "Where is my traffic coming from?" (by showing top referrers), and they'll pull out hits that came via search engines; some will show you what search strings people were using to find you. Some of them will notice multiple hits from a particular visitor within a time range (a half hour, usually) and count it all as part of a single visit. They'll all show you nice usage graphs, usually broken down by hour, day, week, and month. Most can run either as CGIs or from the command line. Some can read gzipped (compressed) log files.

Some will keep a record of summary data, usually broken down by month, so that you can feed them log files with partial months or broken down on an irregular schedule (e.g., if you create a new one only when you notice the old one is too big), or if you have to roll them over daily but want only weekly or monthly statistics.

Rick Dyson maintains readily installable VMS versions of three popular log-file analyzers: ANALOG, Webalizer, and WUSAGE. They rely on public-domain libraries for GIF, PNG, and JPG drawing and for compression, so he keeps those libraries up on VMS as well. If you download the complete kit for any of these three, you'll get another copy of those libraries, so you might want to keep only one set of libraries after you've built all the tools you want to use. The libraries are very handy; you may well want them for Perl, Python, and PHP extensions.

Here's a hint for using any of these packages. If you unpack the zip file onto an ODS-5 disk, you may get all lowercase file names. This shouldn't be a problem—ODS-5 is a case-insensitive case-preserving file system—but it turns out that it is. MMS, at least in the version on my test machine, doesn't recognize a ".c" file as being a ".C" file, and it refuses to build these kits. I eventually did

```
$ RENAME [...]*.c *.C
```

at the top of the directory I'd unpacked the tools into, and I was then able to build it with no trouble.

12.6.3 ANALOG

```
http://www-pi.physics.uiowa.edu/~dyson/analog/
```

The program, written by Stephen Turner, has a home page at `www.analog.cx`. It is frequently updated, runs on many platforms, is very popular, and supports many different languages through language files. It can analyze the log file on the fly. (I just tried it on a DS20E, and it took about 90 seconds to process a 77-MB log file—a month's worth, logging over 400,000 requests.) At `www.reportmagic.org` there's a program that can work with ANALOG output and make very pretty results from it. You need MMS (or MMK) and a fairly current DEC/Compaq C compiler.

OSU comes with a nice DCL script to run ANALOG for you. Unfortunately, it works properly only with a very old version of ANALOG and will need rewriting if you want to use it against a current version.

Download the analog.zip file from the URL. I find Mozilla doesn't know how to deal with the FTP URL that gets to the actual zip file; it doesn't recognize the FTP server and can't figure out what commands to issue. The URL given is a page describing ANALOG. I used WGET to fetch the zip file. Unpack the ZIP file, and you get a directory tree under the current one, named ANALOG_5-22 (or whatever the version is). If you're on an ODS-5 disk, fix the case problem as described.

```
$ SET DEFAULT [.ANALOG-5-22.SRC]
$ @BUILD_VMS
```

This'll crank away for a fairly long time—it's building the graphics library as well as the program—and eventually report success. The compiled program is ANALOG.EXE.

ANALOG analyzes the log file you feed it, rather than doing incremental analysis. It can produce reports in any number of languages and very finely detailed reports as well. Although the program itself operates in batch mode (it reads a log file and produces HTML output), it comes with an HTML form and a Perl CGI program that will run ANALOG for you to produce reports on demand. You can also simply run a batch job whenever you roll over your log files and have the output placed in a Web-accessible directory or mailed to you.

Edit the configuration file, analog.cfg. Make at least the following changes:

```
LOGFILE logfile.log
```

Change logfile.log to a UNIXified path to your log file (e.g., /disk/directory/access.log) or leave it like this if your default is set to the directory your log file is in and the file is named logfile.log. For best results don't try to run ANALOG on the log file that's currently being updated.

```
LANGFILE /path-to-langfile
```

If you don't specify this, it defaults to UK, which would be okay except that there's apparently something funky in the subdirectory translation and ANALOG fails to open [ANALOG.ANALOG-5_22]lang/uk.lng and dies horribly. Specify a full path, not a partial one (e.g., "/dkb0/analog/analog-5_22/lang/us.lng").

```
DOMAINSFILE /path-to-domainfile
```

Similarly, ANALOG fails to open the default (lang/ukdom.tab) domain file. I made this "/dkb0/analog/analog-5_22/lang/usdom.tab." These errors occurred on an ODS-5 disk, and it might be different on an ODS-2 disk.

```
HOSTNAME "[my organization]"
```

Replace the contents of the quoted string with the name you want to have show up on the reports (e.g., "Alan's VMS Web server").

Remove or comment out the following line

```
UNCOMPRESS *.gz,*.Z "gzip -cd"
```

(Otherwise, ANALOG, which has been built without pipe support, will complain about not recognizing the UNCOMPRESS command. UNCOMPRESS works by opening a pipe to the UNCOMPRESS command, feeding it the compressed log file, and receiving the uncompressed form through the pipe. It's possible that you could build ANALOG with pipe support by going into BUILD_ANALOG.COM and defining PIPES as part of the CFLAGS definition. I haven't tried that. If it were going to work, you'd probably want to make the extension "*.*-gz", which is what the version of gzip that I got from the freeware CD names the compressed files it creates.)

```
PAGEINCLUDE filename.type
```

If you want filetypes to be counted in page views, you need a `PAGEINCLUDE` statement for each filetype. It comes with `PAGEINCLUDE *.shtml` present but commented out; I'd recommend adding or uncommenting:

```
PAGEINCLUDE *.shtml
PAGEINCLUDE *.htmlx
PAGEINCLUDE *.pl
PAGEINCLUDE *.php
PAGEINCLUDE *.cgi
PAGEINCLUDE *.com
```

and also adding

```
TYPEALIAS .htmlx  ".htmlx [Server-parsed HTML]"
```

so that if you have .htmlx files, they'll be presented in the correct part of the graph.

You can uncomment

```
#OUTFILE Report.html
```

and get the output created in your default directory, or use a UNIXified path name to put the report where you want it. (ANALOG processed the same file that took AWSTATS three hours in under a minute.) If you prefer to run ANALOG in a batch mode, you're now all set. Have your batch job

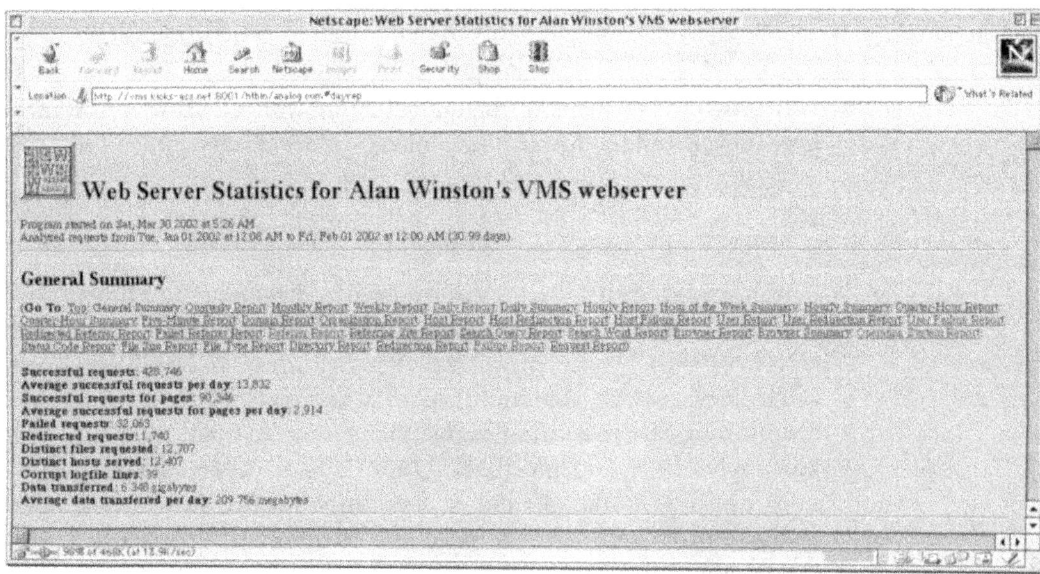

Figure 12.1 *ANALOG Ssummary report.*

mail you the file, or place it in a directory accessible to the Web server; the DCL wrapper can rename it to the month and year log file.

The following page explains in detail what the charts and reports mean: http://www.analog.cx/docs/reports.html.

Figure 12.1 shows the summary report, and Figure 12.2 shows the daily report with images enabled for the bar charts.

You can make ANALOG emit material suitable for import into a spreadsheet by using the line

```
OUTPUT COMPUTER
```

and set the field separator command with

```
COMPSEP separator-character
```

(Typical separator characters are comma for CSV files and "`\t`" for tab-separated files, which Excel seems to like.)

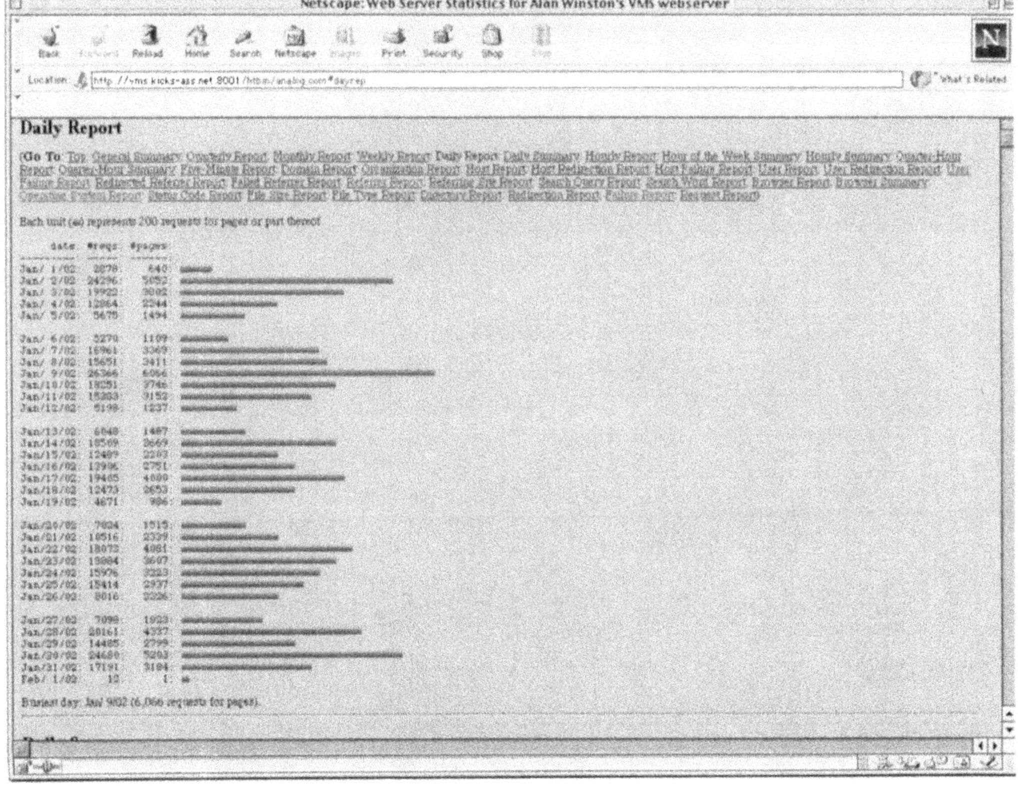

Figure 12.2 *ANALOG Daily Report.*

ANALOG can do incremental processing using cache files, which have a number of confusing features. Read http://www.analog.cx/docs/cache.html if you want to learn about cache files.

ANALOG should not be run directly as a CGI program; the distribution provides a Perl wrapper, which makes sure that it's passed no dangerous options. There's also a sample HTML form for selecting options. To run it you need to edit the Perl program and tell it where it can find ANALOG; it's going to open a pipe to it. The program is anlgform.pl. But there's nothing magic about Perl; you could examine the analog.com program that comes with OSU and tweak it to make it work with a modern ANALOG version. Figure 12.3 shows the OSU ANALOG menu.

The easiest way to edit the OSU program is to delete the configuration file included in the program and replace it with the contents of the configu-

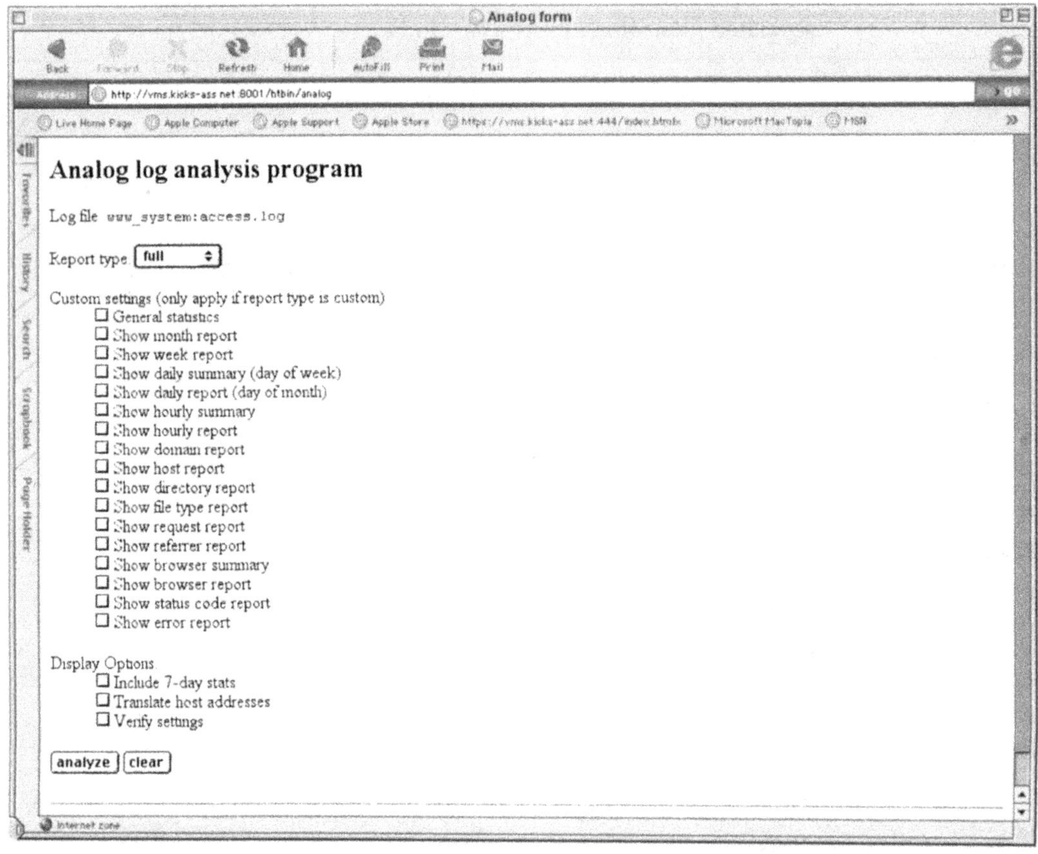

Figure 12.3 *OSU ANALOG menu.*

ration file you used to get it running in batch_mode. Change OUTPUT to NET_LINK: (for OSU, and for the OSU-compatible scripting in CSWS and WASD). If you want graphics, you need to put the provided bar-chart graphics in a Web-available directory and tell ANALOG where they are using IMAGEDIR. If you want ANALOG to make pie charts for you when the output is a nondisk device, you need to give it

```
CHARTDIR /URL-path-to-chart-directory/
LOCALCHARTDIR /file-system-path-to-chart-directory/
```

Remember to set `LOCALCHARTDIR` so that the Web server can read and write to it, and map the `CHARTDIR` path. (The charts will be in PNG format, so look at them with a PNG-capable browser. Alternatively, add `JPEGCHARTS ON` to get JPEGs instead.) Figure 12.4 shows what the pie charts look like.

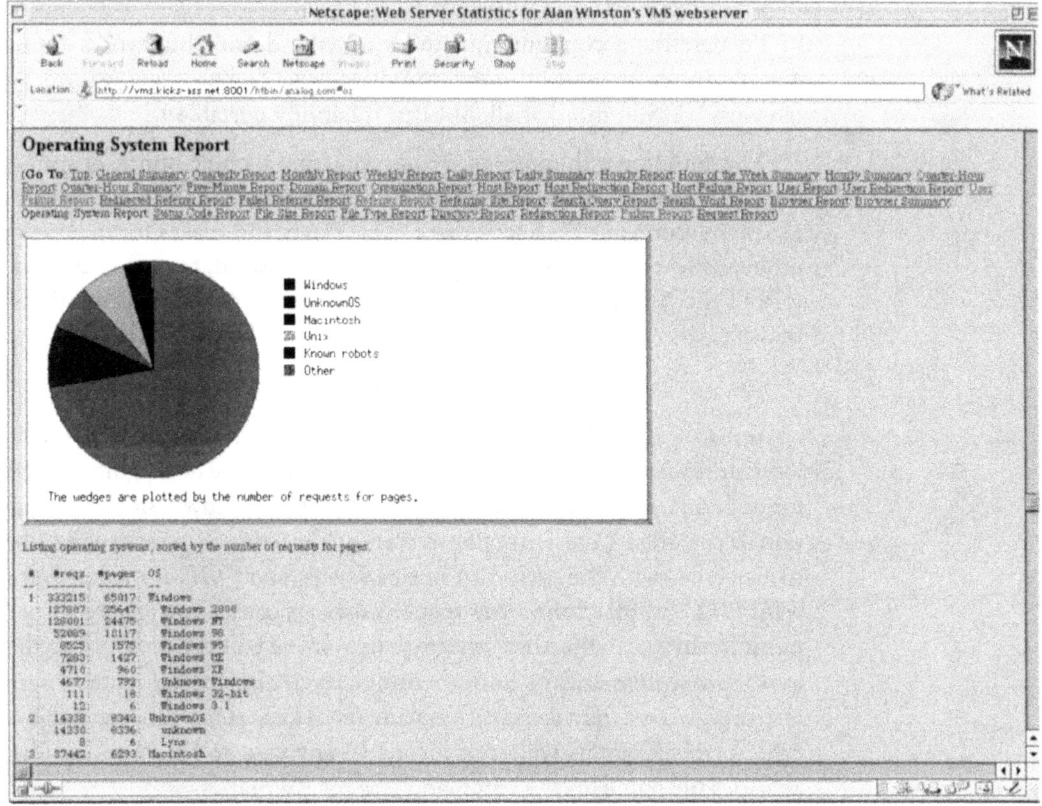

Figure 12.4 *ANALOG Operating System Report with pie chart.*

12.6.4 AWStats

```
http://awstats.sourceforge.net
```

AWStats (Advanced Web Statistics) is a large Perl program for reading log format files and producing interesting and useful charts and info. It handles Combined, Common, IIS, and Webstar formats and lets you define your own as well. I collected the gzipped tar archive, awstats-4_0.tgz, from sourceforge. I presume you've already gotten the gzip/gunzip and VMS tar tools from the freeware CD; they're pretty handy.

```
$ gunzip awstats-4_0.tgz
$ vmstar /extract awstats-4_0.tar /verbose
```

This creates a directory tree below the current level including all the scripts and icons needed. It's okay to set protection w:re on the entire tree—there's nothing very secret in there.

I'll describe a configuration that's not the default but works fine and doesn't clutter up your htbin/cgi-bin directory. (The program was not written with VMS in mind at all, but Perl is handily portable.)

The author was thinking of having you copy a whole bunch of stuff—all the icons, a whole subdirectory full of browser information, robot signatures, and so on into your Web server tree. That's ugly and makes for maintenance problems when you upgrade your Web server. Instead, map the icons directory of the AWStats tree into /awstatsicons/ (or some other value that you can specify in the AWStats file). For OSU or WASD, that looks like

```
map /awstatsicons/* dkb0:[awstats.awstats-4_0.wwwroot.icon]
```

You can have either a separate configuration file for each virtualhost/localaddress/service, which you certainly want if you're logging separately for each one, or a single configuration file. I'll show how a single configuration file works. (The virtualhost config file name is awstats.virtualhost-name.conf—with the periods. You can do this on an ODS-5 volume, if you want.) The vanilla config file name is awstats.conf. (You'll need either to put it in the same directory awstats.pl lives in, or edit the program so that it looks somewhere else, or do something clever with logical names to make /etc/opt/awstats, /etc/awstats, or plain /etc exist, since those are the only other places AWStats will look for it.) In any case you have to specify the statistics file name on the command line for AWStats.

Edit awstats.model_conf into awstats.conf, making these changes:

```
LogFile="/UNIXified path to log file"
```

Examples:

```
CSWS: LogFile="/apache\$specific/logs/access_log."
OSU:  LogFile="/www_root/000000/access.log"
WASD: LogFile="/ht_logs/access.log"
```

The CSWS example looks so odd because the file name is going into a Perl program, and when Perl encounters a dollar sign, under some conditions it will attempt to interpret what follows as a variable name. Therefore, we have a backslash in front of the `$` to "escape" it. Remember this trick, if you do much Perl programming this will come up a lot. (AWStats supports interpolating time elements into log-file names; read the comments in the config file for details.)

```
DNSLookup=1
```

This is set at zero by default; use this if you want it to resolve numeric-IP addresses in the log files. LogResolve might be faster.

```
DirData="."
```

This indicates where to store the data files it uses for incremental log analysis. This is set to /var/cache/awstats by default, which, of course, doesn't exist unless you want to define var as a rooted logical name pointing somewhere and create a cache subdirectory to it. A "." (quotes are needed) says put it in the same directory the file is in; if you prefer, create a subdirectory and use a relative path to it.

```
DirCGI="/Web server-path-to-this-directory"
```

This comes as "/cgi-bin," but that only works if you're in the Web server's own CGI directory. Use whatever directory name you mapped, (e.g., "/awstatbin").

```
DirIcons="/Web server-path-to-icon-directory"
```

This shows whatever you decided to alias the icons file to, such as "/awstaticon."

```
SiteDomain="server.domain.tld"
```

Leaving this blank is okay too. AWStats uses it to generate links in URLs in the report.

```
HostAliases="server.domain.tld 127.0.0.1 localhost"
```

This is a blank-separated list of other names the server might be called. It's used in order to be able to recognize referrer names that are actually this same server.

```
AllowToUpdateStatsFromBrowser=0
```

1 = yes, 0 = no. The update job may take a very long time, allowing the browser to time out. You're better off doing updates from a regular batch job. If you want to update from the browser, note that the DirData directory needs to be writeable by the Web server account (apache$www, http_server, http$server), and if you change your mind and do this later, you need to make the existing data files writeable.

```
SaveDatabaseFilesWithPermissionsForEveryone=1
```

This will store the database files world readable, allowing the Web server to get at them without your going through any special ACL setup. If you don't want them world readable, create an Access Control List, allow the Web server appropriate access, and set this value to 0.

You can go through the other items in the optional section of the configuration file and set them for yourself; they're described in the config file. For example, there's a value called `NotPageList`, which is a space-separated list of filetypes not to count as page views; by default that's "css js class gif jpg jpeg png bmp," but you might want to add more. The parameters I've listed are the mandatory ones to get this running.

AWStats would like to run with taint detection and suppression. (This is a Perl-specific thing that notices when the program is doing particular kinds of operations on data that could be hazardous because the data came from outside the program and haven't been laundered.) This is a good thing, but it complicates your life a little bit. AWSTATS.PL has a -T flag on the first line of the program. This means that it will refuse to run unless you invoke Perl with the same "-T" flag. (The flag has to be in literal double quotes because the C run time will otherwise automatically lowercase it, and Perl doesn't recognize a -t flag.) However, it may not work with the "-T" flag either. You can—and this is, I should admit here, bad advice—edit AWSTATS.PL and remove the -T flag from the first line of the code.

Now you should be able to run AWStats. Here's the command line (which will create the database files, which are confusingly named with the .TMP extension. They need to be permanent.) You can override the log file specified in the configuration file with -logfile file name.

```
$ perl awstats.pl -config=awstats.conf -update
```

Be aware that this can be really slow, which is why you don't want to do the update run from the browser. It took about three hours to process a 77-MB file on my 533-MHz EV56 Alpha.

If you're getting your historical data into the databases, make sure you run it on old log files in chronological order. The database files remember where they left off, and you can't go backward.

To get AWStats running as a CGI program, you'll need to write a DCL wrapper that lives in your standard CGI-BIN directory. (This is because AWStats insists on command-line variables such as the config file name. That means you can't readily run it in a higher-performance persistent Perl environment such as mod-perl, Webperl, or PERLrte.) The DCL can do the appropriate setup (discussed in general in Chapter 14), then $ SET DEFAULT to the AWStats directory and invoke Perl with the right command-line arguments.

Figure 12.5 shows AWStats running as a CGI on a UNIX system.

You'll have to do quite a bit of work to get AWStats running properly as a CGI on your VMS system. It does nicer graphs than ANALOG, but I'm

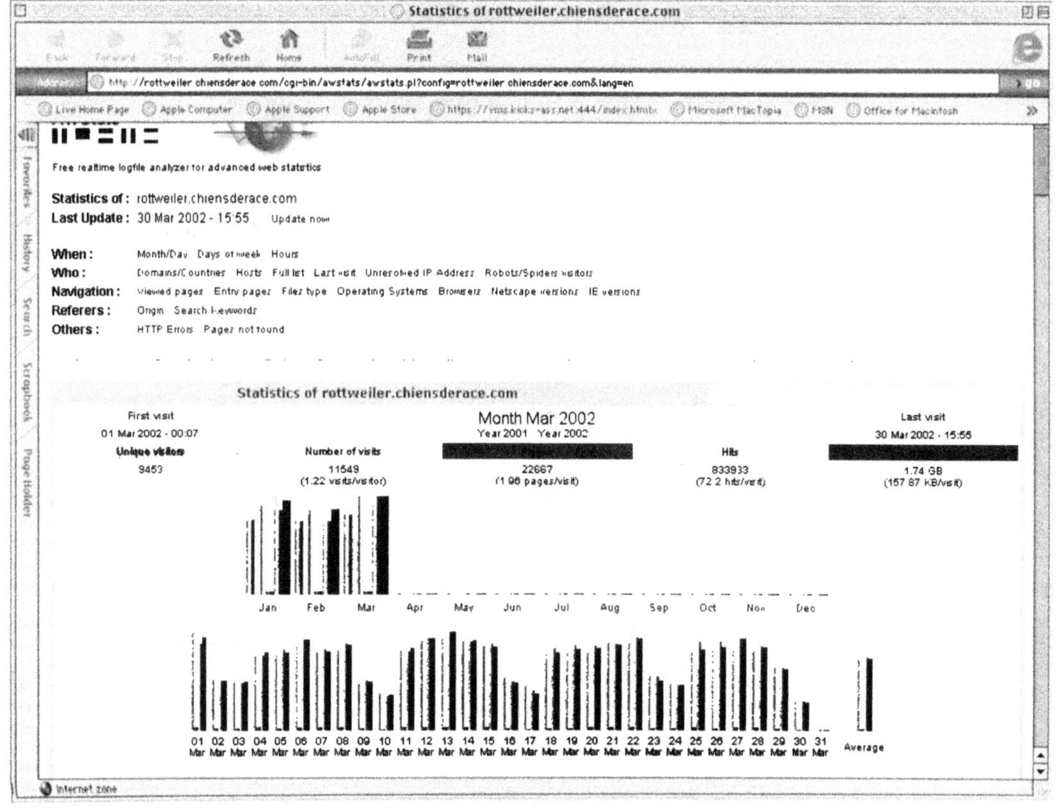

Figure 12.5 *AWStats.*

not sure you'll find it worth it, at least until the AWStats package works right out of the box.

12.6.5 Webalizer

```
http://www-pi.physics.uiowa.edu/~dyson/Webalizer/
```

The Webalizer is a log-file analysis program designed to be run in batch mode or from the UNIX command line. It creates HTML pages and graphics for charts. It can retain a summarized history file or do incremental processing on large log files. You'll get a big zip file; unzip it, and you'll get several libraries (lib-gd, lib-jpeg, etc.) and a Webalizer directory.

In the directory you unpacked everything into, do

```
$ MMS
```

to build the version that uses .PNGs, and

```
$ MMS jpeg
```

to build the version that uses JPEGs instead. The images are, respectively, WEBALIZER-PNG.EXE and WEBALIZER.EXE.

In the directory named after the version (currently [.WEBALIZER-2_01-09]), you'll find sample.conf. You should read all the readmes, but just to get a quick start, copy sample.conf to Webalizer.conf and then edit Webalizer.conf. You'll need to uncomment and change at least these settings.

```
LogFile    /var/lib/httpd/logs/access_log
```

Replace the path to the log file with an appropriate UNIXified path to your log file.

```
LogType clf
```

Actually, just uncomment this. CLF is an abbreviation for the Common Log Format.

```
OutputDir    /var/lib/httpd/htdocs/usage
```

This gives a UNIXified file-system path to a directory that your Web server can see and read. (I just made this `/dkb0/Webalizer`, which was the top level of the directory tree Webalizer was in, and mapped the directory.)

```
HistoryName          Webalizer.hist
```

If you want to build Webalizer summary history files, you specify the path here. If it's just a bare file name, it goes into the `OutputDir`.

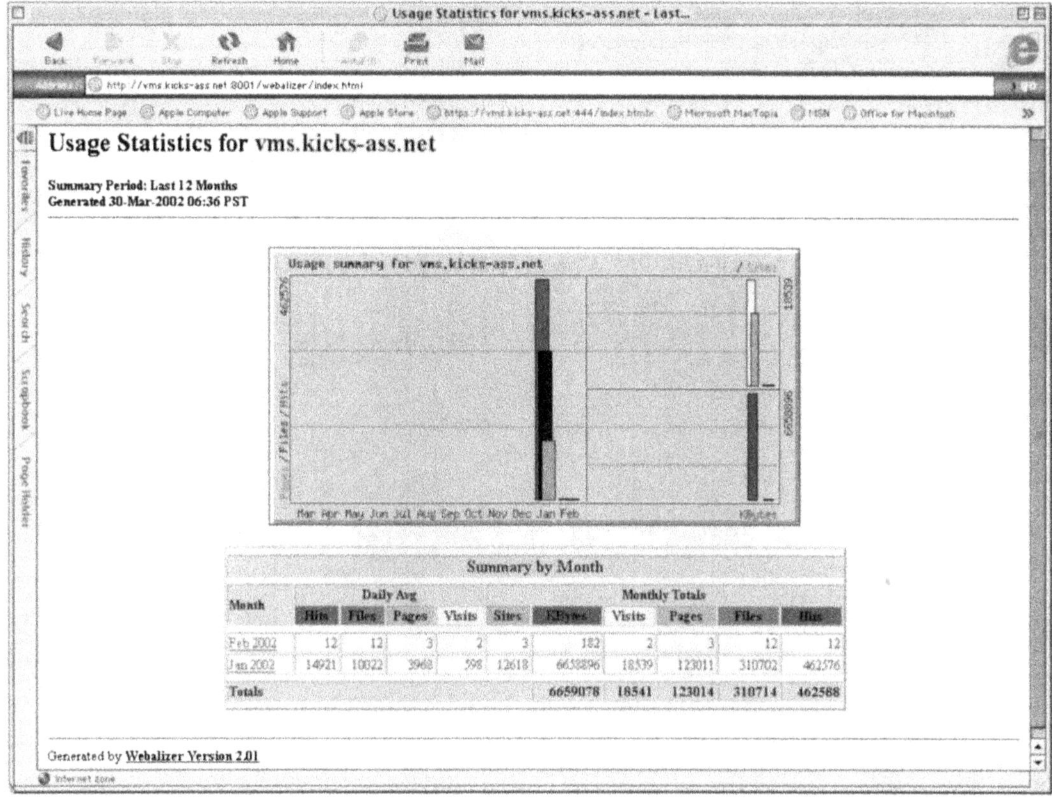

Figure 12.6 *Webalizer's index.html.*

```
HostName              localhost
```

Change this to the host name you want to show on the report. If you don't specify anything, Webalizer will do reverse DNS lookups and may not come up with the answer you want.

```
PageType              extension
```

If you want to make sure your view of pages agrees with Webalizer, add as many `PageTypes` as you need to cover the kinds of files you think count—shtml, htmlx, php*, pl, for example.

At this point, you can just `$ RUN WEBALIZER` and it will populate the OutputDir. Look at it with a browser. Figure 12.6 shows the generated index.html—I fed it only a January log file, so usage spikes in January. The summary line nicely shows the difference between computed page views and total hits. Figure 12.7 shows the 3-D graph summarizing the daily statistics.

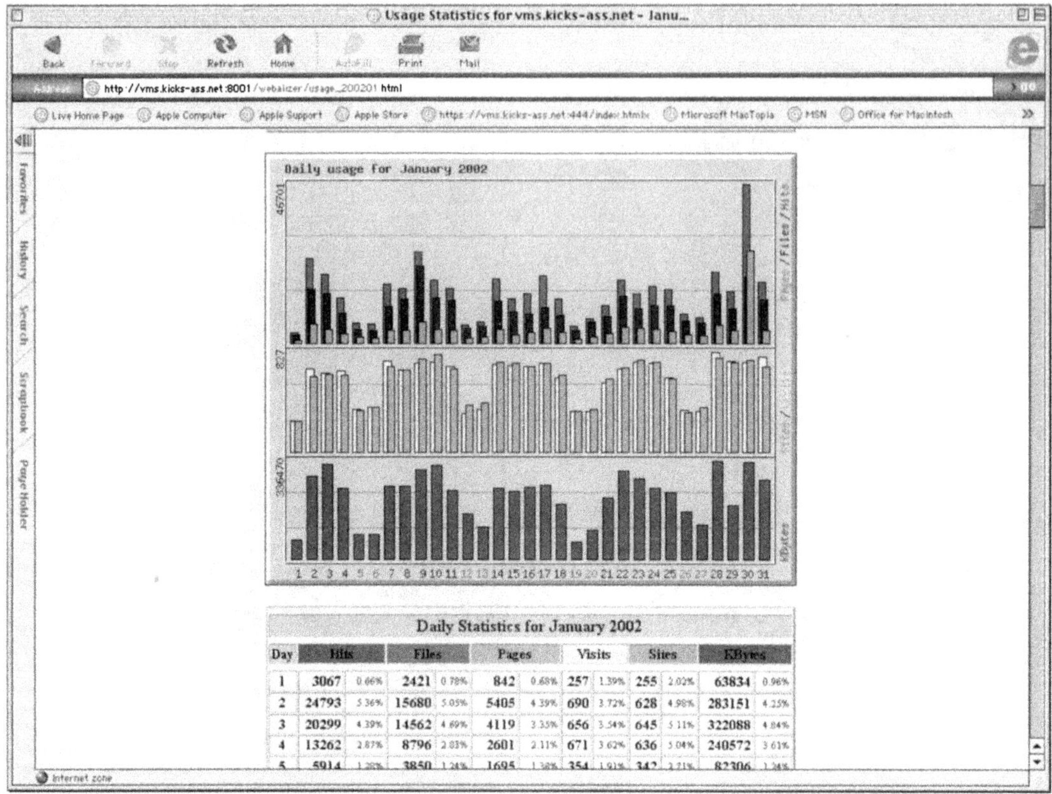

Figure 12.7 *Webalizer's 3-D graph of daily statistics.*

12.6.6 WUSAGE

```
http://www-pi.physics.uiowa.edu/WUSAGE-3_2-VMS.ZIP
```

Download the zip file from this URL. If you put it in $DISK1:[WUSAGE] and unpack it, you'll get [WUSAGE.WUSAGE-3_2A-VMS], so set the default there. (Alternatively, you can rename the lower-level directory to a higher level.)

To build with DEC/Compaq C, run

```
$ @MAKE_VMS
```

or with VAX C, run

```
$ @MAKE_VMS VAXC
```

or with GNU C (although I couldn't test this), run

```
$ MAKE_VMS GNUC
```

WUSAGE is a pretty old program and the most recent format it recognizes is the Common format. Run it in batch to prepare static HTML pages summarizing weekly usage. It will incorporate prefix and suffix files you specify to make the pages fit in with the standard look of your site, and it will place them in the directory you specify. It will also need to know how that directory is mapped to the Web server, since the pages will refer to image files (pie charts) that it creates and will need to know what URLs to precede them with. All this information is determined in the configuration file; if you want to do different servers, create different configuration files.

Edit wusage.conf, find the lines identified with the comments, and make the appropriate changes. Don't introduce any blank lines in your editing.

```
#Name of your Server as it should be presented
IowaSP
```

(Change `IowaSP` to your server, cluster, or institution name as you want it to show on the Web pages.)

```
#File to use as a prefix; MUST BE A COMPLETE FILE SYSTEM PATH.
#REALLY. NOT A URL.
/disk$www/www/wusage/prefix.html
```

That's a UNIXified file-system path; I used `/wusagedisk/wusage/wusage-3_2_vms/prefix.html`.

```
#File to use as a suffix; MUST BE A COMPLETE FILE SYSTEM PATH. REALLY.
#NOT A URL.
/disk$www/www/wusage/suffix.html.
```

That's another UNIXified file system path. I used `/wusagedisk/wusage/wusage-3_2_VMS/suffix.html`

```
#Directory where html pages generated by usage program should be located
/disk$www/www/wusage
```

That's another UNIXified file-system path; the directory needs to be mapped into the space the Web server can see, but this is the file system not the URL. I used `/wusagedisk/wusage`.

```
#URL to which locations of html pages should be appended for usage reports
#(the same as the first line, but in Web space, not filesystem space)
/wusage
```

This is whatever you decide to map in the Web server; it doesn't need to have wusage in the name anywhere if you don't want it to.

```
#Path of httpd log file
/disk$www/Web/logs/access.log
```

That's a UNIXified file-system path; for OSU it could be /www_root/access.log. However, WUSAGE won't read a log currently being updated, so you might want to put this in some other directory. It doesn't understand logs named by date, so this value is fixed unless you want to create an enclosing command procedure that defines the name specified in the configuration file to point somewhere else.

```
#Default domain (for named sites with no domain; should be
#our own domain)
#Top-level domain only (i.e., org not cshl.org)
edu
```

(Make this your own top-level domain.)

```
#Directories/items that should never register in the top ten
#To inhibit everything on a path, use /path*
{
}
```

The values here are URL paths, not file-system indicators, and wildcards are supported.

```
#items that should never register at *all*, even
#for the total access count
{
*/gifs/*
*/bckgrds/*
*/icons/*
*/usage_graph_small.gif
*/usage_graph.gif
}
```

Again, these are URL paths. If you want to count only page views, you're limited to figuring out what pages are (shtml, htmlx, html, htm, php, asp, .pl, cgi) and defining everything else in between the curly braces, one item per line. Suggested values would be

```
{
*.gif
*.jpg
*.jpeg
*.png
*.css
}
```

plus anything else on your site that you never want to count.

```
#Sites that should never register in the usage statistics
{
localhost
}
```

You might also include the host names of the workstations used by your Web developers and your Webmaster, if you want to avoid statistics polluted by the upload-view-tweak-upload cycle of development. Check your log files to see what the host names actually look like.

When you run WUSAGE, it will create a page for the statistics of every week with an entry in the log file and every week since then, so if you run it on old log files, you'll get a bunch of pages that show zero activity. See Figure 12.8 for a sample weekly page with pie chart.

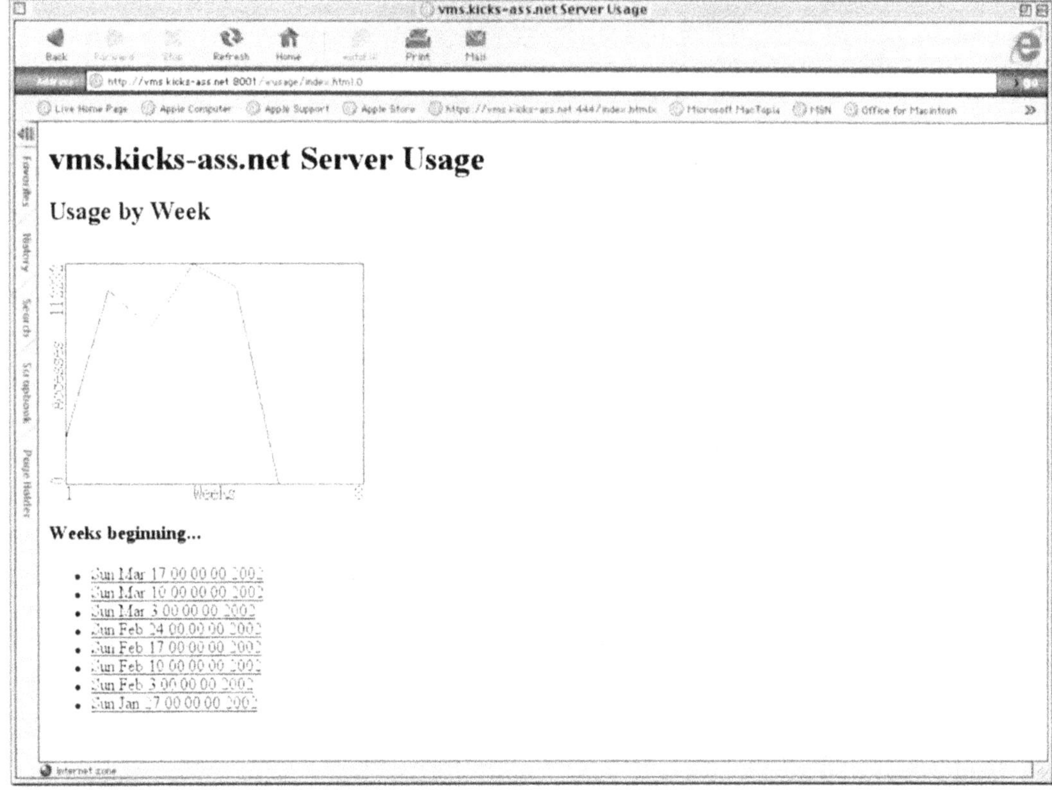

Figure 12.8 *WUSAGE's weekly page.*

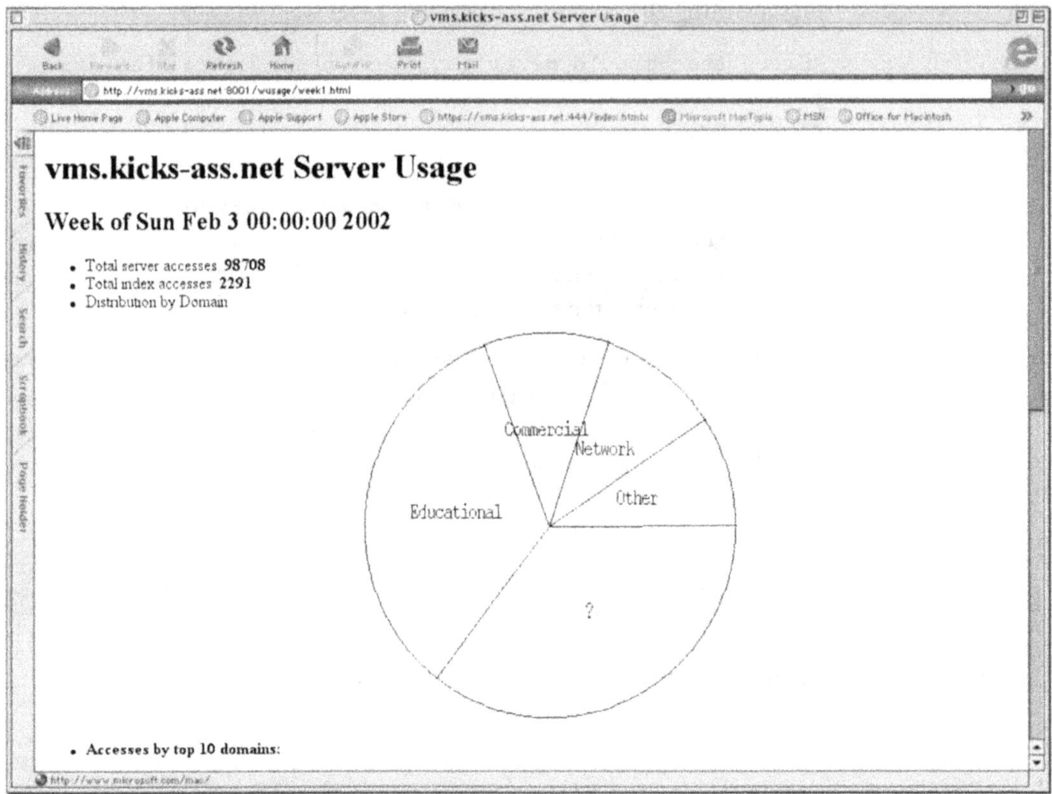

Figure 12.9 *WUSAGE's index.html.*

It also creates an Index.html, which lists each of the weekly pages it created. See Figure 12.9 for the Index.html page. The simplest mode, if you turn your log files over monthly, is probably to run WUSAGE immediately after rolling over the log file and just keep the statistics for that month online.

Arranging cumulative log file usage reports takes some cleverness, and you'll probably have to rename a bunch of the weekly pages and edit the index.html every time. This is a simple tool for reporting all the weeks in one log; if you push it past that, you'll end up doing a lot of work you wouldn't need to do using another tool.

13

Dynamic Content: Directory Browsing and Server-Side Includes

In this chapter, we'll discuss two ways to generate dynamic content on your site without getting fully into CGI scripting (covered in Chapter 14). Directory browsing displays the files that are currently present—or some subset—and different views may be available. Server-Side Includes (SSI) allow highly variable content presentation with a wide variety of techniques.

13.1 Directory browsing

In general, if the URL path translates to a directory name (without a "/"), the server automatically issues a redirect to the path with a "/" appended. If it's a directory with a "/" but no file name, the server looks for files matching the defined names of "Welcome" or "Index" files, and, if it finds one, serves it. If no Welcome file is found, servers will (if permitted to do so), dynamically generate a directory listing as an HTML document with clickable file names that will enable downloading the files, and serve that document out. The form of this document varies from server to server and may include icons representing the filetypes. You have some ability to configure the format in which file information is presented, the order the files are presented in, whether the listing is generated at all (either serverwide or for the particular directory), and whether the directory listing includes a prologue from a particular file.

A caveat: Users who know about directory browsing typically expect their actual file list to be completely hidden if a welcome file is present. WASD can be configured to allow directory browsing to be forced by strings in the URL even if a welcome file is present, so if you allow that, you need to be sure to educate your users.

A historical note: The original function of the World Wide Web was to facilitate easy exchange of files on unlike platforms, so directory browsing was present very early on. A directory listing was referred to as an index; it could either be automatically generated or be prepared in advance by the owner of the files. Thus, index.html is the name to look for in a directory if only the directory name has been presented—thus, also, ModAutoIndex and options `DirectoryIndex`, `Index`, and `FancyIndexing` in Apache. Let's look at the options available.

13.1.1 Apache

In Apache, if the URL path refers to a directory name, a query string can set the primary sort field and the direction of the sort if indexes are allowed on the directory at all. (That's "`/path/?query-string`", and the strings are of the form "`field=direction`"; the fields are "`N`" for file name, "`M`" for modification date, "`S`" for file size, "`D`" for description, and the directions are "`A`" for ascending and "`D`" for descending, so the values are "`N=A`", "`N=D`", "`M=A`", "`M=D`", and so on.)

I briefly discussed the `DirectoryIndex` command in Chapter 5. This is where you can set the names of index or welcome files, or set an action (overriding the server's automatic index generation) if you wish. The command can be used serverwide, virtual-hostwide, within a `<Directory>` or `<DirectoryMatch>` container, or within an .htaccess file in the directory itself if overrides are configured for that directory.

```
DirectoryIndex local-URL [local-URL ...]
```

`local-URL` can be just a file name (index.html, wilkommen.html) or a path; if you wanted to, you could make every file that doesn't have an index.html of its own present a default index.html from somewhere else—for example,

```
DirectoryIndex index.html /defaultfiles/index.html
```

or you can run a program of your own to generate the directory listing—for example,

```
DirectoryIndex /cgi-bin/mylistingprogram.pl
```

or return an `ErrorPage` if you like.

If you don't want automatic indexes at all, use an `Options` directive that doesn't include indexes on the most expansive container; you can use the whole document tree. If you want them in general but want to turn them off in certain trees use

```
<Directory /filesystem/path>
Options -Indexes
</Directory>
```

Or, to let the users turn them off, allow `Overrides` and let them disable the `Index` option in the .htaccess file.

But assuming you want to do standard directory indexing, this will be handled by mod_auto_index. This can sort the directories in ascending or descending order by file name, file size, modification date, or description. (Description is something you can set by filetype with the `AddDescription` directive; as shown further on. By default you don't get any. In addition, if you enable `ScanHTMLTitles` in `IndexOptions` and you haven't set up a general description for .HTML files, Apache will pull out the contents of the `<TITLE>` tag and list that as the description.) Apache on UNIX includes the case when sorting by file name (so "Apache" comes after "zebra") but Apache on VMS does not, even when serving from an ODS-5 disk, where the file names can display in mixed case.

The `FancyIndexing` option produces listings with clickable headers for those columns that will enable the user to request the directory sorted in any of those ways, but you can also set the default order with `IndexOrderDefault`.

Figure 13.1 shows a user directory with a `FancyIndex` with name as the default index order. Figure 13.2 shows the same directory after I clicked on "Last Modified", showing the new order.

These are the available directives:

```
IndexOptions    [+|-]option    [[+|-] option ...]
```

As with the other directives in this section, this can go serverwide, virtual-hostwide, in a directory container, or in an .htaccess file. These options control how your directories will look.

Multiple `IndexOptions` directives for a single directory are merged together. Options can be prefixed with "+" or "-", which adds or subtracts them to current `IndexOptions` settings, either from previous `IndexOptions` directives in the same directory or from inherited settings from some upper level. You can't usefully mix prefixed keywords with unprefixed ones; whenever an unprefixed keyword is found, Apache clears all the inherited options, not just those for that keyword. Incremental options found on subsequent (same level or lower level) `IndexOptions` directives will be applied.

The options for `IndexOptions` are discussed in the following text.

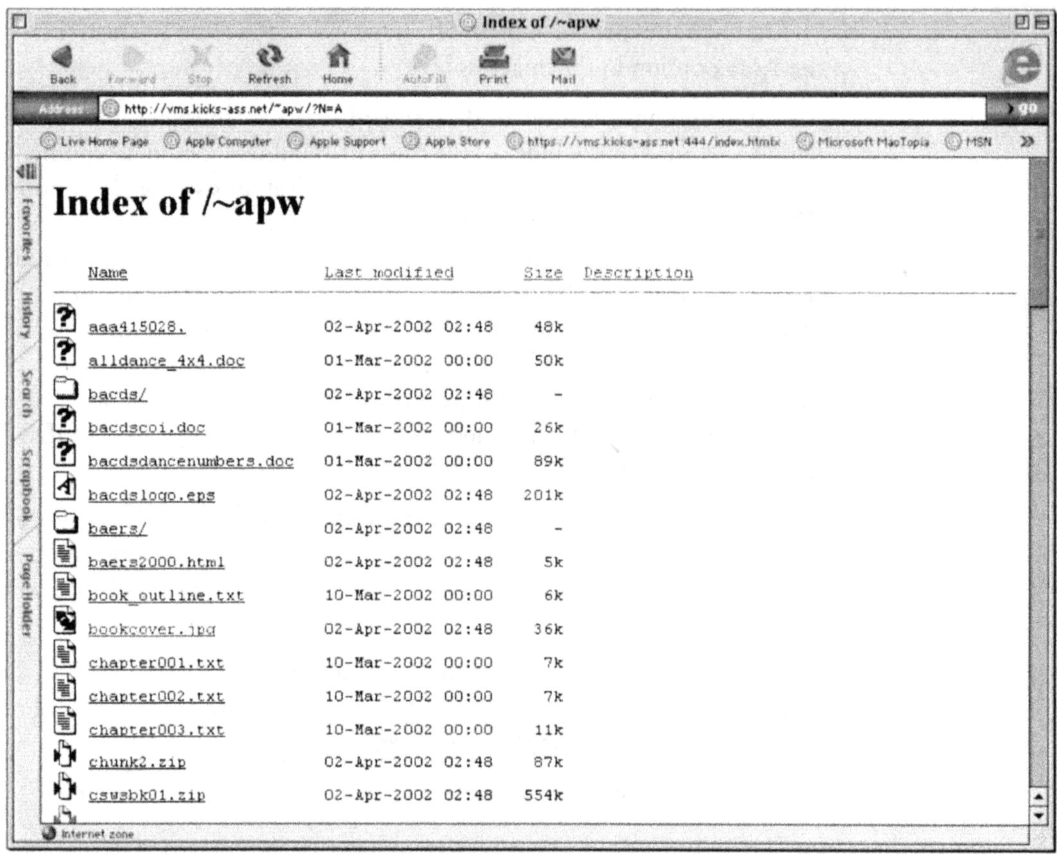

Figure 13.1 *A fancy index from Apache.*

```
DescriptionWidth=[number | *]
```

specifies the width of the description column in characters, or if "*" automatically sizes the description to the length of the longest description in the display.

```
FancyIndexing
```

This turns on fancy indexing of directories, as described previously. If you turn off `FancyIndexing`, you'll get something that looks like Figure 13.3. There is a separate `FancyIndexing` directive, but its use is deprecated.

```
FoldersFirst
```

If `FancyIndexing` is enabled, all subdirectories will be listed before any normal files in any listing, regardless of sort order. The subdirectories will

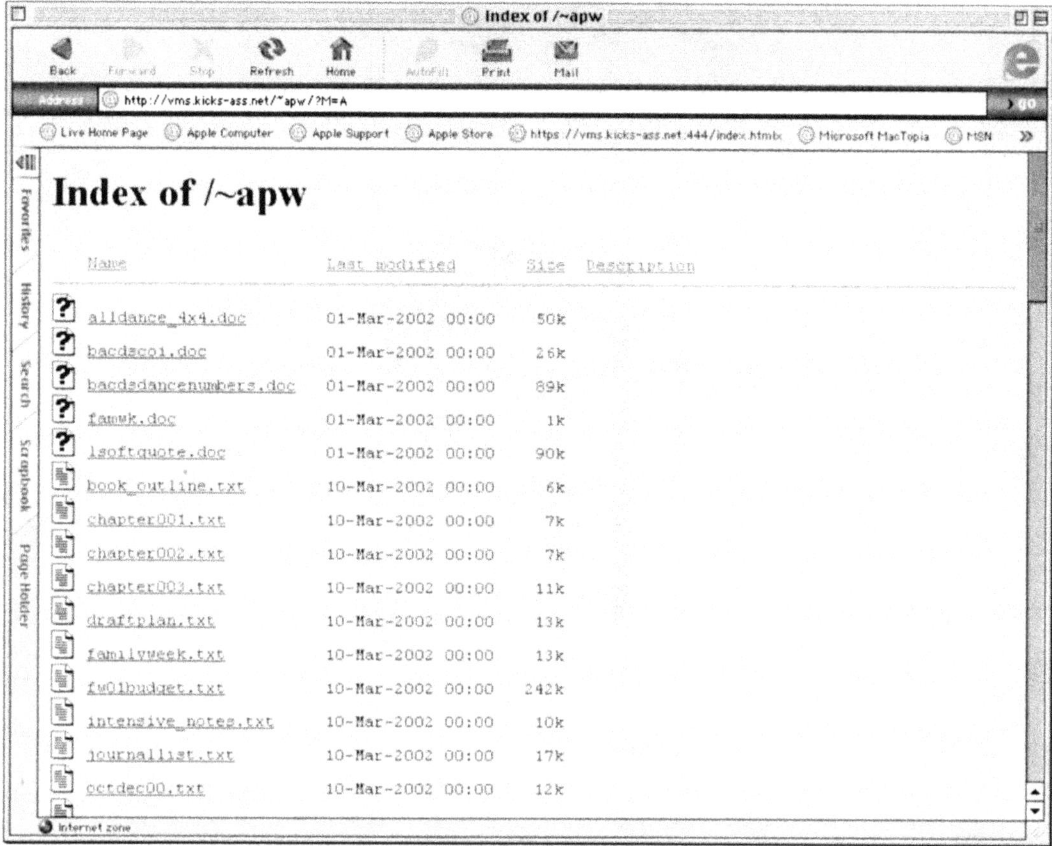

Figure 13.2 *The same index in last-modified order.*

appear sorted in the prevailing sort order, and after them the regular files, sorted independently in the prevailing sort order.

```
IconHeight[=number-of-pixels]
```

If you specify this and `IconWidth`, the server will include "`HEIGHT`" and "`WIDTH`" attributes in the `<IMG>` tag for the file icon. This lets the browser calculate the page layout before receiving all the icons, enabling faster initial display with slow links. If you leave out the "`=number-of-pixels`", the server will give the standard values for the standard supplied icons.

```
IconsAreLinks
```

In fancy indexing, this makes the icons part of the anchor for the file name, so that the user can click on the icon to get the file.

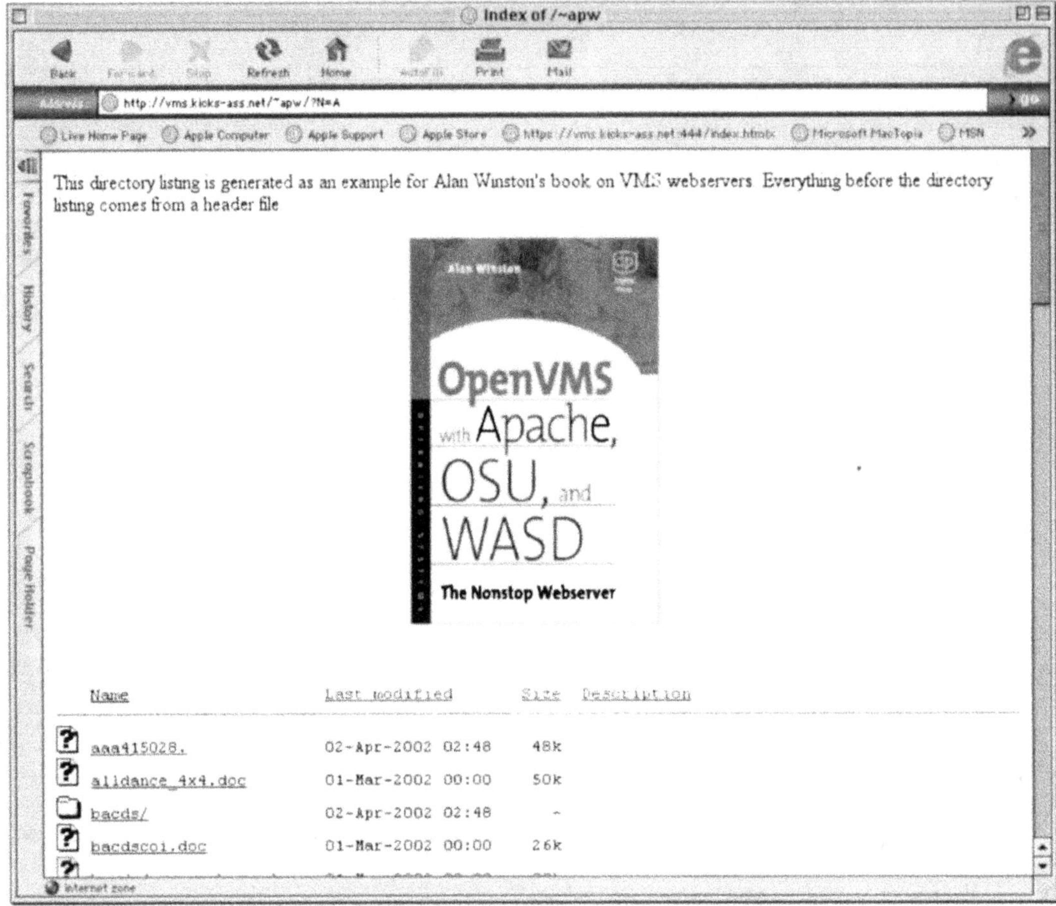

Figure 13.3 *Index header with FancyIndex enabled.*

```
IconWidth[=pixels]
```

See `IconHeight`.

```
NameWidth=[number-of-characters | *]
```

specifies the width of the file-name column in bytes (which for ASCII is equivalent to the number of characters, but may change when you have a file system that supports Unicode). If you specify "`*`", then the server sizes the columns to the length of the longest file name in the display.

```
ScanHTMLTitles
```

In `FancyIndex` mode this tells the server to pull the contents of the `<TITLE>` tag from any HTML files and put that in the "Description" area, although if there's an `AddDescription` item for HTML files, this won't be applied. This is a potentially expensive option, since the server has to read the file and parse the HTML therein.

```
SuppressColumnSorting
```

If you specify this, it disables the `FancyIndex` behavior of making the column headings into links for sorting.

```
SuppressDescription
```

eliminates the description column in `FancyIndex` listings, which gives you back some screen real estate.

```
SuppressHTMLPreamble
```

If you've got a header file (specified by the HeaderName directive) that actually includes the usual HTML preamble (`<HTML>`, `<HEAD>`, `<BODY>`), use this command to tell the server not to generate that stuff itself. (Your header file can't be a completely valid HTML document, because if it includes a `</BODY>` tag, the generated file listing that follows will confuse the browser, so it's more standard to leave off the `<HTML>`, `<HEAD>`, and so on. However, if you want a custom `<TITLE>` for your directory page, you need to do this.)

```
SuppressLastModified
```

In `FancyIndex` listings this suppresses the display of the last-modified date.

```
SuppressSize
```

In `FancyIndex` listings this suppresses the display of the file size.

```
TrackModified
```

This returns the `Last-Modified` and `ETag` values for the listed directory in the HTTP header, so clients can check whether anything has been updated in the directory via a `HEAD` request.

This ends the `IndexOptions` options.

```
HeaderName partial-URL default: "header"
```

This directive sets the name of the file that, if present, will be inserted at the top of the index listing. (See Figure 13.3 for an example with `FancyIndex` and Figure 13.4 for an example without `FancyIndex`.)

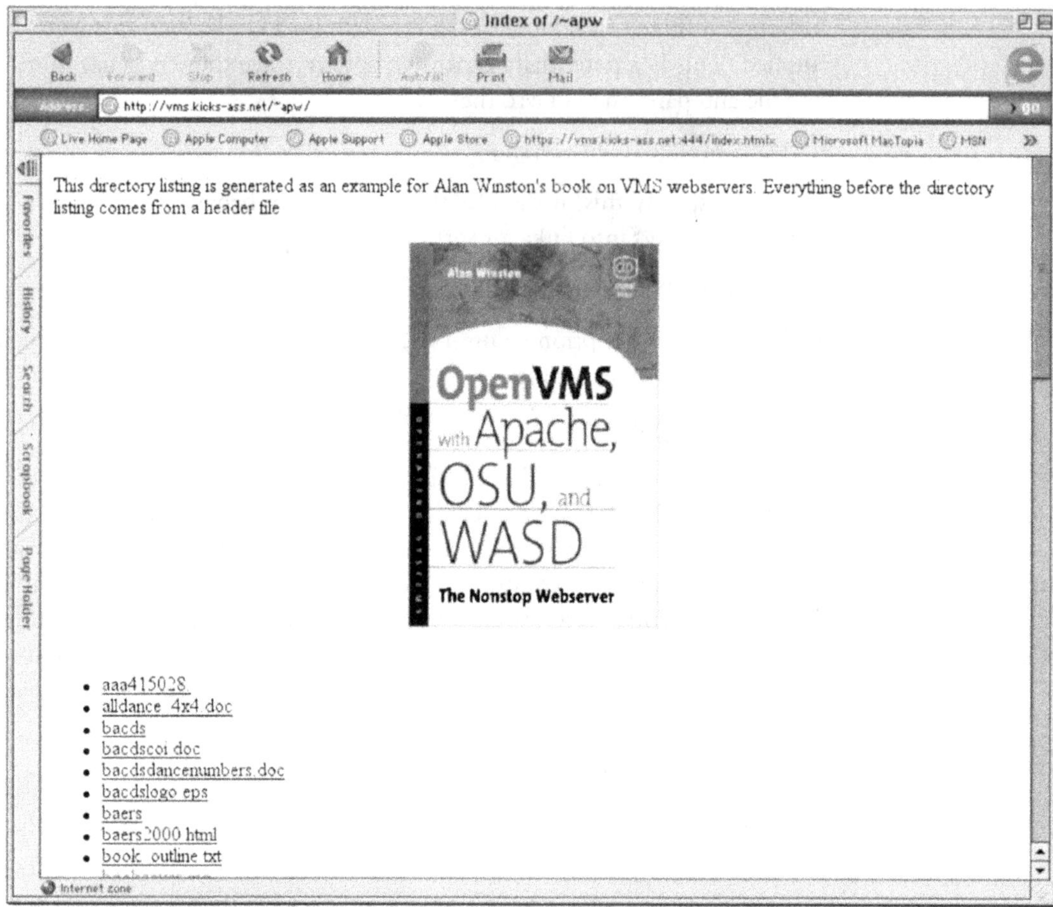

Figure 13.4 *Index header with FancyIndex disabled; shows format of plain index.*

The partial URL can be a file name; if it's a plain file name (such as "HEADER"), Apache will look for a file of a type that is mapped as text/html (i.e., not only header.html but header.shtml or other language variants) and include it in the output; if it's an SSI file and the directory permits `Includes`, the server-side includes in the file will be processed.

If there isn't a text/html-type file there, Apache looks for a text/plain-type file (such as header.txt) and includes it in the output, wrapped in `<PRE>` tags and with any included tags escaped so the browser won't interpret them.

Very trickily, the partial URL can go to a script that generates the header, but only if the script is marked as a text/html file (rather than merely having code in it to generate a text/html header). If you want to do this, you have to use an `AddType` to mark the filetype of the script as text/html.

```
ReadmeName partialURL (default: README)
```

This works just like the `HeaderName` directive, except that the `ReadMe` is a trailer, rather than a header—it follows the generated directory listing.

It's worth noting that the HEADER and README processing will occur even if you don't include these directives and aren't tied to `FancyIndex` at all. You may be able to defeat this processing, if you want to, by defining `ReadmeName` and `Headername` to impossible or unlikely names, but you can't readily turn it off.

```
IndexIgnore wildcarded-file-specifier [wildcarded-file-
specifier]
```

If you want to hide files when listing directories, you list them in `IndexIgnore`. You can list multiple files on a single line or have multiple `IndexIgnore` directives. Each one adds to the list of files rather than replacing the list. The file specifier can be a fully specified file name or wildcarded string, such as "`*.gif`".

```
IndexOrderDefault Ascending|Descending
Name|Date|Size|Description
```

The `IndexOrderDefault` directive works only with `FancyIndex` listing; it allows you to override the initial display order, which is otherwise "ascending order by file name."

The first argument is the order (`Ascending` or `Descending`); the second is what field to sort by. (If it isn't `Name`, file name will always be the secondary sort key after the one you specify.)

The remaining directives are the ways you specify what shows up as icons, what shows up as ALT tags for the icons, and what shows up in the Description column. (The text in ALT tags will show up in place of the image in image-incapable browsers or those with image loading disabled; some browsers will display it when the cursor moves over the image.)

```
AddAlt "String to include as ALT tag" wildcarded-file-
specifier ...
```

sets the value of the ALT tag for files matching the specifier (or any of the specifiers included on the line). The string must be enclosed in double quotes.

```
AddAltByEncoding "String to include" MIME-encoding [MIME-
encoding] ...
```

sets the ALT tag based on the MIME-encoding of the file; the tag string must be in double quotes. (The encoding, as distinct from the type, is something like "x-compressed" or "x-gzip.")

```
AddAltByType "String to include as ALT tag" MIME-type
[MIME-type]
```

Sets the ALT tag based on what MIME-type the file is, based on MIME.TYPES or your `AddType` directives.

```
AddDescription "Description string" file-specifier [file-
specifier...]
```

sets what will be displayed in the Description column under fancy indexing. The file specifier can be a file extension, partial file name, or wildcard expression of full filename; the description string must be in double quotes.

(If you have a directory full of binaries and want to describe each one, you can do this with an .htaccess file that contains an `AddDescription` for each file. It might make more sense to just create an index.html that describes each one, where you can have as many lines as you need for each description.)

Apache doesn't stop you from putting HTML markup in the description, but it doesn't guarantee to display the whole description if it's too long. If some closing tag gets cut off, the rest of the page may look pretty strange.

```
AddIcon [ALT-text,]/URLpath-to-icon filename-or-keyword
[filename-or keyword...]
```

Use `AddIconByType` instead of `AddIcon` if possible, which it usually is. `AddIcon` sets the icon (and, optionally, the ALT-tag text) to show in the directory listing next to files of the type or types specified.

The two special keywords are `^^DIRECTORY^^` for directories in general (which you could usually accomplish in VMS with a .DIR filetype, but that doesn't work everywhere Apache runs) and `^^BLANKICON^^` for blank lines. These are already defined in HTTPD.CONF when you get it, so you won't have to worry about them. Otherwise, the file name can be a file extension, a wildcarded file name, or a complete file name.

```
AddIconByEncoding [alttext,]/URL-path-to-icon MIME-
encoding [MIME-encoding...]
```

In `FancyIndex` listings this directive specifies which icon to display (and, optionally, what ALT-tag text to use) based on the MIME-encoding of the file.

```
AddIconByType [alttext,]/URL-path-to-icon MIME-type [MIME-
type ...]
```

In `FancyIndex` listings this directive specifies which icon to display (and, optionally, what ALT-tag text to use) based on the MIME-type of the file. This can be a wildcard expression, so you can set, for example, a text icon for everything matching "text/*".

```
DefaultIcon /URL-path-to-default-icon
```

specifies the icon to display on `FancyIndex` listings if no icon is otherwise specified for the file. In the distributed HTTPD.CONF this is set to an icon with a picture of a question mark, but if you want to change it, this is the directive to use.

I notice what appears to be a bug in Apache 1.2. The generated index listing for a directory containing an ODS5-only name, Journallist^.sylk.slk, simply dropped that name from the listing.

13.1.2 OSU

OSU offers a choice of external directory browsers—an MST version and a DECnet-accessed scriptserver version. They accept the same configuration directives but require different support to work.

To use the MST, you find the following in your http_suffixes.conf:

```
.ITERATE ThreadPool $pname $qf $a2 $a3
.NEXT dsrv q_flag=1 limit=20 stack=162000
#
.ITERATE Service $sname $parg $darg $iarg
.NEXT dirserv pool=dsrv dynamic=(dirserv,http_dirserv_mst)\
  info=www_system:http_directory.conf
```

This translates to

```
ThreadPool dsrv q_flag=1 limit=21 stack=162000
Service dirserv pool=dsrv dynamic=(dirserv,http_dirserv_mst) \
 info=www_system:http_directory.conf
```

Add the following presentation rule:

```
presentation text/file-directory %dirserv
```

Alternatively, you could make sure the MST stuff is all commented out and use the presentation rule to get the DECnet-based browser:

```
presentation text/file-directory \
 sys$node::"0=WWWDIR"www_system:http_directory.conf
```

You can turn off directory browsing completely with a

```
DirAccess off
```

in HTTP_MAIN.CONF. (If you use the presentation rule, your HTTP_MAIN.CONF `DirAccess` rule will be ignored.) Note that if you mess up the configuration badly enough that the directory server isn't invoked, you still get a list of files—but it's just plain file names, as shown in Figure 13.5. In addition, the DECnet-based browser doesn't go away

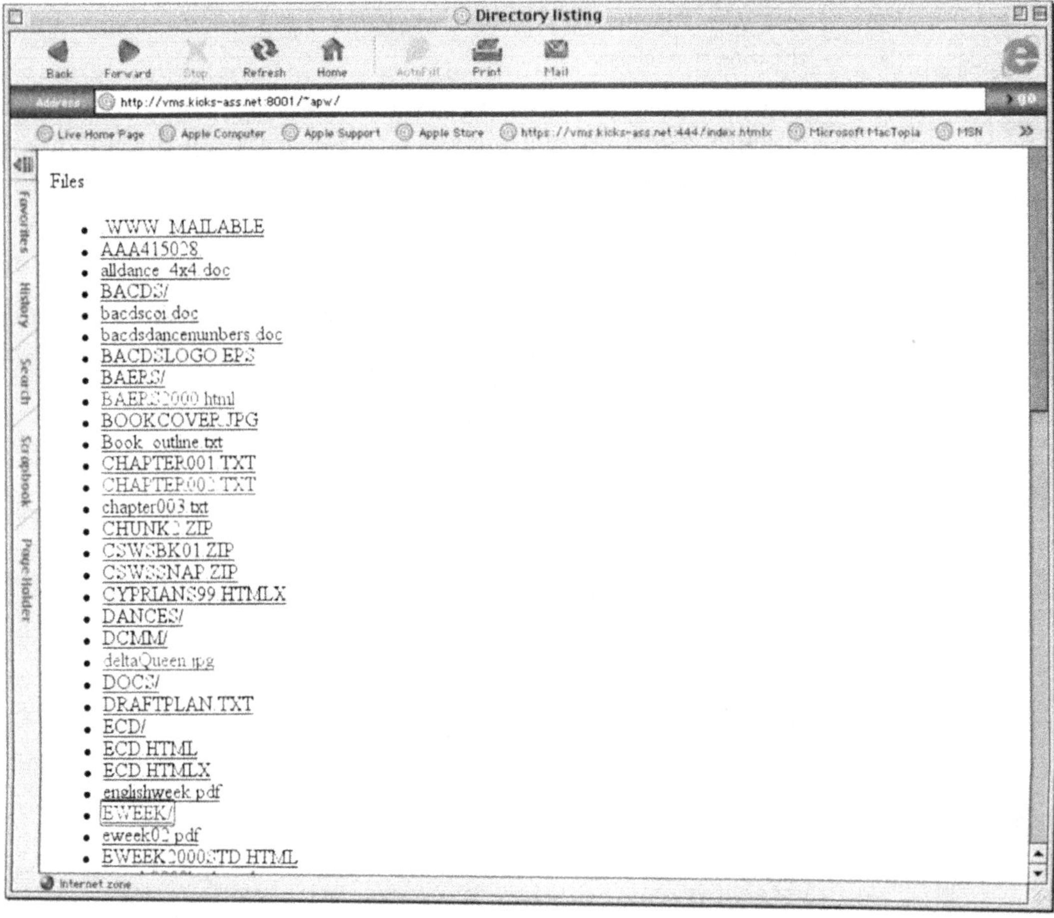

Figure 13.5 *Output from OSU's internal directory list.*

immediately when the server is restarted; consequently, if you change the configuration file, restarting the server won't make the change take effect. You need to find the process the directory server is running in (it'll be named TASK-something) and kill it; the next directory browse will create a new task that reads the configuration file anew.

Each directory server will deal with WWW_SYSTEM:HTTP_DIRECTORY.CONF.

Here are the available directives in that file. (The same directives can be used in a per-directory control file if `DirAccess Selective filename OverRide` is specified in this master file.)

```
DirAccess on | off | selective [controlfile [OVERRIDE]]
```

If on, permits directory browsing; if `off`, rules it out. If "`selective`", permits directory browsing only if the specified control file is present in the directory. (The name if you don't specify is .WWWBROWSABLE.) If `OVERRIDE` is specified, the control file will be read and any directives in it will be interpreted and applied to the directory listing.

```
Include filename
```

If specified, reads the specified file and treats the contents as though they were part of the current file.

```
DirDefLangEnable language
```

enables a default language setting, which, in multilanguage environments, allows different directories to be processed in different languages. (The default setting is "`en`".)

```
Welcome file-name [lang-list]
```

adds file names that will be served as the index file; this can be conditional based on language code. Multiple instances of the directive are allowed. If the relevant welcome file is found, that file will be served and no directory listing will be generated. For example,

```
Welcome welcome en,en-*
Welcome vilkommen de,de-*
```

```
DirReadme [OFF|TOP|BOTTOM] [readme-file]
```

OSU offers a header or trailer, or neither, but not both. Unless it's explicitly turned off, this capability is on, and the default file name is "README." The contents of the `ReadMe` file are wrapped with `<PRE>` but

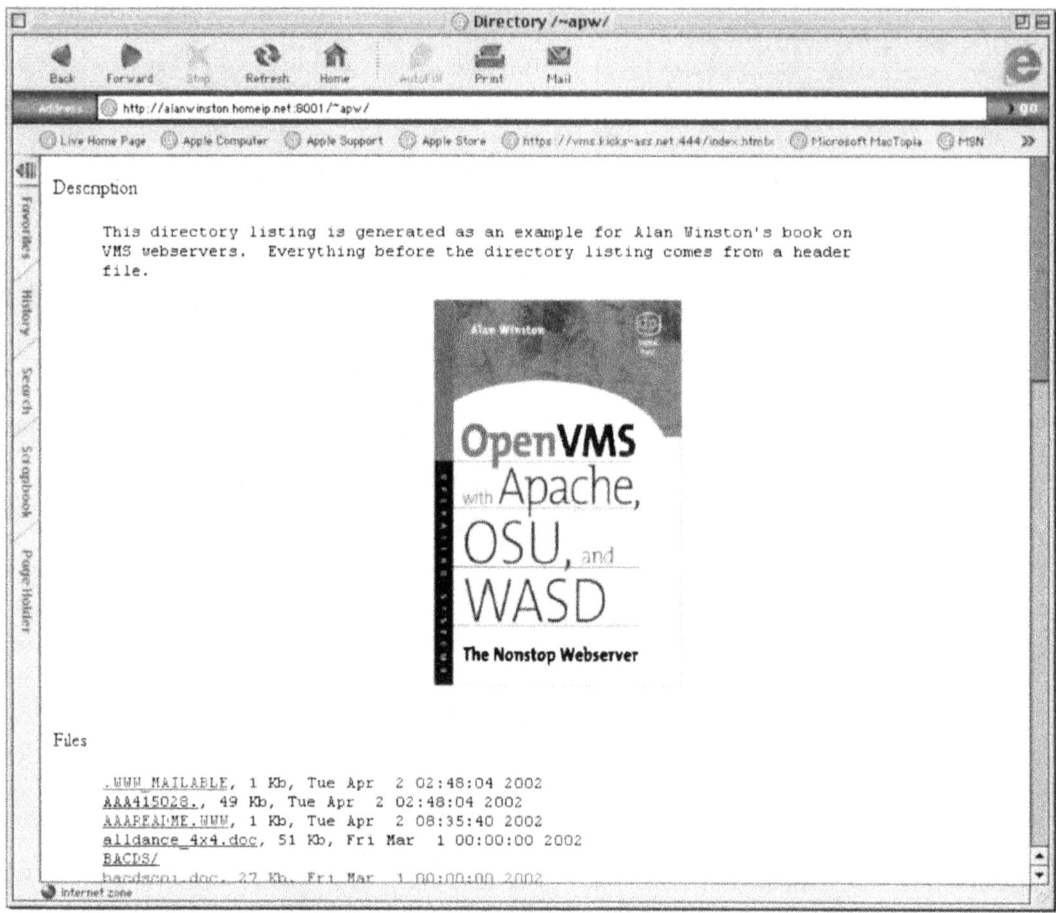

Figure 13.6 *OSU's full listing with README TOP.*

not escaped, so tags may be interpreted. Figure 13.6 shows a directory listing with `DirReadme TOP` and every possible field listed.

```
DirShowDate [ON|OFF]
```

Include last-modified date in listing (off by default).

```
DirShowSize [ON|OFF]
```

Include file size in listing (off by default).

```
DirShowBytes [ON|OFF]
```

If `DirShowSize` is on, report file size in bytes rather than kilobytes.

```
DirShowHidden [ON|OFF]
```

If on, will suppress the listing of files that have extensions but no names (e.g., .WWW_BROWSABLE).

13.1.3 WASD

Remember that userdirs in WASD don't work for accounts that are privileged or disusered or have expired passwords; those directories can't be browsed either, even if diraccess is enabled. (That is, not as userdirs; if the same directories are mapped some other way, they can be seen.)

Quite a lot of flexibility is available to the user through query strings that control the directory browser and through wildcard file specifications at the end of the path. More information on that follows, after the configuration directives. These directives go in HTTPD$CONFIG.CONF

```
[DirAccess] ENABLE | DISABLE | Selective
```

`Enable` turns directory browsing on for every directory, `Disable` turns it off for everybody, `Selective` turns it on only for directories containing a ".WWW_BROWSABLE" file.

Even if `DirAccess` is enabled, the presence or absence of the following files in those directories affects the behavior of directory browsing.

The presence of the file ".WWW_HIDDEN" means that the files in the directory can't be listed, but individual files are accessible (can be linked to if you know the name); this is the equivalent of (W:E) access on the directory. If a subdirectory of the current directory has a ".WWW_HIDDEN", it won't be listed in the directory of the parent folder.

The presence of the file ".WWW_NOWILD" means a wildcard file specification won't work even if configured to work. The presence of the file ".WWW_NOP" suppresses listing of a parent directory. The presence of the file ".WWW_NOS" suppresses listing of subdirectories. The presence of the file ".WWW_NOPS" suppresses listing of either.

```
[DirLayout] layout-string (I__L__R__S:b__D supplied in
conf file).
```

This enables you to specify the layout of each line of generated directories. (You can experiment with the look of different strings by specifying them in entered URLs as part of the query string, rather than editing your config files over and over.)

Straight from the comments in the code that interpret the layout string, Table 13.1 lists the official descriptions:

Table 13.1 *Codes for WASD Directory Layouts*

Element	Meaning
_	(underscore) each underscore provides one space between fields
`C`	creation date
`D`	content-type description (if specified, should be the last field specified)
`D:L`	content-type description as a link
`I`	icon
`L`	file anchor (link, including name as link)
`L:F`	file anchor, ODS-5 file-system name (e.g., spaces, not %20)
`L:N`	file anchor, name only, do not display the file's extension
`L:U`	file anchor, force the name to uppercase (these can have multiple specifications—e.g., "__L:U:N__")
`N`	file name (without anchor)
`O`	file owner (only when SYSUAF authenticated and profile accessed)
`P`	file protection (only when SYSUAF authenticated and profile accessed)
`R`	revision date
`S`	file size
`S:B`	file size to be in comma-formatted bytes
`S:D`	express file sizes in 1,000 (decimal) KB not 1,024 (binary) KB
`S:F`	file size MB and KB to be expressed to one significant place
`S:K`	file size to be in KB
`S:M`	file size to be in MB
`U`	file/directory name in uppercase (MUST be the FIRST directive)

These values are actually case-insensitive, so the lowercase letter in the string that's in your configuration by default has no special meaning. The default string is `I__L__R__S:b__D`, which translates as "Icon, two spaces, file name with extension as a link, two spaces, revision date, two spaces, size given as bytes in a comma-separated string, two spaces, description."

Most popular file types have preconfigured descriptions; HTML files are searched for the contents of the title tag. Figure 13.7 shows the output of a

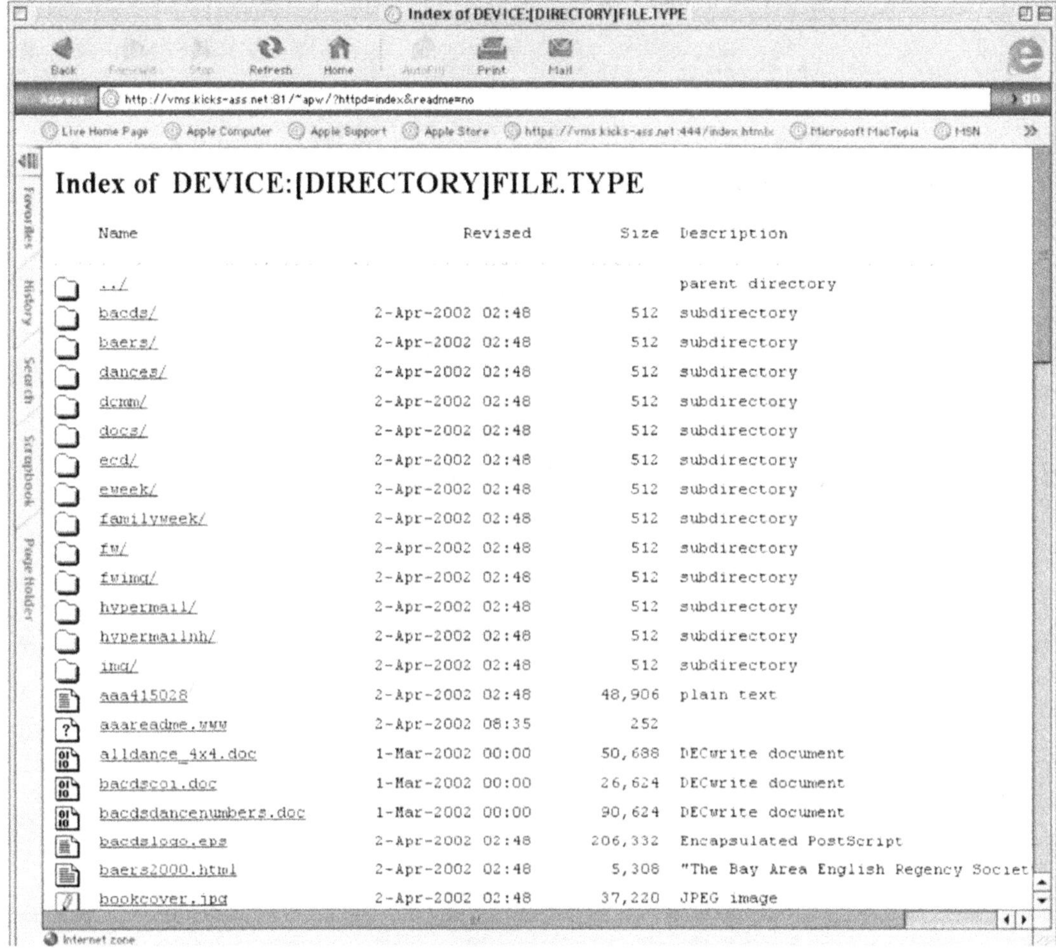

Figure 13.7 *Directory listing in WASD's supplied format, showing config error.*

directory listing in the default format with README processing suppressed.

```
[DirMetaInfo] ENABLED | DISABLED
```

If enabled, the server will include META tags in the generated HTML of directory listings showing the server version, date, host name, and the VMS-style lookup string that generated the listing. (This is for the benefit of humans looking at the system via "view source.") (See Figure 13.8.)

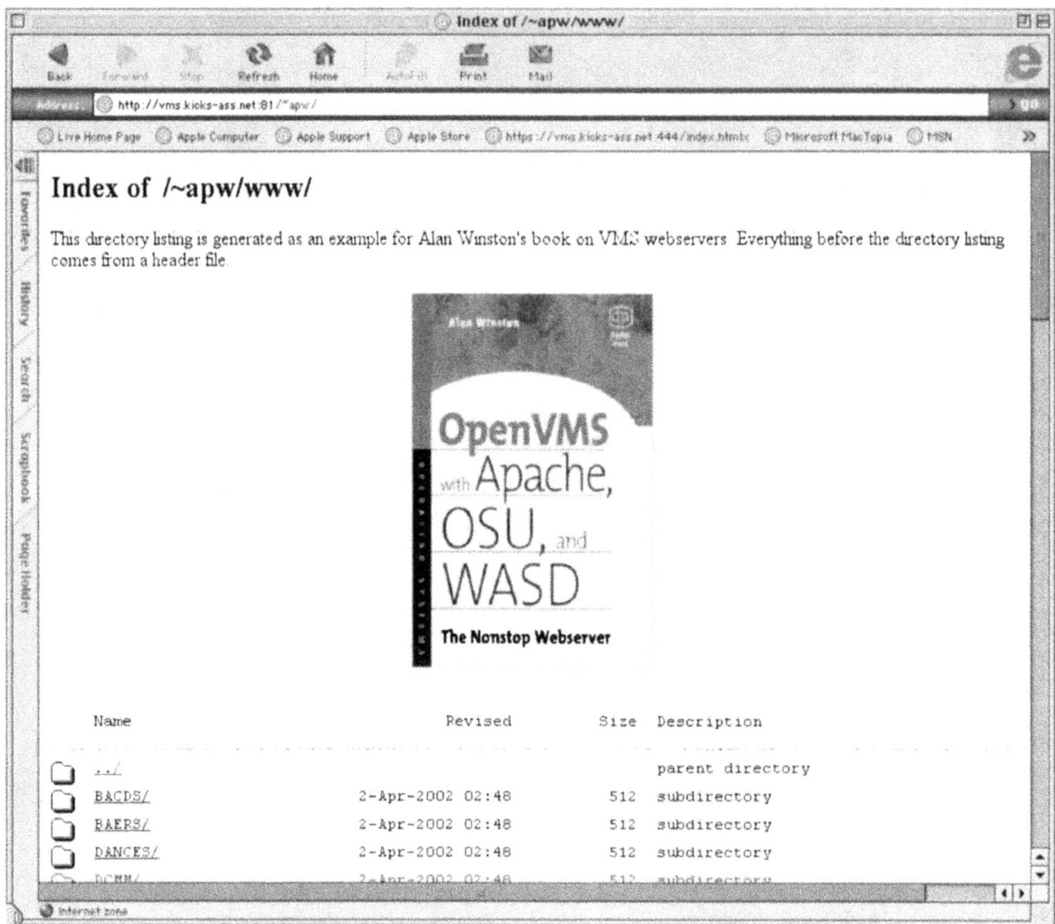

Figure 13.8 *Directory listing in WASD's supplied format—sans config error.*

```
[DirReadMe] DISABLED | TOP | BOTTOM
```

specifies whether to do readme processing at all, and if the function is not disabled, whether to make the readme a header or a trailer.

```
[DirReadMeFile] filename.ext
```

This directive allows multiple readme file names, one per line. The file names in the directory will be matched against the list of readme file names, and the alphabetical first match will be processed as the readme file, so there may be some vanishingly small performance advantage in putting multiple `[DirReadMeFile]` directives in alphabetical order by the file name they specify. The supplied file names are README.HTML, README.HTM, README.TXT, and README.

If the content type of the selected readme file is nontext, it won't be processed. If it's text/html, it's included in the output as is; if it's text/plain, it's wrapped in <PRE> and </PRE> tags to preserve the formatting. If it has a server-side include type, it will be preprocessed by the SSI processor before going out. (See following discussion.)

```
[DirWildcard] ENABLE | DISABLE
```

specifies whether wildcards in file names are enabled at all. (If this is enabled, and `DirAccess` is enabled, then any user can force a directory listing even of directories that have welcome pages by specifying a wildcard, unless the directory has a ".WWW_HIDDEN" or a ".WWW_NOWILD" file in it.)

```
[DirBodyTag] body-tag-string
```

enables you to customize directory listings to more closely resemble the rest of your site design. Must be at least "<BODY>" but can include an additional parameter in the BODY tag and an additional HTML after the tag.

```
[DirDescriptionLines] number-of-lines
```

The server gets the Description line for a file of type text/html by searching through the file looking for a title tag, which is obviously fairly expensive, what with having to open and read each file instead of just listing the name. It's even more expensive if you have long documents, which, perhaps, never specify a title. This directive, which is set to 30 out of the box, says how many lines to read looking for the title tag before giving up. You set it to 0 to disable this behavior altogether.

```
[DirNoImpliedWildcard] ENABLE | DISABLE
```

If enabled, the directory browser won't add wildcards to request if they're not present in the path. (It still gives full directory listings on a bare "/" with no wildcards at all.)

```
[DirNoPrivIgnore] ENABLE | DISABLE
```

Ignore (i.e., do not report) privilege violations on files/directories.

```
[DirOwner] ENABLE | DISABLE
```

If enabled, the O format specifier that lists file ownership will be processed if the access itself is SYSUAF authenticated; otherwise, it will not be.

```
[DirPreExpired] ENABLE | DISABLE
```

If enabled, the HTTP headers on listings will show them as already having expired, so browsers or intermediate caches that honor those headers won't cache the responses and will request a new listing each time.

```
[AddIcon]
/path-to-icon Alt-Tag content-type
[...]
```

specifies the URL-type path to the icon you want to display for a particular content type, the contents of the ALT tag for the icon image, and the content type itself—for example,

```
httpd/-/text.gif [TXT] text/plain
```

says to apply the server-supplied text.gif with the ALT tag "[TXT]" for every file with a content type of text/plain.

Popular content-types are already defined in the out-of-the-box configuration; this directive takes multiple lines of specification.

The following directives are already usefully defined out of the box, and you probably don't want to mess with them unless the specific directory browser icons are really important to the look of your site.

```
[AddBlankIcon] /URL-path-to-blank-icon Alt-text

[AddDefaultIcon] /URL-path-to-default-icon Alt-text

[AddDirIcon] /URL-path-to-directory-icon Alt-text

[AddParentIcon] /URL-path-to-parent-icon Alt-text

[AddUnknownIcon] /URL-path-to-icon-for-unknown-content-
type Alt-text
```

If directory browsing is permitted at all, you can specify quite a lot of the directory formatting through a query string in the URL, overriding your default directory formatting. The format for the query string is "`?httpd=index&`" followed by one or more of the following name and value pairs, such as "`?httpd=index&expired=yes¬ype=yes`".

Table 13.2 shows the options, adapted from the comments in the directory browsing module.

Autoscripts are scripts that execute when you click on them directly. `autoscript=no|false|0` tells the browser to tweak the anchor so that the link brings you to the script contents, not the result of running the script.

Table 13.2 *WASD Parameters for Directory Browsing*

Value	Legal Values
`autoscript=`	yes (default), no, true, false, 1, 0
`delimit=`	header, footer, both (default), none
`expired=`	yes, no, true, false, 1, 0 (listing preexpired)
`filesys=`	yes, no (default), true, false, 1, 0 (ODS-5 file-system name)
`layout=`	see format string definitions
`nop=`	yes, no (default), true, false, 1, 0 (as if .WWW_NOP found)
`nops=`	yes, no (default), true, false, 1, 0 (as if .WWW_NOPS found)
`nos=`	yes, no (default), true, false, 1, 0 (as if .WWW_NOS found)
`notype=`	yes, no (default), true, false, 1, 0 (do not display filetype)
`readme=`	yes, no (default), true, false, 1, 0
`type=`	force file content type (e.g., "&type=text/plain")
`upper=`	yes, no (default), true, false, 1, 0

`filesys`, in practice, specifies what to do about embedded blanks in file names: allow them (setting is no, false, 0) or interpolate %20s. By definition `no|false|0` means ODS-5 file names, and `yes|true|1` means ODS-2 file names. `upper=yes|true|1` forces the output file names to uppercase. Figure 13.9 shows directory output using query string values to suppress the readme file filetypes and force output to uppercase.

WASD's directory browsing is extremely capable and very configurable, although what you can configure is different from what Apache lets you configure. (WASD puts subdirectories first if it shows them at all and sorts only in ascending file-name order.)

Figure 13.7 shows a configuration error that's corrected in Figure 13.8. I include this because I found this an easy mistake to make and hope to spare my readers that problem. The generated title and header tags say "Index of DEVICE:[DIRECTORY]FILE.TYPE" rather than the directory name or URL path. This is because I failed to provide a reverse mapping rule for user directories. (Future versions of WASD will say "NO:[REVERSE.MAPPING.FOR.THIS]FILE.PATH," which may give more of a clue.)

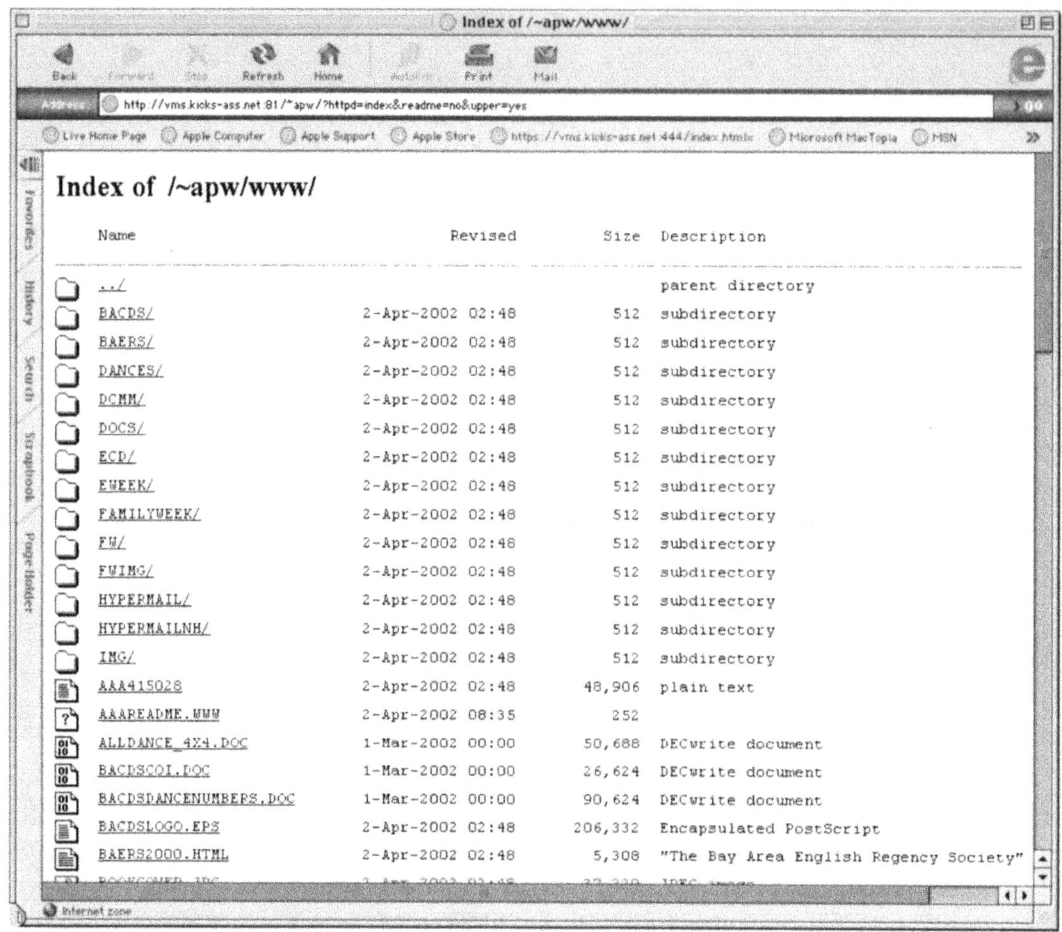

Figure 13.9 *WASD directory browser output using query string values to affect formatting.*

The reverse mapping in this case, which is a userdir, went in the HTTPD$MAP.CONF file, and looked like:

```
pass /~*/www/* /$disk1/*/www/*
```

I also learned in this exercise that if you're serving an ODS-5 disk, you need to tell WASD about it; otherwise, it'll give you errors when you tell it to report files with names that are illegal on ODS-2 drives. The command for that, also in HTTPD$MAP.CONF, was:

```
SET /$disk1/* ODS-5
```

(This is covered in Chapter 7.)

13.2 Dynamic content with SSI

Static Web pages are the same every time you look at them, at least until somebody edits them to make changes. Dynamic pages can change each time they're viewed without additional editing.

One way to do this is to write a special program that generates the HTML for a page with variable content computed and inserted in the right places; we'll discuss this approach in another chapter.

Another way is with server-side includes (SSI), where a component of the Web server parses special tags in the HTML code and replaces them with other data, whether the content of a file referred to in the code; the results of executing a program named in the tag; or a special value, such as today's date, the file date, or the IP address of the browser.

This can be useful for a number of reasons. Including a standard header and footer can make all your pages consistent; it's then easy to change the look of all the pages just by changing the included files. Conversely, you can have a single template page and fill in the body based on a command included in a tag; this approach is used by tools such as PHP, but can be productive in the SSI environment as well. Automatic last-updated date gives the user some idea of how fresh the information presented is. If you have conditional logic, you can take advantage of the special capabilities of particular clients.

One possible drawback of the SSI process is that it no longer works, as it does with plain HTML, to view a page in the browser, save it, edit it, and upload it. (Well, it works, but afterward all the formerly dynamic parts are static forever. For good or ill, the client can't tell which parts were generated by SSI and which were static in the original document.) If your site uses server-side includes and has numerous people updating documents, make sure they're educated about how to deal with SSI files.

SSI can also let users who aren't entirely trusted to write CGI programs have a limited capability to provide dynamic content in their own pages. There are some general concerns with the ability to execute any arbitrary command in the context of the Web server; a curious/malicious/prankish user could delete configuration or log files, shut down the server, or worse. I'll discuss how each server deals with that in the configuration sections that follow.

All three servers have SSI capability, with CSWS and WASD exceeding the tag-replacement model to allow some program logic, presenting or hiding different parts of the page based on conditional statements in tags. I'll discuss SSI configuration for each server, then review the tags and definitions.

13.3 Configuring SSI

13.3.1 CSWS

The relevant options in Apache are `Includes` and `IncludesNOEXEC`, which can go on directory containers and file containers. If you want to prohibit SSI processing altogether, configure your directory containers without `Includes`. If you want to permit SSI processing but don't trust the users to execute arbitrary commands in the context of the server, configure `IncludesNOEXEC` instead.

The relevant directives for fully enabling the common types of SSI files are these:

```
AddType text/html .shtml
AddType text/html .htmlx

AddHandler server-parsed .shtml .htmlx
```

The `AddType` directives let the server know that these will be compliant HTML files once they've been processed; the `AddHandler` directive says that the filetypes should be processed by mod-include.

(Another way of handling this, on UNIX, is to mark the files you want to be preprocessed as executable by setting the execute bit on them; then you can have all the files be named ".html" and only the ones with execute bit set will be preprocessed, saving the server resources that would be required to preprocess all ".html" files. But "the execute bit" is a meaningless concept under VMS, so ignore anything you read about the `XBitHack` directive, and use a different file type for SSI files than for regular HTML.)

13.3.2 OSU

OSU's SSI doesn't support running arbitrary programs in server context, so there's no need for configuration to restrict that ability. SSI is available either to everybody or to nobody. To enable it, the following rules go into HTTP_SUFFIXES.CONF:

```
Service preproc pool=dsrv
dynamic=(preproc,http_preproc_mst)\
```

```
    info=www_root:[000000]accesses.dat

presentation text/htmlx %preproc:
```

By default, HTTP_SUFFIXES defines the text/htmlx type for .htmlx and .htx extensions; you could add

```
SUFFIX .shtml text/htmlx 8BIT 0.5
```

if you wanted OSU to take its best shot at parsing Apache SSI files as well, or change the .html type to text/htmlx if you wanted every HTML file to run through the preprocessor.

13.3.3 WASD

Here are the configuration directives to get WASD to do SSI.

```
[SSI] DISABLE | ENABLE
```

Enabled, anybody can do SSI but without the ability to execute programs from SSI tags (except for include virtual, which can run a configured CGI script.)

```
[SSIAccesses] DISABLE | ENABLE
```

If enabled, WASD will (like OSU) maintain a little RMS indexed file that tracks access counts for pages using the accesses directive.

```
[Scripting] DISABLE | ENABLE
```

For SSIexecs to work, scripting must be enabled. (You most likely want this enabled anyway, and it's enabled in the default configuration file. CGIs won't work if this is disabled.)

```
[SSIexec] DISABLE | ENABLE
```

If disabled, nobody can execute programs from SSIs. If enabled, `SSIexecs` will work, but only for documents owned by UIC [1,4] (SYSTEM) on the theory that anyone with enough privilege to make a page owned by SYSTEM can make so much trouble that any ability granted to such a person by running an `SSIexec` is superfluous.

If you want to grant the ability to do execs to trusted users who aren't [SYSTEM], you can set that up on a URL-path basis. (See Chapter 7 for more on the SET command.)

```
Set /URL-path SSI=PRIV
```

Documents found in this URL path can execute "privileged" commands; see the directive list for details. (This goes in HTTPD$MAP.CONF, as does the next.)

```
Set /URL-path SSI=NOPRIV
```

Documents found in this URL path can execute only "unprivileged" commands; see the directive list for details.

WASD supports setting up an unprivileged "sandbox" account that doesn't have write access to the server's files, and running SSI and scripts under that, which more or less immunizes the server from the ill effects of user scripts. If you want to do that—and it's an extremely good idea to do that if you're going to let unvetted `SSIexec` pages run—you need the following additional configuration.

In your server startup:

```
/PERSONA=sandbox-username
```

In HTTPD$CONFIG.CONF:

```
[DCLDetachProcesses] ENABLE
```

13.4 SSI directives

The directives in SSI documents are all wrapped in HTML comment tags—for example,

```
<!--#directive [tag[="value"]] ... -->
```

Not all directives are supported on all servers, and not all functionality of supported directives is the same on all servers. Here are some major differences.

While all three servers can do "`#include virtual`", Apache's "`#include virtual`" can reference a CGI program, and the server will actually run the program and include the output from running the program. (If the program returns a `Location:` header for a redirect, Apache will convert that into a link.) OSUs and WASDs will just translate the path to a file and return the file contents.

Apache and WASD support flow-control directives, with `#if` and `#else` directives, which can actually test conditions and include different parts of the document in the generated file depending on the results. They can both also set environment variables and print all environment variables with `#printenv`.

Apache and WASD also allow `#exec` (WASD synomym #dcl) directives, which can run DCL commands, scripts, or images. WASD has fairly fine-grained control, with innocuous DCL commands available to unprivileged users and potentially hazardous ones available only in paths marked as privileged or in documents owned by SYSTEM and not world-writeable.

OSU and WASD preprocessor documents can include only parts of other documents; the parts are tagged with `#begin` and `#end` directives. (This can be really handy when you want to include, say, preformatted database output. Rather than having, for example, last night's inventory report for each item required to be in a separate document, you can write a database report that puts each item into a separate part of the same document, and each beautifully formatted page that describes the item can include just the relevant part of the document. The OSU config files demo also shows an extremely ingenious use of this feature.) OSU and WASD also support access counting and display, which Apache doesn't do directly. WASD has an OSU-compatibility mode for documents whose content-type maps to "OSU SSI HTML", which in the supplied configuration file is only .HTMLX files.

OSU processes the entire document before writing any of it to the screen. If you give it an unsupported directive, the only thing sent to the browser is an error message identifying the directive. CSWS/Apache will send the document with the string "`[an error occurred while processing this directive]`" (or a replacement you specify with the `#config errmsg` directive) in place of any bad directives. WASD will process and emit the document from the top down until it encounters a bad directive; it will then emit a big red "`SSI error`" message and stop processing the document.

Here are the SSI directives the three servers support, grouped by functionality.

13.4.1 Access counts (WASD and OSU)

```
<!--#accesses [ordinal] [since=""] [timefmt=""] -->
```

(WASD-only in this format.) This increments and echoes the count of accesses to this document (by VMS-file name). `Since` is a string that will be echoed between the access count and the time of the first access in the access database if the since string is specified; the time is formatted according to the format string in `timefmt`, and means accesses since that time. (Ordinal means appending "st", "nd", "rd", or "th" to the returned access count.) So something like `<!--#accesses ordinal since=" time since initial access on " -->` will produce text like "13th time since initial access on 01-Jan-2002 13:21:15". To forestall your trying it, the increment part works only once per load of the document—you can refer to the access count repeatedly in one document and increment it only once.

To include access counts in OSU, which WASD also supports, do:

```
<!--#echo "accesses[;versionnumber]"--> or
<!--#echo "accesses_ordinal[;versionnumber]"-->
```

(If you've drastically changed your document and want to reset the access count to zero, include the version number in the document. This is not necessarily the file system version number; this is a version number retained in the access file. If you make a new version of the document and don't change the access file reference, the counts will continue incrementing.)

13.4.2 File information

All the servers can fetch the last-modified date or the size of a file by file name or URL path, using the `file=` or `virtual=` tags, respectively. On Apache and OSU, file paths are relative to the current directory; on WASD, they must simply be readable by the server. In Apache, URL paths must be relative to the current directory—you can't get out of the document tree and you can't go any higher in the document tree than you already are. For OSU and WASD, URL paths just have to be mapped by the server and result in a readable file.

```
<!--#flastmod file="VMS-path"|virtual="URLpath"
[fmt="format-string"] -->
```

This directive is replaced with the value of the last-modified date (RMS revision date) of the file named or mapped via the file or virtual tag. Apache doesn't support the `fmt="format-string"` tag; OSU does if it was compiled with DECC but not if it was compiled with VAX C.

```
<!--#fsize file="VMS-path"|virtual="/URLpath" -->
```

This directive is replaced with the size of the file named in the VMS path or mapped in the URL path. On Apache and WASD, the value is formatted according to `#config sizefmt:`—on OSU, it's bytes.

```
<!--#fcreated file="VMS-file-spec"|virtual="/URLpath"
[fmt="format-string"] -->
```

(WASD-only.) This is replaced with the file creation date/time of the file with the VMS path shown in the `file=` tag, or mapped in the `virtual=` tag, formatted according to either the default format string or the format string specified with the optional `fmt=` tag.

13.4.3 File/document includes

```
<!--#include file="filename"|virtual="/URLpath"
  [type="content-type"] [fmt="?"] [part="partname"] -->
```

All three servers support includes, but with some differences. Apache and OSU will only do "file" includes relative to the current path; WASD will allow anything that it can read. All three will allow a "/URLpath" that goes out of the document tree; Apache allows that URL path to be a CGI program (including URL-encoded query string) and will automatically execute it and place the results in the generated document. Neither OSU nor WASD allow that.

The `type` and `fmt` tags are WASD-only. WASD automatically wraps the included content in `<PRE> </PRE>` tags unless the content-type is text/html; the type tag lets you dictate that a file called, say, something.inc, be treated as containing HTML. Alternatively, if you want to include something with text/html and have it treated as text, you can set `type="text/plain"`. If `fmt="?"` is set, the WASD server, instead of halting processing with an SSI error message when it doesn't find the file you specified, will simply continue processing without inserting anything into the generated document.

The `part=` tag is OSU and WASD-only. OSU supports labeled file parts, and WASD endeavors to support them compatibly, although this takes some hacking.

OSU supports referring to a particular named part of a file by using the syntax `filename.part.extension`. On ODS-5 disks it's possible to have multiple dots in a file name, so this is ambiguous, and the ambiguity is resolved in favor of multiple dots, meaning that there's a part name in it.

However, the part name is permitted to be null. The somewhat surprising result of this is that if you want to include a file with multiple dots in the name, you need to double the last dot so that OSU will take it as a null part name and accept the rest of the file name.

If you attempt to include `multipart.include.firstpart.htmlx`, OSU will try to open the file named multipart.include.htmlx, and if that fails, report an error. If it succeeds, it will look for the part labeled "first-part", and if that fails, it will report an error. If you want to include the entire file `multipart.include.htmlx` you have to specify `multi-part.include..html`.

If you want to allow the part-in-filename hack on WASD, you need to configure a redirect in HTTPD$MAP.CONF:

```
Redirect /*.*.htmlx /*.htmlx?httpd=ssi&__part=*
```

but this will work only for files with no dots in the file name and only on `#include virtual`. If you use every feature of OSU-type part includes and are including multidotted ODS-5 files (which I think is a self-inflicted wound, but one that someone with a UNIX background might have thought was a good idea), you're best off sticking with OSU rather than trying to make WASD fake it. (You can run the html_preproc component of OSU as a CGI script under the OSU-compatibility environment of CSWS or WASD if you really, really want the functionality.)

13.4.4 File parts (OSU and WASD)

```
<!--#begin "partname" -->
```

The part name is an alphanumeric label unique within the document. Parts can overlap; there's no hierarchy of parts enclosing parts. Including a part just says to include the file from where it says "`#begin partname`" to where it says "`#end partname`", and the server doesn't care how many irrelevant "begin" and "end" directives it finds in the process; it won't echo them. If there is no matching "`#end`" directive the part is assumed to end at the end of the file. This stuff works in WASD only when in OSU-compatibility mode, triggered either by a `#config OSU="1"` directive or by appearing in a file whose content-type description has "OSU" in it, which, in the supplied configuration, means an .HTMLX file.

```
<!--#end "partname" ["partname"] ... -->
```

OSU lets you end multiple parts with the same `#end` directive. (WASD allows only one per directive.) An `#end` directive appearing before the `#begin` directive matching that part name (or if there is no matching #begin at all) is ignored.

`config` (Apache, WASD, OSU)

The `#config` directive instructs the SSI processor how to behave while processing this particular document. Each server supports a different set of directives.

```
<!--#config buffersize="largest-SSI-directive-length" -->
```

(WASD-only.) SSI directives can take up multiple lines of the file (especially with the WASD #SSI, which supports multiple directives within one comment tag), and very long ones can potentially overflow the statement-processing buffer, which is set by default to the longest record length in the file (as reported by RMS). If you're going to have long SSI strings, set the buffer size high; it can go up to 32,767. This should be the first directive in the file.

```
<!--#config verify="1|0" -->
```

(OSU and WASD.) If verify="1" is set, this instructs the processor to include directives as comments in the generated document; if "0", to stop doing so. This can appear anywhere in the document.

```
<!--#config errmsg="message-string" -->
```

(Apache and WASD.) This changes the default message string to whatever you direct.

```
<!--#config sizefmt="abbrev|bytes|blocks" -->
```

(Apache and WASD.) This sets the default output format for file sizes (as displayed by the `#fsize` directive). The "`blocks`" option is WASD-only. "`bytes`" is a byte count; "`abbrev`" is kilobytes or megabytes.

```
<!--#config timefmt="format-string" -->
```

This sets the default time format for directives that echo time. (See Table 13.3.) Times, incidentally, are formatted in each server by the C library routine strftime, which is why the format codes are the same for all.

```
<!--#config OSU="1|0" -->
```

(WASD-only: set to 1 to require OSU-compatibility.)

```
<!--#config trace="1|0" -->
```

(WASD-only: set to `1` to have each statement displayed, highlighted at the browser, before SSI processing, providing a clear trace of of the SSI directives and their output; set to `0` to disable the trace. Useful if you're trying to debug flow-control statements.)

Table 13.3 *Time Formats*

Element	Meaning
%a	three-letter abbreviated weekday name (e.g., Mon)
%A	full weekday name (e.g., Monday)
%b	three-letter-abbreviated month name (e.g., Jan)
%B	full month name (e.g., January)
%c	preferred date and time format for current locale (per C library)
%d	day of month as a two-digit number
%H	hour of the day as a two-digit number on the 24-hour clock
%I	hour of the day as a two-digit number on the 12-hour-clock
%j	day of the year as a three-digit number
%m	month as a two-digit number
%p	AM or PM (or locale equivalent if different)
%S	second as a two-digit number
%w	day of the week as a one-digit number (Sunday is 0)
%x	preferred date (but not time) format in current locale
%X	preferred time (but not date) format in current locale
%y	year as a two-digit number
%Z	name of the current time zone (if available)
%%	a literal percent sign

13.4.5 Directory/index generation (WASD-only)

```
<!--#dir file="wildcardable-filespec" [par="directory-parameters"] -->
<!--#index file="wildcardable-filespec" [par="directory-parameters"] -->
<!--#dir virtual="URL-path" [par="directory parameters"] -->
<!--#index virtual="URL-path" [par="directory parameters"] -->
```

(WASD-only.) This invokes the directory browser to include a directory or autoindex of the file or path you specify. (`#index` and `#dir` are synonyms. As implemented at present, file and virtual are synonyms; either one will translate a file-system path or a URL path.) The directory parameters are the same ones you can pass as a query string to a generated directory; see the first part of this chapter for details.

Note that the links in the index you generate are just file names, which works fine when you generate a directory based on the URL because your default path gets you to that directory. If you specify a path that leads to a different directory, you'll generate an index page with links that don't work, because they're relative to the directory you specified—not to your current path.

13.4.6 Echo directives

```
<!--#echo var="varname"-->
```

All three servers support the #echo directive, whose general form is shown above. This allows you to include the value of a variable provided by the server in your document; each server has some special variable names that may result in some action. See Table 13.4 for the names.

OSU and WASD permit you to skip the var="varname" step for their special SSI variables; you can get to any that are supported on the particular server with

```
<!--#echo varname -->
```

This syntax will make Apache very unhappy indeed, and it may swallow any part of your document that follows a use of this syntax, so if you're trying to be cross-server compatible, don't use this format. Other formats to avoid are the WASD-only equivalence of #echo and #" (that's "hash-doublequote" without a corresponding closing quote), and the WASD-only equivalence of "var=" and "value=". WASD also allows a trailing "=formatstring" on the ends of date variables, where the contents of the format string matches the values in Table 13.3.

WASD and Apache allow you to echo any CGI variable name with the var="varname" syntax; OSU allows only the special variable names in Table 13.4 but lets you get at any environment variable with

```
<!--#echo getenv="environment-varname"-->
```

which WASD also supports for OSU compatibility. Note that "environment variable" on VMS pretty much means "anything that the C-language initialization routine has stuffed into the C run-time library's environment array at program startup," which will not necessarily be updated in real time. You can't change the value of a global symbol or logical after program startup and expect an already running instance of a program to see it if the program uses getenv; such programs need to do a LIB$GET_LOGICAL to get the current system value.

Apache permits an optional encoding tag, which must precede the `var="varname"` tag in the directive to be effective. The syntax is

```
<!--#echo encoding="none|URL|entity" var="varname" -->
```

The default encoding is "`entity`". "`none`" will give you the unmodified value of the variable, even if that will screw up your HTML page; "`URL`" will do "%" encoding, suitable for including in a generated link.

Table 13.4 *Special SSI Variables Provided by the Servers*

Variable	Servers	Meaning
DATE_GMT	All	The current date and time in Greenwich Mean Time
DATE_LOCAL	All	The current date and time in local time
DOCUMENT_NAME	All	The file name of the current document (that's the top-level document)
DOCUMENT_URI	All	The URL path that reached the top-level document
LAST_MODIFIED	All	Last-modified date for the current document
ACCESSES	OSU+WASD	The number of times this document has been accessed
ACCESSES_ORDINAL	OSU+WASD	As above, with a suffix of st, nd, rd, or th
HW_NAME	OSU+WASD	The server hardware (as returned from GETSYI)
SERVER_NAME	OSU+WASD	The `ServerName` or `localaddress` name portion of the URL to which the server responded
SERVER_VERSION	OSU+WASD	The server software name and version
VMS_VERSION	OSU+WASD	The version of VMS running on the server
CREATED	WASD	Creation date of current file
FILE_NAME	WASD	VMS file spec of the file that was in the path the user requested
THE_FILE_NAME THIS_FILE_NAME	WASD	File name only of the file the reference is in
PARENT_FILE_NAME	WASD	File name only of file that included me, if any
QUERY_STRING_UNESCAPED	WASD	Same as CGI value

13.4.7 Flow-control directives (Apache, WASD)

WASD and Apache both allow for reasonably complex logic in conditional processing via what amounts to a block-structured programming language implemented as directives. Each one supports `#if`, `#elif`, `#else`, and `#endif`, so their capabilities come out about equal. However, the syntax is so different that it'll be clearer to discuss them separately.

Flow control in Apache

```
<!--#if expr="test_condition" -->
<!--#elif expr="test_condition" -->
<!--#else -->
<!--#endif -->
```

At this point even DCL has IF ...THEN ... ELSE ... ENDIF, so I'm not going to spend a lot of time discussing how that stuff works. A sequence of conditionals begins with `#if` and ends with `#endif`. If the `#if` condition wasn't satisfied, a subsequent `#elif` (if any) will be evaluated. If no `#if` or `#elsif` was satisfied, then an `#else` block (if any) will be selected.

The "`expr`" in the `#if` and `#elif` directives is literally the string expr, which is somewhat confusing. It's there because the syntax of SSI directives in Apache requires `tag="quoted string"`, not because it makes it easier to read. If it helps, imagine that you're setting expr equal to the truth value of "`test_condition`" and testing that.

The syntax for "`test_condition`" is pretty familiar to Perl or C programmers. I won't try to do a full Backus-Naur Form rendition here. The contents of test_conditions are literals, variables, and operators. Variables are indicated with `$varname`, so dollar signs in literals must be escaped with a backslash. Compound conditions are made up of elementary conditions connected with `&&` (logical AND; all must be true for the compound condition to be true) or `||` (logical OR; at least one must be true for the compound condition to be true.) The unary condition is `$varname`, which is true so long as that variable has any value at all. All other conditions are comparisons; you can compare variables to literals, variables to other variables, literals to literals (although that's kind of pointless). A special case of literal is a regular expression; you can test whether the contents of a variable match the pattern specified by the regular expression. (Render a regular expression as `/regexp/`, with the slashes.) The operators are `!` (negation), `=` (is equal to), `!=` (is NOT equal to), `<` (is less than), `<=` (is less than or equal to), `>` (is greater than), `>=` (is greater than or equal to), and `~=` (matches).

You can use parentheses for grouping. Basically, put a Perl conditional in the quotes and you'll be fine.

An example follows:

```
<!--#if expr="$HTTP_USER_AGENT ~= /^Mozilla/" &&
        !($HTTP_USER_AGENT ~~ /MSIE/)" -->

  You are using Netscape or Mozilla

<!--#elif expr="$HTTP_USER_AGENT ~= /MSIE/" -->

  You are using Microsoft Internet Explorer

<!--#else -->

  I don't know what you're using. Here, you figure it
out: 

  <!--#echo var="HTTP_USER_AGENT" -->

<!--#endif -->
```

Here's the explanation. The HTTP_USER_AGENT variable gets whatever the client wants to put in it. Netscape claims to be Mozilla; Internet Explorer starts with the Mozilla string too (and adds "compatible" somewhere in there, before admitting that it's "MSIE" somewhere in the string). This means that "if the value of HTTP_USER_AGENT starts with "Mozilla" AND if the value of HTTP_USER_AGENT doesn't contain "MSIE" anywhere in it, then it really is Mozilla. Failing that, if it does contain MSIE somewhere, it's IE; otherwise, take the catch-all case.

WASD

WASD doesn't have a full expression parser but manages to be reasonably expressive nonetheless. Multiple conditionals can occur in a single directive, and the overall evaluation is as though they were ANDed together. To do OR tests, add the `#orif` directive. The use of `#elif`, `#else`, and `#endif` are the same as in Apache, although the conditional syntax is different.

```
<!--#if conditional [conditional] ... -->
<!--#orif conditional [conditional] ... -->
<!--#elif conditional [conditional] ... -->
<!--#else -->
<!--#endif -->
```

A variable reference is `{variable_name}`. The unary conditional is `VALUE=variable-reference-or-literal`. If the variable contains "0" or is empty, this evaluates to false; otherwise, it is true.

The other conditionals are comparisons. All have the format

```
VALUE=what-you're-testing comparison-operator=what-you're-
comparing-it-to
```

The comparison operator tags are `eqs=` (string equal to), `srch=` (string compare with wildcards, `*` for match 0–*n* characters, `%` for single-character match), `lt=` (numeric less than), `gt=` (numeric greater than), and `eq=` (numeric equality).

(Numeric operators call `atoi` on both the value parameter and the comparison parameter—that is, use the C library routine to convert each to integers—and then compare as indicated.)

If you precede a comparison operator tag with an exclamation point, it will logically negate the tag.

```
<!--#if value="0" !eq="0" -->
```

evaluates to false.

Here's a variant of the example I gave for Apache:

```
<!--#if value={HTTP_USER_AGENT} srch="Mozilla*"
        value={HTTP_USER_AGENT} !srch = "*compatible*" -->

  You are using Netscape or Mozilla

<!--#elif expr="$HTTP_USER_AGENT ~= /^Mozilla/" -->

  You are using Microsoft Internet Explorer

<!--#else -->

  I don't know what you're using. Here, you figure it
out: 

  <!--#echo var="HTTP_USER_AGENT" -->

<!--#endif -->


<!--#printenv -->
```

(Apache and WASD.) This inserts all assigned variables into the current document, one name/value pair per line. (This has no special formatting—

it isn't a table or anything—so if you want it to be legible, you need to wrap the `#printenv` in a `<PRE> </PRE>` pair.)

13.4.8 SET directives

```
<!--#set var=varname value=value -->
```

(Apache and WASD.) This sets the variable named `varname` to the value specified by "`value`," creating the variable if need be. However, this is done differently enough that you have little hope for compatibility unless you restrict yourself to setting variables to string values.

Apache

```
<!--#set var="varname" value="value-string"-->
```

`Varname` is, by convention, a variable name in lowercase, which doesn't appear as an Apache variable in Table 13.4. You put value-string in quotes whether or not you want variable substitution. For variable substitution, use a $ in front of the variable name, such as `value="$LAST_MODIFIED"`. (As a result of this syntax choice, if you want to use a literal dollar sign in a string, you have to escape it by putting a backslash in front of it, as in `value="\$57.60"`.) If you use the syntax `value="$(varname)"` the value will be delimited by braces.

WASD

WASD has extended `#set` capability. You can't reset the value of any of the variables in Table 13.4 ("server variables"), but you can set the value of any others ("user variables"). You don't need to use quotes around the `varname`, and you want to use quotes around the value string only if it's a literal quoted string. You can substitute the contents of either kind of variable in place of any tag value in an SSI directive; the syntax for a variable reference is to wrap the variable name in curly braces, with some options that let you select only an extract of the value:

```
{variable_name}
{variable_name,character_count}
{variable_name,offset_from_zero,character_count}
```

Here's an example from the comments in the SSI.C routine:

```
<!--#set var=EXAMPLE1 value="This is an example!" -->
<!--#set var=EXAMPLE2 value={EXAMPLE1,0,10} -->
<!--#set var=EXAMPLE3 value="{EXAMPLE2}other example ..." -->
```

```
<!--#set var=EXAMPLE4 value="{EXAMPLE1,10}other example!" -->
<!--#echo "<P>" var={EXAMPLE3} "<BR>" var={EXAMPLE4} -->
```

The output from the "#echo" would be

```
<P>This is another example ...
<BR>This is another example!
```

```
<!--#ssi |#directive|...] -->
```

(WASD only.) This makes a neater-looking source document by allowing multiple SSI statements inside only one set of comment delimiters. The "#" of each new directive lets WASD know to stop processing the previous directive. This can enhance readability considerably when you're using structured flow-control statements, although if you're going to end up with a large multiline statement, you may want to `#config buffersize` larger. Here's an example from the WASD SSI.C comments, which also nicely shows `#set` and `#if` processing.

```
<HTML>
<!--#ssi
  #set var=HOUR value={DATE_LOCAL,12,2}
  #if value={HOUR} lt=12
      #set var=GREETING value="Good morning"
  #elif value={HOUR} lt=19
      #set var=GREETING value="Good afternoon"
  #else
      #set var=GREETING value="Good evening"
#endif
-->

  <TITLE><!--#echo value={GREETING} -->
    <!--#echo value="{REMOTE_HOST}!" -->
  </TITLE>
  </HEAD>
  <BODY>
    <H2>Simple XSSI Demonstration</H2>
    <!--#echo value={GREETING} --> <!--#echo
value={REMOTE_HOST} -->,
    the time here is <!--#echo value={DATE_LOCAL,12,5} -->.
  </BODY>
</HTML>
```

Note that only directives and their tags can be wrapped in an `#SSI` directive; no HTML code is permitted unless as part of an `#echo` statement.

13.4.9 Exec directives (Apache and WASD)

Both Apache and WASD give you the ability to execute server-based commands, images, command procedures, or scripts. The syntax is quite different.

Apache

```
<!--#exec cmd="command to execute, with parameters" -->
```

The command string is passed to DCL and the output included in the constructed document. Variable substitution works inside the quotes; just preface the variable name with a $. (And, as usual, that means you have to escape any literal dollar signs with a backslash.) It is extremely important not to allow `Includes` (as distinct from `IncludesNOEXEC`) to users you don't trust, as the command executes in the context of the Apache server account.

"`@SYS$STARTUP:APACHE$SHUTDOWN`" could be pretty annoying—funny, whenever anybody loads my SSI document the server crashes—but "`DELETE APACHE$COMMON:[000000...]*.*;*`" would definitely have you testing your backups.

```
<!--#exec cgi="/URLpath-to-CGI-program"-->
```

executes the CGI program—the specification can include a query string with URL-encoded parameters—and puts the results into the generated document. (All the Apache documentation I've seen recommends using `#include virtual` instead, but I don't know why.)

WASD

The possible commands to execute have been divided into an unprivileged set of mostly harmless commands and a privileged set of potentially quite dangerous commands. Note that WASD makes `#dcl` an exact synonym of #exec.

Also note that unless the content-type of the file you execute is text/html, WASD will wrap the output in `<PRE> </PRE>` in the generated document. If you're running executables or scripts that output stuff with embedded HTML markup tags, you can get WASD to drop the `<PRE> </PRE>` tags by including a `type="text/html"` directive in any of the `#exec` directives.

13.4.10 Unprivileged directives:

```
<!--#exec dir=filespec [par=/qualifier[/qualifier-2]] -->
```

replaces the directive with the output from issuing a `$ DIRECTORY filespec [qualifiers]`.

There might be some nuisance value in `par="/output=ht_root:[local]httpd$config.conf"`.

```
<!--#exec vdir=/URL-path [par=/qualifier[/qualifier]...] -->
```

replaces the directive with the output of `$ DIRECTORY URL-path-translated [qualifiers]`.

```
<!--#exec show=WHAT-TO-SHOW -->
```

replaces the directive with the output of `$ SHOW WHAT-TO-SHOW`. (`$ SHOW USERS` or `SHOW SYSTEM` potentially pose a security exposure risk in showing would-be intruders real user names to try to crack.)

```
<!--#exec say=WHAT-TO-SAY -->
```

replaces the directive with the output of `$ WRITE SYS$OUTPUT WHAT-TO-SAY`. Entertaining values for what-to-say are symbol names, lexical functions, and the like.

13.4.11 Privileged directives:

```
<!--#exec exec="DCL-Command-String" -->
```

replaces the tag with the output of `$ DCL-Command-String`. This permits the privileged user to execute any DCL command, including parameters.

```
<!--#exec file=VMS-command-procedure-filespec
[par=parameters] -->
```

replaces the tag with the output of `$ @ VMS-command-procedure-filespec parameters`.

```
<!--#exec run=VMS-executable-image-filespec
[par="parameters"] -->
```

replaces the tag with the output of `$ RUN VMS-executable-image-filespec parameters` (which is quite likely to be an error message about unrecognized parameters).

```
<!--#exec virtual="URL-path-to-command-procedure"
[par=parameters] -->
```

replaces the tag with the output of `$ @ translated-URL-path-command-procedure-filespec parameters.`

```
<!--#exec vrun="URL-path-to-executable-image"
[par=parameters] -->
```

replaces the tag with the output of `$ RUN translation-of-URL-path-to-executable-image parameters`

(which is quite likely to be an error message about unrecognized parameters).

13.4.12 Miscellaneous WASD-only directives

```
<!--#exit -->
```

In an included file, this gets the server to quit processing that file right now and to return to the parent file and continue, if there's more to do. Most useful inside conditional blocks to avoid needless processing to end of file.

```
<!--#stop -->
```

Wherever encountered, stop processing the generated document immediately. Again, most useful inside conditional blocks to avoid needless processing to end of file.

#modified directives

This directive controls the generation of headers based on modification dates of this or other files. This will work only if it appears in the file prior to anything that will produce HTML output, since the headers can't be understood after HTML output begins.

```
<!--#modified file=VMS-filespec [fmt="?"] -->
<!--#modified virtual=/URL-filespec [fmt="?"] -->
```

Each of these directives gets the revision date of the file referred to. The `fmt="?"` tag instructs the server not to complain if the file referred to doesn't exist. At the end of a series of these directives the modified-date value is that of the most recently modified file referred to in the series.

```
<!--#modified if-modified-since -->
```

If the client sent an if-modified-since header and the modified-date produced by the earlier tags is prior to the date/time sent in that header, the server will produce a "`304 not modified`" response rather than generating the page.

```
<!--#modified last-modified -->
```

a "`Last-Modified:`" header with the modified date produced by the earlier tags.

```
<!--#modified expires=expiration-string -->
```

This is here with the `#modified` directives rather than having multiple directives that produce headers, but logically it doesn't have much to do with the other `#modified` forms. This one generates an "`expires:`" header with whatever value you have in the expiration string.

```
<!--## comment string -->
```

(WASD-only.) This lets you put a comment in the source document that won't make it into the generated document unless you've set `<--#config verify=1-->`, which echoes all directives as comments.

14

Running CGI Programs

This chapter is intended to show the differences and similarities in running CGI programs on the three Web servers on VMS. Although I don't intend it as a tutorial on CGI programming in general, the content may venture perilously close to it some of the time, since I hope to give enough context so that the rest of the discussion makes sense.

For general information on CGI programming, you might want to check out these books:

CGI Programming in C & Perl: Featuring C and Perl 5 Source Code
By Thomas Boutell
ISBN: 0-201-42219-0

The Official Guide to Programming with CGI.PM
By Lincoln Stein
ISBN: 0-471-24744-8

Some useful Web resources are the CGI interface definition at http://hoohoo.ncsa.uiuc.edu/cgi/ and, for CSWS, the "Dynamic Content with CGI" chapter in the on-line Apache manual at http://yourserver.domain.tld/manual/howto.cgi

14.1 CGI defined

CGI stands for Common Gateway Interface, which, as the name suggests is a standard interface for programs to be run by Web servers. The CGI specifies some environment variables that the program can interrogate to find out about the caller, two methods of argument passing (POST and GET), and a very simple method by which to return results.

It's entirely possible to have a CGI program that doesn't take any arguments—a program that displays the current temperature in the computer room, for example, probably doesn't need anything of the kind, but it does need to execute when requested, perform some processing, and output HTML.

If a CGI is specified as the ACTION in an HTML form (which also specifies the GET or POST methods), the client will pack up the form variables. (Or a client can just do the same thing as though it were called from a form without a form being involved—it doesn't matter to the CGI definition.) In either case, the variables are "URL encoded," which means that they are turned into a long string consisting of `fieldname=value` (for each field) stuck together with ampersands. Values that aren't letters of the alphabet or numeric digits get replaced with a representation of their ASCII value; probably the most familiar one is %20 (the hexadecimal value of the ASCII code for blank).

```
field1=value1&field2=value2%20value22
```

In a GET method, this is appended to the URL of the program after a question mark and is called the query string. GET is the method clients use to ask for pages in any case, and they may use query strings even on static page requests. Most servers ignore that. On a request OSU recognizes as a script (because the path includes a defined script directory such as HTBIN), it will take the string as a query string; on a static page OSU by default treats it as a search string and if you don't have a search script enabled will produce an error. The limitation with using the GET method with OSU is the 4-KB limit on the HTTP request header—large form input will make the URL too long.

```
http://server.domain.tld/cgiscriptpath?field1=value1%20value12
```

The value of the query string will be found in the `QUERY_STRING` environment variable and will typically also be passed on the command line that invokes the program.

With the POST method, the server collects the URL-encoded form fields and provides them to the CGI program (or a wrapper for that program executing in the CGI process) upon request.

You can use a POST method and still have a query string with additional information; some of the CGI utilities will combine the information from the query string with the form fields passed via POST.

All the information sent as form fields comes back as text. Numerical data are passed as text, not as binary data, and the CGI program is responsible for converting it back to a number before doing any calculation. Some languages, such as Perl, just don't care, and will silently do the numeric conversion for you; this is one of the reasons Perl is such a popular language for CGI. After parsing the input, the CGI program does whatever it's meant to do—it inserts records into a database, submits a batch job, targets and fires nuclear missiles, and writes HTTP headers and HTML, plain text, or binary to its output.

Pretty much all CGIs work this way. There are various high-performance options that use different means to communicate with their servers; they may not be fully CGI compliant. If they have API in the name (such as ISAPI), you can figure they use a different application programming interface. There are also CGI accelerators, which spare the cost of spinning up a brand-new process and loading up a brand-new CGI environment; they provide a CGI-compliant environment to the scripts that run under them (such as the RTEs in WASD or HPSS processes in OSU). We'll talk about these in Chapter 17.

Incidentally, while GET and POST are the only methods supported for CGIs that are the Action of a form, clients can invoke CGIs with HEAD or PUT methods, so it may be worth coding to deal with that. It's unlikely that a client will choose to use a HEAD on a CGI that takes parameters, since the client can guess that the output of the CGI is script output rather than a document, but it's fairly likely to happen on output from parameterless CGIs unless the CGIs issue "pragma no-cache" or "expires:" headers, which let the client know the output is expired already so there's no point in doing a HEAD to get the last-updated date. PUT as a rule only involves uploading files. WASD makes sure that CGI scripts comply with HEAD requests by suppressing any output following the CGI header response from a script. An exception is with non-parsed-header scripts, which, by definition, take care of all the HTTP responses themselves; their output is not adjusted at all.

OSU uses DECnet to communicate with the worker processes that execute CGI programs, and so requires talking to SYS$NET instead of the default SYS$INPUT. Except for a little wrapping at the beginning of the program, OSU CGIs function the same as WASD or CSWS. This wrapping is automatically provided for Perl programs by the WWWEXEC.COM script, so Perl CGIs can run unmodified on OSU, WASD, and CSWS. It's also very straightforward to write a little DCL wrapper for a compiled program that runs on CSWS or WASD to make the SYS$NET assignment before running the program, thereby avoiding source code changes. If you have a compiled program that runs under OSU, you can use the mod_OSUscript CSWS component to run it under CSWS or the OSU compatibility scheme to run it under WASD. You can also configure WASD to run CGIs in DECnet processes, either with or without OSU compatibility.

There are various CGI subroutine libraries defined; they simplify the work of parsing the data stream from the server, but they don't do anything particularly magic (such as giving your program access to shared memory with the server; that's what modules are for in CSWS); you can still write CGI programs even if you don't have a CGI library available, and you can use a CGI library other than the one that came with your server. However, for some capabilities you do at least need a CGILIB that knows how to talk to your server. Probably the best advice if you're programming in C is to grab Mark Daniel's CGILIB, which knows how to talk to all three of these servers.

14.2 Environment variables

Environment variables are how the server tells the CGI program about the environment it's running in. Environment variables are the UNIX mechanism addressing the same problem space as symbols and logical names in VMS, and sometimes the concept has to be force-fitted into VMS. (The VMS Perl people have all kinds of fun trying to appropriately populate and manipulate the %ENV array in Perl, given that there can be symbols and logicals with the same name and multiple definitions of logical names in different logical name tables.)

A host (or horde, if you don't like the double meaning of "host") of environment variables are available to the CGI process. Many are provided to give access to the HTTP headers provided by the client; these are typically named HTTP_headername. Others provide more information about the transaction or the environment, or give configuration information that might otherwise be unavailable to a process that doesn't have rights to read the server configuration files.

While there's a core of CGI environment variables supported by each server, not all variables are supported by all servers. In addition, while CSWS and OSU simply don't define any blank variables, WASD will allow certain variables to be blank and define them anyway; therefore, cross-platform scripts must test for both existence and contents of these variables before using them.

These variables may be named as shown or named WWW_name-as-shown. (OSU has a means for prefixing them with anything you like, while the same may be accomplished by either startup option or mapping rule on a per-path basis with WASD.) They default to the plain name in CSWS. The following list doesn't include optional variables that include the contents of form fields; see section 14.6 for more information about them.

AUTH_ACCESS (WASD)

Only defined for authenticated users. Returns with what kind of access they're authorized: "READ" or "READ + WRITE."

AUTH_AGENT (WASD)

Only defined during authentication by an agent. Not for general CGI use. (See Chapter 7 for more details on authentication.)

AUTH_GROUP (WASD)

Only defined for authenticated users. If the user's membership in an authorization group (see Chapter 7 for details) is what got the user to this resource, returns the name of the authorization group.

AUTH_PASSWORD (WASD)

Only defined for authentication performed via the "EXTERNAL" realm (which means the script itself is going to do the authentication). This returns the password the user entered, since the script will presumably need it.

AUTH_REALM (WASD)

Only defined for authenticated users. Returns the name of the realm in which they were authenticated. (This means scripts can be configured not to give up their secrets even when running in "PROMISCUOUS" mode, although anybody who has the privileges to run the server PROMISCUOUSly probably has the privileges to change the scripts not to do that.)

AUTH_REALM_DESCRIPTION (WASD)

Only defined for authenticated users. Returns the (optional) description specified for the real, which is the string displayed when credentials are requested by the browser.

AUTH_REMOTE_USER (WASD)

Only defined for authenticated users. When user name proxying changes an authenticated remote user name into a local SYSUAF equivalent, this variable contains the original, remote user name supplied by the client.

```
AUTH_TYPE (All)
```

Contains the type of authentication used to limit access to the current document, such as "BASIC" or "DIGEST." Undefined if none used for CSWS and OSU; defined but blank in WASD.

```
AUTH_USER (WASD)
```

Details of user authenticated with a CGIplus authentication agent (see Chapter 7 for authentication information). For instance, with SYSUAF authentication this variable will contain any owner string.

```
CONTENT_LENGTH (All)
```

Defined only on POST requests. Contains the length of information provided by a client POST as an ASCII string representing the number of bytes.

```
CONTENT_TYPE (All)
```

Defined only on POST requests. Contains the content type supplied by the client with POSTed data.

```
DATE_GMT (CSWS,WASD)
```

Current date and time according to the server, represented as Greenwich Mean Time.

```
DATE_LOCAL (CSWS,WASD)
```

Current date and time according to the server, shown as local time.

```
DOCUMENT_NAME (CSWS, WASD)
```

Applies only in SSI processing (but CGIs can be called from CSWS SSI documents, so it's available to CGIs).

In CSWS, translates to the file name portion of the path specification (e.g., "preproc.shtml"), while in WASD it translates to a full VMS file specification (e.g., "DKB0:[VMS]PREPROC.SHTML").

```
DOCUMENT_PATH_INFO (CSWS)
```

Applies only in SSI processing. Same as PATH_INFO. If any additional path is included after the document name—that is, http://server.domain.tld/document/more/stuff/here—it ends up in DOCUMENT_PATH_INFO as /more/stuff/here.

```
DOCUMENT_ROOT (CSWS, WASD)
```

In CSWS, this is the document root specified in the configuration for this virtual host—a UNIXified VMS device and directory spec. In WASD this will always be empty.

```
DOCUMENT_URI (CSWS)
```

Applies only in SSI processing. The whole path to the document, including any additional material; http://server.domain.tld/document/more/stuff/here, ends up in DOCUMENT_URI as /document/more/stuff/here.

```
GATEWAY_BG (WASD)
```

Contains the socket BG device name.

```
GATEWAY_INTERFACE (All)
```

Contains "CGI/version" (e.g., "CGI/1.1" for WASD and CSWS, "CGI/1.0" for OSU).

```
GATEWAY_MRS (WASD)
```

Maximum record size of mailbox into which output is written—probably useful to know if you're writing binary files.

```
HTTP_ACCEPT (All)
```

Contains the contents of any "Accept:" headers supplied by the client, otherwise undefined.

```
HTTP_ACCEPT_CHARSET    (All)
```

Contains the contents of any "Accept-Charset:" headers supplied by the client, otherwise undefined.

```
HTTP_ACCEPT_ENCODING (All)
```

Contains the contents of any "Accept-Encoding:" headers supplied by the client; otherwise undefined.

```
HTTP_ACCEPT_LANGUAGE (All)
```

Contains the contents of any "Accept-Language:" headers supplied by the client—for example, "en-us" for U.S. English.

```
HTTP_AUTHORIZATION (All)
```

Contains the contents of any "Authorization:" headers supplied by the client, otherwise undefined.

```
HTTP_CONNECTION (CSWS)
```

Contains the contents of any "Connection:" header supplied by the client. This is typically supplied only if the client supports keep-alives, and can be rendered as "keep_alive" or, in newer Netscape versions, "Keep-Alive".

```
HTTP_COOKIE (All)
```

Contains the contents of any "Cookie:" header supplied by the client (and may not exist if there were no cookies).

```
HTTP_EXTENSION (CSWS, OSU)
```

Contains the contents of any "Extension:" header supplied by the client. A typical value is "Security/Remote-Passphrase."

```
HTTP_FORWARDED (All)
```

Defined if the "Forwarded:" header was supplied by the client (as is the case with proxy servers); contains the contents of that header.

```
HTTP_FROM (All)
```

Defined if the "From:" header was supplied by the client, and contains its contents. (If defined, it contains the completely unvalidated e-mail address of the client user and shouldn't be counted upon.)

```
HTTP_HOST (All)
```

Contains the contents of the "Host:" header supplied by the client. This should contain one of the aliases for the host on which the server is running. It should be the host name from the URL that the client is requesting. Thus a client seeking http://www.serverhost.com:8000/foo.html should supply "www.serverhost.com" in this header. Many browsers do not do this. It is required in HTTP/1.1.

```
HTTP_IF_MODIFIED_SINCE (All)
```

If the client supplied an "If_modified_since:" header, contains the date specified in that header.

```
HTTP_PRAGMA (All)
```

If the client supplied any "Pragma:" headers, contains the pragmas specified.

`HTTP_RANGE (All)`

If the client supplied a "Range:" header, contains the contents. (Useful for stuff like the byterange program in OSU, which enables large files to be supplied chunk by chunk.)

`HTTP_REFERER (All)`

If the client suppled a "Referer:" [sic] header, contains the contents. This is supposed to contain the URL of the form or page from which a link to this script was activated, and the script may refuse to run if it doesn't come from the correct referer. However, clients such as WGET allow users to specify these headers, so the HTTP_REFERER value may be forged.

`HTTP_UA_CPU (CSWS and OSU)`

CPU on which the client is running (e.g., PPC), if that information is supplied by the browser. Handy when downloading client-side software.

`HTTP_UA_OS (CSWS and OSU)`

OS on which the client is running (e.g., MacOS), if that information is supplied by the browser.

`HTTP_USER_AGENT (All)`

If the client supplied a "User-Agent:" header—which it generally does—this contains the contents of that header. This is typically the name of the browser or other tool being used along with some information about the platform it runs on.

`PATH (CSWS)`

This contains the VMS file path to where the CSWS files are stored; in my tests, it returns consistently as apache$root:[000000]. Included for UNIX compatibility, where the PATH variable is similar to the value of DCL$PATH, it can include a list of directories to search to find any executable file name mentioned.

`PATH_INFO (All)`

If any additional path—as distinct from query string—is included after the document name—that is, http://server.domain.tld/script/more/stuff/here—it ends up in PATH_INFO as /more/stuff/here, and if there isn't any additional path, it's blank or not present.

`PATH_ODS (WASD)`

Contains 0, 2, or 5 indicating whether the path of the script has been set as ODS-5 ("5"), ODS-2 ("2"), or not set ("0," which defaults to ODS-2). Could be used to instruct the script on what kind of file name parsing to do.

`PATH_TRANSLATED (All)`

On CSWS, if PATH_INFO is nonblank—that is, if there was an additional path after your script name—then PATH_TRANSLATED gives you the UNIXified (starts with a "/") VMS file name path with the PATH_INFO contents stuck on the end; so for http://server.domain.tld/cgi-bin/scriptname/more/stuff/here PATH_TRANSLATED is /$diskname/directoryname/more/stuff/here, where /$diskname/directoryname is the DOCUMENT_ROOT for this particular virtual host, if PATH_INFO is blank and PATH_TRANSLATED is blank or undefined. On WASD it's the same story except that the translated path is a VMS-style filespec beginning with the device name, not with a /.

On OSU, when PATH_INFO is nonblank, OSU sets PATH_TRANSLATED to the result of passing PATH_INFO's value through the server's translation rules. When PATH_INFO is blank, the translation is mishandled and you see an internal string showing the script path and script directory. It's best not to even look at PATH_TRANSLATED if PATH_INFO is blank.

`QUERY_STRING (All)`

If there was a query string in the URL—a question mark followed by some text—this variable gets the stuff after the question mark. This is how variables are passed in a GET request. The values are URL-escaped, with blanks converted to %20.

`QUERY_STRING_UNESCAPED (CSWS)`

The query-string with URL-escaping reversed, so %20 is converted back to blank. Field-delimiting ampersands are escaped in this string with a backslash, so you can split the string into name = value pairs based on "\&".

`REMOTE_ADDR (All)`

Contains the IP address of the client or proxy making the request.

`REMOTE_HOST (All)`

Contains the host name of the client or proxy making the request, if the server can determine it; otherwise, it contains the IP address. If you have

DNS lookups disabled, the host name will definitely not be determinable, but it can also be unavailable for other reasons.

```
REMOTE_PORT (All)
```

The port on the remote client to which replies should go (of academic interest only, except when debugging a server).

```
REMOTE_USER (All)
```

If the CGI script is password protected, this will contain the user name provided by the client. In WASD, this is defined but blank if the script wasn't password protected; in other servers, it's undefined.

```
REQUEST_METHOD (All)
```

Contains "GET," "HEAD," "PUT," or "POST," depending on the method of the client request. (Forms can only generate GET and POST, but CGIs that don't require forms will sometimes get a HEAD request from browsers looking to see whether a request can be served from cache.)

```
REQUEST_TIME_GMT (WASD)
```

The time the request was received on the server, according to the server's clock, rendered as GMT.

```
REQUEST_TIME_LOCAL (WASD)
```

The time the request was received on the server, according to the server's clock, rendered as local time.

```
REQUEST_URI (WASD and CSWS)
```

The path to the request http://server.domain.tld/cgi-bin/scriptname/whatever yields /cgi-bin/scriptname/whatever.

```
SCRIPT_FILENAME (CSWS, WASD)
```

In CSWS, contains a UNIXified full VMS file path (e.g., /apache$root/cgi-bin/test-cgi-vms.exe) that gets to the script file. In WASD, contains a non-UNIXified full VMS file path that gets to the script file.

```
SCRIPT_NAME (All)
```

Contains the URL path from the root of the CGI script being executed. (So /htbin/dcl_env_rm.com in OSU, not /bin/.)

```
SCRIPT_RTE (WASD)
```

The Run-Time Environment (persistent scripting environment in CGI-plus) in which the current script is being executed.

```
SCRIPT_URI (CSWS)
```

A fully qualified, host name and scheme included, Uniform Resource Identifier that points to this script (e.g., http://server.domain.tld/cgi-bin/scriptname.ext).

```
SCRIPT_URL (CSWS)
```

The URL path to this script—for example, /cgi-bin/scriptname.ext.

```
SERVER_ADDR (WASD)
```

Numeric IP address of the host serving the request.

```
SERVER_ADMIN (CSWS, WASD)
```

The ServerAdmin value from the configuration, which may be an e-mail address; useful to plug into error page scripts and so on.

```
SERVER_CHARSET (WASD)
```

Default server character set (e.g., "ISO-8859-1").

```
SERVER_GMT (WASD)
```

The offset of the server's local time from Greenwich Mean Time; my California-based server shows "-07:00" for Pacific Daylight Time.

```
SERVER_NAME (All)
```

The host name of the host/service/local address that responded to the request; should match HTTP_HOST if the client supported the HOST header.

```
SERVER_PORT (All)
```

Contains the number of the port on which the client accessed the server.

```
SERVER_PROTOCOL (All)
```

Contains "HTTP/level" (e.g., "HTTP/1.0," "HTTP/0.9," or "HTTP/1.1") depending on which protocol the client and server negotiated. (With the same browser, I find CSWS saying "/1.1" while the other two say "/1.0".)

```
SERVER_SIGNATURE (CSWS, WASD)
```

The server signature from the configuration files, useful in error pages and the like. (If you want to be crafty, you can use the server signature only when you detect an HTTP_FORWARDED variable, which is when there might be some confusion about which server the client connected to.)

```
SERVER_SOFTWARE (All)
```

Returns a string describing what software is running on the server. (Unless you've configured it to be something else, which you can do in WASD if you want to hide what server you're running.) Sample values: "HTTPd-WASD/7.2.2aw OpenVMS/AXP SSL," "OSU/3.10alpha;UCX," "Apache/1.3.20 (OpenVMS) PHP/404p11 mod_perl/1.25 mod_ssl/2.8.4 OpenSSL/0.9.5a."

```
UNIQUE_ID (CSWS, WASD)
```

Magically returns a unique value for this request, which can then be used as a temp-file name (in the case of WASD, which uses the same unique_id generator as Apache but substitutes "_" for "@" in the resultant string) or a database key.

14.3 Necessary HTTP headers

Your CGI script actually talks to the server, which relays what you pass along to the client. Because the server doesn't know what the script is going to do or say, the script has to provide the HTTP headers that the server ordinarily provides for static content.

HTTP headers are separated from the rest of the output by one blank line—that is, there's the header, than carriage-return linefeed, then carriage-return linefeed again.

You need at least one header to tell the client what's coming; that's the "Content-type:" header. Some popular values are "Content-type: text/plain" for ASCII text with no markup codes, which the browser will typically display without reformatting, and "Content-type: text/html" for HTML pages, which the browser can render as it sees fit. See the discussion in section 14.5 for more detail.

14.4 Configuration for CGI

Here's a brief summary of the script configuration highlights from Chapter 7. This should be enough to get a directory defined in which you can put scripts that will be executed.

14.4.1 CSWS

```
ScriptAlias url-prefix file-system-path
```

Same syntax as `Alias`, but marks the directory as containing executable CGI scripts. A typical usage example would be a url-prefix of "`/cgi-bin`" and a file-system-path corresponding to "`/$cgi-disk/cgi-bin`". (You could achieve the same effect by using Alias and specifying "`Options +ExecCGI`" in a container directive for that directory or path.)

```
ScriptAliasMatch url-pattern file-system-path
```

Same meaning as `ScriptAlias`, but uses regular expression for the url-pattern.

14.4.2 OSU

OSU's script-directory commands weren't covered very fully in Chapter 7, so this is new material. The directive to establish a path (which may be to an individual script or to a directory) as containing executable scripts is:

```
EXEC /path VMS-path-or-MST-processor-spec
```

`HTBIN` is an obsolete directive that still works.

```
HTBIN WWW_ROOT:[BIN]
```

is equivalent to:

```
EXEC /HTBIN/* WWW_ROOT:[BIN]
```

`EXEC` is considerably more flexible, since it allows multiple script directories. You can define processors (either high-performance script server [HPSS] or MST processors) for anything with a particular path; the processor itself must be configured to know how to map the path and find the script it's meant to execute.

If you just give a VMS directory path as the second argument to the directive, scripts in that directory will be processed via the DECnet object WWWEXEC. You may need to copy WWWEXEC and some supporting files (CGI_SYMBOLS.EXE) from WWW_ROOT:[BIN] into other script directories, or tweak WWWEXEC so it knows to run CGI_SYMBOLS from WWW_ROOT:[BIN].

There'll be more discussion of MST and HPSS processes in Chapter 17; the rest of this chapter will discuss DECnet-based CGI scripting in OSU.

14.4.3 WASD

In previous chapters I've discussed the possibilities of using some account other than the default WASD account for scripting. While this is crucial when letting users write scripts, it's not a bad idea even for scripts you get to bench-check first. See the /PERSONA startup qualifier and the SET path SCRIPT=AS=username directive; there's a somewhat fuller discussion in Chapter 13.

WASD offers three mapping rules that relate to CGI scripting. Exec and uxec rules map script directories; the script rule maps a specific script. We'll discuss UXEC fully in Chapter 19, so we're skipping it for now.

```
EXEC[+] template [(RTEname)]result
```

The template should include a wildcard so that named scripts will be matched, resulting in something like "/htbin/*". The result can have the wildcard substituted in, resulting in something like "/ht_root/bin/*". This instructs the server both where to look for files in htbin and that those files should be treated as executables.

This means that any script in the directory can be executed, which means that anybody who can contrive to put a file in that directory can get the server to execute anything he or she wants. Make sure permissions are set appropriately.

If the "exec+" form is used, the CGIplus persistent scripting environment will be used. If a Run-Time Environment name is given, that environment (e.g., a persistent Perl process) will be used. (More discussion on CGIplus and RTEs can be found in Chapter 17.)

```
SCRIPT template  file-system-path-to-script
```

The script rule maps a URL to a particular file and makes that file executable. This can be used to make a script look like a static Web page—for example,

```
SCRIPT /status.html  /cgi-bin/status.pl
```

or for making sure only specific named scripts in particular locations are run. Typically the template will look like "/scriptname*", and the path to script like "/Web/myscripts/bin/scriptname.exe*"; the wildcards here are to pass along path names on which the scripts should operate.

Before you go into production, go back to Chapter 7 and read about the WASD SET commands with SCRIPT options.

14.5 CGI environment

14.5.1 CSWS

When a CGI process is activated under CSWS, it has a full complement of symbols defined, with the names of the environment variables.

SYS$OUTPUT points to a socket that will be read by the server. The socket is a BG device. If you use writes from DCL, the C RTL, or any language that goes through RMS, the carriage-control attribute of the socket will be applied, whether you're writing text or binary data, and can mess up your binary data.

HTTP headers must be separated with carriage-return followed by linefeed. If you need to send binaries, use APACHE$FLIP_CCL.EXE to change the state of the carriage-control attribute (initially "ON"). Run it after sending the headers, or make sure to use explicit carriage-return linefeeds on your headers if you emit them after running APACHE$FLIP_CCL. The release notes recommend using the F$FAO lexical function, like so:

```
$ write sys$output f$fao("!AS!/!/","Content-type: image/
jpeg")
```

(`"!/"` will produce the explicit CRLF needed.)

Use APACHE$DCL_BIN.EXE to copy binary files from within DCL scripts. If you're running a C program that needs to copy a large binary file, you can link to the APACHE$FIXBG shareable image and call the routine to change the socket characteristics to work with large binary files. See the release notes for details.

Nothing special is done to SYS$INPUT; if you're in a DCL program it points to SYS$COMMAND (the DCL file itself). If you need to accept PUT or POSTed data (since you can get the stuff sent with GET from the QUERY_STRING variable), you can assign SYS$INPUT to APACHE$INPUT, or read directly from APACHE$INPUT. (You then have to parse the results yourself, which is annoying in DCL but straightforward enough.)

14.5.2 OSU

OSU runs scripts in separate processes to which the server has a logical link via DECnet. The processes can be kept around for multiple script executions, saving process start times. OSU makes the connection to the

WWWEXEC DECnet object, which runs the command procedure WWWEXEC.COM; you can (and should) read the command procedure to see exactly what's going on. There's built-in support for executables, DCL procedures, Perl scripts, and PHP pages; you can edit the procedure to support other languages if you like.

The command procedure can have a dialog with the server over the DECnet link. (The device name is SYS$NET, but WWWEXEC.COM opens NET_LINK, so both it and scripts it runs can read and write to that.) The server always starts by sending WWWEXEC, the method (GET, POST, PUT, etc.), protocol, and URL (file portion of the URI) from the request.

Special `<DNETxxx>` tags are used to send commands to the server, as follows; these notes are based on the comments in the WWWEXEC file.

`<DNETARG>`

Instructs the server to send script process the search argument (that is, the query string) parsed from the URL of request. If the argument was generated by an HTML form, the response message may be quite long—possibly even too long for DCL, which has an upper limit of 255 characters for a symbol value or 1,024 for a symbol value with all the translations done.

`<DNETARG2>`

Same as `<DNETARG>` except that the argument is truncated to 255 characters to fit in a DCL symbol.

`<DNETBINDIR>`

Instructs the servers to send the htbin directory string as defined in the rule file—that is, tell it where to find executables.

`<DNETCGI>`

Instructs the server to read DECnet data "raw" and interpret data sent by Scriptserver as CGI (Common Gateway Interface) script output. If first line is `location: <URL>`, a redirect is performed. End of data is flagged by `</DNETCGI>`.

`<DNETHDR>`

Instructs the server to send the HTTP request header lines sent by the client to the server. Last line sent will be a zero-length line. (This allows the setting of the HTTP_xxx environment variables.)

`<DNETHOST>`

Instructs the server to send the http_default_host environment variable (host name to use in constructing URLs).

`<DNETID>`

Instructs the server to send the server version, the http_default_host environment variable, the local port for the connection, and the remote port and host address. A single message is sent with the items separated by spaces. Note that the remote address is sent as a signed value.

`<DNETINPUT>`

Instructs the server to read data from the client TCP connection and pass it on to the script process. Only one DECnet message will come back in response; if more data are still needed, the script process needs to ask for these data. (This is how arbitrarily large PUT files can be uploaded.)

`<DNETPATH>`

Instructs the server to send the matching portion of the translated URL that caused the script to be invoked—in other words, what ends up in the PATH environment variable. This will be truncated to 255 characters to fit in a symbol and converted to uppercase.

`<DNETRAW>`

Instructs the server to read DECnet data "raw" from the script process and send to the client. The script process is responsible for formatting the entire response in conformance with the HTTP protocol (including carriage control characters). End of data is flagged by a DECnet message consisting solely of "`</DNETRAW>`", which will cause the server to close the connection.

`<DNETRECMODE>`

Instructs the server to process any subsequent `<DNETRAW>` or `<DNETCGI>` using "record" mode rather than "stream" mode. In record mode, an implied CRLF is added to the end of every DECnet record. The maximum record length is reduced to 4,094 bytes (because the cr/lf takes up two bytes out of the 4,096).

`<DNETRECMODE2>`

Forces "alternate" record mode, which means it tries to use longer records.

<DNETREUSE>

Instructs the server to try to reuse this script process (which will work up to the specified maximum number of times from the configuration).

<DNETRQURL>

Instructs the server to pass along the actual URL (prior to rule file transformations) specified in the client's request; the server returns a single DECnet message.

<DNETTEXT>

Instructs the server to send the client an HTTP protocol response with a content-type of "text/plain" and follow with data provided by the scripting process. The script process will first send an HTTP status line (e.g., "200 sending doc") and then follow it with text that is to appear in the user's output window.

Data are sent assuming implied carriage control; the server appends a new line (CRLF) to each DECnet message it receives over the logical link. The script process marks the end of the text data by sending a line consisting solely of the string "</DNETTEXT>", upon receipt of which the server will close the connection.

<DNETXLATE>

Instructs the server so that the next thing coming from the script process is a URL to translate according to the rules file, after which it should send the results back to the script process.

<DNETXLATEV>

Works the same as <DNETXLATE> but honors any document protection rules in force for this particular connection. If the user isn't entitled to see the document based on the URL passed, the translation comes back blank.

You'll mostly have to pay attention to these <DNETxxx> headers only if you're doing DCL scripting or if you don't want to use the provided CGILIB. If you're running Perl or PHP, WWWEXEC will quietly set up the environment on your behalf.

To get the environment symbols defined, run CGI_SYMBOLS. (WWWEXEC defines this as a foreign command, since it takes command-line arguments.) The usage is either:

```
$ CGI_SYMBOLS prefix [form_prefix] [field=filenamepairs]
[bitmask]
```

or

```
$ CGI_SYMBOLS logical-name-table  [temp-file-
name.extension]
```

In the first style, CGI_SYMBOLS defines local symbols using whatever prefix you specified—for example, WWW_ will create symbols named WWW_xxxx; if you specify a form_prefix, symbols will be created for the form fields that came back in this request. Assuming you used FORM_ as the form_prefix, you'll get a symbol called FORM_FIELDS containing a comma-separated list of field names specified in the form return, a symbol for each field named FORM_FLD_name, and a FORM_FLD_nnnn (that is, the number of the matched field in the list of form fields), which contains the value of the form field. The third argument is a hack to get around the problem of field values, which can be longer than 255 characters; you can specify a comma-separated list of "fieldname=filename" pairs, and CGI_SYMBOLS will write the values of each of those fields into the file name specified for it, defining the value of the FORM_FLD_nnnn symbol as the file name for that field.

CGI_SYMBOLS by default will issue a `<DNETCGI>` to the server, which puts the link to the HTTP server into CGI mode and sets the environment so that WWWEXEC will automatically send the CGI terminator when the DCL script exits. In this mode writes must have explicit carriage-control characters; also, the first line output must be either a `content-type:` header or a `location:` header, followed by a blank line. If you don't want to be in CGI mode after the symbols are defined, you can tell CGI_SYMBOLS not to do that by using as the fourth argument a bitmask with bit 0 set (e.g., "1").

In the second style, CGI_SYMBOLS defines logicals instead of symbols for the environment variables, and it defines them in the logical-name table you specify. If a file name is defined (which must include the "." so that CGI_SYMBOLS can tell it's a file name), the request content (query string or post block) will be put into that file. (WWWEXEC uses this second style to set up the environment for Perl scripts to run portably.)

It's typical to run CGI_SYMBOLS explicitly only in DCL scripts, but you could do it for any script that didn't want to bother parsing the data itself.

WWWEXEC knows what to do with .COM, .EXE, .PL, and .PHP files. If you want to execute files with some other extension, you need to edit WWWEXEC and tell it what to do—there's no configuration option such as `AddHandler`.

14.5.3 WASD

Environment variables include form fields, which are defined as WWW_FORM_fieldname. The prefix of environment variables is WWW_ by default, although this may be changed on a serverwide basis using the /CGI_PREFIX startup qualifier or selectively on a per-path basis using the CGIPREFIX mapping rule. This latter method allows scripts requiring different or no prefixes to be configured without disrupting other scripts that expect the prefix. If you need to read POST information, the device to read is HTTP$INPUT.

WASD pays attention to the `content-type:` header produced by the scripts and attempts to treat the output appropriately.

The kind of communication handled with `DNETxxx` headers in OSU is handled through callouts in WASD. (It can also be approached via the `Script-Control:` header, which is discussed next.)

CGI/CGIplus callouts are initiated by the script process. The script writes a special escape character or sequence to the server mailbox; the value of the sequence is the translation of the logical CGIPLUSESC. Once the dialog is opened by the script process, it can consist of any number of (script request: server response) pairs until the script ends the callout. (Requests can suppress responses, so there can legitimately be more requests than responses in a callout dialog.)

Requests look like this:

```
[!|#]keyword: parameters
```

(The optional exclamation point or hash tells the server not to bother responding.)

Responses look like this:

```
status-code  response
```

Here are the keywords. (Some of these really apply only to CGIplus, not CGI, but it makes sense to describe the mechanism completely here.)

```
AUTH-FILE: file specification
```

If /PROFILE is enabled, this determines whether the user name associated with the request is authorized to access the file specified.

```
CGIPLUS: struct|record
```

tells the server that this CGIplus script can process the CGI variables in "struct" mode. By default each CGI variable is transferred to a CGIplus script one "record" at a time. In "struct" mode all variables are transferred in a single, binary I/O, which the script then has to parse.

```
GATEWAY-BEGIN: status-code
```

If you're using the raw TCP/IP socket for output—which there is rarely a good reason to do; it's not even noticeably faster—this callout tells the server about it and gives an HTTP status code.

```
GATEWAY-END: integer
```

If you're using the raw TCP/IP socket for output, this callout tells the server the quantity of data transferred directly to the client by the script.

```
LIFETIME: minutes-to-live|0|-1|none
```

sets or resets a script process lifetime (in minutes). It can extend the lifetime before rundown of frequently used scripts, overriding the `[DclCgiPlus-LifeTime]` configuration parameter. Zero resets to configuration default; `-1` or `none` makes the script process immortal.

```
MAP-FILE: file specification
```

Maps a file back to its URL-style path equivalent; it doesn't guarantee that the file name is legal.

```
MAP-PATH: URL-style path
```

Maps the URL-style path against the server's rule database into a VMS file specification. Note that this does not verify the file name's legality or that the file actually exists.

```
NOOP:
```

No operation. Just return a success response. (You probably won't be using this one much.)

```
TIMEOUT-BIT-BUCKET: number-of-minutes
```

tells the server how long to let a script continue after the client disconnects. Overrides the HTTPD$CONFIG `[DclBitBucketTimeout]` configuration directive.

```
TIMEOUT-OUTPUT: minutes | 0 | -1 | none
```

sets or resets a script request lifetime (in minutes, overrides the `[Timeout-Output]` configuration parameter), even if the script doesn't generate any output in that time. Specifying `none` (or `-1`) gives it an infinite lifetime; zero resets to default.

```
TIMEOUT-NOPROGRESS: minutes | 0 | -1 | none
```

sets or resets a script request no-progress timeout counter. The no-progress period is the maximum number of seconds for which there may be no output from the script before it is aborted. Specifying `none` (or `-1`) gives it an infinite lifetime; zero resets to default.

```
Script-Control
```

is a proposed CGI/1.2 header, with the directive `no-abort`; WASD implements not only that but an assortment of WASD-specific extensions, as follows (in a list based on the WASD documentation).

```
no-abort
```

forbids the server from terminating the script process even if it isn't producing any output. Possibly useful if you've got an incredibly slow script, but dangerous because such scripts can accumulate and clog up your server.

```
X-buffer-records
```

tells the server to buffer records written by the script until there are `[BufferSizeDclOutput]` bytes available, then write it as a single block to the client.

```
X-crlf-mode
```

tells the server to add a trailing CRLF on each record that doesn't have one. That's standard VMS carriage-control, but it's also what's needed for HTTP headers.

```
X-lifetime=number-of-minutes|0|NONE
```

sets the idle lifetime of the current script process; if it doesn't get any work before the number of minutes specified, it's deleted; zero sets the lifetime to the configuration default; `none` exempts it from idle-process pruning.

```
X-record-mode
```

tells the server to add a trailing LF on each record that doesn't have one, regardless of content type. This is what is usually required by browsers for carriage-control in text documents.

```
X-stream-mode
```

tells the server to leave the carriage-control strictly alone; regardless of content type, what it sends the client is exactly what the script writes.

`X-timeout-noprogress=number-of-minutes|0|NONE`

The length of time the process will be allowed to go without any output before the server decides it's wedged and deletes it. Zero sets this length back to the configuration default; `none` keeps the server from tracking this info.

`X-timeout-output=number-of-minutes|0|NONE`

The length of time the process will be allowed to continue if it hasn't finished before being deleted by the server, regardless of whether it's still processing the request. Zero sets it back to the default; `none` disables this functionality.

WASD provides the CGIUTL utility, a Swiss army knife that does a bidirectional assortment of things on behalf of DCL scripts. Define HT_EXE:CGIUTL as a foreign command and you can use these qualifiers (based on the list in the comments of the program):

`/2QUOTE`

Double up the quotes in the symbol given as a parameter (when you want the quotes to actually be part of the definition).

`/BODY`

Output the request body.

`/CGIRESPONSE[=status-code]`

Send CGI header with this status code (default 200).

`/CHARSET=character-set-name`

Tells CGIUTL to explicitly specify a "text/" response character set (to suppress just supply an empty string).

`/CONTENT=content-type`

Sets the content-type for the response (default "text/plain").

`/COPY`

Copy the file given as a command-line parameter out to the client.

`/DBUG`

Turns on all "if (Debug)" statements.

`/EXPIRED`

Add a preexpired "`Expires:`" header to the output.

`/FIELD=fieldname`

Just output the value of this particular field.

`/FORMAT=HEADINGS|NAMES|NONE`

applies when writing a form-URL-encoded body as a file; "`HEADINGS`" says to use underlined headings, "`NAMES`" says to use "`field-name: field-value`", while "`NONE`" suppresses field names completely.

`/LOCATION=new-location-URI`

sends a `302` HTTP header (redirect) with the specified location.

`/MAXSYM=maxchars`

sets the maximum number of characters per output symbol value (and will spill over values to additional symbols).

`/MULTIPART`

Body is multipart/form-data—used to enable file uploading.

`/OUTPUT=filespec`

Output to specified file; filespec is a VMS file specification.

`/PREFIX=string`

Use this prefix for all the created symbol names; defaults to "CGIUTL."

`/[NO]QUIETLY`

When an error occurs, exit with the status inhibited (allowing the procedure to do its own error recovery).

`/RESPONSE[=status-code]`

Send a nonparsed header—that is, not interpreted by the server—with this status code (default 200).

`/SOFTWAREID`

A synonym for `/VERSION`; displays CGIUTL and CGILIB versions.

`/SYMBOLS[=LINES,NOCONTROL]`

Put the parsed input into DCL symbols, optionally one line per symbol (<LF> delimited), optionally strip control characters (e.g., <HT>). (This is for the benefit of scripts dealing with forms that have TEXTAREAs, which can be much longer than will fit into a single symbol.)

`/URLDECODE`

Read and decode a form-URL-encoded, POSTed body; use with `/SYMBOL` or `/OUTPUT` to specify whether to decode it into DCL symbols or to write the output to a temp file.

14.6 Languages for CGI

The VMS calling standard means that any compliant language can call code in any other compliant language. Perl, Python, and DCL aren't compliant languages, more's the pity, but C, FORTRAN, COBOL, BASIC, MACRO, PL/I, and Dibol can all interoperate and, because of the simplicity of the CGI, all do Web work. (Perl and Python are extensible, so you can write some glue to call subroutines in C or, with more trouble, other languages.)

This may not be worth your while, but is at least a theoretical possibility, and might become a reasonable thing to do if you have extensive application-specific subroutine libraries already and want to Web-enable those capabilities.

14.6.1 DCL

The simplest workable CGI needs to put out a header followed by a blank line, and then some actual text. This looks different on each server. Here's how you could show your current system uptime on each one:

CSWS

```
$ write sys$output f$fao("!AS!/!/","Content-type: text/
plain")
$ SHOW SYSTEM/NOPROC
```

OSU

```
$ define sys$output net_link
$ write sys$output "<DNETRECMODE>"
$ write sys$output "<DNETCGI>"
$ write sys$output "content-type: text/plain"
$ write sys$output " "
$ SHOW SYSTEM/NOPROC
$ write sys$output "</DNETCGI>
```

WASD

```
$ write sys$output f$fao("!AS!/!/","Content-type: text/
plain")
$ SHOW SYSTEM/NOPROC
```

Each server comes with at least one example DCL CGI. (Many of the OSU examples use a clever strategy of including the form text in the script, using a `$ CREATE` command to copy the form to the output. This is quite handy and can be used with the other servers as well.)

14.6.2 C/C++

Get the WASD-CGILIB from the WASD site and you should be able to link C programs or C++ programs for other servers and have them work, provided that they were written portably enough to run on VMS. If you're running OSU, you can also just use the OSU-CGILIB (it's a bit confusing because both packages supply a collection of different functions to interact with the scripting environment).

OSU and WASD come with lots of C-based scripts if you want to go through them in detail and figure out how they do what they do.

14.6.3 FORTRAN

You can certainly write CGI programs in FORTRAN. A splendid example is Jonathan Boswell's HYPERMAIL, which serves mail archives to the Web. You can find it at http://www.newtrumpet.org/jsb/hypermail/.

(I've used this program to serve mailing list archives for about five years and been quite happy with it. Mark Daniel's yahMAIL is a complete mail user agent as well as an archive server, so I use that as well.)

This was written specifically for OSU and uses the `<DNETxxx>` dialog shown previously. Here's an example of that dialog:

```
C  Connect to network link established by WWWEXEC.COM
   Open (unit=1, file='net_link:', status='old',
   1     carriagecontrol='list', recl=4096)

   Write(1,10) '<DNETRECMODE>'
10 Format(a)
   Write(1,10) '<DNETRQURL>'
   Read (1,20,end=30) RqurlL,Requested_URL
20 Format(q,a)
```

```
30 Write(1,10) '<DNETCGI>'
   Write(1,10) 'status: 200 Sending document'
   Write(1,10) 'content-type: text/html'
   Write(1,10) !Yes, that's right! A null record. Take THAT, C.
   Write(1,10)
$   '<html><head><title>HYPERMAILV1.4</title></head><body>'
```

The program also has handy, swipeable code for URL-encoding and decoding and request parsing as well, using calls to the STR$ run time library rather than the fairly weak native FORTRAN string manipulation capability. This approach can be emulated even in Macro code. If you've got a FORTRAN program you want to Web-enable, or if you just like FORTRAN, get HYPERMAIL and study it.

Another approach, which should work for WASD and OSU, is to run CGI_SYMBOLS or CGIUTL and make symbols out of form fields, and then do calls to LIB$GET_SYMBOL to get the values.

14.6.4 Perl

Perl is an extremely handy scripting language, and the CGI.PM module makes it a splendid CGI language. CGI.PM takes care of most of the bookkeeping; you can use it to define forms or you can use it with static forms. The Perl cabal have recognized CGI as a core utility, so you get it with each Perl distribution and don't even have to download it separately.

On UNIX systems the Perl scripts are usually named "name" rather than "name.pl," and have the execute bit set. The shell reads the first line of the script, which has a `"#!/path-to-perl"` at the top (sometimes called "the shebang line") and invokes the processor it finds at that path.

No part of this scheme works on VMS—there is no execute bit, DCL won't parse a shebang line, and so on. If you're porting Perl scripts from UNIX, you will at the very least need to change the name from "name" to "name.pl."

If the script is pure Perl, that may well be all you need to do. If it makes system( ) calls to utilities that don't exist on VMS, uses extensions you haven't installed, and so on, then you have more work to do. (Some Perl scripts explicitly open a pipe to sendmail when they want to send mail, which is completely unnecessary, as well as flagrantly unportable; it won't even work on UNIX systems that run exim or qmail instead of sendmail.)

In CSWS, if you've installed mod_perl and defined a handler for the .PL data type, the .pl scripts will be executed reasonably if they're in a directory

CSWS expects to find Perl scripts in. (To see if you've got this working, rename the "printenv" script you find in CGI-BIN to "printenv.pl" and copy it to apache$common:[perl]; then run it as yourserver/perl/printenv.pl.) As mod_perl comes configured out of the box, it expects to find Perl scripts in apache$common:[perl], not in cgi-bin.

Similarly, in WASD, if you've mapped .PL under `[DclScriptRunTime]`, it knows to use the Perl interpreter on your script. (At least if you haven't specified one of the higher-performance server options.)

In OSU, the distributed WWWEXEC knows what to do with a .PL extension. (It looks for webperl, then looks for perl, then looks for miniperl, and invokes the script with output redirected to NET_LINK.)

Here's printenv from the Apache distribution, which should work on any of the Web servers. It gives a little bit of the flavor of Perl:

```
#!/usr/local/bin/perl
##
##  printenv -- demo CGI program which just prints its
environment
##

print "Content-type: text/html\n\n";
print "<HTML>\n";
print "<HEAD><TITLE>All the environment variables</
TITLE></HEAD>\n";
print "<BODY>\n";
print "<PRE>\n";

foreach $var (sort(keys(%ENV))) {
    $val = $ENV{$var};
    $val =~ s|\n|\\n|g;
    $val =~ s|"|\\"|g;
    print "${var}=\"${val}\"\n";
}

print "</PRE>\n";
print "</BODY>\n";
print "</HTML>\n";
```

(The central loop is very characteristic of Perl. %ENV is an associative array, which they call a hash; it's an array of environment-variable values indexed by environment variable names. keys(%ENV) creates a temporary array of the names of the variables; sort(keys(%ENV)) creates a temporary array of those names sorted in alphabetical order. So this says, for each environment variable taken in alphabetical order, which we'll refer to as the scalar $var, look up the value (that's what $val=$ENV{$var} does), then escape any new lines or quotes in the value so they don't mess up the display, then print a line showing the name/value pair. That's quite a lot for six lines, one of which consists entirely of a right curly brace. And this isn't even getting into CGI.PM.

14.6.5 PHP4

In December 2001 Compaq announced a beta release of MOD_PHP, the module that makes PHP work with CSWS. There are literally dozens of books on how to use PHP, so I'll gloss over this briefly here. PHP can also be used with OSU—indeed, David Jones of the OSU server did the first VMS port of PHP—and WASD.

PHP is an annoying recursive acronym; it stands for PHP Hypertext Processor. It's basically a template language; a PHP page is HTML with special tags (similar to server-side includes) that are interpreted by PHP and replaced with the results of various actions, which can include database lookups, script executions, and so on. The PHP scripting language is pretty complete, and in fact you can write fully functional PHP scripts that aren't embedded in HTML pages and still have them be useful.

A very typical use of PHP is to show catalog pages. Where the SSI approach would require one page for each item (which dynamically included the standard headers and footers), the PHP approach would have only one page, with the item number passed as a parameter that would cause PHP to do a database lookup, fetch the specific content for that item, and plug it into the page. PHP is also used to display newspaper stories and in forums. The free software news and rumors site, Slashdot, is run in PHP.

In general, this approach lets you separate the data from the representation. An artistic HTML developer can make the pages look gorgeous while the actual information is maintained elsewhere, usually by somebody else.

In CSWS, if you've installed mod_php, PHP will handle .PHP or .PHTML files wherever it finds them.

In OSU, WWWEXEC knows to run WWW_SYSTEM:PHP.EXE against any .PHP script it finds in an EXEC (HTBIN) directory. It can also be configured as a presentation rule for .PHP files found anywhere. You can either just run the PHP from the command line as the presentation rule, or use the high-performance server script (HPSS), specifying

```
presentation text/php %hpss:hpss_srv_php
```

WASD has a persistent PHP engine (implemented using CGIplus/RTE) supported in the same manner as all of the others. Just install the engine interface and either David Jones's PHP port or the mod_PHP package (which gives you the ability to run PHP from the command line) and have the PHP command defined systemwide. You should be able to get PHP pages processed by adding the following rule to the `[DclScriptRunTime]` configuration directive in HTTPD$CONFIG.CONF:

```
.php PHP
```

Here's the MOD_PHP demo page. It doesn't show off many of the features of PHP but does demonstrate the basic idea of PHP programs embedded in tags that can be included in HTML pages. It happens that in this one the HTML page is entirely generated by the PHP program. PHP can do arithmetic, looping, and all the other programming language stuff you'd expect, and can be extended with plug-ins to do graphics, database lookups, and so on.

```
<?php
echo "<HTML>";
echo "  <HEAD>";
echo "    <TITLE>Mod_Php Rules</TITLE>";
echo "  </HEAD>";
echo "  <BODY>";
echo "    <P>";
echo "    <H1 ALIGN=\"CENTER\">Mod_Php Rules !!</H1>";
echo "    <P>";
echo "    Resistance is futile....";
echo "    <P>";
echo "    <HR>";
echo "  </BODY>";
echo "</HTML>";
?>
```

14.6.6 Python

Python is yet another scripting language. It's known to work well with WASD. There's a report of a successful port of the UNIX mod_python to VMS, but it's not distributed by the CSWS group. Python has a capable CGI module. As with Perl and PHP, it can be extended.

I'm not sure how best to make Python scripts run in CSWS without mod_python. You can do DCL wrapping, but you need to be sure that the query string ends up on the command line if it was a GET request.

In OSU, you need to edit WWWEXEC and tell it to run Python on .PY scripts, possibly with the same kind of wrapping as Perl gets, or embed your script in a DCL wrapper.

On WASD, you just need a `[DclScriptRunTime]` entry if you have the Python command defined systemwide.

```
.py PYTHON
```

14.6.7 Java

Java applications typically run as "servlets" in a special scripting environment, so I will discuss them in Chapter 17.

15

RDB Database Access from CGI Scripts

Most serious Web applications have an underlying database. On a UNIX system this might be MySQL, PostgresSQL, Oracle, DB2, or another database package. On VMS, it could be Oracle Server, Oracle (formerly Digital) Rdb, Cache, or Mimer. But I'm only going to talk about Rdb—first, because that's the database that I have experience with; second, because that database has only fairly recently acquired most of the Web connection tools needed; and, third, because there's all kinds of documentation available for tools such as Oracle Developer and you don't need this book to get the information. Some of the concepts discussed in this chapter may be useful with other databases, but the specifics are all for Rdb.

Without any special database connectivity software you can still communicate databases by having your program write database update or query scripts, spawning them, and parsing the results. This is both ugly and slow, but it could be good enough for very occasional use. (You could even write Datatrieve scripts, taking advantage of Datatrieve's ability to write HTML output to skip the parsing step.) Here are the special tools available to connect Rdb to the Web.

15.1 Rdb Web Agent

Don't confuse this with the Oracle Web Cartridge, which works only if you're running the Oracle Web Server. The Rdb Web Agent, which can run under any of the Web servers, is a CGI package that stands between the Web server and the database, invoking a program that's written as a stored procedure in the database. (More precisely, the RdbWeb executable runs as a CGI and connects to a SQL Services service that you specify in the RdbWeb.cfg file. A useful result of this implementation is that it can connect to SQL Services on servers other than your Web server, allowing you to segregate your exposed-to-the-world Web machines from your database machines.)

Oracle provides a lot of SQL functions for generating HTML output elements, but in my experience those functions don't add much convenience. It's possible to call compiled code as an external function. You have to go through a shareable image library, which is a pain, but at least that mechanism allows you to call any RTL routine you need to.

Rdb Web Agent routines, as with any other CGIs, can generate their own input forms or can just be called as the action routine from prewritten forms. A drawback of having them generate their own forms is that there's no equivalent of the Perl HERE document or the DCL $DECK command, so you can't stick the unmodified HTML for the form into the program; you need to write it out, line by line. (You can have multiple-line writes, but you're still concatenating quoted strings to build the page, and it's very tiresome for complicated pages.)

Rdb Web Agent works reliably, but it has a number of limitations. The fact that programs are stored procedures in the database means that they can't cross databases—your application may deal only with tables in the same physical database as the program. For some applications this is a fatal drawback. In addition, you have to shut down all access to the database to make a change in the stored procedures, which is very inconvenient. If you want to use the same code against different databases, each database must have its own copy.

It's all SQL code. SQL is not the best application language possible. The means by which you find out if your code even compiles is to attempt to store it as a stored procedure. The entire program is rescanned. If there's an error, you get a message that there's an error—somewhere, but there are no hints about line numbers or quotations of invalid syntax. Since you can't update the stored procedure when there's a client, you need to shut down the SQL Services service that serves this database when you want to update the program. If you then find an error after you've dropped the old but presumably working version and then found that your new version doesn't compile, panic may ensue.

RDB Web is definitely better than nothing, and I've used it successfully for a couple of small applications. But it has severe limitations and can't be the only tool in your box for database programming; you'll eventually need to validate against tables in one database for entry into another.

15.2 Embedded RDO or SQL module language

If you have experience writing FORTRAN, C, Pascal, or BASIC that connects to your database using either the RDO precompiler or the SQL module language, you can do the same thing; you just need to hook the program up to the Web. (I discussed doing that in Chapter 14.) Of course, all of these languages take more effort to hook to the Web than Python or Perl. (I give no examples of embedded RDO or SQL Module language here because if you don't already know what they look like, you probably don't want to start messing with them now.)

15.3 Perl, DBI, and DBD::RDB

Perl has a good design to make multiple plug-ins available at the same time. These make it easy to do CGI programming with Perl. There's a whole architecture (DBI—DataBase Interface) for plugging in database connectivity to Perl. DBI is the general Perl-to-data-source interface; individual databases are hooked up using the database driver (DBD) modules. Andreas Stiller has put together `DBD::RDB`, a database driver module for RDB. You must have a recent version of Perl—the CSWS_PERL or the prebuilt kit are both at 5.6.1, which is fine. `DBD::RDB` needs to link against the SQL module language libraries, so your machine must have the RDB development kit—not just the run time—installed in order to build and run `DBD::RDB`.

You must first have DBI installed. It comes in the prebuilt Perl; if you're running CSWS Perl, you can install the prebuilt and then install DBI from that directory tree into CSWS Perl. (This is a good idea only because any VMS configuration/compilation difficulties have been ironed out already. In theory, you can also fetch the module from www.cpan.org, but in practice the version you get from CPAN may not build properly, so it's worth sticking with the prebuilt Perl kit.)

The way to install any module or distribution in Perl is the same. With your default set to the directory the module is in, and your PERL_ROOT and PERLSHR defined in terms of the Perl you want to install into, do

```
$ PERL makefile.pl
$ mms
$ mms test
$ mms install
```

MMK can be used here instead of MMS, if you have MMK and don't have MMS. Don't run `MMS INSTALL` if `MMS TEST` produced any alarming test failures.

Next, you need to fetch the `DBD::RDB` module from CPAN, the Comprehensive Perl Archive Network. Point a browser at WWW.CPAN.ORG, do search-by-author, and look for `ASTILLER`. Download the ZIP file for the package and unzip it. You can do this to produce the same thing:

```
$ PERL makefile.pl
$ mms
$ mms test
$ mms install
```

Please note here that there are `DBD::` modules for many databases that run on VMS; RDB is just the example I'm used to. You can get the `DBD::Oracle` or `DBD::Sybase` module from CPAN just the same way and try to build it. You can't just get the module and build it if you don't have the database installed; the way these modules work is to act as glue, using the callable SQL interface from the database to make a connection with your Perl scripts. If you have more than one database product, you can have more than one `DBD::` module and you can connect to both database products in the same script, which is very handy for data extraction activities even aside from CGI programs. There are also `DBD::` modules for comma-separated variable files and xBase file formats; these include SQL parsers and code to actually do the data extraction and update themselves.

Here's an excerpt from the test script from the `DBD::RDB` module, just to give you an idea of what Perl DBI code looks like. If you want to do DBI coding, you should buy the O'Reilly book, which is enormously helpful. If you don't know Perl at all and you don't know SQL at all, you should just skip this excerpt. This test script creates a database, creates a table, retrieves the field names for the table, populates the table, retrieves the contents, and makes sure it got what it expected.

```
use DBI;
use strict;

my $print_error = 0;
print "1..45\n";


#
# load driver
#
```

```
my $ok = require DBD::RDB;
printf("%sok 1\n", ($ok ? "" : "not "));

#
# create test database;
#
eval {
    my $dbh = DBI->connect( 'dbi:RDB:', undef, undef,
                { RaiseError => 0,
                  PrintError => $print_error,
                  AutoCommit => 0 } );
    $dbh->do('create database filename test');
    $dbh->disconnect;
};
printf("%sok 2\n", ($@ ? "not" : ""));


#
# connect to fresh test database
#
$dbh = DBI->connect( 'dbi:RDB: ATTACH FILENAME TEST.RDB', undef, undef,
                     { RaiseError => 0,
                     PrintError => $print_error,
                   AutoCommit => 0,
                   ChopBlanks => 1 } );
printf("%sok 4\n", ($dbh ? "" : "not "));


#
# create test table
#
$ok = $dbh->do( "set transaction read write" );
printf("%sok 5\n", (( $ok && !$DBI::errstr) ? "" : "not "));

$ok = $dbh->do( q/create table dummy (
              col_char char(15),
              col_varchar varchar(30),
              col_int int,
              col_float float,
              col_date date vms,
              col_decimal decimal(5),
              col_quad bigint,
              col_intp2 int(2) ) / );
printf("%sok 6\n", (( $ok && !$DBI::errstr) ? "" : "not "));

$ok = $dbh->commit;
printf("%sok 7\n", (( $ok && !$DBI::errstr) ? "" : "not "));
```

```
#
# get back default dateformat
#
my $df = $dbh->{rdb_dateformat};
$ok = ( $df eq "|!Y4!MN0!D0|!H04!M0!S0!C2|" );
printf("%sok 8\n", (( $ok && !$DBI::errstr) ? "" : "not "));


#
# start read write again to insert something
#
$ok = $dbh->do( 'set transaction read write');
printf("%sok 10\n", (( $ok && !$DBI::errstr) ? "" : "not "));


#
# prepare insert
#
my $st_text = q/
insert into dummy (
   col_char,
   col_varchar,
   col_int,
   col_float,
   col_date,
   col_decimal,
   col_quad,
   col_intp2 )
values ( ?, ?, ?, ?, ?, ?, ?, ? )/;
my $st = $dbh->prepare( $st_text );
printf("%sok 11\n", (( $ok && !$DBI::errstr) ? "" : "not "));


#
# now two inserts
#
my $col_char_t1      = 'Abcdef';
my $col_varchar_t1   = 'skjdsdalskhd';
my $col_int_t1       = 12345;
my $col_float_t1     = 7654.12E12;
my $col_date_t1      = '19630709';
my $col_decimal_t1   = 54321;
my $col_quad_t1      = '123456789012';
my $col_intp2_t1     = '321.12';

$ok = $st->execute(
    $col_char_t1,
    $col_varchar_t1,
    $col_int_t1,
```

```
    $col_float_t1,
    $col_date_t1,
    $col_decimal_t1,
    $col_quad_t1,
    $col_intp2_t1 );
printf("%sok 15\n", (( $ok && !$DBI::errstr) ? "" : "not "));

my $col_char_t2       = 'BCDEFGHJ';
my $col_varchar_t2    = 'jhfjsdhfshfkljhd';
my $col_int_t2        = 4242442;
my $col_float_t2      = -123.5678E100;
my $col_date_t2       = '20000229 120030';
my $col_decimal_t2    = -54321;
my $col_quad_t2       = '-98765432101';
my $col_intp2_t2      = '-44.44';

$ok = $st->execute(
    $col_char_t2,
    $col_varchar_t2,
    $col_int_t2,
    $col_float_t2,
    $col_date_t2,
    $col_decimal_t2,
    $col_quad_t2,
    $col_intp2_t2 );
printf("%sok 16\n", (( $ok && !$DBI::errstr) ? "" : "not "));


$ok = $dbh->commit;
printf("%sok 17\n", (( $ok && !$DBI::errstr) ? "" : "not "));


#
# prepare select to check the inserted values;
#
$ok = $dbh->do( 'set transaction read only');
printf("%sok 18\n", (( $ok && !$DBI::errstr) ? "" : "not "));

$st = $dbh->prepare( q/
select col_char, col_varchar, col_int, col_float as col_floating,
       col_date, col_decimal, col_quad, col_intp2
  from dummy
 order by col_char /);
printf("%sok 19\n", (( $st && !$DBI::errstr) ? "" : "not "));


#
# check the NAME attribute (name of the select columns)
#
```

```
$ok = ( $st->{NUM_OF_FIELDS} == 8 );
printf("%sok 20\n", (( $ok ) ? "" : "not "));

my $names = $st->{NAME};
$ok = ( 8 == @$names &&
        $$names[0] eq "COL_CHAR" &&
        $$names[1] eq "COL_VARCHAR" &&
        $$names[2] eq "COL_INT" &&
        $$names[3] eq "COL_FLOATING" &&
        $$names[4] eq "COL_DATE" &&
        $$names[5] eq "COL_DECIMAL" &&
        $$names[6] eq "COL_QUAD" &&
        $$names[7] eq "COL_INTP2" );
printf("%sok 21\n", (( $ok ) ? "" : "not "));

$names = $st->{NAME_uc};
$ok = ( 8 == @$names &&
        $$names[0] eq "COL_CHAR" &&
        $$names[1] eq "COL_VARCHAR" &&
        $$names[2] eq "COL_INT" &&
        $$names[3] eq "COL_FLOATING" &&
        $$names[4] eq "COL_DATE" &&
        $$names[5] eq "COL_DECIMAL" &&
        $$names[6] eq "COL_QUAD" &&
        $$names[7] eq "COL_INTP2" );
printf("%sok 22\n", (( $ok ) ? "" : "not "));

$names = $st->{NAME_lc};
$ok = ( 8 == @$names &&
        $$names[0] eq "col_char" &&
        $$names[1] eq "col_varchar" &&
        $$names[2] eq "col_int" &&
        $$names[3] eq "col_floating" &&
        $$names[4] eq "col_date" &&
        $$names[5] eq "col_decimal" &&
        $$names[6] eq "col_quad" &&
        $$names[7] eq "col_intp2" );
printf("%sok 23\n", (( $ok ) ? "" : "not "));


#
# bind columns
#
my ( $col_char, $col_varchar, $col_int, $col_float, $col_date, $col_decimal,
     $col_quad, $col_intp2 );
$ok = $st->bind_columns ( \$col_char,
                \$col_varchar,
                \$col_int,
                \$col_float,
```

```
                \$col_date,
                \$col_decimal,
                \$col_quad,
                \$col_intp2 );
printf("%sok 29\n", (( $st && !$DBI::errstr) ? "" : "not "));

$ok = $st->execute;
printf("%sok 30\n", (( $st && !$DBI::errstr) ? "" : "not "));


#
# first fetch and compare
#
$ok = $st->fetch;
printf("%sok 31\n", (( $st && !$DBI::errstr) ? "" : "not "));

#print "col_char      $col_char\n";
#print "col_varchar   $col_varchar\n";
#print "col_int       $col_int  \n";
#print "col_float     $col_float \n";
#print "col_date      $col_date  \n";
#print "col_decimal   $col_decimal\n";
#print "col_quad      $col_quad  \n";
#print "col_intp2     $col_intp2 \n";

$ok = ( $col_char eq $col_char_t1 &&
        $col_varchar eq $col_varchar_t1 &&
        $col_float == $col_float_t1 &&
        $col_int == $col_int_t1 &&
        $col_date =~ /^$col_date_t1/ &&
        $col_decimal == $col_decimal_t1 &&
        $col_quad eq $col_quad_t1 &&
        $col_intp2 eq $col_intp2_t1 );
printf("%sok 32\n", (( $ok ) ? "" : "not "));


#
# second fetch and compare
#
$ok = $st->fetch;
printf("%sok 33\n", (( $st && !$DBI::errstr) ? "" : "not "));

#print "col_char      $col_char\n";
#print "col_varchar   $col_varchar\n";
#print "col_int       $col_int  \n";
#print "col_float     $col_float \n";
#print "col_date      $col_date  \n";
#print "col_decimal   $col_decimal\n";
#print "col_quad      $col_quad  \n";
```

```
#print "col_intp2     $col_intp2 \n";


$ok = ( $col_char eq $col_char_t2 &&
        $col_varchar eq $col_varchar_t2 &&
     $col_float == $col_float_t2 &&
     $col_int == $col_int_t2 &&
     $col_date =~ /^$col_date_t2/ &&
     $col_decimal == $col_decimal_t2 &&
     $col_quad eq $col_quad_t2 &&
     $col_intp2 eq $col_intp2_t2 );
printf("%sok 34\n", (( $ok ) ? "" : "not "));

$ok = $st->fetch;
printf("%sok 35\n", (( !$ok && !$DBI::errstr ) ? "" : "not "));

$ok = $dbh->commit;
printf("%sok 36\n", (( $ok && !$DBI::errstr ) ? "" : "not "));

$ok = $dbh->disconnect;
printf("%sok 37\n", (( $ok && !$DBI::errstr ) ? "" : "not "));
```

15.4 Python and the Rdb plug-in

Python, discussed in Chapter 14, also has an Rdb plug-in. Here's the URL for a presentation from a company that's made Rdb access via Python running on a WASD server its strategic platform: http://wasd.vsm.com.au/other/wasd-tlt-exec-council-1a.htm.

Jean-François Pièronne developed the Rdb interface for Python. It works beautifully. At the time of writing, it's not really in distributable condition; it works, but it's not packaged well. Jean-François has promised to package it and make it available on his Web site, http://www.pi-net.dyndns.org/, by the time this book is published. I can't give you the exact link. Go there and browse around for it; he's got some other interesting tools and utilities as well.

Just to show what Rdb-enabled Python code looks like, here's the installation verification procedure for the Rdb plug-in installation. This attaches to the current default database, defined by the logical sql$database—which is the same way the SQL utility works—then reads all the nonsystem relations from Rdb$relations and prints out the names and does the same for all the system tables. The IVP demonstrates support for filling in variable values in statements, cursors, and transacton control, as well as working with database values from Python.

```
#
#
import string
import sys, traceback
import rdb
#

attach = rdb.statement("attach 'filename sql$database'")
commit = rdb.statement("commit work")
readonly = rdb.statement("set transaction read only")
curs = rdb.statement("""select rdb$relation_name from
rdb$relations
where rdb$system_flag = ? order by rdb$relation_name""")

attach.execute()

readonly.execute();
print 'User Tables'
curs.execute(0)
x = curs.fetch()
while (x[0] == 0):
     print "user relation name = ", x[1][0]
     x = curs.fetch()
curs.close()
commit.execute()

readonly.execute();
print 'System Tables'
curs.execute(1)
x = curs.fetch()
while (x[0] == 0):
     print "system relation name = ", x[1][0]
     x = curs.fetch()
curs.close()
commit.execute()
```

15.5 Java

Your Java programs/servlets can use JDBC for database access. If you want to connect to Rdb, have your DBA set up SQL*Net (OCI) Services for the databases you need to talk to. (This is basically a means of letting Rdb databases pretend to be Oracle Server databases in order to work with tools that support those.) Now download the "JDBC Thin Client" for Oracle from the Oracle Technology Web site. (You need to register, which is free, and then give the user name and password you selected when you go to download software.) The "Thin Client" is all-Java and runs on multiple platforms, although only Windows NT and Solaris are mentioned. Select a Windows NT JDBC Thin Client that matches the version of the Java Development Kit (JDK) installed on your system. Download it, install it into your Java libraries, and you can run Java programs that access multiple Oracle Server and Oracle Rdb databases on your own system and on any others.

While you're at the OTN site, you can download free developer releases of Oracle RDB for Alpha (a 56-MB zipped file), as well as VAX and various Oracle Server products. Another free development-only database kit is available for Mimer, at www.mimer.com. Mimer offers a JDBC driver as well, along with preprocessors for C, FORTRAN, and COBOL, but I don't know of any Perl or Python modules for that database.

16

Useful Freeware CGI Scripts

With nearly a decade of VMS Web servers behind us, it's not surprising that a number of programs are available free to do useful VMS-specific functions. Here's a grab-bag of programs, organized roughly by function, that I've found useful, along with where to get them. This is only a fraction of the scripts available for VMS, and is limited by two factors: These are scripts written (or adapted) specifically to VMS, rather than, say, Perl CGIs, which are written generically enough to work on VMS, and almost all are scripts I have used myself and found useful. For pointers to other scripts, check out Arne Vaxjhj's page at http://www.levitte.org/~ava/cgiscripts.htmlx.

Incidentally, if you're looking for prewritten Perl CGIs, do yourself and your site a favor and check out http://nms-cgi.sourceforge.net/scripts.shtml for some up-to-date and reasonably secure replacements for the not very good but very popular scripts found at Matt's Script Archive. Documentation is a little rough—though no rougher than the original—and these are models of modern Perl style with attention to security. FORMMAIL.PL continues to be a source of many, many security holes; use the replacement from this site if you're going to use anything, even if you have to tweak it yourself to make it actually send mail. [It opens a pipe to a designated mail program. If you do download the NMS FORMMAIL script, make sure to collect NMS-SENDMAIL, a Perl script that will do the SMTP mail-sending portion of the job.)

16.1 Serving VMS MAIL files

16.1.1 Hypermail

Jonathan Boswell's Hypermail is a great example of a FORTRAN CGI program. It serves VMS mail files (accessed through callable mail functions) to the Web, splendid for serving archives of mailing lists or meeting notes. It's customizable via logical names to make the display look pretty much like the rest of your site. It can serve messages in chronological order or search by a portion of the subject line.

This subject line search can begin to get slow when you have a lot of entries in your mail file. To find the 66th occurrence of a subject line, Hypermail has to look through all the occurrences from the beginning and discard the first 65 occurrences. It's tempting to consider building a mail search tool that saves search result sets so you don't have to do all the searching over again on every message, but managing the temporary files that this would require adds considerable complexity to the program. In any case, Hypermail works very solidly and reasonably quickly on mail files containing thousands of messages; if for some reason you need tens of thousands you may have to put up with some slow response times, divide your archives into multiple mail files, or reconsider whether mail files are the best way to store this information.

You can find Hypermail at http://www.newtrumpet.org/jsb/hypermail/.

16.1.2 yahMAIL (Yet Another Hypermail)

Mark Daniel, author of the WASD server, wrote this package. It's a full-featured Web mail interface to VMS mail files and can also send mail using the callable mail routines (so it isn't limited to interaction with an SMTP server and can use whatever foreign mail transport your host supports). It can decode and download MIME attachments and with many TCP/IP packages upload and include MIME attachments as well. With PMDF all this is supported using the PMDF API, whereas within other mail environments it's accomplished through some workarounds. It's being reworked to use the MIME tools included in the most recent VMS versions so as to be less dependent on such workarounds.

When my users go off to conferences in other countries, they can get at their mail from Internet cafes on any platform with a browser that supports encryption (so their user names and passwords don't go flying by in plain text). Even on-site, the command-line diehards can deal with the attachments that they inevitably get sent using this tool. yahMAIL makes all folders in a mail file accessible, so users aren't restricted to looking solely at new mail; they can file the mail into any folder of their choice or retrieve old mail from folders.

yahMAIL can be configured to use headers and footers of your choice to make the pages resemble the rest of your site. You can find yahMAIL (and many other useful scripts) at http://wasd.vsm.com.au/wasd/.

TurboyahMAIL, at http://kcgl1.eng.ohio-state.edu/www/preview, is a set of patches and new components for yahMAIL written by David Jones, the OSU author, to make yahMAIL use persistent detached processes to access mail files rather than having the same image that talks to the Web server do it (which necessitates frequent opening and closing of the mail files, at concomitantly high I/O cost).

16.2 Sending mail from forms

16.2.1 CGI-MAILTO

CGI-MAILTO is provided with the OSU installation. It parses a GET or POST set of field values—every field on the form, that is—and mails it off to the address you specify in the additional path. You make the Action of the form be `/htbin/cgi-mailto/username`.

CGI-MAILTO will look up the user and ask the server to check his or her [.WWW] subdirectory to make sure that a file named .WWW_MAILABLE is present. If the file is missing, CGI-MAILTO will refuse to send the mail. (This prevents prankish users from using the Web server to generate mail messages to harass other users.)

This can only be used to send messages to users on the same system (or cluster) as the Web server, with SYS$LOGIN directories on disks that are accessible to the system the Web server is running on.

The message subject lines are taken from a "Subject" field on the form, and the message body consists of the fields returned by the client in the order returned, with URL encoding reversed to make them more easily human readable. The messages aren't particularly pretty, but the format is very predictable.

This can be handy if you want form results to be sent to a mail file that will be read by a batch job later.

16.2.2 TMAIL

TMAIL, also in the OSU distribution, plugs field values from a form into a template file whose name you provide in the Action of the form. You can make this as pretty as you like. (Or nearly. If you have the idea of sending a fully filled out HTML form as mail to an HTML-rendering client, you'll have to be cleverer than I am, or at least than I was when I looked at this five years ago, if you want to make radio buttons and menu selections work properly. But you can definitely make a reasonable human-readable, printable, note from it.) In addition to field values you can plug in any CGI variable value, you can specify whether you want the field to be URL encoded or unencoded, and you can specify that a particular string be output if a field or variable is nonnull, rather than just plugging in the contents of the field.

The template specifies recipient, subject, and URLs to return for success or failure. The URL in the form Action needs to be `/htbin/tmail/templatename` and the template file has to be in [.BIN] or in a directory below it, because TMAIL relies on the PATH_TRANSLATED variable value to find the template file, and PATH_TRANSLATED will end up with the equivalent of WWW_ROOT:[BIN]templatename. (Because random users can't use templates from their home directories—unless you've set them up with user scripting capabilities [as discussed in Chapter 19]—TMAIL doesn't check for a .WWW_MAILABLE file in the recipient's Web directory. No untrustworthy user should have enough privilege to write anything in your WWW_ROOT:[BIN] directory.) This means that it's possible to send to an address that's not actually on the local system, most easily by having a FORWARD entry set for the user name on a local system, but possibly by specifying a foreign mail transport in the template.

An advantage of the template-based mail system is that the To: address is never seen and can't be inferred by the client, so you're not exposing any additional addresses to evil spambots. (This is theoretical for me, since I've posted with an unmunged address on mailing lists and newsgroups for many years, and as a result get a couple of dozen spam messages a day. But if you have an address that isn't already known to the world, this is one way to keep it quiet.)

16.2.3 TMAILER

This is Mark Daniel's drop-in replacement for TMAIL, which uses native CGI and runs faster than under OSU emulation. It uses the WASD CGILIB to run under any of the three Web servers. It does all the stuff that TMAIL does and a bit more (which is documented in the comments in the program). If run under WASD or CSWS, it allows the additional path stuff to be an absolute path rather than a relative path from the directory the program is in. This means that users can put forms in user directories and create templates as well, opening up the vague possibility of user-to-user harassment. (However, you can always check the log to see what the referer [sic] was at the time the script was executed, which will point the finger clearly at the offending user, so while it's possible for a user to send unwanted mail without a return address on it, he or she will be found out immediately.)

16.3 System management functions

16.3.1 Changing passwords

There are two different scripts readily available to change passwords via the Web. Both expect the OSU environment but can be run via OSU emulation in CSWS and WASD. They both work the same way: A DCL script puts up a form to collect the user name, old password, and new password, accepts the info, and calls an executable that's been installed with appropriate privilege to update the SYSUAF.

If you're using SSH and it won't allow users to log in with expired passwords, even to change them, it's very handy to have a side door that lets you change the password if you know the old one. Similarly, if you have users who never log in directly and use POP or IMAP to fetch mail from your server, a forms-based password changer is a good thing.

I use Tom Wade's FORTRAN program, available at ftp://picard.eurokom.ie/setpass.zip, which checks password history, updates password history, and so on; it happens to be the first one I tried, and it works very well. I also have a weakness for FORTRAN as a systems programming language, so I recommend this heartily.

It appears that Brian Reed's C program, at http://www.iron.net/~reed/password/, will also do the job.

Jeff Morgan has a super-duper password-change propagator that accepts a password change via OSU and then updates (using DECnet) passwords on a list of other nodes and even Pathworks passwords. You can pick it up at http://www.geocities.com/vmswiz/vms.html.

WASD has a configurable internal mechanism to allow SYSUAF password modification for SYSUAF-authenticated requests.

16.3.2 Monitoring system performance

HyperSPI++, also available from http://wasd.vsm.com.au/wasd/, is a Web-based performance monitoring display tool. There's a data-collection component, HyperSPIxx$agent, which can run on each system you're interested in collecting information about, whether or not it has a Web server running. (The agent writes updated performance information to a data file, which the script component reads and graphs.)

HyperSPI++ was extended by Jean-François Pièronne from Mark Daniel's original HyperSPI program. The script component uses the WASD CGILIB, so it can run appropriately under any of the three Web servers.

This is very handy for getting a graphical feel for what's going on with your VMS cluster or with nonclustered systems with DECnet connections, and it has the considerable advantage of being free.

16.3.3 Displaying disk space utilization

HyperDISK, from the WASD site, does a simple graphical display of how full your disks are. This can be handy if you're figuring out where to put a new directory tree in a fairly full set of disks, or for helping to convince management that you aren't kidding when you say you need more disk space. (Somehow, a diagram showing used space in red is more viscerally convincing than a percentage figure.)

16.4 Presenting documentation

16.4.1 Web-based help browsers

It's helpful to be able to get at VMS help from the Web, especially if you've extended or supplemented your VMS help files with information on local utilities.

VMSHELPGATE

VMSHELPGATE ships with the OSU server and can run under OSU emulation on each server. It uses one of two DCL wrappers, HELPGATE.COM (which with the argument /HELP will return all the HELP topics on your system as clickable links) or VMSHELP.COM, which displays a form to accept a HELP topic, then returns the help entry for just that topic, with no clickable links.

Conan the librarian

Conan, written by Mark Daniel, is a general interface to any text library, so you can use it to browse header libraries, help libraries, or print module libraries. It has keyword search capability and can provide header information about the libraries available. It uses the WASD CGILIB, so should run happily under any of the three Web servers. (Conan is part of the WASD-

SCRIPTS package available at `http://wasd.vsm.com.au`; this is a set of handy scripts that will run on all three of the VMS Web servers I discuss here—and should run under the vanilla CGI environment of Purveyor as well.)

16.4.2 Bookreader servers

If you don't have an InfoServer—a long-discontinued device that let you serve CDs across your network—it's pretty helpful to be able to get at the documentation CDs (or the files from them) with a Web browser. While most new VMS documentation comes in HTML format as well as Bookreader, CDs for older versions and manuals for older software may exist only in Bookreader format. Here are a couple of scripts that can translate Bookreader to HTML on the fly and serve it up. Let me remind you that Bookreader files come in two main flavors: bookshelves, which contain pointers to and descriptions (titles) of multiple volumes on a single topic (e.g., an installation guide, an administrator manual, a getting started guide, a user guide, and a reference manual all for the same product), and books, so a Bookreader server needs to know which it's getting.

WEBBOOK

The WEBBOOK source comes with the OSU server. To build it, you have to set default to WWW_ROOT:[SCRIPT_CODE] and do @BUILD_UNSUPPORTED, or extract the commands to build it from there. It builds by default to run in the OSU CGI environment using the OSU CGILIB, but you can define NOCGILIB to have it take the CGI info from environment variables, which should make it runnable in vanilla CGI on Apache or WASD. (Since the program dates from 1995, this is likely more a result of intended CERN-server compatibility than anything else.)

The build procedure copies the executable to WWW_ROOT:[BIN], so a path of /htbin/webbook/ will get to it. WEBBOOK gets the information about where to find the book or shelf from the PATH_INFO provided by the server, so do /htbin/webbook/path-to-shelf/ (with the trailing slash) to get a bookshelf file, and /htbin/webbook/path-to-book (with no trailing slash) to get to the book.

Hypershelf and Hyperreader

Also part of the WASDSCRIPTS package is a bookshelf reader and a bookreader—Hypershelf and Hyperreader, respectively. These have a functionality similar to WEBBOOK, but have a somewhat prettier interface and make pages that look a little less basic.

For functions that aren't specific to VMS, there are hundreds of free prewritten CGIs available in an assortment of languages. (Not DCL, obviously.) As the C compiler and library get more and more UNIX-compatible, and as the VMS Perl community works to keep Perl cross-platform capable, more and more of these scripts will work unmodified on VMS. So if you need something that isn't here, poke around the Web; see if you can find it. The odds are getting better.

17

High-Performance Scripting Options

17.1 Issues

The basic CGI protocol simply specifies a way for the Web server and the CGI process to communicate; it doesn't say anything about whether that communication is fast or slow.

What makes script processes fast or slow? Assume for the moment that the script program is written efficiently, and the server has enough resources (CPU, memory) to run it without excessive paging to disk or having the process spend too much time on the computable queue waiting for other processes to finish their quantum of computation time. (These are big assumptions, but they're beyond the control of Web server authors.)

High-performance CGI options generally boil down to (a) ways to use the minimum number of different processes to minimize process creation overhead, (b) ways to minimize the number of image activations, generally by creating persistent scripting environments that don't have to be reloaded for each script, and (c) ways to communicate with the Web server faster than the default.

Process creation is a fairly expensive operation on VMS—at least compared with UNIX, where forking a process is pretty cheap. (To be precise to a fault, process creation on VMS isn't all that big a deal, but populating the symbol and logical name tables for the process can be relatively expensive. If it has to run a LOGIN.COM, there's disk access and file parsing time; if it's a subprocess inheriting the environment of its parent, all that information gets transferred through a mailbox, and that is slow.) One general means to avoid paying that penalty, or at least to amortize it over multiple script executions, is to keep your processes around for a while once they've been created—so, for example, the scriptserver processes in OSU live (by default) for ten minutes after the last time anybody spoke to them, and WASD also deliberately keeps its processes around between scripts.

If you want to write a persistent executable that starts up once, makes its database connections or other expensive activities once, and hangs around accepting requests via the server, a different mechanism is offered by each server. For CSWS, you need to write a module. For OSU, an HPSS (high-performance server software) program. For WASD, a program to run under CGIplus. These same requirements are also the requirements to efficiently run interpreted scripts; get a copy of the script interpreter running and pass it a new script name each time. (That's relevant for Perl, PHP, and, surprisingly, Java, but for these purposes the Java virtual machine is an interpreter of the compiled Java byte code.) CSWS provides mod_perl, mod_php, and mod_jk; the persistent Java interpreter now supported is Tomcat (the Jakarta project), which also supports Java Server Pages. (It may very well be possible to use Tomcat with OSU or WASD as well as CSWS; they don't seem to be very tightly coupled.) OSU provides HPSS versions of Perl and PHP and a framework for writing your own HPSS applications and a persistent Java execution environment. WASD supports persistent Run-Time Environments (RTEs), and also provides tweaks for Perl to make it more successfully reentrant.

If your script is in a noncompiled language—not counting DCL, whose interpreter you get with any process unless you explicitly create a detached process without a CLI—you can save time on each script execution by preloading the scripting environment and not exiting from it when the script completes. (This means you need a function in your script environment that can clean up everything a previous script might have done; these are not always provided by scripting environment authors, so the Web server authors have to do something about them.)

Process Software and Microsoft collaborated on a special application programming interface (API) that lets you do scripting in what are essentially shareable images loaded by the server; the term of art is "DLL" for Dynamic Link Library. The Internet Server API (ISAPI) was developed on Purveyor and IIS and is made available on WASD and OSU. This doesn't mean that you can take your NT DLL, put it on VMS, and have anything useful happen; it's still got to be VAX or Alpha object code, which means at least a recompilation and probably more of a port than that. ISAPI applications are fairly tightly intertwined with their servers—they have to be able to communicate by callback with the server. Apache on Win32 platforms has mod_isapi, but this hasn't been ported to VMS as far as I've been able to tell. (There is a similar NSAPI for Netscape Web servers, but nobody's implemented this anywhere but Netscape as far as I can tell.)

There's also a FastCGI (FCGI) specification, which allows for persistent scripting processes with a bidirectional TCP/IP connection between the process and the server. Although this has been around since 1996, it isn't seen as widely in the field as ISAPI. There's a mod_fastcgi for Apache on some platforms, but it's not in VMS; however, there is FastCGI support in OSU. The FastCGI spec is available on the Web at http://www.fastcgi.com/devkit/doc/fcgi-spec.html, and you can also download a C library for FastCGI support from the same site. A DEC BASIC FASTCGI library is available on the Web at http://www.digitalsynergy.inc, although the idea they use there is to use VMS as a back-end application server behind a UNIX or NT version of Apache that actually supports mod_fastcgi.

17.2 Options

Here's a brief review of what's available on which server. This is by no means an exhaustive guide; I hope to tell you enough to get you started with each environment.

17.2.1 CSWS

CSWS provides persistent scripting environments for Perl, PHP, and Java through the Apache modules mod_perl, mod_php, and mod_jk, respectively. Install them according to the installation instructions provided on the CSWS Web site. (Examples for this are shown with the sample CSWS installation earlier in the book.)

MOD_PERL

The configuration file for MOD_PERL is MOD_PERL.CONF, probably located in APACHE$COMMON:[CONF]. The installation modifies HTTPD.CONF to tell Apache to include the MOD_PERL.CONF file. Note that the default installation will result in Perl scripts getting run persistently; if you want to run them as one-off CGIs, you need to choose the Apache::PerlRun module rather than the Apache::Registry module. (If you do that, you still get a win over running DCL wrappers that invoke Perl from the command line, since you avoid image activation costs even if you don't use Apache::Registry, but your scripts need to be reread and recompiled for each use, which may not be ideal.)

Some highlights of the configuration file:

```
#
# Load the dynamic MOD_PERL module
#
LoadModule PERL_MODULE modules/mod_perl.exe
```

(Without this mod_perl won't even be started. The `IfModule` wrapper keeps Apache from trying to execute directives that won't work and will crash the server if the module somehow failed to load; while good practice, this would be more efficacious if the fact the module failed to load didn't crash the server.)

```
<IfModule mod_perl.c>

#
#  PerlSetEnv
#
#  Allow perl modules to reside in the Apache
#  subdirectory under the /perl location.
#
PerlSetEnv PERL5LIB /apache$common/perl
```

Note that this is appended to the PERL5LIB symbol rather than replacing it, so Perl can use anything that's installed in its tree also, as well as anything that the Apache installation, or you, have put into the APACHE$COMMON:[PERL] directory.

```
#
#  Perl-Status
#
#  To enable the location "perl-status" which shows
#  information about the installation of mod_perl,
# uncomment the lines below.

#PerlFreshRestart On
```

`PerlFreshRestart` applies when you restart the server, not with each new script that's handled. It tells mod_perl to flush all existing Perl context when you restart the server.

```
#PerlModule Apache::Status
```

`PerlModule` tells mod_perl to preload the Apache::Status module.

```
#
#<Location /perl-status/>
#  SetHandler  perl-script
#  PerlHandler  Apache::Status
#</Location>
```

This <Location> container directive says to map URLs of /perl-status/ to run using the Perl script handler and to execute the handler subroutine from the STATUS.PM module in the Apache tree, which I find in [.lib.site_perl.apache]. (Or it would if it weren't commented out.) If you enable this you probably want to put some access controls on it.

```
#
# Apache::Registry
#
#  Enable Apache::Registry module
#
PerlModule Apache::Registry

Alias /perl/ "/apache$common/perl/"
```

But note that if you wanted to mix Perl scripts with other kinds of scripts in a single CGI directory, you could make this point to the same directory as cgi-bin, or you could have this go to another disk. Doing this will break the examples unless you copy the contents of apache$common:[perl.apache] into your new /perl/ location.

```
<Location/perl>
   SetHandler perl-script
   PerlHandler Apache::Registry
   Options ExecCGI
   Allow from all
   PerlSendHeader On
</Location>
```

This allows everyone in the world to run Perl scripts from URLs starting with /perl, using the Perl scripts handler; because Apache::Registry is invoked the scripts will be persistent. This makes it very important that scripts be written with strict discipline, since they can leave garbage lying around otherwise. PerlSendHeader On instructs Perl to send out HTTP headers and not leave it up to the scripts.

```
#
# Apache::PerlRun
#
# To setup Apache::PerlRun, uncomment the
# lines below.
#
#PerlModule Apache::PerlRun
#
#Alias /perlrun/ "/apache$common/perl/"
#
#<Location /perlrun>
#  SetHandler perl-script
```

```
#   PerlHandler Apache::PerlRun
#   Options ExecCGI
#   allow from all
#   PerlSendHeader On
#</Location>
#
```

(Apache::PerlRun is the nonpersistent alternative to Apache::Registry. You may need to invoke it if you have sloppily-written Perl scripts.)

```
#
# Mod_Perl Modules
#
#     Two examples of mod_perl modules follow. To enable
#     these modules, uncomment the "location" lines.
#
#
# Hello World example
#
#<Location /world>
#     SetHandler perl-script
#     PerlHandler Apache::Hello
#</Location>
#
#
# Hello World (w/fancy dialog box) example
#
#<Location /world2>
#     SetHandler perl-script
#     PerlHandler Apache::Hello2
#</Location>
```

These are harmless to uncomment, unless you're using the /world or /world2 paths for something else. /world will invoke mod_perl to run apache$common:[perl.apache]hello.pm; it could also do it to invoke modules elsewhere in the perl5lib set of logicals.

```
</IfModule>
```

MOD_PHP

PHP doesn't take a whole lot of configuration. The installation will modify HTTPD.CONF to include the mod_php.conf file; an annotated version follows.

```
##
## Load PHP module
##
```

```
LoadModule php4_module modules/mod_php.exe

AddType application/x-httpd-php .php .phtml
```

This informs CSWS to run anything with a .php or .phtml extension through mod_PHP before serving it out. You might want to add .php3 as an extension here if you need to serve a suite of older .PHP pages.

```
AddType application/x-httpd-php-source .phps
```

This enables you to execute PHP scripts that aren't embedded in HTML pages.

```
Alias /php/ "/apache$root/php/scripts/"
```

And this gives you a reasonable directory to put them in.

```
#PHP_FLAG   engine   ON
```

The Boolean value for engine enables or disables PHP parsing of PHP files. On a serverwide basis, you want the engine ON, which is the default, but you can use this same format (`PHP_FLAG engine OFF`) to disable PHP within a container directive (virtual host, directory, etc.) or in an .HTACCESS file.

```
#PHP_VALUE   error_log   /php_root/logs/error_log
```

You can similarly override the PHP error logging by container directive.

For more information on PHP and Apache, look at the WWW.PHP.NET pages under documentation.

Java

Tomcat is a server that provides a Java Servlet 2.2 container and a Java Server Pages (JSP) 1.1 processor. Apache communicates with the Tomcat server through a mod_jk module, which is included with Tomcat. You need to download and install the most current Java for VMS. (At time of writing, go to http://www.compaq.com/java/download/index.html, but this URL may change to something involving HP.)

Follow the instructions on the CSWS Web site for downloading and configuring Tomcat and mod_jserv—these instructions can currently be found at http://www.openvms.compaq.com/openvms/products/ips/apache/csws_java_relnotes.html.

It's hard to avoid these notes if you download the product. Read them.

17.2.2 OSU

HPSS support

HPSS (High-Performance Server Software) is the mechanism by which OSU supports higher-performance environments. Configuration is similar in all cases; you set up the HPSS executable as a presentation script for the type of script you wish it to execute. (Presentation scripts are configured in HTTP_SUFFIXES.CONF; you specify an HPSS module by giving the name with a percent sign in front of it.)

If you want to write your own HPSS plug-in, study [script_code] hpss_demo.c, as well as the other applications provided. There's hpss_qman, which does VMS queue management functions (and which appears to be completely undocumented), and there's even hpss_mail, a VMS MAIL file server written as an HPSS server in FORTRAN (persistent to avoid the overhead of opening and reopening the mail file, which is a problem for HYPERMAIL).

To allow a generic interface to different HPSS processes, the HPSS_MST.C module is compiled, and (according to the comments in the program), requires some configuration rules in HTTP_SCRIPTS.CONF:

```
ThreadPool hpss stack=120000 q_flag=1 limit=4
```

This rule defines a pool of threads for servicing requests, named HPSS.

```
Service hpss pool=test dynamic=(HPSS,hpss_mst)
info=hpss_srv*
```

This rule defines the service HPSS, assigns it to the HPSS pool, says the start routine is HPSS in the image http_hpss_mst (found in WWW_SYSTEM), and says that the acceptable parameters match the wildcard hpss_*—that is, that the services it can support start with hpss_srv. (Don't confuse these service names with the names of the executables that run them.)

```
Exec /$hpss_exec/* %hpss:
```

This rule says that URLs of the form `/$hpss_exec/*` will be passed to %hpss:, which will execute them if they match the list in info defined in the service. So a URL for this looks like:

```
/$hpss_exec/hpss_name/scriptname
```

Somewhat less generically—and making shorter URLs—you can use a different style of `exec` rule:

```
Exec /$hpss_xxx/* %hpss:hpss_srv_xxx
```

Imagine xxx substituted by Perl or PHP; this results in URLs such as `/$hpss_perl/scriptname` or even `/perl/scriptname`.

You could also configure a presentation rule to execute HPSS applications based on a .hpss suffix, but I don't think it's a good idea.

WEBPERL

WEBPERL isn't a persistent scripting environment, but it does have some performance advantages over a command-line invocation of Perl. If present, WWWEXEC.COM will use it automatically, and pass on the CGI information more efficiently than it will to regular Perl.

WEBPERL.C is in the [.SCRIPT_CODE] directory and should be built with WEBPERL_BLD.COM. As supplied, WEBPERL_BLD.COM didn't work for me. I needed to locate the header files `extern.h` and `perl.h`. To find them, do a $SEARCH starting at your PERL_ROOT and note the location; mine was:

```
PERL_ROOT:[000000.LIB.VMS_AXP.5_6_1.CORE]
```

The build process requires those two headers, PERLSHR_ATTR.OPT (which is in the same directory) and PERLSHR.OPT. PERLSHR.OPT doesn't appear to exist, so you need to create it:

```
$ CREATE PERLSHR.OPT
PERL_ROOT:[000000]PERLSHR.EXE/SHAREABLE
^Z
```

Then edit WEBPERL_BLD.COM so it knows where to find these files; it's looking for PERLSHR.OPT in the directory you pass as the parameter to WEBPERL_BLD and looking for PERLSHR_ATTR.OPT in the default directory; reverse those locations.

```
$ @WEBPERL_BLD PERL_ROOT:[000000.LIB.VMS_AXP.5_6_1.CORE]
```

will now build WEBPERL.EXE and copy it to the [.SYSTEM] subdirectory.

No configuration is necessary to make script processes use WEBPERL—if it's present, it will be used for Perl scripts, which can theoretically run unmodified. If you do this, you'll expose a typo in WWWEXEC.COM, which uses "`protcol`" when it means "`protocol`" in the WEBPERL invocation, so fix WWWEXEC.COM before trying this.

HPSS_PERL

HPSS_PERL.C can be found in the [.SCRIPT_CODE] subdirectory, and needs to be built with HPSS_PERL_BLD.COM. I had exactly the same problems building it as with WEBPERL and solved them the same way, making the same changes to HPSS_PERL_BLD.COM as I described for WEBPERL_BLD.COM in the previous section.

HPSS_PHP

PHP quite sensibly isn't included in the OSU kit; you'll need to download it separately from http://www.er6.eng.ohio-state.edu/~jonesd/php/.

After you unzip the kit (in a separate directory tree), read aaareadme.txt. I found `$ MMS` blew up (because of some pointer mismatch warnings in the STRING.C module, possibly showing that I'm using a more recent and therefore pickier C compiler) and had to run @BUILD_PHP instead; then `$ MMS HPSS` didn't work because the PHP library had compilation errors, so I had to link it by hand. But it worked anyway.

Both PHP and HPSS_PHP link to the shareable image containing the actual guts of PHP.

Follow the instructions in PHP_ROOT:[VMS]aaareadme.txt to load and configure HPSS_PHP.

ISAPI (HPSS)

OSU includes the code for ISAPI_MST.C, which appears to implement ISAPI as an HPSS server. It is not built by default, there are no instructions given for building it, and no command procedures provided for building it. The code does compile, but linking it (using @LINK_MST) produces complaints because of a missing entry point. I was unable to load or test it, so I'm not prepared to swear that it really works. I suspect someone with DLLs already written for Purveyor might be motivated enough to get this going on OSU.

(There is a sample ISAPI.CONF file in the WWW_SYSTEM: directory, which suggests that it was working at some point.)

FastCGI (HPSS)

You can use @BUILD_FASTCGI.COM to compile and link both the FASTCGI MST server and a test client. To enable it to run properly you need to update the main configuration file:

```
ThreadPool fcgi stack=60000 q_flag=1 limit=10
Service testsrv pool=fcgi dynamic=(fastcgi,fastcgi_mst) info=configfile
Exec /$fastcgi/* %fastcgi:
```

and create a configuration file (named in the `info` parameter to the `Service` definition).

The Exec rule means that what looks like different scripts in the URL `/$fastcgi/scriptname` are actually processed by different application servers (which could be on some other machine). The config file lets you specify, for each scriptname, what port on what host the FASTCGI_MST should communicate with to execute the request and if necessary what VMS command to pass it.

To quote the comments in FASTCGI_MST.C, the format of the configuration file is that each line is either a comment or has the form:

```
role name [+]host:port [command]

e.g., "responder test localhost:2301 "

Where:
role      FastCGI role name, must be 'responder'

name      If virtual script name (element after /$fastcgi).

[+]host:port  Host and port to make connections to. The
              optional plus indicates duplicates are
              selected round-robin.

command   VMS command to invoke to start the FastCGI
          application.
```

In addition, setting the environment variable FCGI_RESPONDER_FLAGS to 1 will keep the connections open.

You can examine the TESTFCGI.C sample application to see how the FastCGI communication works, or use Perl, C, or BASIC libraries available elsewhere on the Net to write FastCGI applications.

Crinoid

Crinoid is a high-performance multithreaded persistent Perl execution environment written for OSU by Charles E. Lane at Drexel University. (I list it last because it isn't part of the OSU distribution and is available separately, at http://www.crinoid.com.) A good discussion of how it works and the (minimal) configuration changes for OSU are at http://www.crinoid.com/ftp/000_readme.txt.

It needs at least VMS 6.0 to run and is better off with 6.2 (where it can use the Persona service to create sandboxed "tentacles" running Perl scripts in unprivileged user names). This faces the same issues as user scripting, discussed in Chapter 19.

Running Crinoid uses a different scriptserver DCL file than the OSU-supplied WWWEXEC. It might be possible to coerce the OSU emulation modes in Apache and WASD to run Crinoid. On CSWS you might have to rename the Crinoid WWWPERL.COM file to WWWEXEC.COM and clobber your ability to run non-Crinoid CGIs.

Java

OSU provides a persistent Java execution environment with some glue code. Look in your [.JAVA_CODE] subdirectory; there are clear instructions in the AAAREADME.JAVA_SCRIPT file.

One minor bug in the instructions is that they refer to BUILD_JAVA_SCRIPTS.COM, while the file provided is named BUILD_JAVA_SCRIPT.COM. Here's the outline:

Set default to WWW_ROOT:[JAVA_CODE]. Invoke @BUILD_JAVA_SCRIPT. This will compile and link the Java script server process and will also compile the example scripts, although on my system the last example script, "echo.java," fails to compile. It will also create a WWW_ROOT:[JBIN] directory and put the compiled Java classes into it, and build a java_mst.

Edit HTTP_SCRIPTS.CONF and make `java_enable` blank instead of "#". The goal here is to get a line that says

```
exec /jbin/* node::"task=wwwjava"
```

where the node is either 0 for this system or the node name of the remote system on which you want Java applets to run.

Use PRIVREQUEST to completely shut down the server and restart it with HTTP_STARTUP.COM, so all the images will be installed again, including the new JAVA_MST image.

The first time you make a request to a path starting with `/jbin/` a new persistent Java server will be created. On the first access you'll suffer the pain of starting up the Java virtual machine, but subsequent execution after that should be speedy.

17.2.3 WASD

CGIplus

CGIplus scripts are persistent. The variables are the same as in CGI, but the means of communication are different. A CGIplus script has to read from CGIPLUSIN, which is actually a mailbox. (If a script uses the WASD-supplied CGILIB or calls the CGIPLUS_CGIVAR routine, the differences between CGIplus and regular CGI can be hidden from the mainline of the script.)

The mailbox stays open between invocations of the script. CGIplus scripts can read in Record mode (one line per CGI variable, and when the script reads a blank line from the mailbox it knows that it's had all the information for the current request and can begin processing) or in Struct mode, in which the script first reads a record size in bytes, then reads a single buffer containing all the CGI variables to be passed. (This has to be parsed to obtain the values for each variable, but that work can be hidden by using the CGIPLUS_CGIVAR C language utility function.) Since there are potentially many fewer I/Os in Struct mode, it can be noticeably more efficient than Record mode.

CGIplus scripts need to be written to clean up after each iteration, rather than relying on image rundown to clean things up automatically, since the image doesn't run down. All scripts can write output in Record mode (line-by-line) or binary mode, which is more efficient because of C-library buffering, but CGIplus scripts have to write a special CGIplus EOF mark as a separate mark to indicate that they're done. (You can find code examples in the WASD on-line documentation.) Note that any language that can read records from a mailbox can be used for CGIplus processes; this definitely includes DCL. For a language that requires an explicitly loaded interpreter it might make more sense to use an RTE (discussed in the next section), but there's no reason you couldn't code up a persistent Perl script and simply have a DCL CGIplus script invoke Perl (or PHP, TCL, or what-have-you) with that script as an argument.

To configure exec directories for CGIplus scripts, use:

```
exec+ /URL-path-to-script-directory/* /VMS-path-to-
executables
```

The trick is in the "+" after exec. More on `exec` in Chapter 7.

To configure specific scripts as CGIplus:

```
script+ /URL-of-script* /VMS-path-to-script*
```

The trailing asterisks on the paths are to allow passing of additional path info for parameters.

When you're messing with CGIplus script mapping, the WASD documentation suggests that you restart the server rather than just reloading the rules file, to avoid any confusion with existing CGIplus processes. On a quiet server the same result could be accomplished via a HTTPD/DO=DCL=DELETE command followed by HTTPD/DO=MAP (see Chapter 5).

RTE

A CGIplus process runs the same script every time it's accessed. A Run-Time Environment process can be passed a new script each time it's accessed, but the script is executed within a persistent environment. (For example, a tweaked version of the Perl interpreter can be preloaded as an RTE, and then be passed different Perl script names on every access, executing a different one each time.)

This not only saves process creation time, as happens in CGIplus, it saves image activation time for the interpreter. However, a special interpreter is required that understands the CGIplus rules. An example RTE is provided (as RTE_EXAMPLE.C), and you can also study the provided Perl RTE, PERLRTE.C.

To configure an exec directory in which everything will be run in a specific RTE, do

```
exec /URL-directory-path/* (vms location of RTE)/vmspath-
to-files/*
```

so, specifically:

```
exec /persistent_perl/* (CGI-BIN:[000000]PERLRTE.EXE)
/ht_root/pperl/*
```

This means that any request that comes in for `/persistent_perl/scriptname` will be translated to HT_ROOT:[PPERL]scriptname and passed to a process that's running the Perl Run-Time Environment.

You could make your RTE be a DCL procedure by specifiying the VMS location prefixed by an `@`.

In this format, the server would check that the passed script name could actually be found in `/ht_root/pperl/` and would report "script not found" if it wasn't. If you have an RTE that does something with the script name other than just open a file of that name, you can suppress this behavior with

```
set /persistent-perl/* script=nofind
```

(See Chapter 7 for more on mapping rules.)

Alternatively, if you wanted every Perl script everywhere to be executed by the persistent Perl RTE, you could add to the HTTPD$CONFIG file

```
[DclScriptRunTime]
.PL (CGI-BIN:[000000]PERLRTE.EXE)
```

RTEs exist for PHP and Python, but neither is integrated into the 7.2 distribution. The PHP RTE is available from the WASD download page and can work with either the David Jones PHP or the CSWS PHP.

Java

Java classes can be run as CGI-like and as CGIplus scripts. Find the WASD CGI interface class and some demonstration scripts in the HTROOT:[SRC.JAVA] directory. To instruct the server on how to run Java, configure the .CLASS file type to be run via the DCL wrapper, like so:

```
[DclScriptRunTime]
.CLASS @cgi-bin:[000000]java.com
```

HTTPD$CONFIG already includes appropriate MIME types for the types .CLASS, .JAVA, .JAR, and .PROPERTIES.

ISAPI

Normal ISAPI DLLs are so intimately bound up with the server that a defective application can crash the whole server. WASD has a mechanism for running the DLLs while holding them at arm's length in autonomous processes. (So does OSU; both are somewhat safer from DLL bugs than IIS would be.)

ISAPI is implemented via CGIplus and a wrapper script. The wrapper is CGIsapi (pronounced, according to the documentation, as "see-gee-eye sap-ee"). CGIsapi complies with ISAPI 1.0 and vanilla ISAPI 2.0.

Configuration for ISAPI DLLs:

In HTTPD$CONFIG:

```
[DclScriptRunTime]
.DLL $CGI-BIN:[000000]CGISAPI.EXE
```

```
[AddType]
.DLL application/octet-stream - ISAPI extension DLL
```

In HTTPD$MAP.

```
exec+ /isapi/* /cgi-bin/*
```

(If you're planning to put your DLLs in the cgi-bin directory.)

This will let you execute an ISAPI.DLL with `server.domain.tld/isapi/isapi.dll`.

If you don't already have DLLs to run, or expertise in writing new ones, it's probably pointless to configure and use CGIsapi. There's no real performance advantage over CGIplus.

17.3 Conclusion

High-performance environments are primarily of need in heavy-use environments, but may be of help in running low-duty-cycle applications with adequate performance. Paying the startup costs of Java or Perl only once may make subsequent requests run quickly. In any case, the virtue of these environments is that they produce their results without a significant cost in additional memory or CPU and can help even low-use sites extend the useful life of their hardware.

18

User-Edited Web Pages

This chapter is aimed more at the departmental system level than at the large commercial site. Large commercial sites had better have some scheme for moving pages from authoring platform to test to production, with appropriate testing and signoffs along the way. They may have somebody whose entire job is to transfer files from the sandbox system to the production system. You, as the Webmaster, don't have to worry much about making life easier for those people. Some of the following discussion may still be helpful.

But if you're in a department, and the authority to write Web pages is delegated to the person in charge of the area the Web page describes, then you're going to end up with a lot of people building Web sites who really don't know what they're doing and don't really have either the time or the interest in learning. If they're Windows or Mac people, they may have a lot of trouble understanding the VMS file system, and some of them will never be able to sort out FTP.

So you need to make it easy for them to get their pages onto the server and as likely as possible that the pages will work properly once they get there. You're probably not that concerned with a formal check-in procedure.

18.1 File-naming standards

If your users create their Web pages on PCs or Macs, they can easily create files with names that will make trouble for you later. Announce early and often that they must restrict their file names to lowercase letters, numeric digits, and underscores—no embedded blanks, no punctuation (except for a period between file name and file type, but that last is supplied by the OS).

This is the single most important thing you can do to make it likely that Web sites that work on users' desktops will still work after they're uploaded to your VMS server. Files with this naming structure can also be served from the VMS Web server, even if they reside on disks mounted on other kinds of machines and served over NFS. Mixed-case file names or those with embedded blanks or other punctuation require some name hacking to make references to them work, and no upload procedure will automatically take care of the name hacking in the links specified in the document.

18.2 File layout

What I've done at my site is to dedicate a disk to the Web tree, with the directory structure matching the general URL layout. Once we get down a few levels, each directory is owned by a group (I mean an organization chart group, not a UIC group). I create an ACL Identifier for that group, make it the owner of the subdirectory that the pages for that group should appear in, give the ACL ID enough disk quota for likely use, have the head of the group tell me who should have the rights to update the group's pages, grant the ACL to the accounts of the updaters, and let them have at it.

```
SYSUAF> ADD/ID/ATTRIBUTE=RESOURCE GROUPNAME_WEB_UPDATE
SYSUAF> GRANT/ID/ATTRIBUTE RESOURCE GROUPNAME_WEB_UPDATE
ONE_USER
DISKQUOTA> ADD DEVICENAME GROUPNAME_WEB_UPDATE 500000
```

If those users leave, I can delete their accounts without messing up the Web tree and grant the ACLs to somebody else. The ACL holders can create Web pages using EVE, EDT, or TECO—although I seem to be the only one who thinks this is a good idea. This also works beautifully if they FTP their files up using their own user name and password—no anonymous FTP. (That's obviously not a good idea if they're working from home, since the password goes in clear text, but inside the corporate firewall we think it's acceptable. Eventually we'll be on Multinet 4.4, which supports an encrypted copy capability via SCP.) But FTP can be a problem. Users needs to understand how to get from their SYS$LOGIN directory to the Web directory, some FTP packages upload extraneous material (WS_FTP creates strange _vti folders), and some users just think FTP is too difficult and complicated. (I'd like to point out here that I work at a national laboratory. The people who work there aren't idiots. They just don't spend all their time managing computer systems.)

18.3 Alternatives to FTP

What are the alternatives to FTP? I can give you a sketchy picture, but I've only used one of these—my solution is usually to go sit with the people who need help with FTP and walk them through it.

Netscape Communicator and Mozilla Composer can publish pages and associated graphics to a Web server via HTTP, using the PUT method. (Users don't have to figure out how to map the URL to a file name, as they do with FTP; the Web server does it for them.) They have to put in a user name and passname. The way the OSU server implements PUT, with a DECnet script, works beautifully with the disk structure I lay out. Because the process trying to write to the disk actually is the VMS user, rather than a privileged program emulating the VMS user, OSU doesn't have to mess with access checking or reproducing VMS security checks. If VMS lets the write succeed, it (axiomatically) satisfies VMS access controls. Once you enable the PUT script, it's available for any file in a mapped directory—equally true for userdirs as for items under the document root.

Although CSWS and WASD support the PUT method, configuration for userdirs is much more painful. (If you take a naive approach to CSWS userdir configuration, you can easily end up enabling any valid VMS user to update anybody's user directory, which is rarely what you mean.) Userdirs, as subdirectories off SYS$LOGIN, are pretty easy to get to using FTP, so not allowing PUT may not be a problem.

There are two drawbacks to using Netscape/Mozilla Composer as a publishing tool. The first is that it may alter files created in other tools in the process of uploading them. (I wouldn't have expected this, but I've seen it make deleterious changes in a clean HTML file created by Dreamweaver.) The second is that Netscape can only download your preprocessor files in their processed state, after the server has filled in any includes. This means that when you go to update a dynamic document you save a static one.

The second drawback is addressed in the UPD utility on the WASD server. This server lets a user in possession of the correct credentials browse directory trees, upload files using PUT, edit unprocessed files in an onscreen text area, and more. To make it work you need to have a "reverse mapping" (see Chapter 7) for the directory tree you're trying to get at. (This is actually a possibility even if you want to make OSU or CSWS your "production" server; you can run WASD on another port and just map the same files, or even on another cluster node. You won't have the benefit of a unified file cache knowing about it the very instant that something's been uploaded, but a few seconds or minutes of latency may be a small price to pay for convenient updates.)

There are FrontPage extensions that are supposed to ease the job of "publishing" stuff to the Web server. These don't, at present, exist on VMS in any form, although they are supported on IIS and Apache on UNIX. Incidentally, FrontPage creates ugly, inefficient HTML—and if you use it you'll find yourself with hundreds of copies of the fphover Java applet cluttering your Web disk. Dreamweaver makes a much cleaner page. However, even FrontPage is better than the "save to Internet" option on Office 2000 packages. I once had to debug a problem where an HTML file Word 2000 had created rendered acceptably in Netscape and showed up blank on Internet Explorer; that was a really hideous file internally.

You can share your VMS disk with a PC network using Samba (free) or PathWorks (not free, but a couple of client licenses included with most recent VMS purchases); with appropriate mapping, in theory, PC users just save their files to network disk and—poof!—they're on the Web.

You could enable the FTP server on the NT disk server system and use an FTP mirroring scheme to keep a Web tree on VMS in synch.

You could pay money for a PC-based NFS client and NFS serve the Web disk from VMS. (This has a lot of system administration overhead in it as you need to map userids from the other system.)

You can pay money to some third-party vendor for NFS server software for your NT server and mount the NT disk from VMS. TCP/IP Services 5.3 (which follows immediately on the heels of 5.1) has an NFS client that's willing to pretend the NFS disk is an ODS-5 disk supporting extended file specifications, so it doesn't have to hack in funny characters to handle uppercase letters. This means that the file names in links have a shot at working.

In a variant on that scheme you can run Samba on a UNIX or LINUX box and have NFS mount the disk, or use an FTP mirroring scheme to make a frequent copy of the Web tree from that box to the VMS server.

In another variant, you could use mod_WebDAV on LINUX/xBSD Apache for easy publishing, and use some scheme to get the disk over to VMS. (It is my profound hope that WebDAV [Distributed Authoring and Versioning] will be ported to VMS in the near future, but I don't know of any plans to that effect.)

You could—this is really unpleasant—run IIS on an NT box inside the firewall, with all external access to it deliberately cut off, use the Pathworks publishing stuff to get files uploaded to it, and then use either NFS or FTP mirroring to get its disk to your VMS server.

You could use a storage appliance on the network that's NFS mounted from both PCs and VMS. (All this NFS stuff seems really slow and ugly, but if you use a caching Web server and give it enough memory, any frequently used file will be in memory most of the time anyway, so the additional network latency won't be that relevant.)

But all the ideas that make a UNIX/LINUX/NT box an essential part of your VMS-based Web server scheme are strategically bad for sites whose technical people are struggling to keep their VMS systems in place against the rising tide of "LINUX is the future!" "NT is ready for the Enterprise!" zealots, so your best bet is probably to standardize on an FTP client and write really, really good instructions on how to use it.

19

User-Developed CGI Scripts

Some of your users may need or want to develop their own scripts, or to play with downloaded scripts without risking the security of your entire system. There are a couple of reasonable choices. It's not a good idea to let them run IIS (or Personal Web Services, or whatever else it's being called today) on their desktop machines, since that opens many windows of vulnerability that can result in bigger problems later (the Nimda worm, among others).

You could run a separate sandbox machine for them. (If you have a Galaxy system, you could run a separate Galaxy instance for them, but this seems like an unlikely circumstance.)

You could make them e-mail you the scripts for uploading, and you could eyeball them and make sure they were completely okay. The problems with this option are obvious (and include you not having all the time in the world).

You can set up separate CGI-BIN directories that individual users have rights to upload files into. They had better be trusted users, because their scripts will run with the same rights the Web server has. (And that might mean users' scripts could update databases or change files that they don't have rights to change as individuals.)

Here are the realistic options. You could have a separate instance of the Web server that runs under a different user name with lesser privileges and allow users to upload their CGIs into a different CGI-BIN directory. This could work reasonably well, although if you have multiple users they could interfere with each other.

You could also, finally, have user CGIs that run with the users' privileges. (That puts their files at risk, but at least it limits the damages, - assuming that they don't have any special privileges.)

A few technicalities should be mentioned. The defined capability to impersonate another user was introduced in VMS 6.0, but the interface really settled down (as the Persona services) only in VMS 6.2. Servers that run acceptably on VMS 5.5-2 (OSU and WASD) will not be able to do some of the tricks involving other user names until you upgrade to a later version. WASD has some hand-rolled support for impersonation under VMS 6.0 and 6.1; OSU support starts with the Persona services at 6.2. (Per-thread security profiles weren't introduced until considerably later, which means that it's now possible to do this in a less complex way than WASD and OSU had to; however, these old ways still work.) The following text describes how it's done.

19.1 CSWS/Apache

This isn't currently supported in Apache on VMS. If you need it in Apache, you'll have to roll your own. This isn't impossible, although it's very fiddly business. You write your own executable that's INSTALLed with IMPERSONATE privilege. It runs as a CGI under the regular Apache Web server account. It reads its parameters to determine who it's supposed to be, then uses Persona services to change identity to that user name, and then spawns a process with that identity to actually run the script and resets its own identity back to the default Apache account. You can probably steal much of the code from WASD or OSU.

UNIX/LINUX–based Apache can be configured with suEXEC support, which (under a very restrictive set of conditions) will allow user scripts. It also has the User directive, which can be different from virtual host to virtual host (according to a CSWS engineer on comp.os.vms); the release notes point out that this is not supported in CSWS 1.2, but it's being considered for the next release of CSWS.

19.2 OSU

User scripting is an optional and perhaps underpublicized feature in OSU. (The only documentation I could find on it is in the comments in the user_script.c and user_script.com files.) Here's what happens: From the SYSTEM account, create a detached process that acts as a gateway between the server and the user script execution processes. (This can't be created by the HTTP_SERVER process because it requires heavy privileges—OPER, SYSNAM, and SYSPRV—which are privileges you definitely don't want HTTP_SERVER to have.)

When the server recognizes that it needs to run a user script, it contacts the gateway and passes it the script and user name it needs to run under. The gateway program uses Persona services to assume the needed user name, and then, through a proxy from that user name to itself, creates another process with which it communicates using DECnet task-to-task communication (and then sets itself back to the original Persona). Because the gateway process doesn't read and parse the server configuration files, it needs to get some configuration information from system globals. The gateway connects to the script execution object, WWWEXEC, and uses a different script object. This process can also be used to run scripts using the user name/password entered as a result of SYSUAF-based authentication, so you can run scripts as the user you're talking to as well as run scripts as their owners.

Here's what you need to do to get that all started up. First, compile (or link, if you have object files but don't have a C compiler) the user_script.c program by going to the [.BASE_CODE] directory and doing

```
$ @USER_SCRIPT.COM  BUILD  [NOCOMPILE]
```

(Giving `NOCOMPILE` as the optional P2 will skip straight to the link stage.)

Next, you need to define appropriate DECnet proxies. You can define a default proxy of every account to itself with a single command, or you can define them user by user. If you want just to give userscript capability to everybody, you want to do the former; if you want to allow this only on a user name-by-user name basis after the user has applied to you for permission, then you add a proxy for each user:

```
UAF>  add/proxy  node-number::* */default  ! proxies for
every account
```

or

```
UAF>  add/proxy  node-number::username username/default !
user by user
```

The node number is (area * 1,024) + node number, so if your DECnet node is 49.1 (which it may well be if you're running only over IP), the node number is 50,177. If you're sharing the UAF among multiple nodes in a cluster that will need this functionality, you'll need to issue the add/proxy for each node. You may be able to use node name instead of number, and you may be able to use 0:: instead of either (which would work on all nodes), but I couldn't get this to work right on my test machine running DECnet Phase V.

Define the following logicals. (You need to include the definitions in some file that will be run in your system startup before you create the detached user_script gateway process.)

```
$ DEFINE /SYSTEM  USER_SCRIPT_ACCESS   node::username [,
node2::username2]
```

(NODE::USERNAME is the node and user name the HTTP server runs under. Node is probably the current node. You're telling the gateway from whom it should accept instructions; this can be a list. Depending on how DECnet is configured, you may need to specify a node number rather than a node name.)

```
$ DEFINE/SYSTEM USER_SCRIPT_LIMIT number-of-concurrent-
threads-allowed
```

How many user-written scripts are you willing to have running at once? Note that quotas on the HTTP_SERVER account don't affect this at all, since the gateway program is running with process quota derived from SYSTEM, and each user process is a new process running with that user name's process quotas. Pick a number appropriate to how heavily loaded your system is and how likely you think it is that user processes will go into infinite loops or go to sleep without giving any response back.

```
$ DEFINE/SYSTEM USER_SCRIPT_OBJECT WWWUEXEC
```

Actually, you could make this some other name, but WWWUEXEC is as good as any, and there is some tradition behind this. Don't get confused by the presence of WWWUEXEC-OBSOLETE.COM in the OSU kit—you don't need a WWWUEXEC.COM. The user_script.exe program will register itself as whatever object name you tell it to here; the server will use whatever object you tell it to in the configuration files (they need to be the same name).

```
$ DEFINE/SYSTEM USER_SCRIPTSERVER 0::"""0=scriptserver-
object-name"""
```

You need this only if you plan to run in the somewhat confusingly named "captive mode," in which the user name from the authenticated user is passed to DECnet to run scripts from the base Web server. (Something you might want to do for a script that changed user passwords.) If they're full-access user accounts, you can just leave this undefined and it will know to use WWWEXEC.COM. The program comments suggest WWWCEXEC as the object name; there is no sample file provided, but I think a copy of WWWEXEC.COM would work.

Create the script gateway detached process. From examining the code you might expect executing

```
@[OSU.BASE_CODE]USER_SCRIPT DETACH
```

would work, but it won't until you go to some trouble. Because it defines most of the environment variables itself, including USER_SCRIPT_ACCESS, if it runs from any account other than the OSU server account it won't be willing to talk to the OSU server account. But if you run it from the OSU server account, it won't work either, because that account doesn't have the privilege to register a DECnet object. So you can either make the global declarations I gave, install the user_script.exe, previously, and then, from SYSTEM, do a

```
$run/detached/UIC=OSU-server-account
```

of the user_script.exe, or you can tweak the USER_SCRIPT.COM so that the link is /NOTRACE, and the DETACH portion will execute the image from WWW_SYSTEM. Then, in HTTP_STARTUP, you can insert (in the SYSTEM portion)

```
$ CALL INSTALL_IMAGE WWW_SYSTEM:USER_SCRIPT -
  /PRIV=(SYSPRV,OPER,SYSNAM,IMPERSONATE)
```

and in the daemon portion of HTTP_STARTUP (which runs as HTTP_SERVER across the DECnet link from SYSTEM) add

```
@[OSU.BASE_CODE]USER_SCRIPT DETACH
```

so that it starts up this process, at least the first time it runs. (Every time you restart the server it'll try to start the process up again, but you won't get a bunch of script processes, because the first thing it does is try to set its name, and it bails out if the name's already taken.)

For a particular user, create a [.wwwbin] directory under the SYS$LOGIN directory. [.www] is the user directory for serving files; [.wwwbin] is the user directory for scripts. Notice that the server has to be able to read the files in the [.www] subdirectory, either by ACL entry or by W:RE protection; it doesn't have to be able to read the scripts in the [.wwwbin] directory, because they'll be executed by the user who owns them. Copy the WWWEXEC.COM from the OSU account's SYS$LOGIN to the SYS$LOGIN of the particular user account.

Edit the HTTP_SCRIPTS.CONF configuration file. This comes by default with

```
.define uscript_enable exec
.define uscript_prefix /htbin-cap/*
.define uscript_task 0::"0=CAPSCRIPT"www_root:[bin]
```

which will eventually be expanded to

```
exec /htbin-cap/* 0::"0=CAPSCRIPT"www_root:[bin]
```

which is the format that enables running scripts actually located in WWW_ROOT:[BIN] (the same directory as /htbin/) as the authenticated user.

You'd need a

```
prot /htbin-cap/*  WWW_SYSTEM:VMSAUTH.PROT !See chapter 7
```

before the exec statement to make sure you got a SYSUAF-authenticated user.

To get the format where you're running scripts as their owners, you need

```
exec /htbin~* 0::"0=WWWUEXEC"wwwbin
```

or you can do this user by user if you only want to authorize it for particular user accounts—for example:

```
exec /htbin~testuser* 0::"0=WWWUEXEC"wwwbin
```

but you can't do

```
exec /htbin~testuser/* 0::"0=WWWUEXEC"wwwbin
```

because the user script gateway program gets a copy of the exec rule from the server, and if the last character of the matched string is a "*" and the next-to-last character is a "/", the gateway program thinks it's meant to be in captive mode.

One gotcha here is that you'd ordinarily put the `exec` statements into http_scripts.conf, but you can't do this if you're multihosting and have a `pass /*` in the multihost configuration. If you're doing that, then the `exec` statements must appear before the first `localaddress` block in the http_paths file, or, as with userdirs, the server will try to map this as part of the /* hierarchy for the localaddress host. Another gotcha is with the privileges needed to use user_script. Although the comments in the code don't mention it, it has to have IMPERSONATE privilege as well as SYSNAM, SYSPRV, and OPER. If it doesn't have IMPERSONATE privilege, it will report that the names you're using are invalid user names. In fact, they're not; it's just that the attempt to assume their personas fails because the user_script program can't do it.

Now that you've made those changes, you can restart the server using PRIVREQUEST. Put a script in the [.wwwbin] directory of your testuser account and try to execute it. (Figure 19.1 shows the output of a copy of

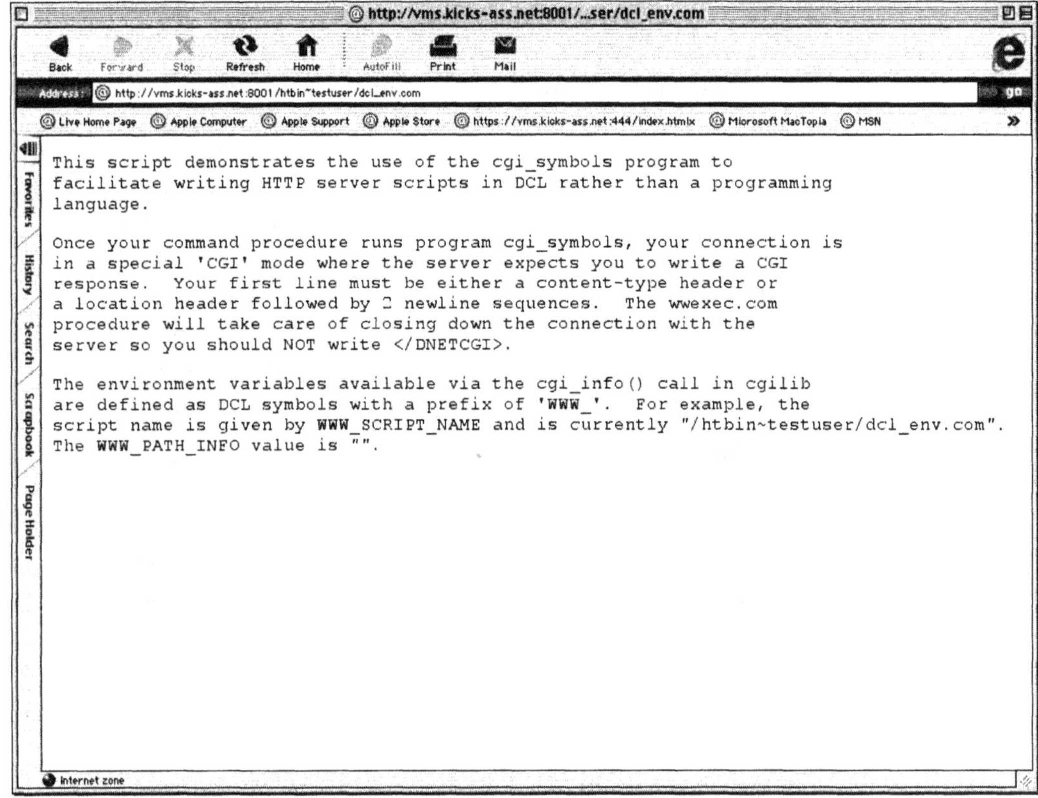

Figure 19.1 *A user script verson of DCL_ENV.*

DCL_ENV.COM, slightly modified so that it knows where to run the CGI symbols from, which I copied into the [.wwwbin] of my testuser account. As you can see, it works.)

19.3 WASD

Use the UXEC mapping rule after a corresponding SET rule, which goes

```
set /~*/www/cgi-bin/*  script=as=~
uxec[+] template [(RTEname)]result
```

This maps script execution for users (running as that user if the Persona services are enabled). The template looks like "/~*/directory/*", and the result looks like "/*/www/cgi-bin/*".

The optional [+], if present, says to run the script in the CGIplus environment. The optional (RTEname) (the parentheses are really part of the command) specifies whether to load a persistent run-time environment, such as a Perl or Python interpreter, and run the script in that.

If you made the template be just /~specificusername/directory/* the result would be /specificdirectory/www/cgi-bin/*, and only the particular user you called out would be able to run scripts. The first wildcard is for user name; the second is for the script name. `Uxec` must be paired with a set rule, as shown previously. The `set` rule in this form tells the server to run scripts from that directory in the Persona—that is, under the user name and with the privileges—of the user it belongs to. You can also specify `script=as=$`, and if you've set up protection so that the user needed to be authenticated against SYSUAF to get to this script, the script will run in the Persona of the authenticated user, not as the user it belongs to.

A third option is `script=as=username`. You can create a VMS user, named perhaps SANDBOX, with minimal privileges (NETMBX, TMPMBX), minimal disk quota, and no rights to write to the Web server files, and then run your untrusted scripts as this safely sandboxed user using `script=as=SANDBOX`. This lets users do even less harm than they would running the script when logged in as themselves, since SANDBOX can't even erase their files for them.

This is not necessary for user-developed scripts, but is perhaps helpful if you want to develop, for example, Web-based management tools that any user (or perhaps just help desk people who may not be trustable with privileged DCL access) can use to start and stop print queues or delete jobs. The solution is to create an account with exactly the necessary privileges—in this case, OPER—and configure only those vetted-and-trusted scripts to run under that user name. The Web allows an easy point-click interface, and if you require a SYSUAF-authenticated user to run the job, you can log who's accessing it, making it easy to tell which user prankishly zapped somebody else's print job.

For any of these run-as-another-user shenanigans to work, the server must be started with the /PERSONA qualifier. If you make that /PERSONA=rightlist-identifier (e.g., /PERSONA=WASD_SCRIPTABLE), then only the accounts to which the system manager has granted WASD_SCRIPTABLE can be used to run scripts. That's probably the method with the least configuration hassle for allowing specific trusted users to run scripts they maintain themselves—if you trust them, you grant them WASD_SCRIPTABLE; if not, you can just use the global `uxec` and `set` rules shown at the beginning of this section.

Perl

The name "Perl" officially stands for "practical extraction and report language," reflecting the original use of the language, but in more than a decade of evolution by open source development, Perl has grown to be far more than that. Perl is a cross-platform Swiss Army knife of software, a veritable toolkit in itself, with applications in reporting, to be sure, but also in system management, database maintenance, and, most dramatically, on the Web.

Perl, not to put too fine a point on it, is the glue that holds the Web together. I'll explain more about that subsequently.

A.1 History

Larry Wall released the first version of Perl in December 1987. The point, to start with, was to extract data from variously formatted text files and to be able to write reports with them. Larry is a linguist, and Perl has grown as a syncretist language, like English, able to adopt idioms from other languages (some `awk`, some `sed`, some C, some `sh`) and become increasingly powerful and expressive, acquiring regular expressions in version 2, binary data in version 3, and considerable extensibility in version 5.

All of this has made Perl into the anti-Pascal. Where one important branch of computer science has concentrated on purity of design (and concomitant aspects, such as the ability to automatically generate code from algorithms and the ability to formally prove that the code matches the algorithm), producing languages of severe beauty such as Pascal and Modula-2, Perl has gone the other way. Philosophical purity is out; pragmatism is in. Pascal is intended to make errors unlikely; Perl is intended to get the job done, and the range of jobs it does has been extended further and further since its birth. A design principle of the Algol-Pascal-Modula-Ada family is to make sure that there's an obvious right way to do any operation. One of the mottos of the Perl community is: There's more than one way to do it!

It's also, philosophically, the anti-UNIX, although it works and plays very well on that platform. The idea with which UNIX was originally developed was that of a big toolbox of little specialized tools, which each did one particular thing. You could use pipes to connect the little tools together, and the only code you'd have to write would be the part really specific to your application. UNIX is rife with little languages and utilities that do really specific things. `awk` reads text files (or line-oriented input streams) and takes actions based on the data. `tr` transmogrifies files, letting you, for example, change a document that's all in capital letters into something with initial caps only. Perl is a big language that does everything.

A.2 A software Swiss Army knife

Part of the original UNIX idea, back when it was growing at Bell Labs, was that the smaller the tool was, the easier it would be to get it right. Perl manages to maintain high quality while incorporating an amazing variety of functionality through three main approaches. It's open source, so that developers can take pride in finding other peoples' errors or feel shame if they leave big errors in their own code. It allows language extensions through modules (such as subroutine libraries: a big chunk of Perl code designed for a particular function—for example, parsing HTML); individual applications can use the routines in the modules without worrying about how they work. It also allows extensions through XS packages; developers can write code in some compiled language to do something that the main Perl engine doesn't do (e.g., making platform-specific operating system calls). Again, the complexity is hidden from the programmer who uses the extension.

Perl is both an applications language and a scripting language. Rather than being rendered into the particular binary code of the processor it runs on, Perl code is interpreted by the Perl engine. (In fact the code is "understood" all at once, before it runs, and rendered into an internal bytecode representation, which executes pretty quickly. That's a bigger win for programs that will process a lot of input than for those that don't go through the inner loop very many times.) This tends to make it slower than highly optimized compiled code, but it makes it much easier to have Perl scripts work across multiple platforms. Perl can spawn any program that runs on the host machine; capture all the output into memory; and, if necessary, parse through it to understand the results. This makes it an excellent glue language for sticking applications together that weren't designed to be stuck together, which has made it very popular with system managers. Because it's an interpreted language, it's quicker and more fun to slap something together than in a compiled language such as C or C++. Because it started out as a text-handling language and has absorbed, over time, most of the richness of the UNIX text-handling tools, it can do extremely powerful things with text in a very few lines of code. There are tools and packages (such as the libwww package) to support all kinds of network interactions.

The very popular and capable—though sometimes annoyingly flaky—majordomo mailing-list software is written in Perl, which is a natural choice for a package that needs to parse requests that come to it in e-mail, reply by mail, maintain text files of subscribers to list, determine whether a mail message comes from somebody who's authorized to post on a list, and so on.

A.3 Web-ready

When the Web came along, Perl was a perfect fit. A common gateway interface (CGI) program connected to a Web form will receive all the input as a text stream from the server; it takes Perl just one line to parse that into an array of field names and values. The HTML it needs to respond with is just text, and Perl is good at that. Even more to the point, Lincoln Stein's CGI.PM module does a lot of the work for you, and it works fine on VMS. Perl has been extended with XS routines to interface with popular database packages (e.g., Oracle and, more recently, Rdb), so it's straightforward to use Perl CGI programs for Web-based database queries and updates—which is basically what e-commerce is all about.

If a program needs to do something that Perl can't do, Perl can open a pipeline to a program that can do it and pass the data along—even a program on some other machine. There's some overhead in starting up the Perl engine and interpreting the scripts, but Apache has resolved this by more or less building in the Perl engine with the mod_perl processor; OSU uses the Webperl script, and WASD uses the PerlRTE. With connections to various freeware plotting packages such as PGPLOT and GnuPlot, Perl can easily output GIF files, charting data on demand. Perl is also good for site maintenance—easily finding stale files, for example—and log file analysis, which is, after all, the practical extraction and reporting it was designed for from the beginning.

A.4 Open source

Perl has been open source from the beginning. It's distributed under Larry Wall's "Artistic License," rather than the GNU Public License (GPL) that so many other tools use. Many people work on each Perl release. How new features will work is determined by rough consensus on the perl5-porters mailing list, or on other lists devoted to specific platforms (e.g., vmsperl). Because source is available and because Perl is so massively useful, it's been ported to many different platforms: various UNIXes and UNIX-like systems; Macintosh; Windows 3.1, 95, NT, NeXT, OS/390 (on big IBM iron), OS/2; and, of course, VMS (VAX and Alpha, although you really need DECC, not VAX C, to compile recent versions). To keep each platform's version from developing incompatibly with the others, all multiplatform stuff is folded into one distribution, under the control of a particular person. (You need to know who has the responsibility, so that person can be thought of as holding a token that indicates responsibility; the Perl developers call this a pumpkin, and sometimes refer to the person holding it as the Pumpking.) Perl distributions, modules, XS packages, and tools are distributed via the Comprehensive Perl Archive Network (CPAN), which has volunteer-hosted mirror sites all over the world. (Naturally, Perl scripts are used to keep the sites in synch.)

The development of Perl has been greatly aided by O'Reilly and Associates (Sebastopol, CA), which has not only published the definitive books on the language—the famous "camel" book is *Programming Perl* by Larry Wall, Tom Christiansen, and Randal L. Schwartz—but hosts the perl.com Web site and has organized Perl conferences. The spread of Perl is also a tribute to Larry Wall's original vision.

Important players on Perl for VMS include Craig Berry (who packaged up a prebuilt kit for 5.6.1 that includes an assortment of useful extensions, including the database interface) and Dan Sugalski (who wrote a number of VMS-specific extensions for system management with Perl and ported mod_perl to VMS, and whose personal site, www.sidhe.org, hosts the Perl prebuilt kit). Dan is at present a Perl Fellow (with "salary" paid by donations to the Perl Foundation) and acts as system architect for Perl 6. Charles Bailey was responsible for the Perl 5.004 port to VMS and has written CRINOID, a distributed high-performance Perl server for VMS (discussed in Chapter 17).

A.5 Resources for Perl

If you want to read more about Perl and tools that go with it, try the following Web sites.

- www.perl.com is hosted by O'Reilly and Associates; it has documentation, news, transcripts of Larry Wall's speeches, FAQS, and downloads.
- perldoc.com has on-line documentations for Perl—be sure to keep a browser window open here while developing or debugging your Perl scripts.
- www.perl.org is the site of the Perl Mongers, a nonprofit group designed to establish Perl user groups. It offers geeky tee-shirts, job listings, documentation, news, and book reviews. It also hosts the VMSperl mailing list, which chronicles Perl development, and functions as a place for VMS-specific Perl questions.
- www.ora.com is the site for O'Reilly and Associates, offering all the programming books and CDs you could hope for.
- http://www.sidhe.org/vmsperl/index.html is Dan Sugalski's VMS Perl page, which hosts the Perl prebuilt kits among other goodies (although it's not always up-to-date).
- http://www.xray.mpe.mpg.de/mailing-lists/vmsperl/ has searchable archives of the VMSPerl mailing list.
- http://www.cpan.org/modules/by-module/VMS/ tells you how to find VMS-specific Perl modules at CPAN.

B

Python

Yes, Python is yet another scripting language. Perl may be the most popular language on the Web, but you may well want to know about Python.

Scripting languages, you'll recall, have some features that make them important to system administrators and programmers alike. They're interpreted rather than compiled, which means that you can usually develop in them faster than with the edit/compile/run cycle required by compiled languages. (The tradeoff is that the applications generally run more slowly than the equivalent application coded in a compiled language. Sometimes this doesn't matter—do you care if a file scan that runs once a month takes 10 minutes or 20?—and sometimes it does, in which case you can declare the scripting-language version a prototype and recode the application in C now that you know for sure what it's supposed to do.) A good scripting language can function as glue, sticking together otherwise incompatible applications or libraries and making them work together.

Most scripting languages got started before the Web did, but when that came along they turned out to be good fits for CGI programming, whether you're Web-enabling existing applications or putting together new ones. In the rush to be the first to new Internet territory, the fact that you could get your site up faster using scripted CGIs rather than compiled ones made scripting languages more popular than ever.

Perl is probably the best known of these languages, but many script languages are used for CGI programming, including DCL, various UNIX shell languages, Tcl, and Python. Users of Python include NASA, Lawrence Livermore National Laboratories, Infoseek, pobox.com, RedHat (in its installation package), as well as many sites running Zope, a Python-based Web application engine (for which there is currently no VMS port—that would make a good project for someone).

There are lots of Python products and packages available for free (where lots is roughly 10 percent of the huge quantity of stuff for Perl). Typically, where there are several different modules or libraries for doing any particular function with Perl, Python will have one. CGI is a core module for Python. (Enough core modules come with Python to build a simple all-Python Web server and a scripted Telnet client for screen scrapers.)

It's somewhat easier than with Perl to teach Python to call any module from a shareable image library. With Perl, you need to go through a fairly arcane process to produce an extension (.XS) that connects up with a library, including writing and compiling glue code in C. (You're supposed to start by reading a doc called perlguts.) With Python, you still need to write a C interface for each module you want to call, but you need to know much less about the Python internals than you do about Perl internals to do the equivalent thing.

B.1 Python's the meaning of life

When Guido van Rossum started work on Python in 1989—although the first version wasn't released until 1991—he was inspired by software engineering principles (and television sketch comedy; the language is named for Monty Python's Flying Circus, and the documentation is larded with references and jokes).

Python is a complete enough language that there's some way to do whatever you need to do—loop structures, subroutines, and so on—but there's generally only one way to do it. (Compare this with Perl's motto: There's more than one way to do it!) Program block structure is shown by indentation, not by curly braces or other delimiters. (Different authorities suggest at least four different styles for handling curly braces in C, and the language itself doesn't mandate any indentation at all; C code written by different developers can look very different.) This helps to make Python more readable—if it's indented, it's a block; if it isn't indented, it isn't one. (In some ways, this kind of thing makes Python the COBOL of scripting languages. That's not necessarily a bad thing.)

The language was also designed to be object oriented from the beginning. (Perl didn't acquire object orientation until version 5, and purists have complaints about how it's implemented. Purists have complaints about lots of things in Perl. That's part of the joy of Perl for those who love it.) It was also designed without much regard to the specifics of a particular platform. Perl has been ported everywhere, but incorporates various UNIX commands and ideas; Python doesn't do much of that—it was designed for

UNIX, but it was first implemented on Macintosh and runs now on UNIX, 32-bit Windows, big IBM iron, and VMS.

Discipline is the watchword of the Python design. A Perl program can look like line noise—remember line noise, random characters generated by a poor modem connection? If you had a character-based modem control program, you'd actually see these strange characters on your screen, but I suppose most people who got online since Netscape came out have never encountered line noise. It's still there, hidden in the PPP negotiation process—but a Python program uses punctuation in normal ways and is generally less surprising to someone who's unfamiliar with the language. A C or Pascal programmer can pick up a Python script and get at least some idea of what's going on. This is also possible with Perl programs that have been specifically coded for readability, but the language design doesn't particularly encourage it. I don't mean to suggest that you can't write incomprehensible code in Python; just that most parts of the language make it easier to write code other people can understand. (There are arcana in some of the object-oriented portions.)

Perl is an extremely large and powerful language, with quite a few idioms that express the same ideas in different ways. The result is that each programmer learns the set of structures in the language that work the way he or she is comfortable with and becomes very productive. This is good, but the drawback is that most programmers end up speaking their own personal dialect of Perl and may find reading someone else's Perl code to be like reading a different language. It's entirely rational to decide that the productivity gains outweigh the maintainability losses, and it's also possible to gain some maintainability through the use of uncool 1960s methods (e.g., coding standards and structured walkthroughs), but you'll lose some productivity that way. If you're writing one-off scripts or prototypes, this isn't an issue, but it's something that really needs to be considered if you plan to do large, tightly integrated multideveloper projects in Perl.

There's a game called Perl golf. It's a competition for the shortest code to perform a particular function. (Golf, because the smallest number of [key] strokes wins.) This is a viable game because there's always more than one way to do it in Perl, and more than one way to notate each way to do it, so if a game proposal goes up on the Perl Monger's Web site, 20 programmers can produce 20 substantially different programs to accomplish the same thing. There is no such game in Python. You get different programs if you use different algorithms, not from expressing the same ideas in different (and less comprehensible) ways.

Python makes it easier to do consistent and coherent multideveloper projects by not offering you as many choices as Perl does. Some developers will consider that a straitjacket. Others will be happier to have more structure.

B.2 Javawocky

Python and Perl both have, on some platforms, the ability to compile scripts into executable code (or at least into C code that can be compiled and linked into a binary, so developers don't have to distribute source code). One unique advantage of Python is that there's a version of Python that runs under Java.

This is Jython (initially JPython), which compiles Python scripts to Java bytecodes that can execute compatibly on any platform that has a Java Virtual Machine (JVM). Version 2.1 was released December 31, 2001. Jython can work in an object-oriented way with any capability the JVM has—importing Java classes, subclassing them, and inheriting their capabilities. (Compiling to Java bytecodes means that the resultant programs run considerably faster than if the C-based Python interpreter had just been reimplemented in Java and had to go through parsing and executing Python scripts every time they needed to be executed.) One result of this project is that whenever the JVM goes on a new platform—a new Palm PC, a set-top box, a refrigerator, OpenVMS—Python is automatically there. Another result is that Python coders can write downloadable applets. This is a very significant development, in my opinion, and may herald considerable growth for Python. The instant availability of Jython applications on VMS may be significant for VMS use as well.

B.3 Java on VMS

Python has been running on VMS for several years. Uwe Zessin made it availabe on the German DECUS Web server, at http://www.decus.de/~zessin/python.html, for some years, although at this writing the material is no longer there. Jean-François Pièrrone is currently hosting the distribution on his server, www.pi-net.dyndns.org; see section B.6 for the URL. The Zessin distribution includes interfaces to the VMS mail library, a SYSUAF reader, an HTML-to-Runoff converter (with which he's made printable documentation from the Web version), an IMAP client (with which it would be pretty straightforward to write a Web mail interface on VMS), and other goodies.

Jean-François Pièrrone and coworkers have developed or ported a number of excellent Python tools to VMS. These include a High-Performance Server System module for Python on OSU and an equivalent Run Time Environment for WASD, along with an interface to Rdb for Python. One company's successful use of Python CGI scripts with Rdb on WASD (is that enough acronyms in a sentence?) can be found at http://wasd.vsm.com.au/other/wasd-tlt-exec-council-1a.ppt.

B.4 Always look on the bright side of life

Guido van Rossum has received funding for a project called "Computer Programming for Everybody." The idea is to teach real programming with real programming languages to schoolchildren and others. The language of choice for this project, of course, is Python. The funding is meant to produce teaching materials more appropriate than the O'Reilly books for sixth-graders. I have no idea how well this will work out, but if it's successful, there will be a large pool of Python developers in ten years.

B.5 Conclusion

I'm trying to avoid the religious argument between Perl and Python. Like most computer-based religious arguments, both sides are right and wrong, because there is no universal right answer. Perl is much more popular than Python, and there are more Perl developers. If you're a manager who decides to use Python because you want your new hires to be able to read the code of the people who've moved on, you do have to consider that it'll be harder to find new hires with Python experience than candidates who have some Perl background. But it may be easier to train people in Python than in Perl.

If you're a developer or system administrator, I can give you some advice. You should definitely check out Python, so that you have it in your toolbox when you come across a project for which Python is the right answer. The learning curve is pretty short if you know C or Pascal, and it's a rich and powerful language—if you can take the discipline.

B.6 Resources

- http://www.python.org is the official Web site for Python users and developers, with documentation, tutorials, FAQs, how-tos, modules, and interviews.

- http://www.python.org/~guido is Guido van Rossum's home page, with articles, interviews, essays, and philosophy.
- http://www.jython.org is the Jython (Python for Java) project home page.
- http://www.cnri.reston.va.us is the site for the Corporation for National Research Initiatives, which employs Guido van Rossum and hosts Jython development.
- http://www.pi-net.dyndns.org/anonymous/jfp/python-2_1_1-vms-src.zip is the site for Python for VMS.
- http://wasd.vsm.com.au/other/wasd-tlt-exec-council-1a.ppt provides presentation on Python with RDB and WASD.

C

PHP

You've got a Web site. You want dynamic content. That particular buzzword means that the content your site presents to an individual user changes either with the passage of time or depending on the identity of the person accessing it. A good example would be a newspaper Web site, where the top story changes when there's breaking news, and the site might also allow users to customize their view of the site so that only tech stories are presented. You don't get dynamic content by having HyperText Markup Language (HTML) coders sitting at terminals 24/7 frantically editing the pages to include only the stories the current users want.

Once you've got a good and recognizable page layout, you don't want to keep messing with it. Hand-editing pages to change the top story is inefficient and error prone. (And, conversely, when you do change your page layout, you want to change it across the whole application, not page by page.)

You could write CGI programs in any language that has a database connection—Perl, C, Python, server-side Java, Visual BASIC, DCL on VMS using command-line utilities for the database lookup, whatever—to do this work. The trick, basically, is that the browser doesn't know where the content comes from. So long as it gets a stream of text that looks like proper HTML, the browser doesn't care how many programs it took to produce it; whether it was in a file or generated in real time; or what computer language, operating system, or hardware produced it. A common gateway interface (CGI) program just has to write valid HTML to its output, and that ends up at the browser. (In some cases this means emitting a content-type header that informs the browser that what's coming is to be interpreted as HTML.)

A program of this kind has a bunch of formatted WRITE or PRINT statements to put out the static parts of the form, code to do database lookups and PRINT the results, and more output statements to clean up at the bottom. Whenever you want to change the Web page this kind of program produces, you need a programmer to go into the code and change the output statements. You can't use a WYSIWYG editor to make the page layout the way you want it. You need to keep tweaking the program code and rerunning the program.

(Perl, incidentally, has one feature that makes this easier than in some other languages. The "HERE document" lets you include an arbitrary amount of unmodified HTML source in your program in a single output statement, rather than needing a new output statement for each line, having to quote each line separately, and so on. This kind of thing is harder in C, but pretty straightforward in a shell script or DCL.)

You can't easily use Web design support tools such as Dreamweaver, FrontPage, or Netscape Composer to develop pages that are constructed this way. It can take a long time to get your pages looking good when they come out of programs like these. It's even worse if your Web pages need to incorporate JavaScript; you can't easily edit the broken JavaScript code and instead have to edit the program that emits the JavaScript. This is tedious and error prone.

The solution? Web page templates, which can be developed with WYSIWYG editors by page designer, and contain directives to tell a server-side processor what kind of content to insert. That processor reads the template, sends the unmodified parts to the browser, and replaces the directives with the results of following the instructions they contain. Those directives can be database lookups, stores, or other kinds of programming logic not based on databases. Your graphics designer can lay out the pages, not worrying about the programming, and the programmer can insert the appropriate directives.

Commercial products that do this include Microsoft's Active Server Pages (ASP) and Cold Fusion from Allaire (Newton, MA). Microsoft provides ASP on Windows NT servers, but there is a UNIX/LINUX version from Chili!Soft (Bellevue, WA—a division of Cobalt Networks). ASP allows the use of VBScript or JScript as the scripting language, even on non-Microsoft platforms. If you see a URL that ends in .asp, you're probably getting something that's been put through an ASP processor. If you see one that ends in .cfm, it's probably Cold Fusion. These aren't options on VMS.

Interestingly enough, the acronym ASP also refers to application service providers, vendors to whom companies outsource some of their IT load. This type of technology—server-side templated scripting languages—is very helpful in developing the kind of applications ASPs need. (A dynamically created page can display a different company logo depending on which client company the connection is coming from. The database connection is also vital.)

In the open source world, PHP is the templating language of choice. On VMS, it's the only choice of which I'm aware. PHP is an annoying recursive acronym; it stands for PHP Hypertext Processor. (You find this a lot in the free software world. GNU stands for GNU's Not UNIX, for example.) Rasmus Lerdorf created the first version of PHP in 1995. Now, the PHP Group Web site credits the language design and concept to Andi Gutmans, Rasmus Lerdorf, and Zeev Suraski. Gutmans and Suraski are developers who got involved while students at the Technion University in Israel and have gone on to run Zend. Lerdorf is now employed by LinuxCare.

PHP became very popular with version 3. It provides an extensible architecture; you can write plug-in libraries to extend the capabilities of the base product, including making it able to talk to different kinds of databases, or for that matter to do anything it doesn't already know how to do. With the aid of libraries—not yet ported to VMS—PHP can talk to Oracle, Adabas, dBASE files, filePro, Informix, InterBase, SQL Server, Oracle, PostgreSQL, Sybase, and anything it can access through a generic open database connectivity (ODBC) driver. There's an XML parser library. There's even an IMAP library, so PHP scripts can function as proxies to read a user's mail via IMAP and present it over the Web. (The mail host needs only to speak IMAP and doesn't even have to have a Web server of its own.)

PHP can run either as a CGI program (which means that when a PHP request is encountered, the PHP program is loaded into memory and executed, at whatever cost in processing time), as an Apache module, or as an HPSS module on OSU. On WASD it's available as a CGI, a CGIplus program, or an RTE, depending on how the mapping rules invoke it. The guts of PHP are in the PHPSHR shareable image library; the PHP program is a small front end that links to it, and so is mod_php.

The PHP scripting language is somewhat reminiscent of Perl, and should be pretty easy to pick up for any programmer. It's somewhat object oriented, supporting the most basic features—classes, constructors, and inheritance. (This isn't the place for a tutorial on object-oriented programming, so if you don't know what that last sentence means, just ignore it.)

A pair of developers—Boris Erdmann and Kristian Kuhntopp—found PHP3 wanting in support for many of the things typically needed by a Web application. Their PHPlib provides classes (that's an object-oriented thing) that hide the differences between the libraries to support different databases—thus making it much easier to write portable scripts—and do user session management (which means that it can automatically keep track of what user you've been talking to and where in your process you were; this takes care of the problem of someone bookmarking a page in the middle of your application).

PHP3 is still in wide use. However, PHP4 came out in 2001, incorporating much of the functionality of PHPlib. PHP4 is the first version of PHP to run on VMS. Dave Jones—the OSU author—did the first port of PHP and has been tracking changes and new releases. CSWS provides a packaged, supported, mod_php, with a PHP front end so you can use it from the command line.

PHP users include the geek news site Slashdot, the automaker Honda, and many other familiar names. If you need dynamic content, PHP may well be the way to go.

C.1 Resources for PHP

- The PHP Association, home of PHP—www.php.net
- High-profile PHP users—www.php.net/sites.php
- Zend Technologies, Ltd., home of commercial PHP development—www.zend.com
- Under the hood of PHP4—www.zend.com/zend/art/under-php4-hood.php
- PHP Builders, offering lots of PHP help and advice—www.phpbuilder.com
- PHPlib—phplib.netuse.de
- Slashdot, a ridiculously popular PHP application—www.slashdot.org
- O'Reilly Associates's PHP DevCenter—www.oreillynet.com/php
- Excerpts from the PHP Pocket Reference—www.oreillynet.com/pub/a/php/excerpts/intro.html

D

Apache

Writing a Web server is easy. You just parse URLs, return files—nothing to it. (http://www.nenie.org/cpcip/httpd.txt has the source code of a minimal Web server in only 481 lines of Z80 assembly language, including plenty of white space for readability. It runs only on the Amstrad CPC, though. Web servers of comparable length have been written in Perl and Python.)

On the other hand, if you want the server to be fast, secure, robust, and capable, the job is a good deal harder.

You may recall that Tim Berners-Lee at CERN, the European high-energy physics research lab, invented the World Wide Web. (Not to be confused with the Internet, which predated the Web by many years. The Web is a set of protocols that runs on top of the Internet.)

The Web uses the HyperText Transfer Protocol (HTTP), so a typical name for a Web server is HTTPd, with the "d" standing for "daemon." (A "daemon"—an essential concept on UNIX systems—is a program that runs in the background, listening until it recognizes that it needs to do something, and then doing it.) The first HTTPd was developed at CERN; the first non-European Web server was installed at SLAC (www-slac.stanford.edu) in December 1991. HyperText had been around as an idea for a long time, arguably since 1945, but Berners-Lee's major insight, articulated in a 1989 proposal, was seamless linking to remote data.

CERN developed servers that ran on big IBM mainframes, on UNIX systems, and on VMS systems. Eventually, however, CERN needed to spend its money on the Large Hadron Collider and ceased WWW software development after December 1994. Various computer science and physics sites had already developed browsers, including SLAC; the National Center for Supercomputing Applications had already developed Mosaic (whose developers went on to found Netscape) and produced an NCSA HTTPd, but development on that product stopped when the primary author, Rob

McCool, left. NCSA HTTPd was the most popular server on the Web, but Webmasters had had to develop their own patches, changes, fixes, and enhancements without any coordination, and the program was wandering in different directions.

In February 1995, a group of Webmasters "got together" via mailing list to support the NCSA HTTPd product. They combined their patches and bug fixes, and by April 1995 made the first official public release of the Apache server (version 0.6.2). Because of all the patches, it was "a patchy server"—I'm afraid that's where the name came from.

The Webmasters developed a methodology for making changes to the core—a method of "lazy consensus," whereby no changes could be checked into the archive without a number of "Yes" votes and an absence of "No" votes. You get voting rights by being recognized as a useful contributor to Apache development.

Now that they had a methodology for working together, the Apache Group really got cooking on improving the server. Version 0.7 involved various new features, but version 0.8 had a new server architecture incorporating features for speed—such as spinning off new processes before they were needed—and extensibility—such as a clearly defined application programming interface (API) and a modular structure. After lots more work, Apache version 1.0 came out in December 1995, extensively tested, ported to lots of platforms, and adequately documented. Within a year, it was the most popular server on the Web, and it has held that leadership position since. In 1999, some 6 million sites ran Apache, including Amazon.com, Hotmail.com (which Microsoft had tried and failed a couple of times to move over to IIS on NT; it just couldn't handle the load), Hewlett-Packard (www.hp.com), *The Financial Times* (www.ft.com), and the English royal family (www.royal.gov.uk).

The module structure was very significant. An Apache module can get a finger in the processing stream wherever it needs it. As a result, the SSI processor can postprocess the results of CGI execution directly rather than running only from files. Other capabilities can be layered on top of other modules; PERL-based extensions are very popular.

Apache runs on LINUX; on FreeBSD; on netBSD; on other UNIX variants; and on Windows NT, MacOS X, OS/2, and the VMS operating system. It powers considerably more sites than all the Microsoft IIS and PWS servers Netcraft can find on the Web, and all the various Netscape servers as well. For FrontPage to be a viable product, Microsoft had to release the

FrontPage publishing extensions for Apache—otherwise, FrontPage wouldn't work with the majority of servers out there.

The most widely used add-ons for Apache are probably the aforementioned FrontPage extensions mod_php, mod_perl, and mod_ssl. Mod_perl means that Apache can be extended with Perl modules, instead of being limited to writing, compiling, and linking additional C modules. A Perl module such as Apache::ASP brings Active Server Pages functionality, developed for Microsoft's IIS, to Perl. There's an embedded Python module for Apache (PyApache), but it hasn't yet been ported to VMS.

Apache is extremely configurable and has been extended and supported by various commercial organizations, including IBM and Compaq. Of course, all this configurability brings with it a lot of complexity, and an Apache Webmaster/sysadmin had really better know his or her stuff. Even Apache.org itself got hacked, more or less benignly, by folks who exploited configuration errors. (Once they had access, they used it to change the configuration so the path they'd used would no longer work, and documented what they'd done. See: http://dataloss.net/papers/how.defaced.apache.org.txt for a detailed account.)

That's not unique to Apache. The administrator of any system that's visible on the Internet had better know his or her stuff. The advantages of Apache (and other freeware servers) include the fact that if you know what you're doing, you can fix security vulnerabilities as soon as you find out about them, rather than waiting for the vendor to develop and release a fix, which may or may not solve the problem.

D.1 Resources

- Tim Berners-Lee—http://www.w3.org/People/Berners-Lee/
- The Web through 1995—http://www.w3.org/History.html
- The Apache Software Foundation—http://www.apache.org
- The Apache HTTP Server Project—
  http://www.apache.org/httpd.html
- Major contributors to Apache—
  http://www.apache.org/contributors/index.html
- Apache Week newsmagazine—http://www.apacheweek.com/
- How Apache.org got defaced—
  http://dataloss.net/papers/how.defaced.apache.org.txt

E

Annotated Sample Configuration Files

These are the configuration files as distributed with each server. You might want to follow along in Chapters 5–7 as we look at the relevant files for each.

E.1 CSWS configuration files

E.1.1 HTTPD.CONF

```
## httpd.conf-dist-openvms
## 1999-12-01 Lee Tibbert
##
## OpenVMS—Httpd.conf-dist modified to have 'reasonable' values on OpenVMS
##
## 2000-03-27   Scott LePage
##
## OpenVMS—Added "Multiviews" to HTDOCS directory for Version 1.3.12
## The default HTDOCS now has multi-language versions of INDEX.HTML
```

Multiviews support automatic content negotiation for multilanguage versions of documents.

```
##
## 2000-06-13   Rick Barry
##
## Change APACHE_ROOT to APACHE$ROOT and username from APACHE to APACHE$WWW.
##
## 2000-06-22   Kevin O'Kelley
##
## Change "/apache$root/htdocs" to "/apache$htdocs" to use the APACHE$HTDOCS
## system-wide logical name that is defined at startup time.
##
## 2000-08-03   Rick Barry
##
## Change AddIcon directive for README file types. Replace second "." with
## "_" and use lowercase for "readme".
##
```

```
## 2000-08-10   Matthew Doremus
##
## Added the SSL configuration support
##
## 2001-01-25   Gaitan D'Antoni
##
## Make README and HEADER lowercase in ReadmeName, HeaderName,
## and IndexIgnore directives.
##
## 2001-02-26   Rick Barry
##
## Add "Listen 80" directive because the single "Listen 443" directive
## in mod_ssl.conf effectively disables the "Port 80" here. According
## to Apache documentation we still need the Port directive (even
## though we now include a Listen directive) for some internal redirects.
#
# Based upon the NCSA server configuration files originally by Rob McCool.
#
# This is the main Apache server configuration file. It contains the
# configuration directives that give the server its instructions.
# See <URL:http://www.apache.org/docs/> for detailed information about
# the directives.
#
# Do NOT simply read the instructions in here without understanding
# what they do. They're here only as hints or reminders. If you are unsure
# consult the online docs. You have been warned.
#
# After this file is processed, the server will look for and process
# /apache$root/conf/srm.conf and then /apache$root/conf/access.conf
# unless you have overridden these with ResourceConfig and/or
# AccessConfig directives here.
#
# The configuration directives are grouped into three basic sections:
#  1. Directives that control the operation of the Apache server process as a
#     whole (the 'global environment').
#  2. Directives that define the parameters of the 'main' or 'default' server,
#     which responds to requests that aren't handled by a virtual host.
#     These directives also provide default values for the settings
#     of all virtual hosts.
#  3. Settings for virtual hosts, which allow Web requests to be sent to
#     different IP addresses or hostnames and have them handled by the
#     same Apache server process.
#
# Configuration and logfile names: If the filenames you specify for many
# of the server's control files begin with "/" (or "drive:/" for Win32), the
# server will use that explicit path.  If the filenames do *not* begin
# with "/", the value of ServerRoot is prepended—so "logs/foo.log"
# with ServerRoot set to "/usr/local/apache" will be interpreted by the
# server as "/usr/local/apache/logs/foo.log".
#

### Section 1: Global Environment
#
# The directives in this section affect the overall operation of Apache,
```

```
# such as the number of concurrent requests it can handle or where it
# can find its configuration files.
#

#
# ServerType is either inetd, or standalone.  Inetd mode is only supported on
# Unix platforms.
#
ServerType standalone

#
# ServerRoot: The top of the directory tree under which the server's
# configuration, error, and log files are kept.
#
# NOTE!  If you intend to place this on an NFS (or otherwise network)
# mounted filesystem then please read the LockFile documentation
# (available at <URL:http://www.apache.org/docs/mod/core.html#lockfile>);
# you will save yourself a lot of trouble.
```

Don't even think about doing this. Your VMS config will be different enough from UNIX configs that you can't share the files, and there's really no point in putting it on UNIX media. Put it on cluster-accessible disk.

```
#
# Do NOT add a slash at the end of the directory path.
#
ServerRoot "/apache$root"

#
# The LockFile directive sets the path to the lockfile used when Apache
# is compiled with either USE_FCNTL_SERIALIZED_ACCEPT or
# USE_FLOCK_SERIALIZED_ACCEPT. This directive should normally be left at
# its default value. The main reason for changing it is if the logs
# directory is NFS mounted, since the lockfile MUST BE STORED ON A LOCAL
# DISK. The PID of the main server process is automatically appended to
# the filename.
#
#LockFile logs/accept.lock
```

Leave this commented out. VMS has a real lock manager, so you won't be messing with a lockfile at all.

```
#
# PidFile: The file in which the server should record its process identification
# number when it starts.

#
PidFile logs/httpd.pid
```

If you're running in a cluster configuration, it needs to end up in system-specific storage, so if your logs are directed to APACHE$SPECIFIC, you'll be fine. You just don't want to be trying to shut down Apache on one node and picking up the process ID of an instance on another cluster node.

```
#
# ScoreBoardFile: File used to store internal server process information.
# Not all architectures require this.  But if yours does (you'll know because
# this file will be  created when you run Apache) then you *must* ensure that
# no two invocations of Apache share the same scoreboard file.
#
## Scoreboard file not used on OpenVMS. Use shared memory instead.
#ScoreBoardFile logs/apache_runtime_status

#
# In the standard configuration, the server will process this file,
# srm.conf, and access.conf in that order.  The latter two files are
# now distributed empty, as it is recommended that all directives
# be kept in a single file for simplicity.  The commented-out values
# below are the built-in defaults.  You can have the server ignore
# these files altogether by using "/dev/null" (for Unix) or
# "nul" (for Win32) for the arguments to the directives.
#
#ResourceConfig conf/srm.conf
#AccessConfig conf/access.conf

#
# Timeout: The number of seconds before receives and sends time out.
#
Timeout 300


#
# KeepAlive: Whether or not to allow persistent connections (more than
# one request per connection). Set to "Off" to deactivate.
#
KeepAlive On
```

There are few circumstances where you'd want this off. You save some overhead per request if you don't need to set up a new connection, and pages may load noticeably faster if it's on.

```
#
# MaxKeepAliveRequests: The maximum number of requests to allow
# during a persistent connection. Set to 0 to allow an unlimited amount.
# We recommend you leave this number high, for maximum performance.
#
MaxKeepAliveRequests 100
```

Depending on system load it may be profitable to play with this number. If you don't get more requests within the KeepAliveTimeout number, it doesn't matter what the setting is here.

```
#
# KeepAliveTimeout: Number of seconds to wait for the next request from the
# same client on the same connection.
#
KeepAliveTimeout 15
```

```
#
# Server-pool size regulation.  Rather than making you guess how many
# server processes you need, Apache dynamically adapts to the load it
# sees-that is, it tries to maintain enough server processes to
# handle the current load, plus a few spare servers to handle transient
# load spikes (e.g., multiple simultaneous requests from a single
# Netscape browser).
#
# It does this by periodically checking how many servers are waiting
# for a request.  If there are fewer than MinSpareServers, it creates
# a new spare.  If there are more than MaxSpareServers, some of the
# spares die off.  The default values are probably OK for most sites.
#
## OpenVMS-If raising number of servers, changed reduced MaxClients below.
MinSpareServers 5
MaxSpareServers 10


#
# Number of servers to start initially-should be a reasonable ballpark
# figure.
#
StartServers 5

#
# Limit on total number of servers running, i.e., limit on the number
# of clients who can simultaneously connect-if this limit is ever
# reached, clients will be LOCKED OUT, so it should NOT BE SET TOO LOW.
# It is intended mainly as a brake to keep a runaway server from taking
# the system with it as it spirals down...
#
## OpenVMS-Be paranoid
MaxClients 20
#MaxClients 150
```

You almost certainly want to enlarge the MaxClients number from 20 if you expect any significant simultaneous load. If you do, go back and increase MinSpareServers, MaxSpareServers, and the number of servers you spin up to start with in StartServers.

```
#
# MaxRequestsPerChild: the number of requests each child process is
# allowed to process before the child dies.  The child will exit so
# as to avoid problems after prolonged use when Apache (and maybe the
# libraries it uses) leak memory or other resources.  On most systems, this
# isn't really needed, but a few (such as Solaris) do have notable leaks
# in the libraries. For these platforms, set to something like 10000
# or so; a setting of 0 means unlimited.
#
# NOTE: This value does not include keepalive requests after the initial
#       request per connection. For example, if a child process handles
#       an initial request and 10 subsequent "keptalive" requests, it
#       would only count as 1 request towards this limit.
#
```

```
MaxRequestsPerChild 0

# Listen: Allows you to bind Apache to specific IP addresses and/or
# ports, in addition to the default. See also the <VirtualHost>
# directive.
#
#Listen 3000
#Listen 12.34.56.78:80
Listen 80

#
# BindAddress: You can support virtual hosts with this option. This directive
# is used to tell the server which IP address to listen to. It can either
# contain "*", an IP address, or a fully qualified Internet domain name.
# See also the <VirtualHost> and Listen directives.
#
#BindAddress *

#
# Dynamic Shared Object (DSO) Support
#
# To be able to use the functionality of a module which was built as a DSO you
# have to place corresponding `LoadModule' lines at this location so the
# directives contained in it are actually available _before_ they are used.
# Please read the file README.DSO in the Apache 1.3 distribution for more
# details about the DSO mechanism and run `httpd -l' for the list of already
# built-in (statically linked and thus always available) modules in your httpd
# binary.
#
# Note: The order is which modules are loaded is important.  Don't change
# the order below without expert advice.
#
# Example:
# LoadModule foo_module libexec/mod_foo.so
```

While MOD_PERL and MOD_PHP load modules, those commands will end up in their respective include files, so don't go here. You'll only be putting a module here if it's not one of the ones distributed with the CSWS package. (The DSO support to which they refer is what VMS users call shareable image libraries.)

```
#
# ExtendedStatus controls whether Apache will generate "full" status
# information (ExtendedStatus On) or just basic information (ExtendedStatus
# Off) when the "server-status" handler is called. The default is Off.
#
#ExtendedStatus On

### Section 2: 'Main' server configuration
#
# The directives in this section set up the values used by the 'main'
# server, which responds to any requests that aren't handled by a
# <VirtualHost> definition.  These values also provide defaults for
# any <VirtualHost> containers you may define later in the file.
```

```
#
# All of these directives may appear inside <VirtualHost> containers,
# in which case these default settings will be overridden for the
# virtual host being defined.
#

#
# If your ServerType directive (set earlier in the 'Global Environment'
# section) is set to "inetd", the next few directives don't have any
# effect since their settings are defined by the inetd configuration.
# Skip ahead to the ServerAdmin directive.
#

#
# Port: The port to which the standalone server listens. For
# ports < 1023, you will need httpd to be run as root initially.
#
Port 80
```

The same comment (well, "run as root" means "run from a privileged account") applies to the Listen directives. Port will be used in constucting self-referential URLs.

```
#
# If you wish httpd to run as a different user or group, you must run
# httpd as root initially and it will switch.
#
# User/Group: The name (or #number) of the user/group to run httpd as.
#   . On SCO (ODT 3) use "User nouser" and "Group nogroup".
#   . On HPUX you may not be able to use shared memory as nobody, and the
#     suggested workaround is to create a user www and use that user.
#  NOTE that some kernels refuse to setgid(Group) or semctl(IPC_SET)
#  when the value of (unsigned)Group is above 60000;
#  don't use Group #-1 on these systems!
#
```

Ignore the entire previous comment.

```
## OpenVMS --
User APACHE$WWW
##User nobody
##Group #-1

#
# ServerAdmin: Your address, where problems with the server should be
# e-mailed.  This address appears on some server-generated pages, such
# as error documents.
#
ServerAdmin you@your.address
```

You may want to make this webmaster@node.domain.tld rather than using your personal e-mail address. Spam harvesters will probably pick up this address at some point. It's also convenient to have a forward for this kind of mail that you can point to somebody else when you're going on vacation without forwarding your personal mail as well.

```
#
# ServerName allows you to set a host name which is sent back to clients for
# your server if it's different than the one the program would get (i.e., use
# "www" instead of the host's real name).
#
# Note: You cannot just invent host names and hope they work. The name you
# define here must be a valid DNS name for your host. If you don't understand
# this, ask your network administrator.
# If your host doesn't have a registered DNS name, enter its IP address here.
# You will have to access it by its address (e.g., http://123.45.67.89/)
# anyway, and this will make redirections work in a sensible way.
#
#ServerName new.host.name
#
# DocumentRoot: The directory out of which you will serve your
# documents. By default, all requests are taken from this directory, but
# symbolic links and aliases may be used to point to other locations.
#
DocumentRoot "/apache$common/htdocs"
```

By default, this has the Apache documentation in it. You may or may not want to put your main document tree in there. Don't use symbolic links (VMS equivalent: SET FILE/ENTER) to splice other document trees into the DocumentRoot; use Alias.

```
#
# Each directory to which Apache has access, can be configured with respect
# to which services and features are allowed and/or disabled in that
# directory (and its subdirectories).
#
# First, we configure the "default" to be a very restrictive set of
# permissions.
#
<Directory />
    Options FollowSymLinks
    AllowOverride None
</Directory>
```

FollowSymLinks isn't going to do much for you.

```
#
# Note that from this point forward you must specifically allow
# particular features to be enabled—so if something's not working as
# you might expect, make sure that you have specifically enabled it
# below.
#

#
# This should be changed to whatever you set DocumentRoot to.
#
<Directory "/apache$common/htdocs">
```

```
#
# This may also be "None", "All", or any combination of "Indexes",
# "Includes", "FollowSymLinks", "ExecCGI", or "MultiViews".
#
# Note that "MultiViews" must be named *explicitly* --- "Options All"
# doesn't give it to you.
#
    Options Indexes FollowSymLinks Multiviews
#
# This controls which options the .htaccess files in directories can
# override. Can also be "All", or any combination of "Options", "FileInfo",
# "AuthConfig", and "Limit"
#
    AllowOverride None


#
# Controls who can get stuff from this server.
#
    Order allow,deny
    Allow from all
</Directory>

#
# UserDir: The name of the directory which is appended onto a user's home
# directory if a ~user request is received.
#
UserDir public_html
```

If converting from OSU, you'll want to change this to WWW.

```
#
# Control access to UserDir directories.  The following is an example
# for a site where these directories are restricted to read-only.
#
#<Directory /home/*/public_html>
#    AllowOverride FileInfo AuthConfig Limit
#    Options MultiViews Indexes SymLinksIfOwnerMatch IncludesNoExec
#    <Limit GET POST OPTIONS PROPFIND>
#        Order allow,deny
#        Allow from all
#    </Limit>
#    <Limit PUT DELETE PATCH PROPPATCH MKCOL COPY MOVE LOCK UNLOCK>
#        Order deny,allow
#        Deny from all
#    </Limit>
#</Directory>
```

This `Directory` container assumes a UNIXism—that all your users will have directories in the /home file system, which is not at all standard on VMS. See the discussion in Chapter 8 on how to handle this, but be aware that it's very much installation specific. The example here isn't going to work at all, but there is no one-size-fits-all solution for this problem.

```
# DirectoryIndex: Name of the file or files to use as a pre-written HTML
# directory index.  Separate multiple entries with spaces.
#
DirectoryIndex index.html
```

"Prewritten HTML directory index" means "default file name to serve if the URL ends with a slash," and doesn't have to be a directory index (list of files) at all. If you allow multiple names for welcome pages, try to put the most likely names first in the list. Possible names include index.html, welcome.html, and .htm variants thereof; you could also allow .shtml and .htmlx or even .php versions.

```
#
# AccessFileName: The name of the file to look for in each directory
# for access control information.
#
AccessFileName .htaccess

#
# The following lines prevent .htaccess files from being viewed by
# Web clients.  Since .htaccess files often contain authorization
# information, access is disallowed for security reasons.  Comment
# these lines out if you want Web visitors to see the contents of
# .htaccess files.  If you change the AccessFileName directive above,
# be sure to make the corresponding changes here.
#
# Also, folks tend to use names such as .htpasswd for password
# files, so this will protect those as well.
#
<Files ~ "^\.ht">
    Order allow,deny
    Deny from all
</Files>

#
# CacheNegotiatedDocs: By default, Apache sends "Pragma: no-cache" with each
# document that was negotiated on the basis of content. This asks proxy
# servers not to cache the document. Uncommenting the following line disables
# this behavior, and proxies will be allowed to cache the documents.
#
#CacheNegotiatedDocs
#
# UseCanonicalName:  (new for 1.3)  With this setting turned on, whenever
# Apache needs to construct a self-referencing URL (a URL that refers back
# to the server the response is coming from) it will use ServerName and
# Port to form a "canonical" name.  With this setting off, Apache will
# use the hostname:port that the client supplied, when possible.  This
# also affects SERVER_NAME and SERVER_PORT in CGI scripts.
#
UseCanonicalName On
```

This is an especially good idea if you're doing virtual hosting. It can help you funnel all your requests into the preferred (fully configured) host name.

```
#
# TypesConfig describes where the mime.types file (or equivalent) is
# to be found.
#
TypesConfig conf/mime.types

#
# DefaultType is the default MIME type the server will use for a document
# if it cannot otherwise determine one, such as from filename extensions.
# If your server contains mostly text or HTML documents, "text/plain" is
# a good value.  If most of your content is binary, such as applications
# or images, you may want to use "application/octet-stream" instead to
# keep browsers from trying to display binary files as though they are
# text.
#
DefaultType text/plain

#
# The mod_mime_magic module allows the server to use various hints from the
# contents of the file itself to determine its type.  The MIMEMagicFile
# directive tells the module where the hint definitions are located.
# mod_mime_magic is not part of the default server (you have to add
# it yourself with a LoadModule [see the DSO paragraph in the 'Global
# Environment' section], or recompile the server and include mod_mime_magic
# as part of the configuration), so it's enclosed in an <IfModule> container.
# This means that the MIMEMagicFile directive will only be processed if the
# module is part of the server.
#
<IfModule mod_mime_magic.c>
    MIMEMagicFile conf/magic
</IfModule>
```

Don't worry about this. Mod_mime_magic isn't part of the server on VMS. If it were—well, by default, the configuration file is included right where this says it is.

```
#
# HostnameLookups: Log the names of clients or just their IP addresses
# e.g., www.apache.org (on) or 204.62.129.132 (off).
# The default is off because it'd be overall better for the net if people
# had to knowingly turn this feature on, since enabling it means that
# each client request will result in AT LEAST one lookup request to the
# nameserver.
#
HostnameLookups Off
```

If you're going to do any log-file analysis (see Chapter 12), you'll have to do lookups later anyway, since some percentage of lookups will fail (either because clients don't have DNS entries or because the DNS servers that are authoritative for them aren't reachable at the moment). It's handy for domain-based security to have the lookups on, but worse for performance. The right choice is installation specific.

```
#
# ErrorLog: The location of the error log file.
# If you do not specify an ErrorLog directive within a <VirtualHost>
# container, error messages relating to that virtual host will be
# logged here.  If you *do* define an error logfile for a <VirtualHost>
# container, that host's errors will be logged there and not here.
#
ErrorLog logs/error_log

#
# LogLevel: Control the number of messages logged to the error_log.
# Possible values include: debug, info, notice, warn, error, crit,
# alert, emerg.
#
LogLevel warn
```

warn incorporates every condition worse than a warning, so this means to log error, critical errors, alerts, and emergencies as well.

```
#
# The following directives define some format nicknames for use with
# a CustomLog directive (see below).
#

LogFormat "%h %l %u %t \"%r\" %>s %b \"%{Referer}i\" \"%{User-Agent}i\"" combined
LogFormat "%h %l %u %t \"%r\" %>s %b" common
LogFormat "%{Referer}i -> %U" referer
LogFormat "%{User-agent}i" agent

#
# The location and format of the access logfile (Common Logfile Format).
# If you do not define any access logfiles within a <VirtualHost>
# container, they will be logged here.  Contrariwise, if you *do*
# define per-<VirtualHost> access logfiles, transactions will be
# logged therein and *not* in this file.
#
CustomLog logs/access_log common

#
# If you would like to have agent and referer logfiles, uncomment the
# following directives.
#
#CustomLog logs/referer_log referer
#CustomLog logs/agent_log agent

#
# If you prefer a single logfile with access, agent, and referer information
# (Combined Logfile Format) you can use the following directive.
#
#CustomLog logs/access_log combined
```

The combined log is my personal preference, and all log-file analysis tools can deal with it. See Chapter 12 for an explanation of the custom log-file format specifiers.

```
#
# Optionally add a line containing the server version and virtual host
# name to server-generated pages (error documents, FTP directory listings,
# mod_status and mod_info output etc., but not CGI generated documents).
# Set to "EMail" to also include a mailto: link to the ServerAdmin.
# Set to one of:  On | Off | Email
#
ServerSignature On
```

This is useful when you're part of a proxy chain and have a problem to report—without the server signature the client doesn't know what system is having the problem.

```
#
# Aliases: Add here as many aliases as you need (with no limit). The format is
# Alias fakename realname
#
# Note that if you include a trailing / on fakename then the server will
# require it to be present in the URL.  So "/icons" isn't aliased in this
# example, only "/icons/"..
#
Alias /icons/ "/apache$root/icons/"

<Directory "/apache$root/icons">
    Options Indexes MultiViews
    AllowOverride None
    Order allow,deny
    Allow from all
</Directory>
```

The icons file is primarily used with FancyIndexing to show pretty pictures representing filetypes on automatically generated directory listings, as discussed exhaustively in Chapter 13.

```
#
# ScriptAlias: This controls which directories contain server scripts.
# ScriptAliases are essentially the same as Aliases, except that
# documents in the realname directory are treated as applications and
# run by the server when requested rather than as documents sent to the client.
# The same rules about trailing "/" apply to ScriptAlias directives as to
# Alias.
#
ScriptAlias /cgi-bin/ "/apache$root/cgi-bin/"

#
# "/apache$root/cgi-bin" should be changed to whatever your ScriptAliased
# CGI directory exists, if you have that configured
```

You aren't restricted to a single `ScriptAlias`; you can have as many different ones as you like. This default lets you conveniently run a couple of small test CGIs distributed with the server.

```
#
# The /htbin directory invokes the OSUscript module, The DECnet task string
# should be customized to invoke the OSU web server's scriptserver object.
#
<Location /htbin>
    SetHandler osuscript-handler
    OSUscript 0::"0=WWWEXEC" www_root:[bin]
    Order allow,deny
    Allow from all
</Location>
```

Note that the OSUscript command lets you specify a node, which doesn't have to be this one. However, you do have to be able to reach it via DECnet, and you need to have the correct proxies set up. WWWEXEC is the right name for the DECnet object if your OSU setup has been done normally.

```
<Directory "/apache$root/cgi-bin">
    AllowOverride None
    Options None
    Order allow,deny
    Allow from all
</Directory>

#
# Redirect allows you to tell clients about documents which used to exist in
# your server's namespace, but do not anymore. This allows you to tell the
# clients where to look for the relocated document.
# Format: Redirect old-URI new-URL
#

#
# Directives controlling the display of server-generated directory listings.
#
```

See Chapter 13 for extensive discussion and examples about this.

```
#
# FancyIndexing is whether you want fancy directory indexing or standard
#
IndexOptions FancyIndexing

#
# AddIcon* directives tell the server which icon to show for different
# files or filename extensions.  These are only displayed for
# FancyIndexed directories.
#
AddIconByEncoding (CMP,/icons/compressed.gif) x-compress x-gzip

AddIconByType (TXT,/icons/text.gif) text/*
AddIconByType (IMG,/icons/image2.gif) image/*
AddIconByType (SND,/icons/sound2.gif) audio/*
AddIconByType (VID,/icons/movie.gif) video/*

AddIcon /icons/binary.gif .bin .exe
AddIcon /icons/binhex.gif .hqx
```

```
AddIcon /icons/tar.gif .tar
AddIcon /icons/world2.gif .wrl .wrl.gz .vrml .vrm .iv
AddIcon /icons/compressed.gif .Z .z .tgz .gz .zip
AddIcon /icons/a.gif .ps .ai .eps
AddIcon /icons/layout.gif .html .shtml .htm .pdf
AddIcon /icons/text.gif .txt
AddIcon /icons/c.gif .c
AddIcon /icons/p.gif .pl .py
AddIcon /icons/f.gif .for
AddIcon /icons/dvi.gif .dvi
AddIcon /icons/uuencoded.gif .uu
AddIcon /icons/script.gif .conf .sh .shar .csh .ksh .tcl
AddIcon /icons/tex.gif .tex
AddIcon /icons/bomb.gif core

AddIcon /icons/back.gif ..
AddIcon /icons/hand.right_gif readme
AddIcon /icons/folder.gif ^^DIRECTORY^^
AddIcon /icons/blank.gif ^^BLANKICON^^

#
# DefaultIcon is which icon to show for files which do not have an icon
# explicitly set.
#
DefaultIcon /icons/unknown.gif

#
# AddDescription allows you to place a short description after a file in
# server-generated indexes.  These are only displayed for FancyIndexed
# directories.
# Format: AddDescription "description" filename
#
#AddDescription "GZIP compressed document" .gz
#AddDescription "tar archive" .tar
#AddDescription "GZIP compressed tar archive" .tgz

#
# ReadmeName is the name of the README file the server will look for by
# default, and append to directory listings.
#
# HeaderName is the name of a file which should be prepended to
# directory indexes.
#
# The server will first look for name.html and include it if found.
# If name.html doesn't exist, the server will then look for name.txt
# and include it as plaintext if found.
#
ReadmeName readme
HeaderName header

#
# IndexIgnore is a set of filenames which directory indexing should ignore
# and not include in the listing.  Shell-style wildcarding is permitted.
#
IndexIgnore .??* *~ *# header* readme* RCS CVS *,v *,t
```

```
#
# AddEncoding allows you to have certain browsers (Mosaic/X 2.1+) uncompress
# information on the fly. Note: Not all browsers support this.
# Despite the name similarity, the following Add* directives have nothing
# to do with the FancyIndexing customization directives above.
#
AddEncoding x-compress Z
AddEncoding x-gzip gz tgz
```

"Certain browsers" is now most browsers; you definitely want to have this turned on unless your server is grossly underpowered (since on-the-fly compression is a tradeoff of CPU for bandwidth).

```
#
# AddLanguage allows you to specify the language of a document. You can
# then use content negotiation to give a browser a file in a language
# it can understand.  Note that the suffix does not have to be the same
# as the language keyword—those with documents in Polish (whose
# net-standard language code is pl) may wish to use "AddLanguage pl .po"
# to avoid the ambiguity with the common suffix for perl scripts.
#
AddLanguage en .en
AddLanguage fr .fr
AddLanguage de .de
AddLanguage da .da
AddLanguage el .el
AddLanguage it .it
```

Note that the UNIX-style language suffix produces file names such as "file.html.fr", which doesn't work on ODS-2 file systems. CSWS will look for files using, not the period, but an underscore, so "file.html_fr".

```
#
# LanguagePriority allows you to give precedence to some languages
# in case of a tie during content negotiation.
# Just list the languages in decreasing order of preference.
#
LanguagePriority en fr de

#
# AddType allows you to tweak mime.types without actually editing it, or to
# make certain files to be certain types.
#
# For example, the PHP3 module (not part of the Apache distribution—see
# http://www.php.net) will typically use:
#
#AddType application/x-httpd-php3 .php3
#AddType application/x-httpd-php3-source .phps
```

Mod_PHP is, of course, available as part of the CSWS project.

```
AddType application/x-tar .tgz

#
# AddHandler allows you to map certain file extensions to "handlers",
```

```
# actions unrelated to filetype. These can be either built into the server
# or added with the Action command (see below)
#
# If you want to use server side includes, or CGI outside
# ScriptAliased directories, uncomment the following lines.
#
# To use CGI scripts:
#
#AddHandler cgi-script .cgi
```

That is, Perl scripts written with the CGI.PM module.

```
#
# To use server-parsed HTML files
#
```

Also known as server-side include files. (If porting from OSU, you may wish to add .htmlx as well as .shtml.)

```
#AddType text/html .shtml
#AddHandler server-parsed .shtml

#
# Uncomment the following line to enable Apache's send-asis HTTP file
# feature
#
#AddHandler send-as-is asis
```

These documents are obliged to include all their HTTP header information—CSWS won't add anything, not even a Content-type: text/plain.

```
#
# If you wish to use server-parsed imagemap files, use
#
#AddHandler imap-file map
```

The world has pretty much moved on to client-side image maps.

```
#
# To enable type maps, you might want to use
#
#AddHandler type-map var

#
# Action lets you define media types that will execute a script whenever
# a matching file is called. This eliminates the need for repeated URL
# pathnames for oft-used CGI file processors.
# Format: Action media/type /cgi-script/location
# Format: Action handler-name /cgi-script/location
#

#
# MetaDir: specifies the name of the directory in which Apache can find
# meta information files. These files contain additional HTTP headers
# to include when sending the document
```

```
#
#MetaDir .web

#
# MetaSuffix: specifies the file name suffix for the file containing the
# meta information.
#
#MetaSuffix .meta
```

The Meta features are very rarely used.

```
#
# Customizable error response (Apache style)
#  these come in three flavors
#
#    1) plain text
#ErrorDocument 500 "The server made a boo boo.
#  n.b.  the (") marks it as text, it does not get output
#
#    2) local redirects
#ErrorDocument 404 /missing.html
#  to redirect to local URL /missing.html
#ErrorDocument 404 /cgi-bin/missing_handler.pl
#  N.B.: You can redirect to a script or a document using server-side-includes.
#
#    3) external redirects
#ErrorDocument 402 http://some.other_server.com/subscription_info.html
#  N.B.: Many of the environment variables associated with the original
#  request will *not* be available to such a script.
```

Error documents are discussed in Chapter 5.

```
#
# The following directives modify normal HTTP response behavior.
# The first directive disables keepalive for Netscape 2.x and browsers that
# spoof it. There are known problems with these browser implementations.
# The second directive is for Microsoft Internet Explorer 4.0b2
# which has a broken HTTP/1.1 implementation and does not properly
# support keepalive when it is used on 301 or 302 (redirect) responses.
#
BrowserMatch "Mozilla/2" nokeepalive
BrowserMatch "MSIE 4\.0b2;" nokeepalive downgrade-1.0 force-response-1.0

#
# The following directive disables HTTP/1.1 responses to browsers which
# are in violation of the HTTP/1.0 spec by not being able to grok a
# basic 1.1 response.
#
BrowserMatch "RealPlayer 4\.0" force-response-1.0
BrowserMatch "Java/1\.0" force-response-1.0
BrowserMatch "JDK/1\.0" force-response-1.0

#
# Allow server status reports, with the URL of http://servername/server-status
# Change the ".your_domain.com" to match your domain to enable.
#
```

```
#<Location /server-status>
#    SetHandler server-status
#    Order deny,allow
#    Deny from all
#    Allow from .your_domain.com
#</Location>
```

If you uncomment this and change .your.domain.com to your domain, you need to enable Hostname lookups for it to work. This still means that everyone in your domain can see the server status reports, which isn't necessarily bad but shouldn't come as a surprise. You could restrict it to require a particular login.

```
#
# Allow remote server configuration reports, with the URL of
#  http://servername/server-info (requires that mod_info.c be loaded).
# Change the ".your_domain.com" to match your domain to enable.
#
#<Location /server-info>
#    SetHandler server-info
#    Order deny,allow
#    Deny from all
#    Allow from .your_domain.com
#</Location>
```

Also requires host name lookups to be enabled.

```
#
# There have been reports of people trying to abuse an old bug from pre-1.1
# days.  This bug involved a CGI script distributed as a part of Apache.
# By uncommenting these lines you can redirect these attacks to a logging
# script on phf.apache.org.  Or, you can record them yourself, using the script
# support/phf_abuse_log.cgi.
#
#<Location /cgi-bin/phf*>
#    Deny from all
#    ErrorDocument 403 http://phf.apache.org/phf_abuse_log.cgi
#</Location>

#
# Proxy Server directives. Uncomment the following lines to
# enable the proxy server:
```

The proxy server is discussed at length in Chapter 11.

```
#
#<IfModule mod_proxy.c>
#ProxyRequests On
#
#<Directory proxy:*>
#    Order deny,allow
#    Deny from all
#    Allow from .your_domain.com
#</Directory>
```

```
#
# Enable/disable the handling of HTTP/1.1 "Via:" headers.
# ("Full" adds the server version; "Block" removes all outgoing Via: headers)
# Set to one of: Off | On | Full | Block
#
#ProxyVia On

#
# To enable the cache as well, edit and uncomment the following lines:
# (no cacheing without CacheRoot)
#
#CacheRoot "/apache$root/proxy"
#CacheSize 5
```

The unit in CacheSize is kilobytes, so this default is 5 KB. (The cache can grow larger, but garbage collection will be triggered.) This default is almost certainly too small if your site is active at all; any serious use will end up with the garbage collector running all the time, and since this is a disk-based cache that'll be a slow operation. Don't let this be more than 80 percent of your free space.

```
#CacheGcInterval 4
#CacheMaxExpire 24
#CacheLastModifiedFactor 0.1
#CacheDefaultExpire 1
#NoCache a_domain.com another_domain.edu joes.garage_sale.com

#</IfModule>
# End of proxy directives.

### Section 3: Virtual Hosts
```

Virtual hosts are discussed in Chapter 9.

```
#
# VirtualHost: If you want to maintain multiple domains/hostnames on your
# machine you can setup VirtualHost containers for them.
# Please see the documentation at URL:http://www.apache.org/docs/vhosts/
# for further details before you try to setup virtual hosts.
# You may use the command line option '-S' to verify your virtual host
# configuration.
```

Not on CSWS.

```
#
# If you want to use name-based virtual hosts you need to define at
# least one IP address (and port number) for them.
#
#NameVirtualHost 12.34.56.78:80
#NameVirtualHost 12.34.56.78
```

Don't be misled by the above examples; `NameVirtualHost` is also a container directive. The point that they're making is that name-based virtual hosts go by the `host:` header sent from the client, not by a DNS name. You have to be sure to tell CSWS to listen on some numeric-IP address or it won't be listening and won't see the host: headers. Since some (old) clients don't send host: headers, you also need to have a default `VirtualHost` configured so that there's somewhere for those clients to fall through to.

```
#
# VirtualHost example:
# Almost any Apache directive may go into a VirtualHost container.
#
#<VirtualHost ip.address.of.host.some_domain.com>
#    ServerAdmin webmaster@host.some_domain.com
#    DocumentRoot /www/docs/host.some_domain.com
#    ServerName host.some_domain.com
#    ErrorLog logs/host.some_domain.com-error_log
#    CustomLog logs/host.some_domain.com-access_log common
#</VirtualHost>

#<VirtualHost _default_:*>
#</VirtualHost>
```

Again, if you're going to do name-based hosting at all, you must uncomment and populate the default host.

E.1.2 MOD_SSL.CONF

SSL is discussed in Chapter 6.

```
##
##  SSL Support
##
<IfDefine SSL>
##
##  Load SSL module
##
LoadModule ssl_module modules/mod_ssl.exe_alpha
##
##  Listen to the standard HTTPS port
##
Listen 443
```

If you need to listen on additional ports, you can add additional `Listen` directives; they're cumulative.

```
##
##  SSL Global Context
##
##  All SSL configuration in this context applies both to
##  the main server and all SSL-enabled virtual hosts.
##
#
#   Some MIME-types for downloading Certificates and CRLs
#
```

```
AddType application/x-x509-ca-cert .crt
AddType application/x-pkcs7-crl    .crl
#   Pass Phrase Dialog:
#   Configure the pass phrase gathering process.
#   The filtering dialog program (`builtin' is a internal
#   terminal dialog) has to provide the pass phrase on stdout.
SSLPassPhraseDialog  builtin
```

As I've said, I recommend against using certificates that require a passphrase to work—you generally want the system to come back (after a power failure, or whatever) without having to find somebody who knows the secret passphrase and get that person to the system console to type it in (especially true when you have a widely-distributed disaster-tolerant cluster). And if all your operators know the passphrase, then it's not a secret any more—so what's the point? Anyway, `SSLPassPhraseDialog` is only relevant if you have a passphrase.

```
#   Inter-Process Session Cache:
#   Configure the SSL Session Cache: First either `none'
#   or `dbm:/path/to/file' for the mechanism to use and
#   second the expiring timeout (in seconds).
#SSLSessionCache        none
SSLSessionCache        shm:logs/ssl_scache(512000)0
```

In a clustered environment, make that `cshm:` (If your cluster is all on a Galaxy server, `cshm:` will use Galactic shared memory, allowing very fast access; if it's in different boxes, the session cache will be maintained on cluster-accessible disk.)

```
#SSLSessionCache         dbm:logs/ssl_scache
SSLSessionCacheTimeout  300
#   Semaphore:
#   Configure the path to the mutual explusion semaphore the
#   SSL engine uses internally for inter-process synchronization.
SSLMutex  sem
#SSLMutex  file:logs/ssl_mutex
```

The default setting will use the VMS Distributed Lock Manager to arbitrate access to the session cache, which is a good thing. The file: method is a pathetic workaround for systems that don't do locking or support semaphores in the OS.

```
#   Pseudo Random Number Generator (PRNG):
#   Configure one or more sources to seed the PRNG of the
#   SSL library. The seed data should be of good random quality.
#   WARNING! On some platforms /dev/random blocks if not enough entropy
#   is available. This means you then cannot use the /dev/random device
#   because it would lead to very long connection times (as long as
#   it requires to make more entropy available). But usually those
#   platforms additionally provide a /dev/urandom device which doesn't
```

```
#   block. So, if available, use this one instead. Read the mod_ssl User
#   Manual for more details.
SSLRandomSeed startup builtin
SSLRandomSeed connect builtin
#SSLRandomSeed startup file:/dev/random  512
#SSLRandomSeed startup file:/dev/urandom 512
#SSLRandomSeed connect file:/dev/random  512
#SSLRandomSeed connect file:/dev/urandom 512
```

There is no VMS equivalent to /dev/random or /dev/urandom, so just stick with the built-in. (Unless you want to write a driver for the RNAO: device, and even then I wouldn't expect CSWS to work reliably with it.)

```
#   Logging:
#   The home of the dedicated SSL protocol logfile. Errors are
#   additionally duplicated in the general error log file.  Put
#   this somewhere where it cannot be used for symlink attacks on
#   a real server (i.e. somewhere where only root can write).
#   Log levels are (ascending order: higher ones include lower ones):
#   none, error, warn, info, trace, debug.
SSLLog      logs/ssl_engine_log
SSLLogLevel info

##
## SSL Virtual Host Context
##
<VirtualHost _default_:443>

#  General setup for the virtual host
DocumentRoot "/apache$common/htdocs"
#ServerName new.host.name
ServerAdmin you@your.address
ErrorLog logs/error_log
TransferLog logs/access_log

#   SSL Engine Switch:
#   Enable/Disable SSL for this virtual host.
SSLEngine on

#   SSL Cipher Suite:
#   List the ciphers that the client is permitted to negotiate.
#   See the mod_ssl documentation for a complete list.
#SSLCipherSuite ALL:!ADH:RC4+RSA:+HIGH:+MEDIUM:+LOW:+SSLv2:+EXP:+eNULL

#   Server Certificate:
#   Point SSLCertificateFile at a PEM encoded certificate.  If
#   the certificate is encrypted, then you will be prompted for a
#   pass phrase.  Note that a kill -HUP will prompt again. A test
#   certificate can be generated with `make certificate' under
#   built time. Keep in mind that if you've both a RSA and a DSA
#   certificate you can configure both in parallel (to also allow
#   the use of DSA ciphers, etc.)
SSLCertificateFile /apache$root/conf/ssl_crt/server.crt
#SSLCertificateFile /apache$root/conf/ssl_crt/server-dsa.crt
```

You can put the certificate wherever you want it, but you have to make sure it's someplace that the CSWS account (Apache$WWW) has read access to, isn't visible to the entire world, and isn't Aliased or under the DocumentRoot so it won't get served out.

```
#   Server Private Key:
#   If the key is not combined with the certificate, use this
#   directive to point at the key file.  Keep in mind that if
#   you've both a RSA and a DSA private key you can configure
#   both in parallel (to also allow the use of DSA ciphers, etc.)
SSLCertificateKeyFile /apache$root/conf/ssl_key/server.key
#SSLCertificateKeyFile /apache$root/conf/ssl_key/server-dsa.key
```

The same constraints apply to the location of the private key.

```
#   Server Certificate Chain:
#   Point SSLCertificateChainFile at a file containing the
#   concatenation of PEM encoded CA certificates which form the
#   certificate chain for the server certificate. Alternatively
#   the referenced file can be the same as SSLCertificateFile
#   when the CA certificates are directly appended to the server
#   certificate for convinience.
#SSLCertificateChainFile /apache$root/conf/ssl_crt/ca.crt
```

But you only need this if you're using a certificate that didn't come from a known certificate authority.

```
#   Certificate Authority (CA):
#   Set the CA certificate verification path where to find CA
#   certificates for client authentication or alternatively one
#   huge file containing all of them (file must be PEM encoded)
#   Note: Inside SSLCACertificatePath you need hash symlinks
#         to point to the certificate files. Use the provided
#         Makefile to update the hash symlinks after changes.
#SSLCACertificatePath /apache$root/conf/ssl_crt
#SSLCACertificateFile /apache$root/conf/ssl_crt/ca-bundle.crt
```

And you only need SSLCACertificatePath and SSLCARevocationPath if you're acting as a Certificate Authority.

```
#   Certificate Revocation Lists (CRL):
#   Set the CA revocation path where to find CA CRLs for client
#   authentication or alternatively one huge file containing all
#   of them (file must be PEM encoded)
#   Note: Inside SSLCARevocationPath you need hash symlinks
#         to point to the certificate files. Use the provided
#         Makefile to update the hash symlinks after changes.
#SSLCARevocationPath /apache$root/conf/ssl_crl
#SSLCARevocationFile /apache$root/conf/ssl_crl/ca-bundle.crl

#   Client Authentication (Type):
```

Discussed in Chapter 7.

```
#   Client certificate verification type and depth.  Types are
#   none, optional, require and optional_no_ca.  Depth is a
#   number which specifies how deeply to verify the certificate
#   issuer chain before deciding the certificate is not valid.
#SSLVerifyClient require
#SSLVerifyDepth  10

#   Access Control:
#   With SSLRequire you can do per-directory access control based
#   on arbitrary complex boolean expressions containing server
#   variable checks and other lookup directives.  The syntax is a
#   mixture between C and Perl.  See the mod_ssl documentation
#   for more details.
#<Location />
#SSLRequire (    %{SSL_CIPHER} !~ m/^(EXP|NULL)-/ \
#            and %{SSL_CLIENT_S_DN_O} eq "Snake Oil, Ltd." \
#            and %{SSL_CLIENT_S_DN_OU} in {"Staff", "CA", "Dev"} \
#            and %{TIME_WDAY} >= 1 and %{TIME_WDAY} <= 5 \
#            and %{TIME_HOUR} >= 8 and %{TIME_HOUR} <= 20       ) \
#           or %{REMOTE_ADDR} =~ m/^192\.76\.162\.[0-9]+$/
#</Location>

#   SSL Engine Options:
#   Set various options for the SSL engine.
#   o FakeBasicAuth:
#     Translate the client X.509 into a Basic Authorisation.  This means that
#     the standard Auth/DBMAuth methods can be used for access control.  The
#     user name is the `one line' version of the client's X.509 certificate.
#     Note that no password is obtained from the user. Every entry in the user
#     file needs this password: `xxj31ZMTZzkVA'.
#   o ExportCertData:
#     This exports two additional environment variables: SSL_CLIENT_CERT and
#     SSL_SERVER_CERT. These contain the PEM-encoded certificates of the
#     server (always existing) and the client (only existing when client
#     authentication is used). This can be used to import the certificates
#     into CGI scripts.
#   o StdEnvVars:
#     This exports the standard SSL/TLS related `SSL_*' environment variables.
#     Per default this exportation is switched off for performance reasons,
#     because the extraction step is an expensive operation and is usually
#     useless for serving static content. So one usually enables the
#     exportation for CGI and SSI requests only.
#   o CompatEnvVars:
#     This exports obsolete environment variables for backward compatibility
#     to Apache-SSL 1.x, mod_ssl 2.0.x, Sioux 1.0 and Stronghold 2.x. Use this
#     to provide compatibility to existing CGI scripts.
#   o StrictRequire:
#     This denies access when "SSLRequireSSL" or "SSLRequire" applied even
#     under a "Satisfy any" situation, i.e. when it applies access is denied
#     and no other module can change it.
#   o OptRenegotiate:
#     This enables optimized SSL connection renegotiation handling when SSL
#     directives are used in per-directory context.
#SSLOptions +FakeBasicAuth +ExportCertData +CompatEnvVars +StrictRequire
```

```
<Files ~ "\.(cgi|shtml)$">
    SSLOptions +StdEnvVars
</Files>
<Directory "/apache$root/cgi-bin">
    SSLOptions +StdEnvVars
</Directory>

#   SSL Protocol Adjustments:
#   The safe and default but still SSL/TLS standard compliant shutdown
#   approach is that mod_ssl sends the close notify alert but doesn't wait for
#   the close notify alert from client. When you need a different shutdown
#   approach you can use one of the following variables:
#   o ssl-unclean-shutdown:
#     This forces an unclean shutdown when the connection is closed, i.e. no
#     SSL close notify alert is send or allowed to received.  This violates
#     the SSL/TLS standard but is needed for some brain-dead browsers. Use
#     this when you receive I/O errors because of the standard approach where
#     mod_ssl sends the close notify alert.
#   o ssl-accurate-shutdown:
#     This forces an accurate shutdown when the connection is closed, i.e. a
#     SSL close notify alert is send and mod_ssl waits for the close notify
#     alert of the client. This is 100% SSL/TLS standard compliant, but in
#     practice often causes hanging connections with brain-dead browsers. Use
#     this only for browsers where you know that their SSL implementation
#     works correctly.
#   Notice: Most problems of broken clients are also related to the HTTP
#   keep-alive facility, so you usually additionally want to disable
#   keep-alive for those clients, too. Use variable "nokeepalive" for this.
SetEnvIf User-Agent ".*MSIE.*" nokeepalive ssl-unclean-shutdown

#   Per-Server Logging:
#   The home of a custom SSL log file. Use this when you want a
#   compact non-error SSL logfile on a virtual host basis.
CustomLog logs/ssl_request_log \
          "%t %h %{SSL_PROTOCOL}x %{SSL_CIPHER}x \"%r\" %b"

</VirtualHost>
</IfDefine>
```

E.1.3 MOD_PERL.CONF, MOD_PHP.CONF

These files appear, annotated, in Chapter 17.

E.2 OSU Configuration Files

E.2.1 HTTP_MAIN.CONF

```
.ignore .AUTHORIZE .FORM
```

The .ignore directives are for the benefit of the servermaint application.

```
.define HNenable #
```

The hashmark (#) is the comment indicator. When you see something like Hnenable, the way to enable it is to change the hash to a blank.

```
.define hostname preferred.host.name
```

Change to your preferred host name.

```
.define Penable port
.define port 8000
.define ncport 8040
```

ncport is the noncached port; if you're doing SSL on versions prior to 3.10alpha, you need the ncport to be 443 for SSL.

```
.define TraceLevel http_log_level
```

A numeric value with no upper limit, although anything above three will log an awful lot. You can change this dynamically on the running server with the PRIVREQUEST command.

```
.define TraceLog http_error.log
.define AccessLog access.log
.define aclogext
```

Set this to 1 to get the extended log format (which matches the Apache "Common" format, including user-agent and referrer.).

```
.define DNSLookup Off
```

Set to on if you want your log files to show the DNS names of the clients.

```
.define ReqTMO 2:00
.define reqTMOenable TimeLimit Request
.define kaTMOenab TimeLimit Keepalive
.define kaTMO 40
.define kaLIM 12
.define kaScavenge scavenge
.define rspTMOenable #
.define rspTMO 1:00:00
.define searchenable search
```

OSU will take a query string (the part of a URL following the ? as a search string unless you make searchenable "#").

```
#.define search_script www_root:[bin]index_search.exe
.define search_script nullsearch.com
.define authenable authenticator
.define authenticator www_system:ext_authenticator
```

```
.define clientcount EventCounter Clients
.define ecflags 3
.define extdirenable presentation
.define extdirscript %dirserv:
```

See Chapter 13 for a discussion of the directory server options. This default says to use the MST version of the directory server.

```
.define DirAccess off
.define putenable #
.define putscript wwwpost.com
```

Make putenable blank if you want to be able to publish via HTTP from Netscape Composer or similar tools.

```
.define fcsize 2000000
.define fcrefresh 3:00
.define fclimit 48000
.define fcmaxrec 4096
```

The fc parameters are all for the file cache; see Chapter 11 for details on how they work. These defaults are reasonably sensible.

```
.define proxy_action /demo/nogateway.html
.define proxy_enable #
```

Proxying is disabled by default. See Chapter 11 for details.

```
.define proxy_gateway /htbin/proxygw/
.define proxy_scriptserver ProxyScript
.define proxy_task 0::"0=WWWPROXY"
.define proxy_task_prot null
.define proxy_task_pfile www_system:proxy.prot
.define proxy_log_enable null
.define proxy_log_file proxy-access.log
.define file_flags 7
#
# Top-level configuration file for http server.
# The .ignore line and .define lines at the beginning of this file
# were written there by the servermaint script, which edits this file
# via a form interface controlled by the file named in the .form interface
# below.
#
.FORM www_system:http_main.servermaint
#
# define hostname and port number(s), command line args override port numbers.
#
.EXPAND $HNenable $hostname
.EXPAND $Penable $port $ncport
##############################################################################
#
# Define who can update this file via the servermaint script.  There are
# currently 3 .authorize formats:
```

```
#     user[@host-addr]         Allow access if user matches CGI REMOTE_USER
#                              and host-addr (if present) matches client host.
#                             (Must protect script URL).
#    *[@host-addr]Allow access if CGI REMOTE_USER non-null,
#                              indicating script URL was protected.
#    user[@host-addr] password  Allow access if user (and host-addr) matches
#                              server port is non-provileged (>1023).
.ITERATE .authorize $smaint_user $smaint_pwd
.NEXT server maint
.NEXT *
#
# Set trace level to current value of environment variable http_log_level.
# Since second argument in TraceLevel rule is null, trace data will go
# to error log file.  The trace level governs the amount of debugging
# information the server will write to the trace file during its execution,
# common trace levels:
#    0 - No trace, errors only (default).
#    1 - Show connect open and close and URL path info requested.
#    6 - Trace script execution
#    11 - Trace rule file translation steps.
#
.EXPAND TraceLevel $TraceLevel  # $TraceLog
#
# Enable access log file and send data to log file name given by AccessLog
# pre-processor variable.
#
.EXPAND AccessLog $AccessLog $aclogext
#
# Enable/disable reverse host lookup.  When enabled, hostnames appear in log
# file rather than IP addresses.
#
.EXPAND DNSLookup $DNSLookup
.EXPAND FileFlags $file_flags
#
# Set Network timeout values.
# Non-zero keepalive timeout enables keep-alive support.
#
.EXPAND $reqTMOenable $ReqTMO
.EXPAND $rspTMOenable $rspTMO
.EXPAND $kaTMOenab $kaTMO $kaLIM $kaScavenge
#
.EXPAND FileCache size $fcsize
.EXPAND FileCache refresh $fcrefresh
.EXPAND FileCache limit $fclimit
.EXPAND FileCache maxrec $fcmaxrec
#
# Set parameters for privrequest and known script operations.  Localaddress
# rules with host addresses starting with '@' are a hack to pass through
# parameters to the TCP module.  Note that UCX versions prior to 5.0 have
# a hard limit of 5 for the listen backlog.  The segment_size parameter
# is the max size for a write QIO (larger writes are broken up by tserver_tcp
# into multiple QIOs), increase with care due to increased bytlm consumption.
#
include www_system:http_manage.conf
```

```
localaddress @listen_backlog=500
#localaddress @segment_size=4096
################################################################################
#
# Enable/disable and specific search script.
#
.EXPAND $searchenable $search_script
#search  www_root:[bin]dtsearch.com
#
# Comment out the following line to disable the authenticator sub-process.
# The authenticator must be running in order for any 'protect' rules to
# function properly.
#
.EXPAND $authenable $authenticator
#
# Define the put script, which handles non-script PUT requests sent by clients.
#
.EXPAND $putenable $putscript
#
# The proxyscript is effectively a map command applied when a gateway
# request is specified.  Since it is positioned before http_paths, the
# test for proxy will be the first translation rule tested.
#
.EXPAND proxyscript $proxy_action
.EXPAND $proxy_enable $proxy_gateway
.EXPAND $proxy_scriptserver /prxygw111/ ; \
   $proxy_log_enable $proxy_log_file ; \
   $proxy_task_prot /prxygw111/ $proxy_task_pfile ; exec /prxygw111/ $proxy_task
################################################################################
# Enable statistics counters to track number of connections (clients) and\
# host classes.  Note that DNSLookup must be on for non-numeric host masks.
#
.EXPAND EventCounter Flags $ecflags
.EXPAND $clientcount
.ITERATE EventCounter HostClass $class $mask
.NEXT kcgl 128.107.76.*
.NEXT kcgl 164.107.77.*
.NEXT kcgl 164.107.78.*
.NEXT kcgl 164.107.79.*
```

If you're going to use these, change them to netblocks you're likely to use. KCGL is the computer graphics lab at OSU.

```
################################################################################
#
# Turn on directory browsing (on by default) so files that don't have
# directories will get list of files formatted into HTML.
# Note: The Welcome and DirAccess rules only apply when the internal browser
#       is being used, they don't apply if http_suffixes.conf defines an
#       external browser (presenation rule for text/file-directory).
#
.EXPAND DirAccess $DirAccess
#
```

```
# Define list of welcome files (index files) to search for when only a
# directory is specified in the URL, 1 file per welcome directive.
#
.ITERATE Welcome $welcome_file
.NEXT index.html
.NEXT welcome.html
.NEXT index.htmlx
```

Put these in the order you consider most likely to be used, since it'll search in the order they're given here.

```
############################################################################
#
# The suffixes file contains the rules that map file types to the HTTP/MIME
# content-type for the file.  For some mime types it may also define special
# 'presentation' scripts that the server will use to convert the file's
# data to another form for transfer to the client.
#
include www_system:http_suffixes.conf
.EXPAND $extdirenable text/file-directory $extdirscript
############################################################################
#
# The paths file contains the rules that are 'executed' by the server to
# translate the path portion of the requested URL to a filename to return
# or script to execute.
#
.iterate FileExpire $fepath $feinterval
.next /demo/images/* RDT+1:00:00
include www_system:http_paths.conf
```

E.2.2 HTTP_PATHS.CONF

```
.ignore .AUTHORIZE .FORM
.define rootpage /demo/servermaint.html
```

You'll need to change rootpage to your desired home page, unless you want every one who goes to your address to check out the server maintenance page. Note that rootpage is an absolute path, not relative to www_root. (It happens that /demo/ is mapped in terms of the www_root, but that's not necessarily the case.)

```
.define demopath /www_root/serverdoc/*
.define demoenable pass
.define robotenable pass
.define robotfile /www_root/serverdoc/robots.txt
```

See Chapter 7 for what goes in robots.txt.

```
.define sitepath /www_root/documents/*
```

All the discussion in this book makes www_root be the location of documents, but the server design is biased toward making documents in general live in /www/whatever, while only home pages live directly under /.

```
.define scodeenable pass
.define userdirenable userdir
.define userdirname www
.define baduserenable #
.define baduser /www_root/serverdoc/baduser.html
.ITERATE .authorize $smaint_user $smaint_pwd
.NEXT server maint
.NEXT *
.AUTHORIZE server maint
.FORM www_system:http_paths.servermaint
#
# The rules in this file are translation/protection rules that govern how the
# paths in requesting URLs are translated or trigger protection checks.  The
# ordering of these rules can affect the outcome of the translation process.
# Most of the rules assume the logical www_root exists.
#
# Configure multi-homing (ip based and host/cname-based) root pages and
# log files.
#
.ITERATE localaddress cname $hname ;\
      AccessLog $cn_logfile $cn_extflags ;\
      map / $cn_root
.ITERATE localaddress $addr $name ;\
      AccessLog $mh_logfile $mh_extflags ;\
      map / $mh_root
localaddress            # terminate localaddress blocks.
#
# Define error pages:
#    cep_enable          errorpage | #
#    cep_name            protfail | openfail | rulefail | cgiprotocol | code4...
#    cep_path            {url path}
#    cep_code            [*]
#
.ITERATE $cep_enable $cep_name $cep_path $cep_code
.NEXT errorpage protfail /demo/error_403.html
.NEXT # openfail /htbin/openfail.com *
.NEXT errorpage rulefail /demo/error_403.html
.NEXT # cgiprotocol /demo/error_500.html
.NEXT errorpage  code4 /demo/error_preproc.html
```

Error pages are discussed in Chapter 13.

```
#
# Configure access to sample document directory (www_root:[serverdoc]).  Set
# alias /demo to translate to /www_root/serverdoc/ and map the root document
# for the server (/) to return this directory's index.html.
#
filecache exclude *;
.EXPAND map / $rootpage
.EXPAND $demoenable /demo/* $demopath
```

```
#
# Create a special alias used to trigger protection checks to demonstrate
# the protection mechanisms.  Note that protect rules should always have
# templates ending in '*' to avoid problems with version numbers appearing
# as multiple names in a file.
#
protect /protdemo/* www_system:level2.prot
protect /protdemo/conf* www_system:level3.prot
hostprot /protdemo/hostprot.html* www_system:level1.prot
.EXPAND $demoenable /protdemo/* $demopath
#
# Grant access to selected www_root directories.
#
.EXPAND pass /www/* $sitepath
.EXPAND $demoenable /www_root/serverdoc/*
.EXPAND $scodeenable /www_root/script_code/*
.EXPAND $scodeenable /www_root/base_code/*
#
#usermap /~* _ fspec_fixup,fixup,www_system:.exe
#usermap /reverse/* /www_root/script_code/ (revers,reverse_shr,www_system:.exe)
#usermap /* /* escape_special,fname_encode
#
```

The usermap functions are related to support for identifying users based on certificates clients present. This is in a very preliminary form as of 3.10alpha and shouldn't be used in any but an experimental way. You'll have to read ident_map.c if you want to know what this does in detail.

```
# Comment out the follow line to disable user directory access.  The server will
# allow access to the web subdirectory of a user's account if set by the user.
# The argument for the userdir rule is the subdirectory name (www -> [.www]).
#
.EXPAND $userdirenable $userdirname
.EXPAND $baduserenable /~* $baduser
#
#protect /slidepost/* www_system:slideshow.prot
#map /slidepost/* /htbin/slideshow2/*
#
# If not a file directory, see if URL matches a script directory.
#
map /help* /htbin/helpgate/help*
include www_system:servermaint_protection.conf
protect /htbin/yahmail* www_system:yahmail.prot

include www_system:http_scripts.conf
#
# Special mapping for handling crawlers.
#
.EXPAND $robotenable /robots.txt $robotfile
#
# the xrule dummy arg is limited to map, pass, fail, and redirect.
#
.ITERATE $xrule $xtemplate $xpath
.NEXT pass /examples* /sys$sysroot/examples*
```

```
.NEXT pass /javadoc* /sys$sysroot/syshlp/java*
.NEXT pass /axpdoc* /axpdoc*
# Only allow certain of the login directory (www_root:[000000]) files to be
# accessible, then prohibit www_root/000000/* in order to prevent users from
# circumventing the protected files by putting a series of root dirs.
#
.EXPAND $scodeenable /www_root/000000/wwwexec.com
fail /www_root/000000/*
#
# Fail everything else (this is the default, but include for completeness).
#
fail     *
```

E.2.3 HTTP_SUFFIXES.CONF

```
=================================
.ignore .AUTHORIZE .FORM
#
# Define thread pools and MST-based services.
#
.ITERATE ThreadPool $pname $qf $a2 $a3
.NEXT dsrv q_flag=1 limit=20 stack=162000
#
.ITERATE Service $sname $parg $darg $iarg
.NEXT dirserv pool=dsrv dynamic=(dirserv,http_dirserv_mst) \
info=www_system:http_directory.conf
```

This sets up only one service, the dirserv mst, but could be used to set up any number of them.

```
.define forceall suffix
.define PPenable presentation
.define PPscript %preproc:
```

Establishes the MST-based (rather than CGI-based) HTML preprocessor (for server-side includes) .

```
.define pdfbrenab presentation
.define pdfbyterange byterange
```

Sets up the byterange server as the presentation script for PDFs, but could be used for any other large binary file. (Works really well.)

```
#
# Authorization list for servermaint script
#
.FORM www_system:http_suffixes.servermaint
.ITERATE .authorize $smaint_user $smaint_pwd
.NEXT server maint
.NEXT *
#
# Define common suffixes, server must properly distinguish between binary
# and and ascii (8BIT) files in order to transfer them to the client.
#
```

```
.ITERATE suffix $sfx $rep $enc $qual
.NEXT .crt application/x-x509-ca-cert BINARY 1.0
.NEXT .aif audio/x-aiff BINARY 0.8
.NEXT .aifc audio/x-aiff BINARY 0.8
.NEXT .aiff audio/x-aiff BINARY 0.8
.NEXT .gif image/gif BINARY 1.0
.NEXT .txt text/plain 8BIT 0.5
.NEXT .com text/plain 8BIT 0.5
.NEXT .class application/octet-stream BINARY 1.0
.NEXT .jar application/jar BINARY 1.0
.NEXT .htm text/html 8BIT 0.5
.NEXT .html text/html 8BIT 0.5
.NEXT .htmlx text/htmlx 8BIT 0.5
.NEXT .htx text/htmlx 8BIT 0.5
.NEXT .jpg image/jpeg BINARY 1.0
.NEXT .jpeg image/jpeg BINARY 1.0
.NEXT .lis text/plain 8BIT 0.5
.NEXT .mol chemical/x-mdl-molfile BINARY 1.0
.NEXT .mpe video/mpeg BINARY 1.0
.NEXT .mpg video/mpeg BINARY 1.0
.NEXT .mswd application/vnd.ms-word BINARY 1.0
.NEXT .nai application/winstall BINARY 1.0
.NEXT .pac application/x-ns-proxy-autoconfig 8BIT 1.0
.NEXT .pdb chemical/x-pdb 8BIT 1.0
.NEXT .php text/plain 8BIT 1.0
.NEXT .pot application/vnd.ms-powerpoint BINARY 1.0
.NEXT .pps application/vnd.ms-powerpoint BINARY 1.0
.NEXT .ppt application/vnd.ms-powerpoint BINARY 1.0
.NEXT .ppz application/vnd.ms-powerpoint BINARY 1.0
.NEXT .qpw application/quattropro BINARY 1.0
.NEXT .hlp text/plain 8BIT 1.0
.NEXT .ps application/postscript 8BIT 1.0
.NEXT .ps-z application/postscript BINARY/x-compress 1.0
.NEXT .dvi application/x-dvi BINARY 1.0
.NEXT .dcr application/x-director BINARY 1.0
.NEXT .doc application/vnd.ms-word BINARY 1.0
.NEXT .dot application/vnd.ms-word BINARY 1.0
.NEXT .eps application/postscript 8BIT 1.0
.NEXT .gzip application/x-zip-compressed BINARY 1.0
.NEXT .pdf application/pdf BINARY 1.0
.NEXT .hlb vms/help BINARY
.NEXT .tlb vms/tlb BINARY
.NEXT .olb vms/olb BINARY
.NEXT .mcd application/mathcad BINARY
.NEXT .mlb vms/mlb BINARY
.NEXT .mpeg video/mpeg BINARY 1.0
.NEXT .mov video/quicktime BINARY 1.0
.NEXT .moov video/quicktime BINARY 1.0
.NEXT .qt video/quicktime BINARY 1.0
.NEXT .ra audio/x-pn-realaudio BINARY 1.0
.NEXT .ram audio/x-pn-realaudio BINARY 1.0
.NEXT .rpm audio/x-pn-realaudio-plugin BINARY 1.0
.NEXT .spl application/futuresplah BINARY 1.0
.NEXT .rtf application/rtf 8BIT 1.0
```

```
.NEXT .snd audio/basic BINARY 1.0
.NEXT .exe vms/exe BINARY 1.0
.NEXT .pcsi vms/exe BINARY 1.0
.NEXT .zip application/zip BINARY 1.0
.NEXT .bck application/VMSBACKUP BINARY 1.0
.NEXT .au audio/basic BINARY 1.0
.NEXT .avi video/x-msvideo BINARY 1.0
.NEXT .mid audio/x-midi BINARY 1.0
.NEXT .midi audio/x-midi BINARY 1.0
.NEXT .bleep application/bleeper 8BIT 1.0
.NEXT .wav audio/x-wav BINARY 1.0
.NEXT .xbm image/x-xbm 7BIT
.NEXT .bmp image/x-MS-bmp BINARY 0.8
.NEXT .cab application/octet-stream BINARY 1.0
.NEXT .tar application/tar BINARY 1.0
.NEXT .tar-gz application/x-zip-compressed BINARY 1.0
.NEXT .tgz application/x-zip-compressed BINARY 1.0
.NEXT .imagemap application/imagemap 8BIT 1.0
.NEXT .sit application/x-stuffit BINARY 1.0
.NEXT .swf application/x-shockwave-flash BINARY 1.0
.NEXT .bin application/x-macbinary BINARY 1.0
.NEXT .hqx application/mac-binhex40 BINARY 1.0
.NEXT .png image/png BINARY 1.0
.NEXT .word application/vnd.ms-word BINARY 1.0
.NEXT .wpd application/wordperfect BINARY 1.0
.NEXT .wrl model/vmrl BINARY 1.0
.NEXT .xl application/vnd.ms-excel BINARY 1.0
.NEXT .xlb application/vnd.ms-excel BINARY 1.0
.NEXT .xlm application/vnd.ms-excel BINARY 1.0
.NEXT .xls application/vnd.ms-excel BINARY 1.0
# The following line forces the server to send everything.
.EXPAND $forceall *.* text/plain * 0.01
#
# Define converter scripts to handle special representations.  Text/htmlx is
# used for html files with embedded server-side commands.
# Application/imagemap is content-type for mapimage.exe conf files.
.EXPAND $PPenable text/htmlx $Ppscript
.EXPAND $pdfbrenab application/pdf $pdfbyterange
.ITERATE presentation $rep $script
.NEXT application/imagemap www_root:[bin]mapimage
#
# The server makes a special check for text/file-directory when the URL  ends
# in a '/' (directory URL).  If no presentation defined, server will use an internal
# routine to generate a HTML listing of the files in the directory.
#
# The presentation rule below makes the server use a special decnet object
# (task WWWDIR) to perform directory browse functions.  The WWWDIR object
# interprets the script name (http_directory.conf) as the name of a
# configuration file that defines options for the directory layout.
#
#presentation text/file-directory sys$node::"0=WWWDIR"www_system:http_directory.conf
#
# The following rules make the server use the dirserv MST to perform directory
# browse functions.  Note that a separate thread pool must be used because of
```

```
# higher stack requirements.  This rule is mutually exclusive with use of
# the WWWDIR-based browser enabled by the preceding presentation rule, both use
# the same http_directory.conf configuration file.
#
```

This comment is wrong; the dirserv MST was defined previously. The following rules define the HTML-processor service, followed by the MST version of the PHP processor.

```
Service preproc pool=dsrv dynamic=(preproc,http_preproc_mst)\
    info=www_root:[000000]accesses.dat
#presentation text/htmlx %preproc:
presentation text/php %hpss:hpss_srv_php
```

E.2.4 HTTP_MANAGE.CONF

```
.ignore .AUTHORIZE .FORM
.define manhost 127.0.0.1
```

That's localhost, so you can run PRIVREQUEST on this system (whatever it is) and be listened to. If you want to control OSU on a system different from the one you're logged into, adjust manhost accordingly.

```
.define manport 931
```

That's the number you'll be specifying on the PRIVREQUEST command line.

```
.define mhEnable manage port
```

And without this PRIVREQUEST won't work at all.

```
#
# This configuration file controls the management interface parameters
# to the server.  It is included by http_main.conf.
#
.FORM www_system:http_manage.servermaint
.ITERATE .authorize $smaint_user $smaint_pwd
.NEXT server maint
.NEXT *
#
# Management functions on the running server are initiated by connecting
# to the server from a designated IP address and port number, known as
# the manage host and manage port.  The data received by the server from
# the management port (usually a privileged port number) is interpreted as
# a management command rather than an HTTP request.
#
.EXPAND manage host $manhost  # default to local host.
.EXPAND $mhEnable $manport    # arbitrary number (should be less than 1024
manage script /htbin/servermaint/http_manage/
.ITERATE manage script $mscript
.NEXT /htbin/serverman/
#
```

E.2.5 HTTP_SCRIPTS.CONF

Scripts in general are discussed in Chapter 14; user scripts are discussed in Chapter 19.

```
.ignore .AUTHORIZE .FORM
.define script_enable exec
.define script_task www_root:[bin]
.define script_prefix /htbin/*
.define uscript_enable exec
.define uscript_prefix /htbin-cap/*
.define uscript_task 0::"0=CAPSCRIPT"www_root:[bin]
.define java_enable #
.define java_prefix /jbin/*
.define java_task 0::"task=wwwjava"
.define isapi_enable #
.define sdTMOenab #
.define sdTMO 1:00
.define soTMOenab #
.define soTMO 10:00
.define srTMOenab TimeLimit ScriptReuse 2
.define srTMO 300
.define srPERM 0
.FORM www_system:http_scripts.servermaint
.ITERATE .authorize $smaint_user $smaint_pwd
.NEXT server maint
.NEXT *
#
# Define translation rules  for triggering scripts.  The following virtual
# script directories are defined:
#
#    /htbin/*             Runs scripts in www_root:[bin] via DECnet
#    /cgi-bin/*           (unix) fork-based CGI scripts.
#    /$mapimage/*         Builtin clickable image processing
#    /$omnimap/*          Dynamically loaded clickable image processing
#    /$testcgi/*          Test environment for dynamically loaded MST.
#    /tarserv/*           Connects to alternate DECnet-based scriptserver.
#
# Additionally, bind the following suffixes to virtual scripts:
#
#    .mapimage          /$omnimap/ncsa
#    .htimage           /$omnimap/htimage
#    .url               /$omnimap/url
#
#
# Define the primary directories for external scripts.  /htbin is used
# for external VMS scripts and /cgi-bin is used for unix scripts.
#
.EXPAND $script_enable $script_prefix $script_task
.EXPAND protect $uscript_prefix www_system:slideshow.prot
.EXPAND $uscript_enable $uscript_prefix $uscript_task
.EXPAND $java_enable $java_prefix $java_task
```

```
#
# Enable check for image map requests (/$mapimage/*), restrict the config
# files to residing in the /demo or /www directory trees (delete argument for
# unrestricted use of builtin mapimage).
#
.ITERATE ThreadPool $pname $qf $a2 $a3
.NEXT imap q_flag=1 limit=10 stack=120000

.ITERATE $srvenb $sname $p $a2 $a3
.NEXT service mapimage pool=imap builtin=mapimage
.NEXT service forkscript pool=imap builtin=cgifork
.NEXT service omnimap pool=imap dynamic=(omnimap,http_omnimap_mst)
.NEXT service testcgi pool=imap dynamic=(testcgi,http_testcgi_mst)
.NEXT service hpss pool=imap builtin=HPSS info=hpss_srv_*
#.NEXT service hpss pool=imap dynamic=(hpss,http_hpss_mst) info=hpss_srv_*
#.next # fastcgi pool=imap dynamic=(fastcgi,http_fastcgi_mst) info=fastcgi.conf
#
# Only permit the 1 testfork script to execute from cgi-bin.
#
map /cgi-bin/testfork/* /forkcgitest/*
fail /cgi-bin/*
map /forkcgitest/* /cgi-bin/testfork/*
#
# Make list of optional exec directories.
#
.ITERATE $execenb $prefix $task
.NEXT exec /pvbin/* 0::"0=WWWPVEXEC"www_root:[pvbin...]
.NEXT exec /$mapimage/* %mapimage:/www
.NEXT exec /$mapdemo/* %mapimage:/demo
.NEXT exec /$omnimap/* %omnimap:/demo
.NEXT exec /$testcgi/* %testcgi:/bleem
.next exec /$hpss/* %hpss:
.next exec /perlbin/* %hpss:hpss_srv_perl
.NEXT # /$hpss-xxx/* %hpss:hpss_srv_xxx
#.next exec /phpbin/* %hpss:hpss_srv_php
```

This is an alternate way of handling PHP scripts. The presentation script approach (seen in HTTP_SUFFIXES) takes care of it in a way that allows PHP to work on files in any directory.

```
#.next /$fastcgi/* %fastcgi:
.NEXT exec /tarserv/* sys$node::"0=WWWTAR"tar_archive:
.NEXT # /cgi-bin/* %forkscript:/www_root/cgi-bin/
```

Those are all pseudodirectories, not actually mapping directly to real directories on disk. (The %name things are all MST processes.) /tarserv/ is the very cool "targazer" program, which allows browsing tar archives as though they were disk structures; there's an example of this at the OSU home page, where every release ever is online and browseable.

```
.EXPAND $isapi_enable www_system:isapi.conf
#exec /pdf/* ER6S1::"0=PDFCD"pdf_server.conf
```

This appears to be the spoor of a not-yet-implemented feature, maybe something that does a PDF->HTML translation on the fly. But I speculate without adequate evidence.

```
#
# Set global timeout parameters for DECnet connections.
#
.EXPAND $sdTMOenab $sdTMO
.EXPAND $soTMOenab $soTMO
.EXPAND $srTMOenab $srTMO $srPERM
#
# Configure the omnimap MST.  This dynamically loaded service handles mapping
# for multiple input file formats: htimage image maps, NCSA (mapimage) image
# maps, and indirection files (url).  Use same thread pool as  the mapimage
# builtin service.  Note that in use the omnimap script directory must include
# the name of one of its virtual scripts: /htimage/, /ncsa/, /url/.
#
#service omnimap pool=imap dynamic=(omnimap,http_omnimap_mst)
#exec /$omnimap/* %omnimap:/demo

suffix .mapimage application/mapimage
suffix .mapimage2 application/htimage
suffix .url application/url-redirect
presentation application/mapimage %omnimap:/ncsa
presentation application/htimage %omnimap:/htimage
presentation application/url-redirect %omnimap:/url
#
# FastCGI uses separate file (info=fastcgi.conf) to configure its applications.
#
#service fastcgi pool=imap dynamic=(fastcgi,http_fastcgi_mst) info=fastcgi.conf
#exec /$fastcgi/* %fastcgi:
#
```

See Chapter 17 for a discussion of FastCGI.

E.3 WASD Configuration Files

E.3.1 HTTPD$CONFIG.CONF

```
# Configuration:  192.168.0.3:443
#                 HTTPd-WASD/7.2.0 OpenVMS/AXP SSL
# Last Modified:  Saturday,  2-JUN-2001 22:02:23
#                 webadmin.'PROMISCUOUS'@192.168.0.3
```

That header is automatically created during the installation process.

```
# -SERVICE-
```

If you maintain multiple services (roughly equivalent to VirtualHosts), it's probably worth your while to use the separate HTTPD$SERVICE.CONF file.

```
[Service]
[ServiceNotFoundURL]
# -GENERAL-
[Busy]  50
[ServiceListenBacklog]  5
[RequestHistory]  100
[ActivityDays]  28
[CharsetDefault]  ISO-8859-1
[DNSLookup]  disabled
```

Enable it if you want hostnames in your log files.

```
[Monitor]  enabled
[Port]  80
[StreamLF]  250
[SearchScript]  /cgi-bin/query
[SearchScriptExclude]
[PutMaxKbytes]  250
[PutVersionLimit]  3
[MapUserNameCacheEntries]  32
[PersonaCacheEntries]  32
# -LOGGING-
```

See Chapter 12 for information on logging in plenty of detail.

```
[Logging]  disabled
[LogFormat]  combined
[LogNaming]
[LogPeriod]
[LogPerService]  disabled
[LogPerServiceHostOnly]  disabled
[LogFile]  HT_LOGS:
[LogFileExtend]  0
[LogExcludeHosts]
```

User tracking is discussed in detail in Chapter 12 as well. If enabled, WASD produces a unique ID and attaches it to all the activity from the particular user, which enables you to sort out unique users from all the others using the same Web proxy.

```
[Track]  disabled
[TrackMultiSession]  disabled
[TrackDomain]
# -OPCOM-
```

Controls whether messages get sent to the console, in fine detail.

```
[OpcomTarget]  none
[OpcomAdmin]  disabled
[OpcomAuthorization]  disabled
[OpcomControl]  disabled
[OpcomHTTPd]  disabled
[OpcomProxyMaint]  disabled
# -CACHE-
```

See Chapter 11 for a detailed discussion of cache. These defaults should work adequately. Virtually all file access in WASD will go through the cache if it's enabled.

```
[Cache]  enabled
[CacheHashTableEntries]  1024
[CacheEntriesMax]  200
[CacheTotalKBytesMax]  2048
[CacheFileKBytesMax]  64
[CacheChunkKBytes]  8
[CacheValidatePeriod]  00:01:00
[CacheFrequentHits]  3
[CacheFrequentPeriod]  00:02:00
# -TIMEOUTS-
[TimeoutInput]  00:02:00
[TimeoutOutput]  00:30:00
[TimeoutNoProgress]  00:02:00
[TimeoutKeepAlive]  00:00:05
# -BUFFER SIZES-
```

These all have to do with scripting, sometimes advanced scripting.

```
[BufferSizeDclCommand]  6142
[BufferSizeDclOutput]  4096
[BufferSizeDclCgiPlusIn]  6142
[BufferSizeNetRead]  2048
[BufferSizeNetWrite]  4096
# -INDEX PAGES-
```

What to display if only a directory name is given

```
[Welcome]
HOME.HTML
INDEX.HTML
HOME.SHTML
INDEX.SHTML
# -HOST ACCESS-
```

Blocking access from particular hosts or granting it to particular hosts; see Chapter 7.

```
[Accept]
[Reject]
# -REPORTS-
[ServerAdmin]
[ServerSignature]  enabled
[ServerReportBodyTag]  <BODY LINK="#0000cc"
VLINK="#0000cc">
[ServerAdminBodyTag]  <BODY LINK="#0000cc" VLINK="#0000cc">
[ReportBasicOnly]  disabled
[ReportMetaInfo]  enabled
[ErrorReportPath]
[ErrorRecommend]  enabled
# -AUTHORIZATION-
[AuthCacheMinutes]  10
[AuthRevalidateUserMinutes]  0
[AuthRevalidateLoginCookie]  disabled
[AuthFailureLimit]  10
```

Get the password wrong this many times and find yourself locked out of the system.

```
[AuthBasic]  enabled
```

Basic Authorization: supported everywhere, but dangerous because of an absence of encryption.

```
[AuthDigest]  disabled
```

Digest Authorization: safer because encoded, but not supported by all browsers.

```
[AuthDigestGetLife]  0
[AuthDigestPutLife]  0
# -PROXY SERVING-
```

See Chapter 11 for proxy serving discussion, although it's actually pretty safe to just turn on `ProxyServing` and `ProxyCache`.

```
[ProxyServing]  disabled
[ProxyCache]  disabled
[ProxyAddForwardedBy]  disabled
[ProxyReportLog]  enabled
[ProxyReportCacheLog]  disabled
[ProxyHostLookupRetryCount]  4
[ProxyHostCachePurgeHours]  1
[ProxyCacheFileKBytesMax]  0
[ProxyCacheNoReloadSeconds]  30
[ProxyCacheReloadList]  1,2,4,8,12,24,48,96,168
```

```
[ProxyCacheRoutineHourOfDay]  0
[ProxyCachePurgeList]  168,48,24,8,0
[ProxyCacheDeviceDirOrg]  64x64
[ProxyCacheDeviceCheckMinutes]  15
[ProxyCacheDeviceMaxPercent]  85
[ProxyCacheDevicePurgePercent]  1
# -SCRIPTING-
```

See Chapters 14 and 17 for information about scripting.

```
[Scripting]  enabled
[DclDetachProcess]  disabled
[DclDetachProcessPriority]
[CgiStrictOutput]  enabled
[DclSpawnAuthPriv]  disabled
[DclGatewayBg]  disabled
[DclSoftLimit]  15
[DclHardLimit]  20
[DclBitBucketTimeout]  00:00:15
[DclZombieLifeTime]  00:10:00
[DclCgiPlusLifeTime]  00:10:00
[DECnetReuseLifeTime]  00:10:00
[DECnetConnectListMax]  0
[DclCleanupScratchMinutesMax]  10
[DclCleanupScratchMinutesOld]  10
[DclScriptRunTime]
.pl PERL
.dll $CGI-BIN:[000000]CGISAPI.EXE
.class @CGI-BIN:[000000]JAVA.COM
# -SSI-
```

Server-side includes are discussed in Chapter 13.

```
[SSI]  enabled
```

Allows include processing at all:

```
[SSIexec]  enabled
```

Allows execution of programs from within SSI documents:

```
[SSIaccesses]  enabled
```

Allows reading/updating the access counter file from SSI documents.

```
# -DIRECTORY-
```

See Chapter 13 for an exhaustive discussion of directory browsing.

```
[DirAccess]  enabled
[DirLayout]  I__L__R__S:b__D
[DirBodyTag]  <BODY>
[DirDescriptionLines]  30
[DirMetaInfo]  disabled
[DirOwner]  disabled
[DirPreExpired]  disabled
[DirWildcard]  enabled
[DirNoImpliedWildcard]  enabled
[DirNoPrivIgnore]  enabled
[DirReadme]  top
[DirReadmeFile]
README.HTML
README.HTM
README.TXT
README.
# -ICONS-
[AddIcon]
```

As in Apache, icons are mostly used to make directory listings look nicer. The contents of each line is path-to-icon, Alt-tag, content-type.

```
/httpd/-/text.gif  [TXT]  text/plain
/httpd/-/text.gif  [CSS]  text/css
/httpd/-/doc.gif  [HTM]  text/html
/httpd/-/doc.gif  [HTM]  text/x-menu
/httpd/-/image.gif  [IMG]  image/gif
/httpd/-/image.gif  [IMG]  image/x-xbitmap
/httpd/-/image.gif  [IMG]  image/jpeg
/httpd/-/movie.gif  [MOV]  image/mpeg
/httpd/-/sound.gif  [AUD]  application/audio
/httpd/-/x-script.gif  [htm]  application/x-script
/httpd/-/text.gif  [txt]  text/x-ismap
/httpd/-/x-shtml.gif  [htm]  text/x-shtml
/httpd/-/binary.gif  [BIN]  application/octet-stream
/httpd/-/binary.gif  [BIN]  application/x-vms512
/httpd/-/binary.gif  [BIN]  application/x-compressed
/httpd/-/postscript.gif  [PS_]  application/postscript
/httpd/-/gzip.gif  [ZIP]  application/x-gzip
/httpd/-/compressed.gif  [ZIP]  application/x-compress
/httpd/-/uu.gif  [UUE]  application/x-uuencoded
/httpd/-/wp.gif  [WPC]  application/x-wp
/httpd/-/doc.gif  [PDF]  application/pdf
/httpd/-/binary.gif  [BIN]  application/x-ns-proxy-autoconfig
/httpd/-/binary.gif  [BIN]  application/x-x509-ca-cert

[AddBlankIcon]  /httpd/-/blank.gif  _____
[AddDefaultIcon]
[AddDirIcon]  /httpd/-/directory.gif  [DIR]
[AddParentIcon]  /httpd/-/back.gif  [<--]
[AddUnknownIcon]  /httpd/-/unknown.gif  [???]

# -CONTENT TYPES-
```

```
[AddType]
.HTML  "text/html; charset=ISO-8859-1"  HyperText Markup Language
.HTM  text/html  HyperText Markup Language
.MENU  text/x-menu  hypertext menu
.MNU  text/x-menu  hypertext menu
.TXT  "text/plain; charset=ISO-8859-1"  plain text
.GIF  image/gif  GIF image
.XBM  image/x-xbitmap  X-bitmap
.DIR  x-internal/directory  binary
.SHTML  text/x-shtml  HyperText Markup Language (pre-processed)
.SHT  text/x-shtml  HyperText Markup Language (pre-processed)
.ISMAP  text/x-ismap  Clickable-image mapping
.ISM  text/x-ismap  Clickable-image mapping
.  text/plain  plain text
.ACF  text/plain  DCE Attribute Configuration File
.ADA  text/plain  Ada source
.ANNOUNCE  text/plain  plain text
.ASC  text/plain  plain text
.ASCII  text/plain  plain text
.B32  text/plain  BLISS-32 source
.BAS  text/plain  BASIC source
.BKB  application/x-script  /HyperReader  Bookreader book
.BKS  application/x-script  /HyperShelf  Bookreader shelf
.C  text/plain  C source
.CLD  text/plain  VMS Command Line Definition
.CFG  text/plain  configuration file
.CGI  text/plain  Perl source
.CLASS  application/octet-stream  Java class
.CMS  text/plain  Code Management System rules
.COB  text/plain  COBOL source
.COM  text/plain  DCL procedure
.CONF  text/plain  configuration file
.CNF  text/plain  configuration
.CPP  text/plain  C++ source
.CRT  application/x-x509-ca-cert  DER certifcate (MSIE)
.CSS  text/css  W3C Cascading Style Sheet
.DBF  application/x-script  /dbiv  dBASEIV database
.DBT  application/octet-stream  dBASEIV database memos
.DCL  text/plain  DCL procedure
.DIS  text/plain  distribution list
.DLL  application/octet-stream  ISAPI extension DLL
.DOC  application/octet-stream  DECwrite document
.DECW$BOOK  application/x-script  /HyperReader  Bookreader book
.DECW$BOOKSHELF  application/x-script  /HyperShelf  Bookreader shelf
.DVI  application/octet-stream  TeX Device Independent
.EPS  text/plain  Encapsulated PostScript
.EXE  application/octet-stream  Executable
.FDL  text/plain  VMS File Definition Language
.FIRST  text/plain  plain text
.1ST  text/plain  plain text
.FOR  text/plain  Fortran source
.H  text/plain  C header
.HLP  text/plain  VMS help source
.HDR  text/plain  LSE template
```

```
.HLB  application/x-script  /Conan  VMS help library
.HTC  application/x-script  /pcache  WASD proxy cache
.HTMLX  text/x-shtml  OSU SSI HTML
.IMAGEMAP  application/x-script  /htbin/mapimage  OSU Image map
.IDL  text/plain  DCE Interface Definition Language
.IMG  application/octet-stream  DDIF image
.JAVA  text/plain  Java source
.JAR  application/octet-stream  Java JAR
.JPG  image/jpeg  JPEG image
.JPEG  image/jpeg  JPEG image
.LIS  text/plain  plain text listing
.LIST  text/plain  plain text listing
.LOG  text/plain  plain text log
.MAR  text/plain  MACRO-32 source
.MAN  text/plain  U**x man page
.MLB  application/octet-stream  VMS MACRO library
.MMS  text/plain  Module Management System rules
.MPG  image/mpeg  MPEG movie
.MPEG  image/mpeg  MPEG movie
.MSG  text/plain  VMS message source
.OBJ  application/octet-stream  VMS object module
.ODL  application/x-script  /HyperShelf  BNU shelf
.OLB  application/octet-stream  VMS object library
.OPT  text/plain  VMS linker options
.PAC  application/x-ns-proxy-autoconfig  proxy autoconfig
.PAS  text/plain  Pascal source
.PDF  application/pdf  Adobe Portable Document Format
.PEM  application/x-x509-ca-cert  Privacy Enhanced Mail certificate
.POD  text/plain  Perl documentation
.PL  text/plain  Perl source
.PERL  text/plain  Perl source
.PM  text/plain  Perl package
.PRO  text/plain  IDL source
.PROPERTIES  text/plain  Java properties
.PS  application/postscript  PostScript
.PY  text/plain  Python source
.READ*  text/plain  plain text
.RELEASE_NOTES  text/plain  VMS software release notes
.SDML  text/plain  Standard Digital Markup Language—VAX Document source
.STY  text/plain  TeX Style
.TEX  text/plain  TeX source
.TEXT  text/plain  plain text
.TPU  text/plain  Text Processing Utility source—VMS TPU
.TLB  application/x-script  /Conan  VMS text library
.UIL  text/plain  User Interface Language—X Window System
.UID  application/octet-stream  User Interface Definition—X Window System
.UU  application/x-uuencoded  UU-encoded
.UUE  application/x-uuencoded  UU-encoded
.VMS  text/plain  plain text
.WP  application/x-script  /hwp  WordPerfect document
.WPD  application/x-script  /hwp  WordPerfect document
.WP5  application/x-script  /hwp  WordPerfect document
.ZIP  application/x-gzip  ZIP-compressed
.Z  application/x-compressed  compressed
```

```
.HTL  text/plain  plain text
*  x-internal/unknown
[AddMimeTypesFile]
# End!
```

E.3.2 HTTPD$MAP.CONF

```
# example WASD mapping rule file

# paranoid?
# (un)comment appropriate line to restrict access to the /ht_root/ tree
# YOU MAY NEED TO COMMENT-OUT THE FINAL RULE IN THIS FILE ALSO!
# (also consider controlling access via HTTPD$AUTH)
#pass /ht_root/doc/*
#pass /ht_root/src/*
#fail /ht_root/*
pass /ht_root/*
```

You definitely don't want to go in production like this, with all your configuration files browseable.

```
# (template for HTTP proxy serving)
#pass http://*

# (template for FTP proxy serving, currently via proxy agent script)
#redirect ftp://* /fetch/ftp://*
#pass /ftp://*
#script+ /fetch/* /cgi-bin/fetch/*

#(allow stream-LF conversion on these paths)
set /ht_root/* stmLF
set /web/* stmLF

#(disable caching on these paths)
set /ht_root/src/* NOcache

#(next line allows for CERN HTTPd icon compatibility)
map /httpd-internal-icons/* /httpd/-/*
pass /ht_root/runtime/* /ht_root/runtime/*
pass /httpd/-/admin/*
pass /*/-/* /ht_root/runtime/*/*

# generalised "/web..." rules
#pass /web/* /web/*
#pass /web /web/

#just for the example
map /web/* /ht_root/*

#----- scripting rules

exec /cgi-bin/* /cgi-bin/*
```

Vanilla CGI:

```
exec+ /cgiplus-bin/* /cgi-bin/*
```

CGIplus scripts—scripts located in cgi-bin but accessed via /cgiplus-bin/:

```
exec+ /cgiauth-bin/* /cgi-bin/*
```

External authorization agents are CGIplus scripts.

```
exec+ /isapi/* /cgi-bin/*
```

ISAPI wrapper in a CGIplus file—see Chapter 17.

```
# server-internal "scripts"
script /upd/* /upd/*
script /echo/* /echo/*
script /tree/* /tree/*
script /where/* /where/*
script /xray/* /xray/*
```

```
script /query/* /cgi-bin/query/*
script /extract/* /cgi-bin/extract/*
script /print* /cgi-bin/print*
```

Individual script mappings rather than mapping entire script directories

```
script+ /conan* /cgi-bin/conan*
script+ /help* /cgi-bin/conan*
script+ /HyperReader* /cgi-bin/HyperReader*
script+ /HyperShelf* /cgi-bin/HyperShelf*
```

Individual CGIplus (persistent) script mappings for reduced latency, faster response.

```
# rules for RTE examples only (may be commented out if not required)
exec /plbin/* /ht_root/src/perl/*
```

Execute anything referred to in /plbin/ from the HT_ROOT:[SRC.PERL] directory as a vanilla CGI script.

```
exec /plrte/* (cgi-bin:[000000]perlrte.exe)/ht_root/src/perl/*
```

Execute anything referred to in /plrte/ from the HT_ROOT:[SRC.PERL] directory using the persistent run-time environment achieved by loading cgi-bin:perlrte.exe into a persistent process.

```
exec /rtbin/* (cgi-bin:[000000]rte_example.exe)/ht_root/src/httpd/*
```

Execute anything referred to in /rtbin/ from HT_ROOT:[SRC.HTTPD] using the example RTE engine.

```
#----- DECnet-based scripting
# for WASD CGI DECnet scripts
exec /decnet/* /0::/cgi-bin/*
# OSU-specific .HTMLX (SSI) processing
redirect /*.*.htmlx /*.htmlx?httpd=ssi&__part=*
```

See Chapter 13 for an explanation of this.

```
# OSU-specific DECnet scripting
exec /osu/* /0::"0=wwwexec"/cgi-bin/*
exec /htbin/* /0::"0=wwwexec"/cgi-bin/*
map /demo/* /www_root/serverdoc/*
# for 'vmshelpgate' script
pass /help*
# for 'webbook' (maps a VMS file specification jammed into the path)
pass /*[*]*
# if a current/previous installation of OSU then this should map to it
pass /www_root/*

#----- user (DECnet-based) scripting, directories
# based on the assumption user web areas are located in WEB:[USER.<username>]

#exec /~*/cgi-bin/* /0""::/web/user/*/cgi-bin/*
#exec /~*/osu-bin/* /0""::"0=wwwexec"/web/user/*/cgi-bin/*
#pass /~* /web/user/*
```

See Chapters 13 and 19 for a discussion of the issues involved in allowing users to run scripts and how WASD allows this to be done safely.

```
#----- miscellaneous

# uncomment the next line to give free reign to the entire system disk
pass /sys$common/* /sys$common/*
```

Or, more properly, comment it out to avoid giving free reign to the entire system disk.

```
pass /sys$common/syshlp/* /sys$common/syshlp/*
pass /sys$common/syslib/* /sys$common/syslib/*

# used for bookreader books
pass /decw$book/* /decw$book/*
pass /sys$common/decw$book/* /sys$common/decw$book/*
pass /sys$common/decw$defaults/user/* /sys$common/decw$defaults/user/*
# used for BNU environment
pass /disk$vaxdoc* /disk$vaxdoc*
pass /disk$axpdoc* /disk$axpdoc*
```

How you read/serve the bookreader files is discussed briefly in Chapter 16.

```
# just for the demonstration file!
pass /* /ht_root/*
```

You definitely want to change this before going live.

E.3.3 HTTPD$SERVICE.CONF

Note that this file isn't distributed with the server; you have to create it if you want to use it. I have included my own HTTPD$SERVICE to clear up some syntax issues.

The service name goes in double brackets. If the service is HTTP, you leave it off. If the port is 80, you leave it off. If you try to specify those default scheme and ports, the server will fail to parse the services file and refuse to start up. The per-service directives apply to the service under which they most immediately appear. When you want to go back to configuration that affects all services, specify service [*].

```
[[hudson.dyndns.info:81]]
[[https://hudson.dyndns.info:444]]
[ServiceSSLCert] sslcerts:server.pem
[[vms.kicks-ass.net:81]]
[[https://vms.kicks-ass.net:445]]
[ServiceSSLCert] sslcerts:server.pem
[[alanwinston.homeip.net:81]]
[[https://alanwinston.homeip.net:446]]
[ServiceSSLCert] sslcerts:server.pem
[[http://*:81]]
```

E.3.4 HTTPD$MSG.CONF

There isn't that much to say about this configuration file, except that it shows the messages WASD can produce, and how easy it would be to change them (perhaps on April Fool's Day?)

```
# Example message configuration file.
#
# 24-OCT-2000  MGD  V7.1, change "subprocess" to "scripting process"
# 08-APR-2000  MGD  v7.0, report and HTTP messages
# 26-NOV-1999  MGD  v6.1, agent messages, logout message
# 05-MAY-1999  MGD  v6.0, proxy messages
# 02-APR-1998  MGD  v5.1, additional SSI messages
# 12-MAR-1998  MGD  v5.0, additional messages
# 25-OCT-1997  MGD  compatible with HTTPd v4.4 and v4.5
# 09-AUG-1997  MGD  v4.4, initial
#
# The case and punctuation in these messages is quite deliberate and
# varies depending on the type and context of the message being generated
# ... try to reproduce it as closely as possible!

[version] 7.0
[language] 1 en

[auth]

en 01 Authentication required!
en 02 Access denied.
en 03 Authentication failed.
en 04 Scheme not supported.
en 05 authenticating user
en 06 authentication database problem
en 07 VMS authentication problem
en 08 Username too long.
```

```
en 09 Password too long.
en 10 <B>Authorization cancellation has probably not occured!</B>\
<P>Reload/refresh this page, clear the fields, resubmit,\
then cancel the new username/password dialog.\
A failure report indicates successful logout!\
Then navigate backwards.\

en 11 Authorization agent mapping problem.
en 12 Authorization agent not found.
en 13 Authorization agent response problem.

[dir]

en 01 Created|Description|Name|Owner|Protection|Revised|Size
en 02 parent directory
en 03 subdirectory
en 04 Directory layout problem.
en 05 Index of
en 06 Tree of

[general]

en 01 Sanity check failure.
en 02 INTERNAL ERROR
en 03 String overflow.
en 04 Heap allocation failed.
en 05 calloc() failed
en 06 Request calloc() failed.
en 07 Server too busy.
en 08 Server access denied.
en 09 Facility is disabled.
en 10 Wildcard not permitted.
en 11 File
en 12 Document
en 13 Directory

[htadmin]

en 01 Authentication database problem.
en 02 Current password not verified.
en 03 Password details incomplete.
en 04 New password not verified.
en 05 Current and new passwords identical.
en 06 Password processing error.
en 07 User not found.
en 08 Password database problem.
en 09 Change Authentication|Current|New|Verify|Change|Reset
en 10 Authentication for !%% changed.

[http]

# NOTE: messages in (parenthesese) are not used in this version
en 01 The server is reporting an UNKNOWN status code!
en 02 (Continue)
en 03 (Switching protocols)
en 04 The request has been successful.
en 05 The resource has been created.
```

```
en 06 (The request has been accepted for processing.)
en 07 (non-authoritative)
en 08 (The requested resource had no content.)
en 09 (reset content)
en 10 (partial content)
en 11 (multiple choices)
en 12 The requested resource has been moved permanently.
en 13 The requested resource has been moved temporarily.
en 14 (see other)
en 15 The requested resource has not been modified.
en 16 (use proxy)
en 17 The server could not understand the request.
en 18 The request requires authorization.
en 19 (payment required)
en 20 The requested action is not permitted.
en 21 The requested resource could not be found.
en 22 (method not allowed)
en 23 (not acceptable)
en 24 Proxy authentication required.
en 25 (request timeout)
en 26 A resource conflict has prevented processing the request.
en 27 (gone)
en 28 (length required)
en 29 (precondition failed)
en 30 (request entity too large)
en 31 (request URI too long)
en 32 (unsupported media type)
en 33 The server has encountered an unexpected condition.
en 34 The requested action is not implemented by this server.
en 35 External agent did not respond (or not acceptably).
en 36 This service is not (or no longer) available.
en 37 (gateway timeout)
en 38 (HTTP version not supported.)

[ismap]

en 01 Confused
en 02 Client (browser) has supplied an unacceptable coordinate.
en 03 No default path specified
en 04 Incomplete specification
en 05 Incorrect number of coordinates
en 06 Number of coordinates exceeds internal limit
en 07 Region specification problem

[mapping]

en 01 Access denied, no mapping rules loaded!
en 02 Access denied, internal processing problem.
en 03 Access denied, by rule.
en 04 Access denied, by default.

[proxy]

en 01 Proxy services are not configured.
en 02 Proxy services are currently disabled.
en 03 This is not a proxy service!
```

```
en 04 This is not a proxy CONNECT service!
en 05 Only "http:" proxy supported.
en 06 Unknown host.
en 07 Chained proxy server refused connection.
en 08 Host refused connection.
en 09 Chained proxy server not reachable.
en 10 Host not reachable.
en 11 Chained proxy server failure.
en 12 Server response could not be understood.
en 13 Server host was disconnected.
en 14 Server response header error.

[put]

en 01 Multipart MIME-encoded processing problem.
en 02 Multipart/mixed MIME-encoded not supported.
en 03 Multipart file name not specified.
en 04 Multipart field problem.
en 05 Multipart upload file name not specified.
en 06 Directory name not specified.
en 07 Directory already exists.
en 08 Delete file name not specified.
en 09 created
en 10 superceded
en 11 deleted

[request]

en 01 Request format not understood.
en 02 Request method not supported.
en 03 Request body read problem.
#(this is a sys$fao() format string ... be carefull!)
en 04 Attempted !AZ of !UL kbytes exceeds allowed maximum of !UL kbytes.
en 05 Redirection loop detected.
en 06 URL-encoding problem.
en 07 URL-form-encoding problem.

[script]

en 01 Script not found.
en 02 Scripting process hard-limit reached.
en 03 Request pragma problem.
en 04 Request cookie problem.
en 05 creating mailboxes
en 06 creating scripting process
en 07 initializing DCL enviroment
en 08 writing CGIplus variables
en 09 Script did not provide an acceptable response.

[ssi]

en 01 SSI Error!
en 02 line
en 03 access count disabled
en 04 directive not terminated or too large
en 05 directive unknown
en 06 directive tag unknown
```

```
en 07 directive tag invalid
en 08 DCL execution disabled
en 09 DCL command not supported
en 10 document with DCL must be owned by SYSTEM
en 11 document with DCL cannot be world writable
en 12 included file must be "text/..." content-type
en 13 cannot include file (access problem)
en 14 problem with date/time format string
en 15 possible SSI document recursion (including itself)
en 16 variable problem
en 17 [VARIABLE-DOES-NOT-EXIST!]
en 18 flow-control problem

[status]

en 01 SUCCESS
en 02 ERROR
en 03 Document not found
en 04 File not found
en 05 Document protection violation
en 06 File protection violation
en 07 (no information)
en 08 <BR><I>(document, bookmark, or reference requires revision)</I>
en 09 <BR><I>(protection requires revision)</I>
en 10 <BR><I>(no authorization to access the object)</I>
en 11 <BR><I>(invalid file specification, requires correction)</I>
en 12 <BR><I>(try again shortly)</I>
en 13 <BR><I>(correct situation, try again)</I>

# this template is used for all server error and success reports
en 14 <HTML>\
<HEAD>\
!AZ<TITLE>!AZ !UL !AZ</TITLE>\
</HEAD>\
!AZ\
<FONT SIZE=+1>\
<B>!AZ !UL</B>  -  !AZ\
</FONT>\
!%%!%%!%%\
</BODY>\
</HTML>

# server signature formatting
en 15 <P><HR WIDTH=85% ALIGN=left SIZE=2 NOSHADE>\
!AZ

# server signature itself
en 16 <ADDRESS>!AZ/!AZ Server at !AZ Port !UL</ADDRESS>

# if configured this information is added to error and success reports
en 17 <P>Additional information: \
<A HREF="/httpd/-/status1xx.html">1<I>xx</I></A>, \
<A HREF="/httpd/-/status2xx.html">2<I>xx</I></A>, \
<A HREF="/httpd/-/status3xx.html">3<I>xx</I></A>, \
<A HREF="/httpd/-/status4xx.html">4<I>xx</I></A>, \
```

```
<A HREF="/httpd/-/status5xx.html">5<I>xx</I></A>, \
<A HREF="/httpd/-/statushelp.html">Help</A>

[upd]

en 01 Select/enter file name.
en 02 Select/enter directory name.
en 03 Query problem.
en 04 Enter filter specification.
en 05 Select source file name.
en 06 Enter target file name.
en 07 Select current file name.
en 08 Enter new file name.
en 09 File names identical!
en 10 Select action button (do not press [ENTER])
en 11 Not a text file.
en 12 Parent directory not supplied.


en 13 Update|help|Subdirectories|Files\
|select from list|none available|enter name\
|Reset|Goto|List|Tree|Create|Protect|Delete\
|Upload|as|local file\
|select from list|none available|enter name/path\
|Reset|View|Edit|Create|Filter|Rename|Copy|Protect|Delete

en 14 Update|Create|Confirm
en 15 Update|Delete|Confirm
en 16 Update|Rename|to|Confirm
en 17 Update|Copy|to|Confirm

en 18 New Document|Document|Help|Revised\
|Update|Save As|Update|Create|Preview|Undo Editing\
|Change Edit Window

en 19 WORLD accessable|OWNER and GROUP|OWNER only
#(the following is a more technical alternative)
#en 19 S:RWED,O:RWED,G:RE,W:RE|S:RWED,O:RWED,G:RE,W|S:RWED,O:RWED,G,W
en 20 protection changed
en 21 renamed to
----END---
```

Index

Access controls, 135–50
 Apache, 136–40
 OSU, 140–43
 password-based, 144–45
 Robots.txt, 147–50
 SSL and, 145–47
 WASD, 144–50
ALT tags, 245–46
ANALOG, 219, 220–25
 analog.cfg file, 221
 Daily Report, 223
 defined, 220–21
 downloading, 220
 home page, 220
 Opening System Report, 225
 OSU DCL script, 220
 OSU menu, 224
 pie charts, 225
 Summary Report, 222
 UNCOMPRESS command and, 221
 See also Log-interpretation tools
Anonymous authentication, 124
Apache, 6–7
 access controls, 136–40
 `AddAltByType` directive, 246
 `AddAlt` directive, 245–46
 `AddDescription` directive, 246
 `AddIconByEncoding` directive, 247
 `AddIconByType` directive, 246
 `AddIcon` directive, 246
 add-ons, 9
 ambiguities and user tracking, 214–15
 anonymous authentication, 124
 authentication, 120–24
 cache management, 187
 Combined format, 206
 command-line control, 56–58
 Common format, 206
 `CONFIGURE` command, 57
 cookie-based user-tracking features, 203
 `DefaultIcon` directive, 247
 default startup, 25
 `DescriptionWidth` directive, 240
 directory browsing, 238–47
 `DirectoryIndex` command, 238
 echo directives, 269–70
 error logs, 216
 error page with signature, 48
 `exec` directive, 276
 fancy index from, 240
 `FancyIndexing` directive, 240
 flow-control directives, 262–63, 271–72
 `FLUSH` command, 57
 `FoldersFirst` directive, 240
 format specifiers for logs, 205–6
 `GRACEFUL` command, 57
 `HeaderName` directive, 243
 `IconHeight` directive, 241
 `IconsAreLinks` directive, 241
 `IndexIgnore` directive, 245

Apache *(cont'd.)*
- IndexOptions directive, 239
- IndexOrderDefault directive, 245
- log-file formats/locations, 204–8
- log-file rotation, 211–12
- mapping, 98–102
- MIME.TYPES file, 102
- modules on UNIX systems, 120
- NEW command, 57
- password-based authentication, 120–22
- platforms, 7
- proxy management, 193–97
- READ command, 57
- ReadmeName directive, 245
- RESTART command, 57
- RUN command, 57
- ScanHTMLTitles directive, 242
- set directives, 274
- SHUTDOWN command, 57
- SOURCE, 137
- SSL and, 87
- SSL authentication, 122–24
- START command, 58
- starting, 50
- STOP command, 57
- stopping, 50
- Suppress directives, 243
- TrackModified directive, 243
- user-defined CGI scripts, 356
- user directories, enabling/disabling, 154
- userdirs, 153
- version 1.0, 7
- version 2.0, 7
- virtual hosts, 162
- VMS port, 10
- Web-based configuration/control and, 63
- *See also* CSWS

Apache Software Foundation, 7

Authentication, 117–35
- anonymous, 124
- Apache, 120–24
- BASIC, 118, 121
- DIGEST, 118–19, 121, 122
- ident-based, 133–35
- OSU, 124–27
- password-based, 120–22
- SSL, 122–24
- SYSUAF-based, 121, 127
- WASD, 127–35
- X.509, 119

Authorization, 95, 120, 128

Autoscripts, 256

AWStats, 226–30
- command-line variables, 229
- defined, 226
- illustrated, 229
- running as CGI program, 229
- with taint detection and suppression, 228
- *See also* Log-interpretation tools

BASIC authentication, 118, 121

Bookreader servers, 331–32

Cache management, 185–92
- Apache, 187
- OSU, 187–90
- WASD, 191–92

Caches
- directives, 187
- entries as stale, 190
- file expiration date/time, 189
- in-memory chunk size, 188
- maximum file size, 188
- memory allocation, 188
- OSU file, 187
- VCC/VIOC/XFC, 187

Caching
- defined, 183
- distribution, 183
- memory availability, 186
- proxy, 193, 199

C/C++, 307

ProxyForwardedBy directive, 200
ProxyHostCachePurgeHours directive, 202
ProxyHostLookupRetryCount directive, 200
proxy maintenance activities, 202
proxy management, 199–202
ProxyReportCacheLog directive, 200
ProxyReportLog directive, 200
ProxyServing directive, 200
Python, 312
real-time monitoring, 62
REPORT, 110
RMSCHAR, 110
RTE and, 334, 346–47
SCRIPT, 111
Scripting directive, 261
scripting environments support, 13
script rule, 107, 108
server administration, 13
server administrator e-mail, 49
server process priority, 54
set directives, 274–75
set rule, 108, 159, 361
shutdown, 56
speed, 13
SSIAccesses directive, 261
SSI configuration, 261–62
SSI directive, 261
SSIexec directive, 261
SSI=PRIV|NOPRIV, 111
SSL and access control in, 145–47
SSL authentication, 131–33
SSLCGI, 112
SSL configuration, 94–95
SSL installation, 86
SSL renegotiation, 133
SSL services, specifying, 94
startup, 51–56
STMLF (NOSTMLF), 112
SWISH-E and, 176
systemwide logical names, 40
SYSUAF authentication, 55
SYSUAF-mapped userdirs, 158
TCP/IP software and, 16–17
test page, 33
THROTTLE, 112
TIMEOUT, 112
Track directive, 215
TrackDomain directive, 215
TrackMultiSession directive, 215
UPD utility with, 351
user-developed CGI scripts, 361–62
user directories, 157–59
userdirs restrictions, 157
uxec rule, 108, 361
VMS version and, 15–16
WATCH facility, 56
Web-based control, 64–65
Welcome directive, 47
X.509 certificate authentication/ authorization, 95
zip files, 32
See also Web servers
WATCH facility, 56
Wayback Machine, 148
Webalizer, 219, 230–32
3-D graph of daily statistics, 232
defined, 230
home page, 230
index.html, 231
See also Log-interpretation tools
Web-based control, 63–65
WEBBOOK, 331
WebDAV, 352
Web directories, 151–59
pros and cons, 151–52
security risks, 151
Webmaster address, 47–50
WEBPERL, 341

Web servers
access controls, 135–50
ambiguities and user tracking, 213–15
authentication, 117–35
basic configuration, 40–50
cache management, 185–92
CGI configuration, 293
CGI environment, 296–306
choosing, 13–14
command-line control, 56–62
configuration, 86–95
directory browsing, 237–58
disk space, 17–18
document trees, 44–47
error logs, 216–18
error messages, 47–50
functioning of, 185–86
high-performance CGI scripting options, 335–48
hostnames, 40–44
installation, 78–86
installation guidelines, 19–34
log-file formats/locations, 204–11
log-file rotation, 211–13
log interpretation tools, 218–36
network issues, 18–19
options, 9–14
ports, 40–44
preinstallation, 15–19
proxy management, 193–202
security and, 3
SSI, 259–79
starting/stopping, 50–56
TCP/IP software, 16–17
timeline, 8
user-developed CGI scripts, 356–62
Web-based control, 63–65
See also CSWS; OSU; WASD
WUSAGE, 232–36
downloading, 232
home page, 232
index.html, 236
running, 233
weekly page, 235
See also Log-interpretation tools
WWWSSL.COM file, 83–84

X.509 authentication, 95
client, 92
defined, 119
X.509 certificates, 74
authentication/authorization, 95
specifying, 132

yahMAIL, 326–27

CERN, 5–6
Certificate authorities (CAs), 69
  in database, 69
  getting certificates from, 71–75
  picking, 71
Certificates
  getting, from CAs, 71–75
  passphrase, 87
  self-signed, creating, 75–77
  verification lifetime, 132
  X.509, 74, 132
CGI
  as ACTION, 282
  callouts, 301
  configuration of, 293–95
  defined, 281–84
  freeware scripts, 325–32
  high-performance scripting options, 333–48
  HTTP headers, 293
  languages for, 306–12
  routine libraries, 284
  scripts, 283
CGI-BIN directories, 355
CGI environment, 296–306
  CSWS, 296
  OSU, 296–300
  WASD, 301–6
CGI-MAILTO, 327
CGIplus, 107, 295, 345–47
  callouts, 301
  ISAPI implementation, 347–48
  script mapping, 346
  scripts, 345
CGI scripts
  environment variables, 284–93
  freeware, 325–32
  GET method and, 282, 283
  with no arguments, 281–82
  POST method and, 282, 283
  running, 281–312
  user-developed, 355–62
CGI_SYMBOLS, 299–300
CGIUTL utility, 304–5
Clustering, 1–2
ColdFusion Server, 4
Combined format, 204
  Apache, 206
  OSU, 208
  WASD, 210
  See also Log-file formats
Command-line control, 56–62
Common format, 204
  Apache, 206
  OSU, 208
  WASD, 210
  See also Log-file formats
Common Gateway Interface. *See* CGI; CGI scripts
Compaq Secure Web Browser (CSWB), 161
Compaq Secure Web Server. *See* CSWS
Conan, 330–31
Conditional mapping, 112–16
  overhead, 113
  rules using, 112–13
  See also Mapping; Mapping resources
Conditionals
  `AC:accept`, 113
  `AL:accept-language`, 113
  `AS:accept-charset`, 113
  `CK:cookie`, 113
  `EX`, 114
  form, 113
  `HO:host`, 114
  `ME:http`, 114
  multiple, 113
  `QS:query-string`, 114
  `RF:referring`, 115
  `SC:request-scheme`, 114
  `SP:server-port`, 114
  `UA:user-agent`, 115
  `VS:host-name/address`, 115

Configuration, 86–95
basic, 40–50
document trees and index files, 44–47
error messages and Webmaster address, 47–50
ports and hostnames, 40–44
SSL, 86–95
Configuration files, 35–40
CSWS, 35–38
OSU, 38–39
WASD, 39–40
Crinoid, 343–44
CSWS, 9–11
AddType directive, 260
Alias directive, 45
cache management, 187
CGI configuration, 294
CGI environment, 296
choosing, 13
configuration file, 35–36
CustomLog directive, 90
DCL, 306
default Web document directory, 45
defined, 9
directives, 41
disk space and, 17–18
downloading, 9
file instructions, 37
high-performance CGI options, 335–39
home pages, 20
HTTPD.CONF file, 35–36, 41
installation guide, 20–28
listen directives, 41
logicals definition, 22
mod_auth_anon, 124
mod_auth_openvms, 120
mod_perl, 20, 24, 26, 35, 335–38
mod_php, 24, 26, 35, 310, 338–39
mod_proxy, 193
mod_rewrite, 98
mod_ssl, 24, 26, 35, 78–79, 86–92
multihosting/multihoming, 162–64
OpenSSL kit, 86
password files, 37
Perl, 309
PHP, 310
Python, 311
SSI configuration, 260
SSLCACertificateFile directive, 92, 123
SSLCACertificatePath directive, 92, 123
SSLCARevocationFile directive, 122–23
SSLCARevocationPath directive, 122–23
SSLCertificateChainFile directive, 92
SSLCipherSuite directive, 92
SSL configuration, 86–92
SSL installation, 78–79
SSLMutex directive, 91
SSLOptions directive, 89
SSLPassPhraseDialog, 90
SSLProtocol directive, 92
SSLRandomSeed directive, 91–92
SSLRequire directive, 88, 140
SSLRequireSSL directive, 140
SSLSessionCacheTimeout directive, 91
SSLVerifyClient directive, 123
SSLVerifyDepth directive, 123
TCP/IP software and, 16–17
user-defined CGI scripts, 356
user directories, 152–56
VMS version and, 15–16
Web-based administration and, 11
See also Apache; Web servers
CSWS_JAVA, 23

DBD (database driver), 315
DBI (DataBase Interface), 315–22
code, 316–22
defined, 315
See also Perl
DCL, 306–7
CSWS, 306

OSU, 306
WASD, 307
DECnet
configuration, 32
installing, 30
method, 11
Phase IV, 30, 31
proxies, 30, 357
starting, 30
WWWEXEC object, 297
See also OSU
DIGEST authentication, 118–19, 121
defined, 118–19
password-suitable file for, 122
See also Authentication
DII COE project, 4
Directory browsing, 237–58
Apache, 238–47
defined, 237
OSU, 247–51
users and, 237
WASD, 251–58
Disk space, 17–18
RAM disks and, 18
utilization display, 330
Documentation presentation, 330–32
Document trees, 44–47
Downloads, 19–20
DSL, 19

Echo directives, 269–70
Embedded RDO, 315
ENGINE interface, 85–86
Environment variables, 284–93
AUTH_ACCESS, 285
AUTH_AGENT, 285
AUTH_DESCRIPTION, 285
AUTH_GROUP, 285
AUTH_PASSWORD, 285
AUTH_REALM, 285
AUTH_REMOTE_USER, 285
AUTH_TYPE, 286
AUTH_USER, 286
CONTENT_LENGTH, 286
CONTENT_TYPE, 286
DATE_GMT, 286
DATE_LOCAL, 286
defined, 284
DOCUMENT_NAME, 286
DOCUMENT_PATH_INFO, 286
DOCUMENT_ROOT, 287
DOCUMENT_URI, 287
GATEWAY_MRS, 287
HTTP_ACCEPT, 287
HTTP_ACCEPT_CHARSET, 287
HTTP_ACCEPT_ENCODING, 287
HTTP_ACCEPT_LANGUAGE, 287
HTTP_AUTHORIZATION, 287
HTTP_CONNECTION, 288
HTTP_COOKIE, 288
HTTP_EXTENSION, 288
HTTP_FORWARDED, 288
HTTP_FROM, 288
HTTP_HOST, 288
HTTP_IF_MODIFIED_SINCE, 288
HTTP_PRAGMA, 288
HTTP_RANGE, 289
HTTP_REFERER, 289
HTTP_UA_CPU, 289
HTTP_UA_OS, 289
HTTP_USER_AGENT, 289
PATH, 289
PATH_INFO, 289
PATH_ODS, 290
PATH_TRANSLATED, 290
QUERY_STRING, 290
QUERY_STRING_UNESCAPED, 290
REMOTE_ADDR, 290
REMOTE_HOST, 290
REMOTE_PORT, 291
REMOTE_USER, 291
REQUEST_METHOD, 291

Environment variables *(cont'd.)*
REQUEST_TIME_GMT, 291
REQUEST_TIME_LOCAL, 291
REQUEST_URI, 291
SCRIPT_FILENAME, 291
SCRIPT_NAME, 291
SCRIPT_RTE, 291
SCRIPT_URI, 292
SCRIPT_URL, 292
SERVER_ADDR, 292
SERVER_ADMIN, 292
SERVER_CHARSET, 292
SERVER_GMT, 292
SERVER_NAME, 292
SERVER_PORT, 292
SERVER_PROTOCOL, 292
SERVER_SIGNATURE, 292
SERVER_SOFTWARE, 293
UNIQUE_ID, 293
See also CGI; CGI scripts
Error logs, 216–18
Apache, 216
OSU, 216–17
WASD, 217–18
Error messages, customized, 47–50
Exec directives, 276

Fancy indexing, 240–42
FastCGI (FCGI), 335, 343
File layout, 350
File-naming standards, 349–50
Flow-control directives, 262–63, 271–74
FORTRAN, 307–8
Freeware CGI scripts, 325–32
CGI-MAILTO, 327
changing passwords, 329
Conan, 330–31
disk space utilization display, 330
document presentation, 330–32
HyperDISK, 330
Hypermail, 325–26
Hypershelf/Hyperreader, 331–32
HyperSPI++, 329–30
performance monitoring, 329–30
sending mail from forms, 327–29
serving VMS MAIL files, 325–27
system management functions, 329–30
TMAIL, 327–28
TMAILER, 328–29
VMSHELPGATE, 330
WEBBOOK, 331
yahMAIL, 326–27
See also CGI; CGI scripts
FrontPage, 352
FTP
alternatives, 351–53
server, 352

GZIP, 79

High-performance CGI scripting options, 333–48
conclusion, 348
CSWS, 335–39
issues, 333–35
OSU, 340–44
WASD, 345–48
See also CGI; CGI scripts
Hosts
default, 164
virtual, 164, 167
HPSS (High-Performance Server Software), 340–41
HPSS_PERL, 342
HPSS_PHP, 342
Ht://Dig, 179–82
Berkeley database, 179
configuration file entries, changing, 181–82
defined, 179
package, 179

search database, 180–81
See also Indexing
HTTP, 5
defined, 67
headers, 103
services, 167
as stateless protocol, 118
HTTPD.CONF file, 35–36
AddType directive, 102
CustomLog directive, 164
default host, 164
defined, 35
directives, 41
DocumentRoot directive, 163–64
ErrorLog directive, 164
listen directive, 41
NameVirtualHost directive, 163
ServerAdmin directive, 163
server-level directives, 36
ServerName directive, 164
HTTPD$CONFIG.CONF file, 9, 167
authorization failure limit, 128
CacheChunkBytes directive, 191
Cache directive, 191
CacheEntriesMax directive, 191
CacheFileBytesMax directive, 191
CacheFrequentHits directive, 192
CacheFrequentPeriod directive, 192
CacheHashTableEntries directive, 191
CacheTotalBytesMax directive, 191
CacheValidatePeriod directive, 192
DirAccess directive, 251
DirBodyTag directive, 255
DirDescriptionLines directive, 255
DirLayout directive, 251
DirMetaInfo directive, 253
DirNoImpliedWildcard directive, 255
DirNoPrivIgnore directive, 255
DirOwner directive, 255
DirPreExpired directive, 256
DirReadMe directive, 254
DirReadMeFile directive, 254
DirWildcard directive, 255
service definitions, 167
See also WASD
HTTPD$MAP.CONF file, 47, 170, 192
HTTPDMON utility, 53, 62, 94
HTTP_MAIN.CONF, 188–90
HTTPS, 67–78
defined, 67
dialog, 77–78
for multiple node names, 162
port, 77–78
requests, 106
service, 167
services centralization, 77
SSL software, 67–68
transaction log, 88
URL, 77
HyperDISK, 330
Hypermail, 325–26
Hyperreader, 331–32
Hypershelf, 331–32
HyperSPI++, 329–30
HyperText Transfer Protocol. *See* HTTP
HyperText Transfer Protocol Secure. *See* HTTPS

Indexes
automatic, 238
defined, 237–38
fancy, 240–42
last-modified order, 241
Index files, 44–47
Index.html, 238
Indexing
directory, 239
fancy, 240
with ht://Dig, 179–82
with Lynx, 172–75
reasons for, 171–72

Indexes *(cont'd.)*
with SWISH-E, 175–79
with VMSindex, 172–75
Inkromi's Slurp, 148
Installation
CSWS, 20–28
downloads and, 19–20
guides, 19–34
OSU, 28–32
SSL, 78–86
WASD, 32–34
Instant ASP (iASP), 4
Internet Server API (ISAPI), 334, 342, 347–48

Java, 312, 323–24, 347

Languages for CGI, 306–12
C/C++, 307
DCL, 306–7
FORTRAN, 307–8
Java, 312
Perl, 308–10
PHP4, 310–11
Python, 311–12
See also CGI; CGI scripts
LDAP (lightweight directory access protocol), 120
Log-file analyzers, 204, 219–20
ANALOG, 219, 220–25
defined, 219
Webalizer, 219, 230–32
WUSAGE, 219, 232–36
Log-file formats, 204–11
Apache, 204–8
Combined format, 204
Common format, 204
OSU, 208
WASD, 208–11
Log-file rotation, 211–13
Apache, 211–12
OSU, 212
WASD, 212–13
Logging, customizing, 203–4
Log-interpretation tools, 218–36
ANALOG, 219, 220–25
AWStats, 226–30
log-file analyzers, 219–20
LogResolve, 218–19
Webalizer, 219, 230–32
WUSAGE, 232–36
LogResolve, 218–19
Logs
Apache format specifiers for, 205–6
error, 216–18
tools for interpreting, 218–36
Lynx Crawl, 172–75

Mapping
Apache, 98–102
conditional, 112–16
OSU, 103–5
WASD, 106–12
Mapping resources, 97–117
Apache, 98–103
OSU, 103–6
WASD, 106–17
Message-based server thread (MST), 84
META tags, 149, 253
MIME.TYPES file, 102
Mod_auth_anon, 124
Mod_auth_dbm, 120
Mod_auth_kerberos, 120
Mod_auth_ldap, 120
Mod_auth_openvms, 120
Mod_auth_radius, 120
Mod_java, 20
Mod_perl, 20, 24, 26, 335–38
configuration file, 35
test page, 27
Mod_php, 26, 310, 338–39
configuration file, 35
test page, 28

Mod_proxy, 193
  AllowCONNECT directive, 195
  CacheDefaultExpire directive, 196
  CacheDirLength directive, 197
  CacheDirLevels directive, 197
  CacheForceCompletion directive, 197
  CacheGcInterval directive, 196
  CacheLastModifiedFactor directive, 196
  CacheMaxExpire directive, 196
  CacheRoot directive, 196
  CacheSize directive, 196
  NoCache directive, 197
  NoProxy directive, 194
  ProxyBlock directive, 194
  ProxyDomain directive, 195
  ProxyPass directive, 195
  ProxyPassReverse directive, 195
  ProxyRemote directive, 194
  ProxyRequests directive, 194
  ProxyVia directive, 195
Mod_rewrite, 98
  example, 102
  examples, 99
  RewriteBase directive, 100
  RewriteEngine directive, 100
  RewriteLog directive, 100
  RewriteLogLevel directive, 100
  RewriteOptions directive, 100
  RewriteRule directive, 101, 102
Mod_ssl, 24, 26
  configuration, 86–92
  configuration file, 35
  global directives, 86
  installation, 78–79
Mod_WebDAV, 352
Mozilla Composer, 351
MST interface, 86
Multihoming, 161–70
  configuration, 162–70
  CSWS, 162–64
  defined, 162
  OSU, 165–66
  WASD, 167–70
Multihosting, 161–70
  configuration, 162–70
  CSWS, 162–64
  defined, 162
  OSU, 165–66
  WASD, 167–70

Netscape Communicator, 351

Ohio State University DECthreads HTTP Server. *See* OSU
OpenSSL, 12, 68
  binaries, 72
  confirmation, 77
  for generating certificate request, 74
  installation, 72
  instructions, 72
  object libraries, 13
  WASD kit, 86
  See also SSL
OPENSSL.CNF file, 73
OpenVMS
  freeware, 172
  user authorization, 9
OSU, 6, 11–12
  access controls, 140–43
  ANALOG menu, 224
  authentication, 124–27
  cache directives, 188–90
  cache management, 187–90
  CGI configuration, 294
  CGI environment, 296–300
  choosing, 13–14
  Combined format, 208
  command-line control, 58
  Common format, 208
  configuration files, 38–39
  content type, 105–6
  DCL, 306

OSU *(cont'd.)*
DECnet method, 11
default page, 31
DEFPROT rule, 141
`DirAccess` directive, 249
`DirDefLangEnable` directive, 249
directory browsing, 247–51
`DirReadme` directive, 249
disk space and, 17–18
documentation, 12
downloading, 28
`DSPCACHE` command, 58
echo directives, 269–70
editable config files, 39
error logs, 216–17
ErrorPage command, 49
file caching, 12
file/document includes, 265–66
file parts, 266–68
high-performance CGI options, 340–44
host-name command, 41
HOSTPROT rule, 140
HPSS support, 340–41
HTTP_MAIN.CONF, 188–90
HTTP_SCRIPTS.CONF file, 359–60
in-memory cache organization, 186
installation guide, 28–32
internal directory list output, 248
`INVCACHE` command, 59
Java execution environment, 344
log-file formats/locations, 208
log-file rotation, 212
mapping rules, 103–5
MIME types, 105
MST external directory browser, 247–48
multihosting/multihoming, 165–66
multiple parts, 266
multiple versions on different ports, 93
`NEWLOG` command, 59
`NEWTRACE` command, 59
pass command, 46
`pass` rule, 104–5
password-based authentication, 124–25
Perl, 309
persistent scripting environments and, 11
PHP, 105, 310–11
platforms, 11
PROTECT rule, 141
.PROT files, 39
PROT rule, 140
proxygw.c, 198
proxy management, 197–99
Python, 312
`RESTART` command, 59
root directory, setting, 46
server account creation, 29–30
server distribution, 83
server image, building, 29
shutdown, 51
`SHUTDOWN` command, 59
SSI configuration, 260–61
SSL authentication, 126–27
SSL cache configuration directives and, 93
SSL_CHAIN_VERIFY, 126
SSL_CLIENT_VERIFY, 126
SSL configuration, 92–94
SSL_ENGINE, 92, 93
SSL installation, 79–85
SSL support and, 12
SSL_TASK, 92, 93
starting, 50–51
`STATISTICS` command, 60
support, 12
SYSUAF lookup, 156
TCP/IP software and, 16–17
testing, 31–32
threading, 11
trace level, 217
user-developed CGI scripts, 356–61
user directories, 156–57
VMS version and, 15–16

Web-based administration utility – main page, 63
Web-based administrative utility – server commands, 65
Web-based control, 63–64
`Welcome` directive, 249
See also Web servers

Password-based access control, 144–45
Password-based authentication
Apache, 120–22
OSU, 124–25
WASD, 127–31
Passwords, changing, 329
Perl, 10, 20, 308–10
CGI.PM module, 308
CGI programming with, 315–22
CSWS, 309
DBD, 315
DBI, 315–22
OSU, 309
WASD, 309
PHP, 20
in CSWS, 310
defined, 310
error logging, overriding, 339
in OSU, 310–11
parsing, enabling/disabling, 339
PHP4, 310–11
templates, 105
uses, 310
in WASD, 311
Ports, 42–44
as arguments, 42
commands, adding, 42
default, 40, 43
HTTPS, 77–78
listened to, specifying, 42
privileged, 42
Preinstallation, 15–19
Privileged directives, 277–78
Process Software's Purveyor, 7
Proxy entries, 133–35
dedicated, 185
example set of, 134–35
formats, 133
freeware, 185
multiple, 134
Proxygw.c, 198
Proxy management, 193–202
Apache, 193–97
OSU, 197–99
WASD, 199–202
Proxy servers
anonymizing, 184
as big win, 184
DECnet, 30, 357
special purpose boxes, 184
Public key infrastructure (PKI), 71
Python, 311–12
in CSWS, 311
in OSU, 312
RDB plug-in, 322–23
in WASD, 312

RAID storage, 1
RAM disks, 18
RDB
database access, 313–24
plug-in, 322–23
RDB Web Agent, 313–15
limitations, 314
routines, 314
running, 313
Reliability, 2
Resources, mapping, 97–117
Reverse proxying, 193, 194, 199
Robot Exclusion Standard, 148
Robots.txt, 147–50
creation standard, 148
defined, 147
META tags, 149

Run-Time Environments (RTEs), 334, 346–47

Search engines, external, 171
Secure session layer. *See* SSL
Security, 2–3
  record, 18
  Web directories and, 151
Self-signed certificates, 75–77
Server-side includes (SSI), 259–79
  access counts, 263–64
  configuring, 260–62
  CSWS configuration, 260
  defined, 259
  directives, 262–79
  directory/index generation, 268–69
  drawbacks, 259
  dynamic content with, 259–60
  echo directives, 269–70
  `exec` directives, 276
  file/document includes, 265–66
  file information, 264–65
  file parts, 266–68
  flow-control directives, 271–74
  miscellaneous directives (WASD), 278–79
  OSU configuration, 260–61
  privileged directives, 277–78
  `set` directives, 274–75
  unprivileged directives, 277
  variables provided by servers, 270
  WASD configuration, 261–62
`Set` directives, 274–75
  Apache, 274
  WASD, 274–75
Simple Web Indexing System for Humans – Enhanced. *See* SWISH-E
SQL Module language, 315
SSL, 67–68
  access control in WASD and, 145–47
  cache configuration directives, 93
  ENGINE interface, 85–86
  HTTPS support, 68
  library, 83
  MST interface, 86
  renegotiation, 133
  root directory, 76
  TASK interface, 84–85
SSL authentication
  Apache, 122–24
  OSU, 126–27
  WASD, 131–33
SSL configuration, 86–95
  CSWS, 86–92
  OSU, 92–94
  WASD, 94–95
SSL installation, 78–86
  CSWS, 78–79
  OSU, 79–86
  WASD, 86
SWISH-E, 175–79
  custom results page layout, 178
  default page layout, 177
  defined, 175
  documentation index search page, 176
  functions, 175
  package, 175
  source, 175
  WASD and, 176
  See also Indexing
System performance monitoring, 329–30
SYSUAF-based authentication, 121, 127

TASK interface, 84–85
TCP/IP software, 16–17
TEST_SERVER.COM, 31
Time formats, 268
TMAIL, 327–28
TMAILER, 328–29
Tomcat, 339
Tracking, 213–15
  Apache, 214–15
  WASD, 215

UCX, 17
UNIXified file-system path, 233–34
Unprivileged directives, 277
UPD utility, 351
Upgrades, rolling, 2
User-developed CGI scripts, 355–62
  CSWS/Apache, 356
  number running simultaneously, 358
  OSU, 356–61
  WASD, 361–62
  See also CGI scripts
User directories, 151–59
  CSWS, 152–56
  enabling/disabling, 154
  OSU, 156–57
  PASS command for, 158
  pros and cons, 151–52
  WASD, 157–59
User-edited Web pages, 349–53
  file layout, 350
  file-naming standards, 349–50
  FTP alternatives, 351–53

VDDriver, 164
VirtualHost
  containers, 87, 88, 89, 164
  SSL/TLS protocol engine for, 88
Virtual hosts, 164, 167
VMS
  Apache port, 10
  clustering, 1–2
  mod_auth_dbm and, 120
  needs and, 3–4
  reasons for using, 1–4
  reliability, 2
  security, 2–3
  threading implementation, 11
  Web and, 5–8
VMS Engineering, 4
VMSHELPGATE, 330
VMSindex, 172–75
  building with DECC, 173
  example command procedures and, 174
  index building with, 175

WASD, 8, 12–13
  access controls, 144–50
  AddType directive, 116
  ambiguities and user tracking, 215
  authentication, 127–35
  AUTHONCE (NOAUTHONCE), 109
  basic configuration, 43
  cache management, 191–92
  CACHE (NOCACHE), 109
  CGI configuration, 295
  CGI environment, 301–6
  CGIplus, 345–46
  CGIPREFIX, 109
  CGIUTL utility, 304–5
  CHARSET, 109
  choosing, 13–14
  Combined format, 210
  command-line control, 60–62
  command-line options at server startup, 51
  Common format, 210
  conditional mapping, 112–16
  configuration files, 39–40
  CONTENT, 109
  content type, 116–17
  cookie-based user-tracking features, 203
  DCL, 307
  defined, 12
  directory browser output, 258
  directory browsing, 251–58
  directory browsing parameters, 257
  directory/index generation, 268–69
  directory layout codes, 252
  directory listing – sans config error, 254
  directory listing showing config error, 253
  directory tree, 13
  disk space and, 17–18

WASD *(cont'd.)*
DNSLookup directive, 211
DO=AUTH commands, 60
DO=CACHE commands, 60–61
DO=DCL commands, 61
DO=DECNET commands, 61
DO=LOG commands, 61
DO=MAP command, 62
DO=SSL commands, 62
DO=THROTTLE commands, 62
downloading, 32
DO=ZERO command, 62
echo directives, 269–70
error codes, 50
error logs, 217–18
exec directive, 276, 295
exec rule, 107
EXPIRED (NOEXPIRED), 109
file/document includes, 265–66
file parts, 266–68
flow-control directives, 262–63, 272–74
format strings, 209–10
high-performance CGI options, 345–48
HTTPD$AUTH.CONF file, 129, 145
HTTPD$CONFIG.CONF file, 9, 128, 167, 191–92
HTTPD$MAP.CONF file, 47, 170, 192
HTTPDMON utility, 53, 62, 94
HTTPD$MSG.CONF file, 169
HTTPD$SERVICE.CONF file, 95, 132, 168
HTTPD$SSL_CERT file, 94
HTTP$SERVER account, 34
ident-based authentication, 133–35
INDEX, 110
in-memory cache organization, 186
installation guide, 32–34
LogExcludeHosts directive, 211
LogFile directive, 211
LogFileExtended directive, 211
log-file formats/locations, 208–11
log-file rotation, 212–13
LogFormat directive, 210
Logging directive, 210
LogNaming directive, 210
LOG (NOLOG), 110
LogPeriod directive, 212
LogPerService directive, 210
LogPerServiceHostOnly directive, 211
MAPONCE (NOMAPONCE), 110
mapping, 106–12
mapping rules, 107–8
MIME TYPES, 117
miscellaneous SSI directives, 278–79
multihosting/multihoming, 167–70
obtaining, 13
ODS-5 (ODS-2), 110
on-line administration utility, 64–65
OpcomAdmin directive, 217
OpcomAuthorization directive, 218
OpcomControl directive, 218
OpcomHTTPD directive, 218
OpcomProxyMaint directive, 218
OpcomTarget directive, 217
password-based access control, 144–45
password-based authentication, 127–31
Perl, 309
PHP, 311
PROFILE (NOPROFILE), 110
PROMISCUOUS mode, 33
ProxyCacheDeviceCheckMinutes directive, 201
ProxyCacheDeviceDirOrg directive, 201
ProxyCacheDeviceMaxPercent directive, 201
ProxyCacheDevicePurgePercent directive, 201
ProxyCacheFileBytesMax directive, 200
ProxyCachePurgeList directive, 201
ProxyCacheReloadList directive, 201
ProxyCacheRoutineHourOfDay directive, 200

www.ingramcontent.com/pod-product-compliance
Lightning Source LLC
Chambersburg PA
CBHW080129220326
41598CB00032B/5004